D0096600

BROKEN BALLOTS

BROKEN BALLOTS

Will Your Vote Count?

Douglas W. Jones & Barbara Simons

CSLI
PUBLICATIONS
Center for the Study of
Language and Information
Stanford, California

Copyright © 2012
CSLI Publications
Center for the Study of Language and Information
Leland Stanford Junior University
Printed in the United States
16 15 14 13 12   2 3 4 5

Library of Congress Cataloging-in-Publication Data
Jones, Douglas, 1951-
  Broken ballots : will your vote count in the electronic age? /
  Douglas Jones and Barbara Simons.
      p. cm. – (CSLI lecture notes ; no. 204)
  Includes bibliographical references and index.
  ISBN 978-1-57586-637-6 (cloth : alk. paper) –
  ISBN 978-1-57586-636-9 (pbk. : alk. paper)
  1. Voting–United States. 2. Voting–Technological
  innovations–United States. 3. Voting-machines–United States.
  4. Elections–United States–Management.
  I. Simons, B. (Barbara), 1941- II. Title.

  JK1976.J64 2012
  324.6′50973–dc23

                                                    2011050327
                         CIP

∞ The acid-free paper used in this book meets the minimum requirements
of the American National Standard for Information Sciences—Permanence
of Paper for Printed Library Materials, ANSI Z39.48-1984.

CSLI was founded in 1983 by researchers from Stanford University, SRI
International, and Xerox PARC to further the research and development of
integrated theories of language, information, and computation. CSLI headquarters
and CSLI Publications are located on the campus of Stanford University.

CSLI Publications reports new developments in the study of language,
information, and computation. Please visit our web site at
http://cslipublications.stanford.edu/
for comments on this and other titles, as well as for changes
and corrections by the author and publisher.

We dedicate this book

to our spouses,
David Bowen and Beverly Jones,
who have put up with our work on this
book for over half a decade,

our children and grandchildren, who are
inheriting our democracy,

and to everyone around the world who
has worked to guard democratic
institutions and human rights.

Contents

Preface

About the Authors

Douglas W. Jones is on the computer science faculty at the University of Iowa, where he came after obtaining his Ph.D. from the University of Illinois in 1980. At Illinois, his primary interest was the interaction of computer architecture and operating systems. There are major questions in computer security that sit squarely in this intersection. At Iowa, these topics continued to focus his work, but led to unexpected spinoffs in real-time scheduling and data compression algorithms. Real-time scheduling led him further afield, into embedded systems for motion control.

In 1994, he responded to a call for volunteers to serve on the Iowa Board of Examiners for Voting Machines and Electronic Voting Systems. As he was the only volunteer, he was appointed. By 2000, as chairman of the 3-person board, he began to speak out about shortcomings of the current state of voting technology. In the aftermath of the contested 2000 presidential election, he was called to testify before the U.S. Commission on Civil Rights, the House Science Committee, and other boards and commissions. Since 2000, he has had little time to devote to anything but elections. He resigned from the Iowa Board of Examiners in 2004, and in 2005, he and a group of researchers at Stanford, Berkeley, Rice, Johns Hopkins and SRI International were awarded a grant to establish ACCURATE, A Center for Correct, Usable, Reliable and Transparent Elections, by the National Science Foundation. In addition to funded research, he has participated in investigations, consulted and testified about voting systems, and in 2009, he was appointed to the Technical Guidelines Development Committee of the U.S. Election Assistance Commission.

Jones first began to think about writing what became this book in June 2002, during an encounter with Hans von Spakovsky in Atlanta.

While von Spakovsky, a lawyer, and Jones, a scientist, represent opposing political parties, their shared fascination with the many ways in which elections can go wrong led to an enjoyable extended conversation. At one point during this conversation, von Spakovsky quipped, "you know, you should write a book." This is that book.

Jones gratefully acknowledges the support of the National Science Foundation through grant CNS-052431, ACCURATE.

Barbara Simons is retired from IBM Research, which she joined while finishing her Ph.D. from the University of California at Berkeley. At IBM her research focused primarily on scheduling algorithms and compiler optimization. While she has long been interested in the interplay between computing and policy, her involvement with computerized voting began when she was appointed to the National Workshop on Internet Voting, convened at the request of President Clinton. The 2001 workshop report recommended against Internet voting. She also participated on the Security Peer Review Group for the US Department of Defense's Internet voting project (SERVE) and co-authored the report that led to the cancellation of SERVE because of security concerns. Simons co-chaired the Association for Computing Machinery (ACM) study of statewide databases of registered voters, and co-authored the League of Women Voters report on election auditing. She was appointed to the Board of Advisors of the United States Election Assistance Commission in 2008.

Simons was President of ACM, the nation's oldest and largest educational and scientific society for computing professionals, from July 1998 until June 2000. She founded ACM's US Public Policy Committee (USACM) in 1993 and served for many years as the Chair or co-Chair of USACM.

Writing a book had not occurred to Simons until she was approached in early 2005 by Jim Maurer about writing a "trade book" on computerized voting. Simons asked Doug Jones if he was interested in co-authoring a book, he said yes, and here we are. Neither of us knew what a trade book was. (If you are wondering, this is not a trade book). Nor did we expect that we'd be working on this book for the next six years. One problem with writing a book about a topic that is rapidly evolving is that chapters that we had thought were finished have often needed revising and updating. The book is as current as we've been able to make it, given the constraints of the publishing industry. We hope to be able to keep the reader informed of changes that occur after we complete the manuscript via the book's website at http://BrokenBallots.com.

The opinions expressed in this book are solely those of the authors and do not necessarily represent the positions of any organization with which either author might be associated, including the National Science Foundation, the Technical Guidelines Development Committee or the Board of Advisors of the U.S. Election Assistance Commission, the University of Iowa, Verified Voting, IBM, and ACM.

Acknowledgements

We have received incredibly useful feedback and wonderful assistance from many colleagues and friends to whom we are immensely grateful. We hope that anyone whose name we have unintentionally omitted will be understanding. Among the many people who have provided us with assistance are Jim Maurer, Dan Wallach, Andrew Appel, Noel Runyan, David Jefferson, Ion Sancho, Linda Freedman, Max Freedman, Kathleen Bennett, L Peter Deutsch, Jeremy Epstein, Georgeanna Drew, Teresa Hommel, Sam Scharff, Ellen Theisen, Liz Simons, David Bowen, Daniel Seligson, Alexander A. Shvartsman, Jean Armstrong, Shawn Casey O'Brien, Karl Auerbach, Michael Froomkin, Vince Lipsio, Stan Klein, David Chaum, Rebecca Mercuri, Robert Ferraro, Toni Appel, Herb Deutsch, Steve Bolton, Joe Hall, Cindy Cohn, Warren Stewart, Marybeth Kuznik, Merle Kuznik, David Wagner, Beth Hahn, Steven Rosenfeld, Kevin Shelley, Carole Young-Kleinfeld, Martha Mahoney, Dan McCrea, Carma Forgie, Mark Lindeman, Cherrill Spencer, Marlene Potter, Linda Tumbarello, Jason Kitcat, Vanessa Teague, Peter Ryan, Ben Smyth, Mitch Trachtenberg, Philip Stark, Curtis Gans, Rick Drew, Pam Smith, Rebecca Wilson, Kim Alexander, A. J. Devies, William Edelstein, Eddie Hailes, Eleanor Hare, Bob Kibrick, Dave Klein, John McCarthy, Joyce McCloy, Justin Moore, Peter Neumann, Jim Soper, and Isobel Bowen. Also thanks to the many concerned grassroots members of the disability rights community for their insights and wisdom. Finally, a very large thanks to Laura Gould and David Dill. Of course, in offering our thanks to the above people, we do not imply that they endorse all of our conclusions.

1

Introduction:
Why This Book?

A fair and accurate election process is essential to any democracy.
Report on Election Auditing, the League of Women Voters [286]

This book never should have been written. In 1934, the Brookings Institution published a great book by Joseph Harris entitled *Election Administration in the United States.* [431] Had people followed Harris' advice, there would have been no need for our book. Harris began his book with the following stinging critique: "There is probably no other phase of public administration in the United States which is so badly managed as the conduct of elections. Every investigation or election contest brings to light glaring irregularities, errors, misconduct on the part of election officers, disregard of election laws and instructions, slipshod practices, and downright frauds."

Harris' assessment strikes at the heart of one of America's most cherished myths, that our democracy sets the gold standard against which all other nations can be measured. A few states adopted some of the reforms Harris recommended, but his work was largely forgotten. Perhaps those who repeated such criticisms during World War II and the Cold War risked being labeled unpatriotic. But even with the rise of the civil rights movement, criticism of American democracy was largely confined to minority voting rights issues; questions about the overall quality of American elections were largely ignored.

For many of us, the general election of 2000 was a wake-up call. That election showed the world that there was something wrong with the way we count votes in the United States. Naturally, there was strong pressure for reform in the aftermath. Florida moved quickly to abandon punched-card ballots, replacing them with a mixture of newer voting technologies, and many other states soon followed Florida's lead.

1

After problems with the new touch-screen voting machines in Miami, Congress passed the Help America Vote Act of 2002 (HAVA). This act provided a huge infusion of cash so that states could buy new voting equipment. Many states moved quickly to purchase high-tech electronic voting systems, buoyed by the assurance that they were accurate, accessible, reliable, and secure.

Unfortunately, these assurances turned out to be overly optimistic at best, and misleading at worst. In their eagerness to have the most modern and best election equipment, and to take advantage of almost $4 billion in federal funding, well meaning election officials were quick to accept the claims of voting system vendors. Few questions were asked about crucial issues. How secure and accurate are these machines? How easy are they to use? How could an election audit or recount be conducted? There was little or no consultation with independent technical experts on these questions, and remarkably little scientific research. The implicit assumption appears to have been that no recount would ever be needed, because the new systems were so completely secure and reliable that there would no longer be any reason to challenge an election result.

As this book documents, the answers to the above questions are not very encouraging. Many of the new voting systems on the market have serious security flaws, and many are so badly designed that a substantial number of voters have had serious difficulty voting as they intended. Because post election recounts and audits could not or have not been conducted, it has not been possible to explain discrepancies in election results produced by many of these systems. Furthermore, subsequent scientific and engineering research on these voting technologies has revealed that the regulations governing the machines' construction and use are based on flawed assumptions about their operation.

Ironically, legislation that was prompted by a desire to improve our voting systems created a situation in which it became impossible to conduct a post-election audit or recount in many parts of the country. While some things may have improved in the past few years, there are still several states in which there is no way to recount votes. The nation is forced to accept results produced by voting systems that are known to be flawed, inaccurate, unreliable, and insecure.

Our laws have not kept pace with the enormous changes in how elections are being run. Court challenges of questionable results have been thrown out. Sometimes judges are unwilling or legally unable to require a new election; other times they may not understand the underlying technology or statistics on which the court challenge is based. Old laws mandating absurdly short periods of time for certifying election results have created pointless obstacles to conducting post-election audits or recounts. Most states lack legislation mandating sound post-election audits or recounts in very close elections, and some states have laws that make it all but impossible to verify election outcomes.

Meanwhile, states are being pressured to allow military and expatriate voters to return their voted ballots by fax or via the Internet. Here, too, there has been a disconnect. Sometimes policy makers do not understand that email is sent over the Internet, and therefore attaching a voted ballot to an email is in fact Internet voting. Policy makers who strongly support the use of paper ballots in elections may not even realize that pure Internet voting does not produce a paper ballot.

As they had with electronic voting machines, policy makers and election officials have been quick to accept all-encompassing claims of Internet voting vendors about the security, accuracy and usability of this newest voting technology. Perhaps policy makers believe that Internet voting is secure, in spite of widely publicized Internet viruses and successful Internet-based attacks on major corporations and entire nations. Or perhaps they feel that nothing is likely to go terribly wrong. Again, outside independent experts are rarely consulted.

A Book Overview

The recount battles following the November 2000 presidential election in Florida illustrate that the United States remains divided about whether that election properly represented the will of the people. Whatever the truth may be, the recounts and legal conflicts that followed Election 2000 raised serious doubts about the integrity of our system of elections. We are not interested in re-hashing the outcome of that election, but, like Joseph Harris over 75 years ago, we want to answer two questions: How did the United States come to accept voting systems and systems of election administration that could produce such unclear outcomes? And what can we do to improve things?

We are writing about an issue that significantly predates our involvement. Our story begins when inventors first joined the fight against the extraordinary corruption that arose in the Victorian era. Over a century ago the United States led the world in experimenting with using technology to count votes. In most of the world until very recently, people would have thought it absurd to count anything other than paper ballots. America has a longstanding attraction to technology, but the same can be said for Great Britain. As we document in Chapter 2, the British were the first to invent voting machines, but it was in American that saw their first use, starting in the 19th century.

What is special about elections in the United States? We show in Chapter 2 that the answer has two parts: First, U.S. elections are extremely complex because we elect people to so many different kinds of offices, and voting machines can eliminate some of the tedious and error-prone clerical work that follows from this. Second, the incidence of election fraud in 19ᵗʰ century America was astonishingly high, and voting machines were seen as a tool for fighting fraud. Despite their potential advantages, voting machines were subject to serious questions from the very start. Many of these questions apply just as well to today's electronic voting machines.

The rise and fall of punched cards offers interesting lessons, which we discuss in Chapter 3. After election 2000, the shortcomings of punched card voting seemed so obvious that one might ask how this technology was ever thought to be acceptable. It is ironic that one of the primary motives behind the introduction of punched card ballots was that they permitted real audits and recounts; it was the difficulty of conducting the recounts in 2000 that discredited this technology. The irony was compounded when paperless touch-screen voting machines replaced Florida's punched-cards, "solving" the hanging-chad problem while effectively eliminating audits.

Optical mark-sense voting, a technology that was developed in parallel with punched card voting, is described in Chapter 4. Punched-cards and optical-scan or mark-sense voting were the first two computerized vote-counting technologies to make deep inroads into the voting system marketplace. As we show in Chapter 5, the idea of purely electronic voting systems predates the development of national regulations. In Chapter 6 we examine how the problems posed by these technologies inspired the first serious efforts at drafting national voting system standards. It was only after some regulations were in place that direct recording electronic voting systems achieved more than token market penetration.

Unfortunately, HAVA did not succeed at eliminating or even reducing the controversies surrounding elections. Instead, paperless voting machines themselves have become the center of new controversies, as we illustrate in Chapter 7. Questions about the security, accuracy, and reliability of voting machines have resulted in court cases and bitter political battles. California has been a dramatic microcosm of these fights, which we explore in Chapter 8.

In addition to providing funds to update voting technology, HAVA required for the first time that voting systems be accessible for people with disabilities. In Chapter 9 we chronicle issues confronting people with disabilities and how disability rights activists were misled about and disappointed by paperless touch screen voting machines. We also describe how some voting systems have proven to be far more accessible to voters with disabilities than others.

Yet another requirement of HAVA was that states create statewide databases of all registered voters. Voter registration can be used as a tool to prevent fraud, but it can also disenfranchise voters. Chapter 10 examines how citizens have been disenfranchised historically, as well as policy and technical issues surrounding the new statewide databases of registered voters.

Internet voting is being touted as a method for increasing voter participation, especially for young people, as well as for military and civilians living abroad. We give an overview of the history and issues, as well as the risks, surrounding Internet voting in Chapter 11.

Chapter 12 examines how some national good government groups, acting on the belief that the new paperless electronic voting technology would benefit minorities and people with disabilities, became unwitting advocates for insecure voting systems. Several of these organizations modified their positions when they realized that these systems were not what the vendors claimed them to be. We also discuss attempts to pass legislation to reform HAVA at the federal level, and analyze why these efforts failed.

A critical component of all elections is counting the ballots and verifying that those counts are accurate. We address ways in which ballots can be manually counted, recounted, and audited in Chapter 13. We also describe other important aspects of elections that need oversight and auditing.

We close with Chapter 14 in which we present a list of crucial reforms. We hope that this book will provide the reader with the background and knowledge needed to help bring those reforms to fruition.

2

Déjà Vu All Over Again: 19th Century Voting Technology

The three most prominent sources of corruption are, first, intimidation of voters; second, bribery of voters, and third, fraudulent casting of votes, or, as it is commonly called, 'ballot box stuffing.'

Louis Kutscher, U.S. Patent 412,761, 1889.

The disputed 2000 U.S. Presidential election wasn't our nation's first brush with widespread voting problems. Since the birth of our democracy, unscrupulous businessmen, politicians, and voters have occasionally found ways to take advantage of the system. When confronted with problems, U.S. election officials have frequently turned to cutting edge technology as a solution.

The fundamental problems faced by election officials over the past 150 years have not changed. As each new voting technology is adopted, there is an initial period of enthusiasm before flaws begin to emerge. When the public discovers that corrupt voters or politicians have found new and creative ways to commit fraud, the search begins for new technology.

Election fraud is hardly a new invention. In Harrison County, Texas, the federal government moved in to run elections after charges were filed against 65 people for fraudulent voting incidents at 19 of the county's 23 polling places. Forty-five people pled guilty to federal election fraud. The year was 1878, a year after the end of Reconstruction. [710]

After the government stepped in, the true extent of the problems in Harrison County came to light. Since the federal government had no authority over state and local elections, the state passed legislation in 1880 allowing two ballot boxes at each polling place. The federal ballot box, for federal races only, was under the control of U.S. marshals. The state and local ballot box was controlled by county election officials. In

7

the 1888 general election, 2723 ballots were counted from the federal ballot box in Harrison County, while 4548 ballots were found in the state and local ballot box. One could argue that 40 percent of the electorate simply abstained from the federal election even though it was a presidential election year, but ballot box stuffing seems far more likely. Election fraud in the late 19th century was not a secret. Reporters openly covered it and, in some regions, parties openly promoted it.

It is important to note that the extent of historical election fraud is rarely as easy to determine as it was in Harrison County. For the purposes of this book, however, this is not important. What mattered to the development of various election reform movements, including the movement to apply technology to elections, was the perception of fraud, not its reality. Similarly, honest elections alone are not sufficient to establish a sound democracy. The widespread perception of fraud can undermine a government, even if the election that put it in power was conducted honestly.

Our definition of what is and is not fraud has changed with time. Ballot box stuffing and dishonest counting are as fraudulent today as ever, but the lines have shifted in other areas. Registration fraud was impossible in the era before voter registration, and vote selling was once both common and legal.

Regardless of the extent of fraud or its nature, what is clear from the historical record is that most of the innovations in voting technology made during the 19th century were motivated by the perception of fraud. The developers of these technologies made it clear that they saw themselves as reformers. As the 19th century progressed, we can identify several rounds in the battle between technology and election fraud. In each round, the introduction of a new voting technology moved the battle lines, setting the stage for the next round. As we will see in later chapters, many of the ideas first explored in the 19th century continue to resonate to this day.

2.1 The First Round

Before the American Revolution, most voting was conducted by voice vote, or *viva voce* in academic Latin. Voters called out their votes loudly enough that the clerk could write them down, typically adjacent to the voters' names in the pollbook. This created a permanent official record of who voted for each candidate. While the system allowed observers to record the votes and verify the count, it also opened the door to voter intimidation, retaliation, and other strong-arm tactics. Someone who was listening could easily threaten those who voted "the wrong way" or

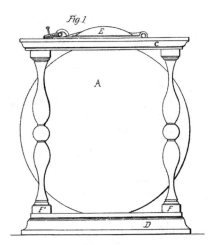

FIGURE 1 Samuel Jollie's glass ballot box. The hollow glass sphere A is mounted in a cast-iron frame CDF with a hinged lid E that has a slot for inserting ballots. From U.S. Patent 21,684.

reward those who voted "the right way," and this was frequently done quite openly.

By the time of the American Revolution, the shortcomings of voice voting were becoming apparent to some, and there was growing interest in exploring alternatives. The original constitution of the state of New York ordained that "a full and fair experiment shall be made of voting by ballot, ... as soon as may be after the termination of the present war between the United States of America and Great Britain." [749] On the other side of the Atlantic, the short-lived French constitution of 1795 required that "all elections are carried on by secret ballot." [357]

The move to paper ballots created opportunities for new forms of election fraud, forms that were impossible with voice voting. In 1856, a vigilance committee in San Francisco found an ingenious ballot box designed so that extra ballots could be stored under a false bottom in the box. The ballot box could be opened before an election to show that it was empty, with the extra ballots hidden under the false bottom. Before opening the box to count the ballots, the false bottom could be slid aside to mix the extra ballots with the legitimate ones. [594]

Such trick ballot boxes were needed only where there were vigilant observers. Where local election officials could exclude observers, they could stuff the ballot box directly. In 1858, Alan Cummings and Samuel Jollie patented competing transparent ballot boxes. [218,518] In 1856,

Jollie sent prototypes of his glass ballot box, shown in Figure 1, to San Francisco for trial use and began to lobby New York City to adopt his box for the 1856 election.[756,757] Cummings was quick to join in the competition, submitting his box to the city.[755]

Jollie's patent contained a clear statement of the benefits of a transparent ballot box: "In this way it will be obvious that the bystanders can see whether every ballot that is put into the hole actually goes into the box, and whether more ballots go into the box than are actually put through the ballot hole at the top. The whole progress of the balloting is clearly in view, and when the ballots are taken out to be counted, it must all be done in open view." This logic remains compelling. Plastic has replaced glass, but transparent ballot boxes remain in use in many nations to this day.

New York City bought 1200 of Jollie's glass ballot boxes for use in the 1857 election, at a cost of $15 each. Unfortunately, the city did not pay for them, and the ensuing lawsuits dragged on into 1860.[758] Jollie's ballot boxes remained in use for decades and went on to become the iconic ballot box of the late 19th century, largely because the noted political cartoonist Thomas Nast used it as a model in all of his illustrations of ballot boxes.

In the early 19th century, voters were expected to provide their own ballots—either handwritten or printed. Handwritten ballots have always posed challenges when it came time to count them. If a voter wanted his ballot to be secret, or if he wanted to assure that it would be easy to read, he could use a pre-printed ballot form, usually provided by a candidate or political party. If he wanted his ballot to be identifiable, he could write distinctively or use an easily identifiable piece of paper.

Pre-printed ballots have been preserved in various collections. For example, consider the ballot shown in Figure 2 from 1839. This ballot was printed as part of Francis Gehon's campaign for non-voting delegate to the U.S. Congress from Iowa Territory. His ballots included just his own name along with write-in blanks for other offices in the election. All surviving examples of this ballot appear to have been torn from the pages of a newspaper. If readers supported Gehon, they could tear out the ballots and take them to the polls.

Francis Gehon's ballot illustrates a central feature of elections in the United States. This ballot contains votes for twelve candidates in races for nine offices. In most parliamentary democracies, there is just one office on the ballot in a general election, member of parliament. Our habit of putting large numbers of offices on one ballot adds a dimension of complexity to all aspects of election administration in the United States that is largely absent elsewhere in the world.

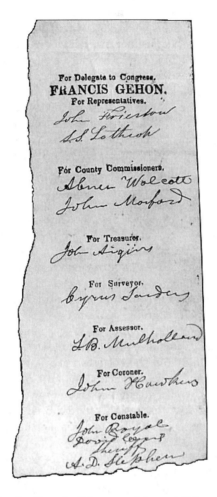

FIGURE 2 Ballot for Francis Gehon, used in an 1839 general election in Iowa City, Iowa. Gehon omitted the office of sheriff, so the voter had to squeeze in that office at the bottom. From the collection of the Iowa State Historical Society, Francis Gehon papers.

By having his own name mechanically printed on a convenient ballot form, Gehon reduced the likelihood that some of his votes would be discounted on the grounds that they were illegible or that voters could not remember or properly spell his name. Pre-printed ballots also helped ensure that illiterate voters could vote. Candidates for different offices who endorsed each other could print joint or party tickets. The fact that Gehon did not include any other names suggests that he was not affiliated with any broad-based political party.

Pre-printed ballots did more than reduce the subjectiveness of counting and extend voting rights to the illiterate. They also reduced election fraud. Honest tellers tend to favor candidates they prefer when they are forced to make judgment calls while counting votes. Dishonest tellers can exploit this, deliberately declaring ballots to be illegible for the sake of discounting them.

As political parties became more organized, better funded, and more directly involved in elections, they began printing and distributing their own ballots to voters. These ballots, known as *party tickets*, included the names of all of the candidates endorsed by the party for election in a particular district. Party tickets were easier to count accurately than ballots printed by individual candidates since there was little need for write-in blanks.

The Republican ticket shown in Figure 3 is quite typical. This ticket has some distinctive typographical features. The party name at the top is bold and legible, but small type and cramped margins are the norm for office and candidate names. This design encourages voters to ignore the details and vote the straight party ticket. The only places where the typography invites attention are those where the party had no endorsements. There, write-in blanks are provided. The typography of such partisan ballots discouraged voters from making changes. A voter could strike out a candidate's name, but doing so left little space to write in an alternative name.

These partisan ballots had a significant effect on the way votes were counted. With handwritten ballots, tellers had to examine each one carefully for every name it might contain. Even without subjectivity or bias, this process was error prone. With party tickets, the vote-counting task was easy as long as most people voted the straight party ticket.

Anyone who has counted a stack of money knows that the best way is to count the bills after sorting them by denomination, a system much easier than trying to add up the denominations on an unsorted stack of bills. Counting party tickets was just as straightforward if the tellers began by sorting the tickets into stacks by party. Once sorted by party, each teller could independently verify the count of ballots in each stack.

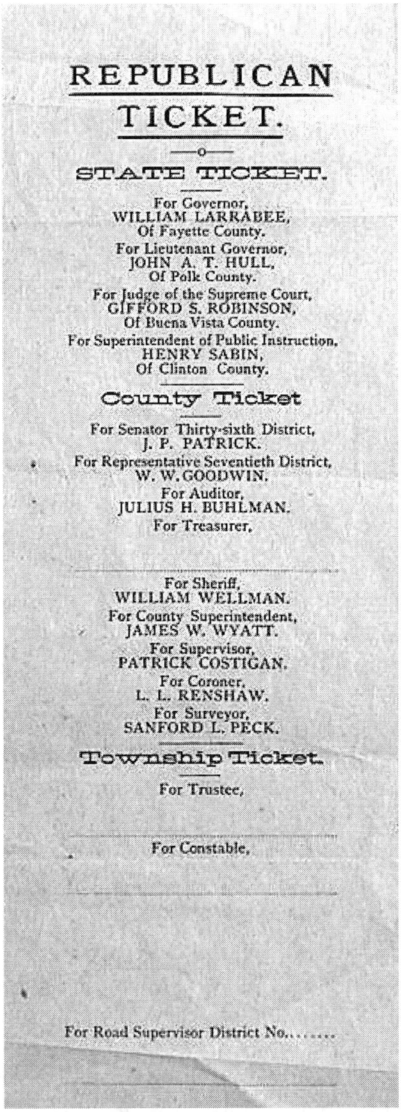

REPUBLICAN TICKET.

—o—

STATE TICKET.

For Governor,
WILLIAM LARRABEE,
Of Fayette County.

For Lieutenant Governor,
JOHN A. T. HULL,
Of Polk County.

For Judge of the Supreme Court,
GIFFORD S. ROBINSON,
Of Buena Vista County.

For Superintendent of Public Instruction,
HENRY SABIN,
Of Clinton County.

County Ticket

For Senator Thirty-sixth District,
J. P. PATRICK.

For Representative Seventieth District,
W. W. GOODWIN.

For Auditor,
JULIUS H. BUHLMAN.

For Treasurer,

For Sheriff,
WILLIAM WELLMAN.

For County Superintendent,
JAMES W. WYATT.

For Supervisor,
PATRICK COSTIGAN.

For Coroner,
L. L. RENSHAW.

For Surveyor,
SANFORD L. PECK.

Township Ticket.

For Trustee,

For Constable,

For Road Supervisor District No........

FIGURE 3 Republican party ticket from the 1888 general election in Iowa. From the collection of the Iowa State Historical Society, William Larrabee papers.

Just as with stacks of money, the ballots for each party could be counted into piles of ten to further help avoid clerical errors. The only ballots requiring close scrutiny and individual attention were those that had been altered with strikeouts or manuscript additions.

While partisan paper ballots reduced the need for many subjective decisions, they introduced new opportunities for abuse. Unless strike-outs were clear and thorough, a dishonest teller could argue that the line through a name was just a stray mark or an accident. A dishonest teller could strike-out candidates he disliked with a single pencil stroke. Altering a manuscript ballot required significantly more work. Of course, it was risky to tamper with ballots when votes were counted in the presence of observers, but observers weren't always allowed.

The net effect of introducing pre-printed ballots was to trade one set of problems for another. In 1887, the *New York Times* estimated that nearly 70 ballots were being printed by various parties for every citizen who actually voted.[760] Not only was this a huge waste of paper, but not all of these ballots accurately represented the party slates of the parties they purported to support. When a political committee printed ballots under the name of one party but omitted some of that party's candidates, the committee was described as "knifing" those candidates. Knifing was widely condemned by the parties, but it was not necessarily illegal. It was possible, after all, that a voter who voted a knifed ballot intended to oppose the knifed candidates.[845]

Ballot box stuffing was an inelegant but effective strategy for cooking an election, but fraud at the ballot box was only one of many problems with voting in the mid-19th century. Voter intimidation and vote buying were also problems. Political parties had little reason to keep ballots secret, since they wanted to know who their supporters were. Parties went out of their way to print distinctive ballots, some on brightly colored paper or in different forms. If you went to the polls holding a bright pink Democratic ballot or a long skinny Republican ballot, everyone knew how you were voting. Even if you carried your ballot into the polling place in secret, the use of a glass ballot box ensured that your ballot was visible to observers when you voted.

By the late 19th century, it was widely believed that election fraud had become a way of life throughout much of the United States, although the actual extent of fraud is hard to assess outside of a few jurisdictions. Some voters, known as floaters, offered their votes to the highest bidder. Reformers charged that campaigns across the rural South and the urban North were focusing less and less on the issues and more and more on promises of protection and patronage.[154]

2.2 The First Voting Mechanisms

The demand for a secret ballot contained in the 1795 French constitution had no immediate impact, but half a century later, revolutionaries across Europe remembered. The most detailed response came from the Chartists, the first mass labor movement in England. The *People's Charter* of 1838 demanded universal suffrage and the secret ballot. To support this demand, the published versions of the charter included as an annex a detailed schedule explaining how to run a polling place and a description of a voting machine. [618,619]

Unlike the Chartists, the next inventors of voting mechanisms attempted to automate roll-call votes in state legislatures, rather than voting in polling places. In 1848, Robert Monaghan patented the first mechanical voting system proposed in the United States. [717] This idea went on to attract several other inventors, including Albert Henderson, who invented the first electrical voting system two years later. [455]

These first legislative voting systems did not count votes, they just recorded them. The idea of mechanical vote counting was present in the Chartist proposal, and it emerged again in the world of fraternal lodges. In 1860, Gilbert Bailey patented a "ballot box" designed for counting yes-no votes in this setting. [74] There was no obvious need for such mechanisms in lodge elections, but inventors continued to file patents in this area for several decades. [779,75]

Popular histories of technology sometimes credit Thomas Edison with the invention of the voting machine. His first patent, granted in 1869, involved an improvement to Henderson's electrical vote recording system. [290] What Edison contributed was the addition of electromechanical counters to Henderson's electrochemical vote recorder. While this was ingenious, Edison's ideas were entirely ignored in the subsequent development of voting technology.

The first mechanical counting technology to achieve any success in the polling place did not count votes, it counted ballots. In 1860, Miles Shinn patented an "apparatus for detecting fraud in ballot boxes." [912] Shinn's ballot box incorporated a "registrar" mechanism to count ballots as they were inserted in the box and a "detector" mechanism to detect whether the box had been opened since the time it was set for the election. Shinn's patent was issued only two years after Jollie's patent on a glass ballot box, and like Jollie, his focus was on defending against ballot box stuffing.

The Civil War diverted the interest of inventors during the 1860s, but the collapse of the Tweed Ring in 1871 refocused the interest of inventors on electoral reform. Boss Tweed and his cronies are estimated

IN COUNTING THERE IS STRENGTH

"THAT'S WHAT'S THE MATTER."

Boss Tweed. "As long as I count the Votes, what are you going to do about it? say?"

FIGURE 4 Thomas Nast's caricature of Boss Tweed's approach to elections. Note that the ballot box in the picture is Samuel Jollie's glass ballot box. From *Harpers Weekly* October 7, 1871, page 944.

to have stolen as much as 200 million dollars during the period they controlled New York City. With glass ballot boxes in use, simple ballot box stuffing was no longer possible, but the Tweed ring had no difficulty fixing elections. Before the 1871 municipal elections, Thomas Nast caricatured Boss Tweed as saying "As long as I count the votes, what are you going to do about it?" [731] Nast's cartoon, shown in Figure 4, proved prophetic. Tweed was reelected, but only by dint of extraordinary fraud. The *New York Times* reported incidents at numerous polling places where observers were expelled or attacked and where ballots went uncounted. In one absurd case, an election inspector was seen chewing up and spitting out ballots for reform candidates instead of counting them. [759] Unfortunately for Tweed, his confederates were defeated and within months, he faced arrest.

Transparent ballot boxes can defend against ballot box stuffing, but they can't guarantee that all of the ballots voted are counted. Shinn and other inventors of registering ballot boxes understood that counting the

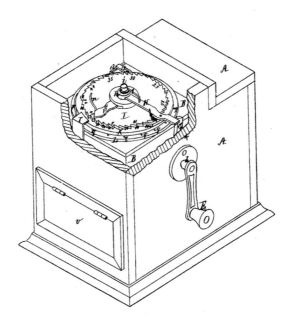

FIGURE 5 James Savage's registering ballot box. The voting slot is in the lid behind the dial (not visible in this illustration). One turn of the crank is required per ballot voted. This counts the ballot on the large dial on top of the box and imprints the ballot with an inked stamp.
From U.S. Patent 142,124.

ballots as they were deposited offered a potential defense. In Shinn's design, the counter was not particularly easy to read, but within three years of Tweed's downfall, this defect was corrected. In 1873, James Savage patented the box shown in Figure 5. This included a mechanical counter that was clearly visible to the public, so that all could see the counter increment as their ballots were inserted, and everyone present at the end of the day could know how many ballots should be found when the box is opened. Savage's box also included a mechanism to cancel each ballot as it was placed in the box, offering an opportunity to distinguish between properly inserted ballots and those that might have been inserted improperly. [877] A year later, George Davis patented a registering ballot box that included a gong, so that everyone in the polling place could easily hear when each ballot was voted. [224] These new ballot boxes were not immediately successful, but by 1884 Massachusetts mandated the use of registering ballot boxes. [119]

2.3 The Australian Ballot

America's problems with honest elections were far from unique. One of the clearest early calls for electoral reform came in 1838 in England. The first great Chartist petition ended with these sentences: "Therefore, we demand universal suffrage. The suffrage, to be exempt from the corruption of the wealthy and the violence of the powerful, must be secret." [618]

The Chartist demand for secret ballots came with a proposal for how to operate a polling place using a simple voting machine appropriate for Britain's parliamentary elections. Chartist influence in the young colony of Australia was significant, but Australia did not have the resources to deploy even the simplest of voting machines.

Many Australians worked on the problem of refining the secret ballot idea. The most important of these innovators was William Boothby, electoral commissioner of South Australia. [117] Boothby proposed that ballots with the names of all qualifying candidates should be printed at government expense, then distributed to voters at polling places equipped with voting booths. By doing this, Boothby hoped to ensure that every voter's ballot would be identical except for the anonymous marks indicating a voter's intent. In 1856, the Australian colony of Tasmania was the first to pass a version of this new system into law, followed quickly by several other Australian colonies. [753]

Some political scholars and philosophers argued forcefully against the secret ballot, chief among them Great Britain's John Stuart Mill.[708] In Mill's England, only male landowners could vote. With the fate of so many in the hands of so few, Mill felt that those who could not vote had a right to know how the few who could had voted, and a right to pressure the voters to act in the interest of the population as a whole. Mill understood that the franchise was being expanded and that class distinctions were on the decline, and he held that voters in the coming egalitarian society with universal male suffrage were unlikely to need the protection of a secret ballot.

There were practical reasons to oppose secret ballots: They significantly added to the cost of elections, because the government had to print the ballots, provide voting booths, and find larger polling places with space for the booths. Before secret ballots, there was no need for government to process nominating petitions or regulate how parties nominated their candidates. Government involvement in the nomination process implied a loss of autonomy for the political parties. Finally, secret ballots required a greater degree of literacy than party tickets. With the latter, an illiterate voter could simply take a party ticket from a representative of a party he trusted. Countering these objections was the widespread belief that the secret ballot was a major tool in the fight against corrupt political machines. [845]

The need for voting booths of some sort was implicit in the Australian plan for polling places, but once the secret ballot was adopted, it quickly became apparent that there was a need for booths that were inexpensive, compact to store, and easy to set up and take down. In the United States, this led to a brief flood of voting booth patents starting in 1892. [423,457,533]

Outside of Australia, the standard printed ballot—widely known as the Australian ballot—was adopted rather slowly. Britain adopted the secret ballot with the *Ballot Act of 1872*. [388] In the U.S., frustration with election fraud grew steadily during the late 19th century, fueled by stories about Tammany Hall and other corrupt political machines. In 1887, the *New York Times* ran a clear demand for a switch to the secret ballot. [760]

The 1888 U.S. presidential election added more fuel to the push for reform. Benjamin Harrison lost the popular vote in this election to Grover Cleveland by a margin of over 90,000, but went on to win the electoral vote by 233–168, amid accusations of election tampering. [10,146] In 1888, Louisville, Kentucky and the Commonwealth of Massachusetts had already adopted the Australian ballot. By 1892, 37 of the 44 states in the United States had switched to the new system.

An Australian-style ballot was printed clearly with the names of qualifying candidates from all parties on a single sheet of paper. To vote for a candidate, voters were required to make a standard mark, typically an X, in the *voting target* printed next to each candidate's name. In U.S. elections, with multiple offices on one ballot, there are many ways to arrange the ballot. *Office-block ballots* deemphasize the role of parties by blocking together all candidates for each office on the ballot. In contrast, *party-column ballots* emphasize the party affiliation of the candidates by listing all candidates from the same party in the same column with one row set aside for each office. Through the early 1890s, party column and office block ballots were in fairly close competition, but by the start of the 20th century, twice as many states had opted to use party-column ballots as office-block ballots. [620]

From the start, most states that used party-column ballots augmented them to allow *straight party voting* by adding a target at the head of each party column. Marking the straight-party target indicated a vote for all candidates from that party. A few states using office-block ballots also allowed straight-party voting. The political parties wanted straight-party voting for partisan reasons, but there were also practical

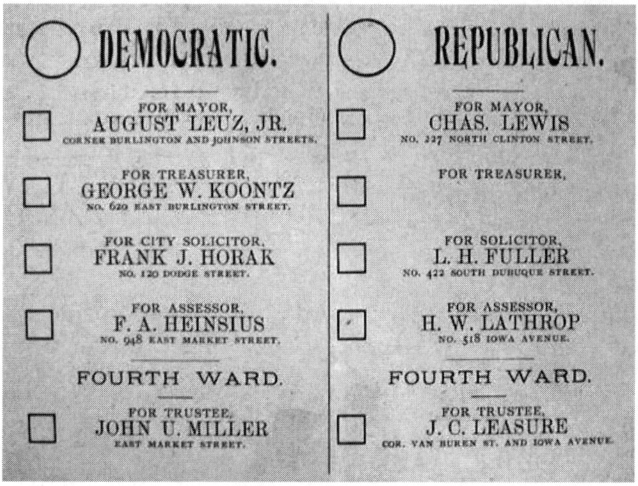

DEMOCRATIC.	REPUBLICAN.
FOR MAYOR, AUGUST LEUZ, JR. CORNER BURLINGTON AND JOHNSON STREETS.	FOR MAYOR, CHAS. LEWIS NO. 227 NORTH CLINTON STREET.
FOR TREASURER, GEORGE W. KOONTZ NO. 620 EAST BURLINGTON STREET.	FOR TREASURER,
FOR CITY SOLICITOR, FRANK J. HORAK NO. 120 DODGE STREET.	FOR SOLICITOR, L. H. FULLER NO. 422 SOUTH DUBUQUE STREET.
FOR ASSESSOR, F. A. HEINSIUS NO. 948 EAST MARKET STREET.	FOR ASSESSOR, H. W. LATHROP NO. 518 IOWA AVENUE.
FOURTH WARD.	FOURTH WARD.
FOR TRUSTEE, JOHN U. MILLER EAST MARKET STREET.	FOR TRUSTEE, J. C. LEASURE COR. VAN BUREN ST. AND IOWA AVENUE.

FIGURE 6 An Australian secret ballot from an 1893 municipal election in Iowa City, arranged in party-column format with a straight-party option. From the collection of the Iowa State Historical Society.

reasons. The straight-party option simplifies voting for illiterate voters and it reduces the average time voters spend in the voting booth, thus reducing the number of booths needed.

2.4 How Secret?

While the United States was two decades behind Great Britain in moving to the secret ballot, the debate over the use of secret ballots had a clear influence on proposals for voting technology that emerged in the late 19thcentury. One issue that remains with us to this day is the question of how secret the secret ballot should be. One side argues that if anyone can reconstruct how a given voter voted, there is the possibility that someone will abuse this to coerce voters. The other side argues that if a problem ballot is found, it should be possible to tie that ballot to the voter who cast it.

Part 1 section 2 of the British Ballot Act of 1872[388] required that "each ballot paper shall have a number printed on the back," and instituted election procedures linking this number to the voter. As a result, the Ballot Act did not guarantee that the voter was anonymous. Rather, Schedule 1 part 1 section 41 stated that "no person ... shall open the sealed packet of counterfoils [linking the voters to the ballot numbers]" except by order of Parliament or an appropriate tribunal. In effect, the British model makes the identity of the voter a state secret.

Alabama, Arkansas, Colorado, Missouri and Texas adopted variants of the British model, requiring that each ballot be tied by a serial number to the corresponding voter. The majority of the states adopting secret ballot laws opted to provide some variation on absolute secrecy. In most states, the right to a secret ballot was statutory, but in Idaho, Virginia, Washington and Wyoming, the state constitutions explicitly addressed the issue. [620] California and Louisiana went so far as to require that voters use rubber stamps to mark their ballots, thus avoiding the possibility of distinctive marks. In most states, serial numbers were still used to help guarantee that voters returned the same ballots they were issued, but those numbers were written on stubs that were torn off before each ballot was put in the ballot box.

Developers of voting machinery have come down on both sides of this divide. Even before the widespread adoption of the Australian Ballot, developers of registering ballot boxes began to develop boxes that conformed to the British model. In 1878, for example, Morris Williams patented a registering ballot box that carefully stored the ballots in exactly the order in which they were voted. [1014] A year later, Steuben Bacon patented a ballot box that automatically stamped each ballot with a serial number as it was voted. [73] Williams offered little rationale for his patent, but Bacon was strident, claiming that his machine "effectually and radically detects and defeats all these frauds and thefts and enables officials" to determine exactly which ballots were lawfully cast.

This question—how secret is enough—continues to vex election reformers and designers of election technologies to this day. As we will see, the first generation of mechanical voting machines included machines that followed each of these models. In coming chapters we will see how this division continues into the era of electronic voting.

2.5   Voting Machines

In 1875, Henry W. Spratt of Kent, England was granted a U.S. Patent on a "voting chamber and mechanism therefor," a voting booth incorporating a voting machine. [936] His goal was to allow secret voting "without the aid of balls, tickets, passes, letters, figures, official stamps, or ballot boxes." In addition, his system assured "absolute secrecy, it being impossible to discover for whom the voter has voted ... [while allowing] all parties, pro and con ... [to] be satisfied that the voter has voted." Finally, "at the close of the poll the result of the voting can instantly be made known ... [with] a complete check as to the numbers voted, preventing any tampering with the apparatus." To this day, this list of goals remains central to the design of voting systems, whether mechanical or electronic. Only one of these goals remains controversial, the elimination of paper ballots and ballot boxes.

Spratt filed for his patent within a few years of the passage of the Ballot Act of 1872 and the trial of Boss Tweed, but we can only speculate as to whether or not there was any connection between these events and Spratt's work. Spratt's reference to eliminating the use of balls, however, suggests that he knew about the Chartist voting machine proposal, since votes were cast on the Chartist machine by dropping a brass ball (the ballot) into the hole next to the appropriate candidate's name on the top of the machine. Like the Chartist machine, Spratt's machine could handle only a single multi-candidate race at a time. This made it unsuitable for a general election in the United States, where general elections always involve multiple offices on the ballot at every level from local to federal.

Spratt's machine did solve a number of problems. It contained a mechanism to prevent the voter from voting for more than one candidate, and the mechanism was interlocked with the voting booth door, so that the machine was automatically set for the next voter when the previous voter left the booth. Spratt also included a public counter showing the total number of votes cast, an idea pioneered with the registering ballot boxes.

In 1878, Alexander B. Roney of Pittsburgh patented a voting machine that allowed multiple candidates to run for multiple offices in a single election. [854] Roney's machine was clumsy, with levers and other controls sticking out of five of the six sides of the box. Roney's stated objectives included the usual desire to eliminate fraud and preserve the purity of the franchise and "to avoid the trouble and waste of time caused by counting the votes." The elimination of the need to count the votes, or as Spratt stated it, the goal of making the results "instantly known" prevents precinct election workers from engaging in the kind of post-election shenanigans that the Tweed Ring had made notorious.

In 1881, Anthony C. Beranek patented the first practical mechanical voting machine to address the needs of U.S. general elections. Beranek's machine adopted a party-column layout as shown in Figure 7. It is interesting to note that conventional histories of the debates over ballot layout typically cite the dates 1888 and 1889 for the introduction of party-column and office-block ballot formats, and discuss the tradeoffs between these two formats largely in terms of partisan considerations. [994] In contrast, Beranek adopted the party-column layout for technical reasons. Specifically, the interlock mechanism used in his machine to prevent overvoting operated using a row of spacers. Press-

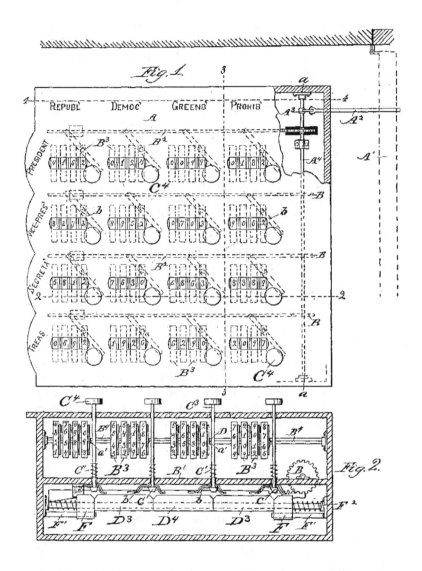

FIGURE 7 Anthony Beranek's voting machine, the first to resemble a modern mechanical voting machine. Linkage A^2 to the door of the voting booth resets the machine for each voter. The counters B^3 behind the panel are advanced by push buttons C^4. Blocks F, D^3 and D^4 interlock the rows to prevent overvoting. From U.S. Patent 248,130.

ing a button for a candidate drove a wedge between two spacers in the row, squeezing the spacers in the row in a way that blocked the wedges attached to the other buttons in the row. This, of course, forced all candidates for each office to be in one row, leading naturally to a party column organization.

Like Spratt's machine, Beranek's machine was never used. The first voting machine to see actual use in a polling place was based on patents issued to Jacob H. Myers of Rochester, New York, granted in 1889 and 1890.[726,727] The *Myers Automatic Booth* followed Spratt's and Beranek's approach by integrating the voting-machine with the booth. Because it incorporated the interlock mechanism from Beranek's machine, it was constrained to use a party-column layout. Myers made several improvements to the mechanism and added a crude straight-party option in the form of a pivoted bar that could be used to push all the voting buttons in one column at once.

Voting machines could not be used without a change to the law. Myers drafted legislation in 1889, and by the end of the year he had collected thousands of signatures on petitions urging trial use of his machine.[762] On March 15, 1892, "an act to secure independence of voters at town meetings, secrecy of the ballot, and provide for the use of Myers' automatic ballot cabinet" was signed into law in New York.[179] This act applied only to town meetings, but that was enough to permit trial use of the new machine. The trial came within a month, on April 12 in Lockport. Newspaper reports of the election make it clear that the public understood that these new voting machines were mechanical implementations of the Australian ballot, and that their purpose was understood in terms of preventing fraud in both the casting and counting of votes. One report correctly compared the mechanism to that of a cash-register, and gave the minimum and maximum time to cast a vote as two minutes for the slowest voter and nine seconds for the fastest, in a twenty-candidate election. The report ended by saying that "one feat in particular is claimed for it [the Myer's machine], and that is, that it will absolutely kill the old 'machine' which counted, falsified and repeated at elections." [763,245]

New York's law authorizing the use of "Myers Automatic Ballot-Cabinets" was renewed in 1893, firmed up with considerable detail in 1894, and broadened to apply to all towns and cities in 1896.[914] The *New York Times* continued its glowing reports of the use of the machine in 1893.[764] By this point, Myers had patented an improved machine that permitted cumulative voting, that is, casting up to some fixed number of votes for any of a group of candidates for the same multi-seat office.[728]

2.6   Industrialization

In 1894, Sylvanus Davis of Rochester, New York patented a voting machine that solved most of the problems Myers had solved using different, and in several cases superior mechanisms. [226] Like Beranek and Myers, Davis used a system of wedges to interlock the buttons for each office, but he completely rethought how these were linked to the buttons, creating an interlocking mechanism that was both more flexible and easier to maintain than its predecessors.

Davis's interlocking mechanism forced the face of the machine to be turned 90 degrees, so that all candidates for each office were arranged in a column, with the straight party lever at the end of the row. This party-row format with the straight-party lever at the end of the row would eventually dominate the mechanical voting machines of the 20th century.

Davis improved his machine, obtaining several patents over the next few years. [227,228] In 1895, Davis founded the United States Voting Machine Company of Jamestown, New York to manufacture his machine, [990] and he hired some very talented engineers. Among them, Henry Cooper and Angus McKenzie are notable. [204] Cooper and McKenzie patented numerous improvements to Davis's machine, all the while staying within the party-row framework imposed by Davis's interlocking mechanism. [666]

In one regard, Davis's machine followed Myers' very closely. Both designed huge machines integrated into wrought iron booths. It is easy to imagine permanently erecting one of these machines in a town hall, but it is hard to imagine setting one up on a temporary basis, and it is not obvious how they could be broken down for storage. McKenzie tried to solve the problem of breaking down the bulky voting booth for storage, but in practice the U.S. Voting Machine was used without the booth. Instead, the face of the machine was simply turned toward the wall and screens were added on each side. [422]

Davis understood that he needed to defend his voting machine not only against voters who might attempt to violate the rules but also against technicians and election workers. Davis asserted that with his machine, "no movement of the counting mechanism is possible, except that imparted to it by the voter." [226] To prevent manipulation of the counters when the back of the machine was open for maintenance, each counter was enclosed in a sealed case, as shown in Figure 8. Unfortunately, this protective measure cost money, and the drawings from later patents held by the U.S. Voting Machine Company omit this protection.

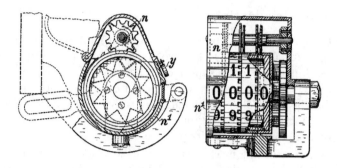

FIGURE 8 Side and front views of a mechanical counter from Davis' voting machine. Case n n^1 is closed by seal y to prevent tampering during routine maintenance. From U.S. Patent 526,668.

Davis followed Myers' lead in pressing New York for legislation permitting the use of his machines. On April 21, 1896, "an act to enable the towns and cities of this state to use the Davis automatic ballot machines at all elections therein" was passed. [914] As a result, both the Myers machine and the Davis machine saw use in New York for the presidential election of 1896. [422]

The Davis and Myers voting machines had competition. John McTammany jumped into the fray in 1892, even before New York passed its first voting machine law. McTammany held a number of patents for player-piano mechanisms. [680,681,682] Given his background, it is no surprise that his voting-machine patents focus on machines that record votes by punching holes in long paper rolls similar to those used in player pianos, [685,686,688] and on tabulating machines that can count votes recorded on such rolls. [683,687,689,690]

McTammany was not the first to propose recording votes on a continuous paper roll. John Rhines of St. Paul, Minnesota had patented a similar machine, the *Votograph*, [761,846] but McTammany's machine saw significant use and he was the first to clearly document the principal shortcoming of recording votes on a paper roll. McTammany said that when votes are recorded sequentially on a roll of paper, "it is possible to identify a man's vote, by counting voters as they go in and afterward counting the rows of marks on the sheet." [684] This puts reel-to-reel vote recorders such as the McTammany and Rhines systems closer to the British model of ballot secrecy than to the absolute secrecy typically required in the United States.

The McTammany voting machine had opponents. In 1895, the Rhode Island Supreme Court was asked whether the McTammany piano-roll was a ballot under state law. The majority held that since the piano-roll was a permanent paper record of the vote and subject to a hand count, if necessary, it met the definition of a ballot. The lone dissenter, Horatio Rogers, held that it is not a ballot since "a voter on this voting machine has no knowledge through his senses" that he has voted, but rather, must trust that "the machine has worked as intended. . .".[853] Rogers' critique applies equally to any opaque voting mechanism, whether the mechanical voting machines of the 19th century or the electronic machines of the 21st. Curiously, Rogers did not comment on the threat to ballot secrecy posed by the McTammany machine, although a contemporary study of voting machines done for the State of California explicitly recognized this issue.[133]

Like Myers, McTammany sought legal approval for the use of his machine. He began in his home state of Massachusetts, where the legislature approved limited use of his machine on June 9, 1893.[640] As in New York, use was limited to local elections. When the law was changed in 1896 to allow use of McTammany's machine in all elections,[620] there were immediate problems. McTammany's machine could accommodate only 50 candidates, while there were 75 candidates for presidential elector on the ballot. Unfortunately for McTammany, Massachusetts law at the time permitted voters to vote for individual electors, as opposed to voting for them by party list.[641]

The 1896 presidential election was the first large-scale test for voting machines, and both the Myers and McTammany machines attracted criticism as a result. Serious undercounts were noted on both machines. In one Rochester precinct, only 237 votes were registered on a Myers' machine after 400 voters had used the machine, clear evidence that something was wrong. In Worcester, Massachusetts, where the long ballot forced the use of multiple machines, many voters apparently failed to notice the races on the second machine.[765,827] Unfortunately, there was no way to recover any votes lost to such failures, and in fact there was no actual evidence of failure. Defenders of such machines can always argue, however implausibly, that the high undervote was due to deliberate abstention on the part of the voters.

In Worcester, there were also problems with McTammany's pneumatic vote tabulator, so the holes in the player-piano rolls had to be counted by hand, One local Massachusetts candidate reported a more surprising failure. While observing at the polls, he learned to identify the sound of the key associated with his name on the McTammany voting machine, allowing him to learn that he had lost the election before the polls closed.[827] This may be the first report of acoustic snooping on mechanical voting machines, but there were others.[766]

2.7   Consolidation and Monopoly

Alfred Gillespie of Atlantic, Iowa entered the voting technology fray in early 1896. Gillespie was a prolific inventor, holding patents on things as diverse as methods for stringing pianos,[376,377] a cord fastener for mailbags,[378] and a pneumatic-tube system.[379] Gillespie's first voting machine patent introduced several new ideas.[380] In most of the previous voting machines, voters could not correct errors. Pushing the button for a candidate was irreversible. The Davis machine allowed voters to pull buttons back out after pushing them by mistake, but pulling on a pushbutton is not obvious. In Gillespie's machine, the voter could correct his selections at any time before he left the booth. Only on leaving the booth and pulling the lever to reset the machine for the next voter was the selection registered.

Gillespie incorporated a modified version of the Davis interlocking mechanism into a second patent,[386] and then moved to Rochester where he made additional improvements in 1898.[381] From the point of view of New York law, his cross-party endorsement mechanism was particularly important.[385] New York allows multiple parties to endorse a single candidate. On a party-row or party-column ballot, a cross-endorsed candidate's name may appear multiple times, once per endorsing party. Gillespie's cross-party endorsement mechanism automatically combined the votes for cross-endorsed candidates. Gillespie also purchased the Myers voting machine patents and founded the Standard Voting Machine Company in 1898.[990]

Where Myers and Davis had used push buttons for voting, Gillespie put one small lever by each candidate's name that could be turned to point to that name and expose an X to vote for that candidate. He also linked the large lever that cast the ballot and reset the machine to a curtain surrounding the front of the machine. This curtain replaced the cumbersome voting booths integrated with other early machines. Opening the curtain incremented the counters and cleared the levers, while closing the curtain unlocked the machine for the next voter. As can be seen in Figure 9, Gillespie adapted parts of his machine from Davis's machines while retaining the party column format of Meyers' machine.[381,386]

Finally, in 1899, Gillespie adopted a practical write-in mechanism. This had a door for each office covering a spool of paper that advanced only when a write-in vote was cast for that office.[382] By this

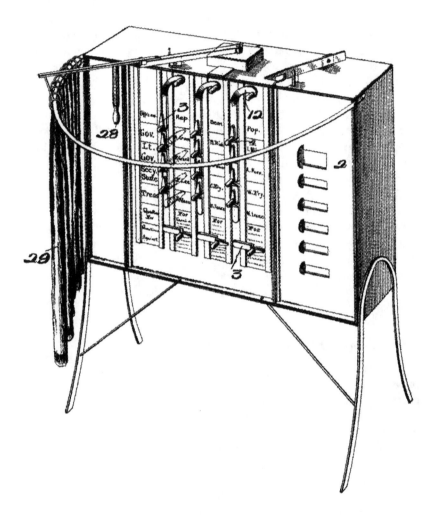

FIGURE 9 Gillespie's voting machine, as of 1899. Lever 28 closes curtain 29 to enable the machine. Voters may use straight party levers 12 or individual candidate levers 3 to cast votes, as well as write-in doors 2, but the votes are not actually counted until the curtain is opened. From U.S. Patent 628,905.

point, it became quite proper to refer to voting machines as being programmable. Before each election, technicians would insert or remove spring clips to set rules such as "vote for one" in one office or "vote for three" in another, and links could be connected or disconnected for cross-party endorsements. All of this programming involved mechanisms that were invisible to the voter and election observers, hidden behind the face of the machine.

By the time of the 1900 presidential election, 442 voting machines based on the Davis and Gillespie patents were in use in upstate New York. On December 14, 1900, Gillespie's Standard Voting Machine Company merged with Davis's United States Voting Machine Company to form the U.S. Standard Voting Machine Company.[990] This company and its descendants would hold an effective monopoly on mechanical voting machines well into the 20th century.

Gillespie was a director of the new company, and he continued to file numerous patents on behalf of the new company over the next decade, covering such details as improved interlocking mechanisms[383] and better linkages between the levers on the face of the machine and the registers that count the votes.[384] Angus McKenzie, from Davis's company, also joined the new company, assigning many of his patents to U.S. Standard[667,668] and to its successor, the Empire Voting Machine Company.[669,670,671]

2.8   Adopting Voting Machines

By the early 1900s, it seemed that mechanical voting systems would prevail over hand-counted paper ballots. Voting machine manufacturers were finding that the greatest barrier to the acceptance of the new machines was not the technology involved, but the cost. With the explosive growth of mass production in the late 19th century and the hundreds of identical mechanisms behind the face of the machine, the cost was bound to fall.

While voting machines were expensive, there were strong economic arguments in their favor. With voting machines, the votes are already counted by the time the polls close, so the only jobs remaining for the poll workers are to record the numbers from the counters, fold up the voting booths, and seal the machines. In contrast, it could take several hours to hand count paper ballots from just one precinct in a general election. Fewer hours of work reduced the cost of poll workers. In many jurisdictions, precincts were kept deliberately small in order to limit the time needed to hand count the ballots. With voting machines, small precincts could be combined, greatly reducing the cost.

In the next chapter, we explore the widespread adoption of voting machines and the slow realization that they were not as foolproof as their proponents claimed. Over the first half of the 20th century, lever voting machines made by successors of Gillespie's company would come to dominate polling places across the United States. The next great wave of technological change in voting would not come until the rise of electronic computers in the 1960s.

3

How Did We Get Here?
From Levers to Punched Cards

*Witness thinks that if he were custodian [of the voting machines] and
had sufficient time, he could produce any result he desired at the following election and could cheat 30,000 or 50,000 or any number of
votes in the course of an election.*

Testimony of O. A. Leutwiler, 1915 [595]

By the early 20th century, communities across the United States were adopting voting machines. The move was not sudden, but by 1925, 60% of the population of upstate New York lived in cities and towns that were using voting machines. Just seven cities in the state were holdouts, including New York City. [1037]

Table 1 gives the dates of adoption and abandonment of voting machines in several cities in the first third of the 20th century. The abandonments are evidence of resistance to voting machines, which tended to be strongest in the bigger cities. New York resisted the move to voting machines until 1925, and opponents of voting machines carried the day in Chicago, holding out against election automation until the second half of the 20th century.

By 1929, 24 states had authorized use of voting machines, and the monopoly built in 1900, later known as the Automatic Voting Machine Company, had sold 11,000 machines. By 1931, New York City alone was using over 3000 machines. [71] By 1933, 80% of the precincts in New York State used voting machines. In Indiana, Iowa and Washington, the figure was closer to 50%. [432]

Among jurisdictions that tried and then abandoned voting machines, the reasons given for abandonment varied. In Wisconsin, after 30% of the electorate was voting on machines, the legislature passed a bill requiring the use of paper ballots for some county questions. Running

TABLE 1 Some cities that adopted voting machines, with years of adoption and, in several cases, abandonment. [1037,1038,432]

Rochester, NY	1896
Buffalo, NY	1899
Milwaukee, WI	1902 – 1920
San Francisco, CA	1904 – 1906
Des Moines, IA	1908
Minneapolis, MN	1908 – 1913
Chicago, IL	1912 – 1912
Seattle, WA	1916
Tacoma, WA	1920
Grand Rapids, MI	1922
New York, NY	1925
Portland, OR	1928 – 1928

mixed paper-mechanical elections was confusing enough that it forced the abandonment of machines by 1920. The story in Minnesota was similar. There, a state law mandated that voters be given a choice between paper ballots and machines, and again, the confusion and expense of the mixed system forced the abandonment. [1037]

San Francisco's experiment with voting machines was ended abruptly by the 1906 earthquake, while Massachusetts abandoned its early use of voting machines because of dissatisfaction with the McTammany machine.

The governor of New Jersey launched a statewide move to voting machines in 1902. The move was initially successful, but by 1905 public opposition was very well organized. Despite support from the Secretary of State, the legislature allowed municipalities to hold referenda on the use of voting machines, and in 1910 the state entirely abandoned machines.

Proponents of voting machines saw a clear pattern. New Jersey Secretary of State S. D. Dickenson wrote that those who object to voting machines were elderly, conservative, indifferent, or party agents who wanted to manipulate votes. [1037] David Zuckerman, a Republican in New York, cynically observed that "In some communities which have begun to consider voting machines seriously the opposition is of a political nature, as it was in New York City. Just as in that city, however, it seems possible that the political machine can retain its hold as readily under use of mechanical voting methods as under any other form. As soon as politicians learn that such is the case, and when they come to feel that they can prevent the reduction in the number of districts which the use of machines makes possible, their opposition will cease." [1038]

3.1 Scandal in Chicago

Considerable money is involved when a city the size of Chicago opts to purchase voting machines. In July of 1911, the Chicago Board of Election Commissioners contracted to buy 1000 voting machines from the Empire Voting Machine Company at a total cost of $942,500. The first 200 machines were delivered and paid for in 1912, with delivery planned over a 3-year period. The City Club of Chicago's Bureau of Public Efficiency quickly concluded that this was an imprudent contract because no preliminary trial had been made and the city council's finance committee had not been consulted. [574] In 1913, after a court ruling against use of voting machines, the Bureau declared that "the Board of Election Commissioners and the Empire Voting Machine Company had disregarded every principle of business prudence," and that the Empire contract was void. Therefore, they argued that the city should cease all payment to Empire. [856]

The legal case against the Empire Voting Machine hinged on a remarkable requirement. The Illinois election statute of 1903 stated that "No voter shall remain within the voting booth or compartment longer than one minute," and therefore, voting machines are legal only if "each elector can understandingly and within a period of one minute cast his vote for all candidates of his choice." [1020] The Empire voting machine could not meet this requirement, but neither could any other conceivable technology, including conventional paper ballots. A typical ballot from the November 1912 general election in Chicago had 53 races* and 258 candidates. [152]

The Illinois legislature launched an investigation in response to the City Club's allegations. [494] Much of the ensuing hearing revolved around Lloyd L. Duke's written statement alleging that over $20,000 in bribes had been paid by Empire's agents in order to obtain the contract. [288] The committee concluded that the machines could be and probably had been manipulated to give a false result, that they could not meet the requirements of Illinois law, and that the purchase had been imprudent. No conclusions were drawn about the alleged fraud, but the committee recommended cancellation of Chicago's contract with Empire and repeal or amendment of the Illinois voting machine law. [127]

The case in Chicago was complicated by the relationship between Mayor Carter H. Harrison, who was elected in 1912, and newspaper

---

*Oversimplified. The ballot actually allowed voting individually for presidential electors, but we have lumped the presidential elector races to count each party's slate of electors as just one candidate.

magnate William Randolph Hearst. Several of the voting machine commissioners were former Hearst employees, and it was alleged that Hearst
controlled a large amount of Empire stock. [767] Hearst was a Harrison
backer, but he denied any connection to Empire. [450] Countercharges
made by Edward E. Marriott, a reporter for Hearst's *Chicago Examiner*, repeated the allegations of bribery against Empire while supporting Hearst's denial of involvement. [768,635]

The business methods of the Empire company helped maintain de-
niability for the company. Salesmen for Empire and its corporate predecessor, the U.S. Standard Voting Machine Company, were paid $50
per week plus personal expenses. In the early days of the industry,
salesmen had to account for their expenses, but under Empire's management, the rules were changed. Salesmen were paid a flat commission
of $135 per machine sold, with no required accounting. Salesmen were
free to keep this money or spend it on the expenses incurred in making
a sale, including any bribes required. [81]

Empire did not survive its attempt to sell voting machines to
Chicago. In 1913 it was taken over by the Triumph Voting Machine
Company, which was then reorganized into the company that eventually became the AVM or Automatic Voting Machine Company, as
summarized in Figure 10.

The scandal in Chicago set back the voting machine industry for
many years in Illinois and several other states, and the temptation
to use corrupt sales tactics similar to those uncovered in Chicago has
continued to the present. A. J. Liebling described a dinner in the late
summer or fall of 1959 at which Earl Long, Governor of Louisiana,
discussed splitting a $12,000 rebate from a voting machine vendor with
the state's Custodian of Voting Machines. [601] In 1969 and 1970, the
Shoup Voting Machine Company paid $40,000 in bribes to officials of
Hillsborough County (Tampa), Florida, in order to induce them to buy
new machines. In a related kickback scheme, bribes were paid in Harris
County (Houston), Texas in order to sell the used Florida machines in
Texas. [415]

Lest anyone conclude that such corruption is a thing of the past
or confined to only one company, there have been similar cases in the
modern era. Bill Culp, former election director of Mecklenburg County
(Charlotte), North Carolina, was convicted for accepting bribes of over
$134,000 between 1990 and 1998. This scandal involved the independent
sales and service representative of Microvote, the manufacturer of the
county's electronic voting machines. [231] In 2000, Louisiana Commissioner of Elections Jerry Fowler pled guilty in a kickback and bribery

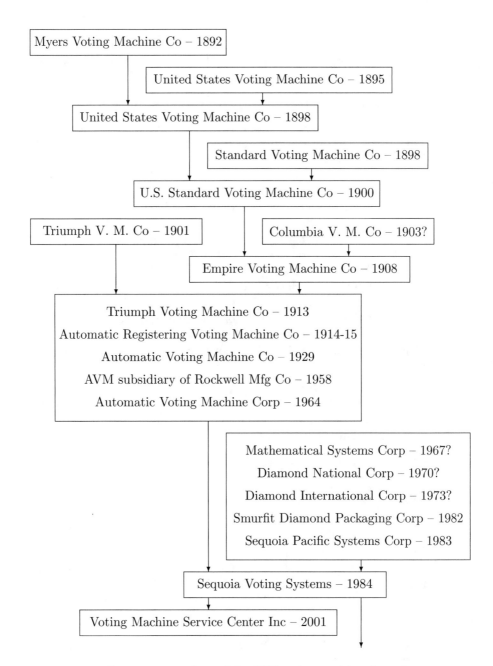

FIGURE 10 Corporate genealogy of the AVM voting machine, from the Myers Voting Machine Company to the Voting Machine Service Center. [71,363,57]

scheme involving old AVM mechanical voting machines after Sequoia
Voting Systems took over AVM. [617,355]

3.2 Fraud and Reform in the Interwar Era

In the 1920s, the biggest battle over the use of voting machines was in
New York City. Both parties identified voting machines with reform.
The Democratic political machine in control of the city, still known as
Tammany Hall, opposed voting machines, while the Republican opposition advocated them. [1037] The story in New York was muddied by the
discovery in 1922 that some of the machines being prepared for ship-
ment to New York by the Automatic Registering Machine Company
were in fact Empire machines that had been rejected by Chicago. [769]
Nonetheless, New York formally adopted mechanical voting machines
in 1925, [1038] and continued to use them into the 21st century.

In 1934, Joseph P. Harris published his landmark book on election
administration in the United States. [431] This comprehensive book included an in-depth review of election problems, both those due to error
and those due to fraud, and it suggested a broad range of reforms targeting these problems. Harris' list of types of election fraud remains
useful today: [433]

1. Registration frauds.
2. Repeating.*
3. Ballot box stuffing.
4. Chain ballots (see below).
5. Voter assistance.
6. Intimidation and Violence.
7. Altering Ballots.
8. Substitution of Ballots.
9. False Count and False Returns.
10. Altering Returns.

Registration fraud, repeating, ballot box stuffing, intimidation, violence, and substitution of ballots were well established techniques long
before the introduction of the Australian ballot. With the advent of
the secret ballot, voter intimidation became more difficult, resulting in
new approaches to fraud.

3.2.1 Improper Voter Assistance

Harris reported that voter assistance had became a major tool for
crooked elections. "In practically every state some provision is made
for assistance to be given to the voters who are unable to mark their

---

*A repeat voter goes to the polls several times, casting one ballot on each visit.

ballots. ... The number of voters assisted in some of the precincts of our large cities is perfectly amazing, there being no effort whatever to confine the assistance to persons unable to read and write, or unable to mark the ballot because of physical infirmity." Because laws allowed voters to bring anyone they wanted into the voting booth as an assistant, voters could be intimidated into allowing scoundrels to assist them. This form of fraud is applicable to any voting technology, and the defenses against it are purely procedural.

In the era of partisan paper ballots, there was little need for voter assistance, but with the move to the Australian paper ballot and voting machines, illiterate voters and voters with disabilities faced serious problems. Before, they could accept a partisan ballot from a party representative they trusted and simply deliver it to the polling place, but with these new voting methods, they were required to read and mark their ballots in secret. Simple justice suggests that such voters are entitled to assistance, but those who did not like universal suffrage saw an alternative, the literacy test. Literacy tests were applied across the South in order to prevent blacks from voting, while grandfather clauses were used to permit illiterate whites to vote. As Governor Earl Long of Louisiana is reputed to have said, "da machines is less important dan who's allowed to vote." [601]

Improper voter assistance has been well documented in many elections. As recently as 2010, eight people in Clay County, Kentucky were convicted on charges that included widespread use of illegal voter assistance as part of an election rigging scheme. [319,1026]

3.2.2 Chain Ballots

In contrast to the other frauds Harris listed, chain ballots are a specific attack on paper Australian secret ballots. To start a chain, the vote buyer must obtain one official ballot. Harris mentioned that absentee ballots could be used to start a chain, but sample ballots or even a blank piece of paper superficially resembling a ballot will sometimes suffice. The crook gives this first ballot to a voter with instructions to smuggle a blank ballot out of the polling place and vote the bogus initial ballot. The crook pays each voter for the blank ballot brought back, and then marks that ballot and gives it to the next voter in the chain. Thus, one blank ballot in the wrong hands at the start of Election Day can be used to bribe a large number of voters, and one sample ballot or blank page found in the ballot box could be evidence of a chain. [433]

Harris considered chain voting to be a secondary threat in 1934, but in the decades that followed, the situation changed. [433] In 1962, Rovert D. Loevy described the chain ballot as "the most spectacular and effective method yet devised to defraud the electorate." The power of chain voting and the "short pencil" led Loevy and others to continue recommending the use of voting machines, despite a growing understanding of the many ways they could be rigged. [610]

Strict security measures for blank ballots can prevent chain voting, but the primary defense is procedural, involving detachable numbered stubs on each ballot that permit the precinct officials to determine that the voter who returns a ballot for deposit in the ballot box is the same voter to whom that particular ballot was issued. Harris outlined this defense in detail, but to this day, many jurisdictions do not follow his advice. [434]

3.2.3 Short Pencils

The "short pencil" method that Loevy referred to was a widespread ballot alteration method in which the tellers counting ballots would conceal a short pencil somewhere on their person, sometimes just a piece of pencil lead carefully parked under a fingernail. Even when observers are present, a skilled teller can avoid detection while adding either stray marks to invalidate ballots or marks for candidates in order to convert undesirable votes to overvotes and abstentions to votes for the political machine's candidate. [781]

Adding a straight-party option to Australian ballots offers new opportunity for alteration. Under the usual rules for straight-party voting, a voter who marks one party may cast cross-over votes by voting in individual races for candidates from other parties. Voters make no marks in races where they intend the straight-party vote to apply, so a short pencil artist can easily add marks to blank races that are indistinguishable from split-ticket votes. [642]

3.2.4 Stray Marks

If voters were allowed to sign their ballots, a vote buyer could look through the voted ballots to make sure that the vote sellers kept their bargains. As a result, if we want to discourage vote selling, we must forbid voters from signing their ballots. Unfortunately, vote sellers and vote buyers could agree on just about any ballot marking to serve as a signature.

Australian secret ballot laws typically deal with the threat of voter signatures by limiting the markings that are legal on a ballot. This creates a new vulnerability. Consider this wording from the Michigan statutes:

168.803 Counting and recounting of votes ...

Sec. 803. (1) Except as otherwise provided in this act, the following rules shall govern the counting and recounting of votes: ...

(a) If it is clearly evident from an examination of a ballot that the ballot has been mutilated for the purpose of distinguishing it or that there has been placed on the ballot some mark, printing, or writing for the purpose of distinguishing it, then that ballot is void and shall not be counted.

(b) A cross, the intersection of which is within or on the line of the proper circle or square, or a check mark, the angle of which is within a circle or square, is valid. Crosses or check marks otherwise located on the ballot are void.

(c) Marks other than crosses or check marks used to designate the intention of the voter shall not be counted.

(d) A cross is valid even though 1 or both lines of the cross are duplicated, if the lines intersect within or on the line of the square or circle.

(e) Two lines meeting within or on the line of the square or circle, although not crossing each other, are valid if it is apparent that the voter intended to make a cross. ... [706]

Clause (a) of Michigan's law can be exploited by a short pencil artist, since all that is needed to invalidate an undesirable ballot is a single random pencil stroke. The threat is sufficiently serious that some states explicitly outlaw any marking on ballots by the tellers, [984] and it is sufficiently alarming that voting machine vendors have used it in their material promoting use of paperless mechanical voting machines. [69]

Clauses (b) through (e) above can also be used to disenfranchise voters. All a teller needs to do is apply very strict standards to ballots containing votes for candidates he dislikes while being lenient with ballots he favors. The extraordinarily high numbers of void and blank ballots reported in the Encyclopædia Britannica article of 1910 is very likely explained by such tactics. [546]

3.2.5   Why Bother with Counting?

Another major form of fraud was to ignore the ballots completely. Most jurisdictions in the 19th and early 20th centuries used precinct-count tabulation; that is, the election workers in each precinct were responsible for counting that precinct's ballots after the polls closed. Counting can be tedious work and in many jurisdictions, particularly where it was difficult to demand a recount, precinct officials simply made up numbers instead of conducting an honest count.

Boss Tweed admitted as much in 1877 in his testimony before the New York Board of Aldermen when he said that his ward bosses would "count the ballots in bulk, or without counting them announce the results in bulk, or change from one to the other, as the case may have been. . . . The ballots made no result; the counters made the result." [751] This pattern was not confined to the 19th century. In his 1934 book, Joseph Harris reported cases from several cities where there was ample evidence that the "precinct officers did not take the trouble to count the ballots at all." [435]

3.3 Problems with Mechanical Voting Machines

By 1927, the development of mechanical voting machines had reached the point that David Zuckerman dismissed most of the objections to the machines, writing: "The only improvements of any importance which may be looked for in the future are refinements intended to convince the individual voter that his vote is being registered in accordance with his desires and to furnish a printed record of the vote for each candidate." [1038] In today's terms, he acknowledged a need for voter verification and the elimination of the need to manually transcribe the results from the machine onto the official report of the canvass.

In 1934, Joseph Harris wrote that "it is sometimes asserted that the machines may be fraudulently set or manipulated, that rubber bands may be place in the machine to alter the count, and that in other ways the machines may be beaten. While it may be possible to manipulate the machine and to steal votes, the experience in many cities seems to indicate that it is not practicable, and in actual practice it is not done." [432]

Louisiana and Chicago, two notoriously corrupt jurisdictions, resisted the introduction of voting machines for many years. In each case, however, there is evidence that corrupt elections were held almost immediately after machines were introduced. This suggests that by the 1950s, voting machines were merely an inconvenience to those intent on election fraud, not a serious barrier.

In late 1959, Governor Earl Long of Louisiana is reputed to have said "Da voting machines won't hold me up, . . . If I have da right commissioners, I can make dem machines play Home Sweet Home. . . . Da goody-goodies bought dose machines to put a crimp in da Longs, . . . Da first time dey was used, in 1956, I won on da first primary. Not even my brother Huey ever did dat." [601] This is in keeping with Joseph Harris' assertion that it is "generally agreed that most voting frauds are committed by the election officers themselves, and in the count. The old form of voting fraud—that of repeating—has largely disappeared. It is safer and cheaper to have the election officers steal the election." [432]

By the time of the 1960 presidential election, Chicago had finally decided to install voting machines. 634 of Chicago's 3,771 precincts still used paper ballots, and evidence of fraud in that election suggests that it was concentrated in the paper precincts. Nonetheless, some older fraud techniques remained in widespread use in precincts that used voting machines. Most notably, improper voter assistance was observed in many voting machine precincts. Some voters do need assistance, particularly when confronted with new voting technology. Assistance becomes improper when the assistant works to ensure that votes are cast for the "correct" candidate. Illinois election laws permitted assistance in the voting booth only for illiterate voters or voters with disabilities, and instruction in the use of the mechanism only on a model voting machine outside the booth. Assistants and instructors had to be election judges, working in pairs, one from each major party. Special record keeping was required for each case of an assisted voter. Violations of these rules were noted in numerous precincts. In one precinct, 310 of 338 voters were improperly instructed. [534]

Many years later, Robert Merriam, the former 5th ward Alderman who had run for mayor against Daley in the 1950s, said that the switch to voting machines had forced many precinct captains to subscribe to Popular Mechanics. [534] The question of what these precinct captains learned in their studies, and when they applied it, is very important but extremely difficult to answer. What we do know is that for many decades, election officials rarely spoke or wrote about voting machine vulnerabilities.

The reluctance of election officials to speak publicly about the shortcomings of voting machinery parallels the reluctance of many locksmiths to speak about the weaknesses of locks. Officials frequently object that open discussion could aid those intent on committing fraud. In the 19th century, Tomlinson and Hobbs argued strongly for open discussion, saying: "Rogues knew a good deal about lockpicking long before locksmiths discussed it among themselves, as they have lately done. If a lock ... is not so inviolable as it has hitherto been deemed to be, surely it is in the interest of honest persons to know this fact, because the dishonest are tolerably certain to be the first to apply the knowledge practically; and the spread of knowledge is necessary to give fair play to those who might suffer by ignorance. It cannot be too earnestly urged, that an acquaintance with real facts will, in the end, be better for all parties." [963]

Public officials are reluctant to speak about voting system shortcomings for another reason. Marie Garber, former election administrator for Montgomery County, Maryland, said that when her county decided to change voting systems, "I wanted to learn all I could from those who had already used it .... If they had made mistakes, if things had gone wrong, I wanted to know why and how we could avoid doing the same things, ... Whatever mistakes we make, I said, let them be original. However, it was not always easy to extract from election officials what was wrong, or even not so good about their voting system. Who wants to admit their choice was less then the best?" [364]

After the 1968 general election, Marie Garber found 3 voting machines out of the 1800 used in Montgomery County which had recorded an unusually low number of presidential votes. When she asked about the low counts, the vendor, AVM, suggested that perhaps people in those precincts simply abstained in the presidential race. When Garber investigated the mechanisms of these three machines, she found that one of the wheels inside the machines' counters had a broken tooth. The mechanism was plastic, and the net effect of the failure was to discard a fraction of the votes recorded on that counter.*

In the 1968 election, Richard Nixon, Hubert Humphrey and George Wallace were the major candidates. Significant losses to any of these three would have been noticeable, so practically speaking, Garber's audit involved just the 3 voting positions for these candidates on each of the 1800 machines in her county. In sum, she studied a total of 5400 counters, out of which she found 3 that had broken gear teeth. This translates to a failure rate of 1 in 1800.

Mid 20th century voting machines had from 270 to 665 counters each. If the failure rate of individual counters really was on the order of 1 in 1800, this would suggest that from 14 to 31% of all voting machines would be expected to have a broken counter, depending on the size of the machine. Of course, with a sample of only 3 out of 1800, these figures should be taken as only the roughest guide to the rate of mechanical counting failure in the lever voting machine era.

An important feature of the failure that Garber discovered is that there is no way to determine after the fact whether the gear teeth broke from normal wear and tear, or whether the break was done deliberately by a service technician. Furthermore, after a gear tooth has broken, the most one can say is that it is broken now. When it broke cannot be

---

*Reconciling Garber's recollection with the mechanism of AVM's machines is not easy. The part that most closely fits her description is called the *transfer pinion*, a gear that transfers carries from the one's place to the ten's place in each counter.

known, and therefore, we can never be sure how many votes might have been lost.

In 1978, Philadelphia's notorious mayor Frank Rizzo faced a term limit imposed by the city charter. A charter amendment to determine if Rizzo could run for another term was placed on the ballot, and Philadelphia's voters went to the polls. During the election, voting machines began to fail, with failures apparently concentrated in precincts where opposition to Rizzo was strong. At the FBI's request, a team led by Ransom F. Shoup II investigated the failures. At the time, the R.F. Shoup Corporation was the largest competitor of AVM Corporation, the old Automatic Voting Machine company. It appears that Shoup was more interested in the possibility that his company could sell voting machines to Philadelphia than he was in making an honest investigation. He offered to let one of the city commissioners review and edit his report in exchange for a deal, and the commissioner turned him in. In the end, Shoup was convicted of conspiracy and obstruction of justice. Unfortunately, the case against Shoup overshadowed the original questions about the selective pattern of voting machine failures, but sabotage remains the most obvious explanation. [13]

During the century after the introduction of mechanical voting machines, speculation about rigged machines was widespread, but there were few public demonstrations of machine rigging. A county election administrator recounted a story from the 1960s about an elderly technician from the county's voting machine vendor who explained how to rig the vendor's machines. Although the incident happened over 40 years ago, the administrator insisted to us that no names be mentioned.

The most dramatic public demonstration that mechanical voting machines could be rigged came in 1979. In a legislative hearing in Louisiana, Representative Emile "Peppi" Bruneau demonstrated in detail how to alter the results on a Shoup lever voting machine without leaving any evidence of the alteration. He defeated the lead seal securing the machine by using a cigarette lighter to heat the seal wires enough to pull them out of the lead, pried off an acrylic cover that was not intended to be removable, prodded the wheels of the counters he wanted to change with a cotton swab so that they held the numbers he wanted, and then put everything back as it had been, including replacing the lead seal by heating the wires until he could push the seal back into place. [415,616] The extent to which these kinds of tricks had been in use over the previous 80 years will never be known because they leave no evidence.

3.4   The Rise of the Punched Card

In his 1934 book on election administration, Joseph Harris concluded that "most claims of the savings which voting machines will effect fail to take into account altogether the capital outlay, with the proper interest and depreciation charges. This indeed is one of the largest charges in the use of machines, and in many cases equals or exceeds the savings made on other items." [434] Harris was sufficiently dissatisfied with the existing voting machines that he developed his own ideas and filed for a patent in 1929. [436] In a 1980 interview, Harris recalled having the idea "that the voting system should record the votes in the precinct, but only record them on a piece of paper or a card, later to be counted by computer." [732]

Harris's 1934 machine was a revival of McTammany's punched-paper player-piano-roll vote recorder, but with a rectangular array of push buttons on the face. This allowed presentation of a party column ballot to the voter, and it led to much deeper mixing and interleaving of the punches corresponding to the different voters' ballots, making it much harder for an observer with access to the vote record to surreptitiously reconstruct individual voters' ballots.

Recording votes by punching holes in paper is an old idea. One of the earliest voting patents issued in the United States, granted to Robert Monaghan of Liverpool, Pennsylvania in 1848, used punches to perforate a paper record of a legislative roll-call vote. [717] This idea was first extended to the polling place in patents granted in 1890 to Kennedy Dougan of Missoula, Montana. [280,281] Voters using Dougan's machine voted with a stylus, piercing holes in paper ballots through holes in the ballot holder. The ballots themselves were blank, but candidate names were printed beside each hole in the ballot holder. Dougan's systems also included ballot readers that attempted to eliminate subjective questions about which ballot positions were punched. Dougan's readers did not tabulate votes, they merely raised and lowered publicly observable flags for each candidate so that observers could do the tabulation.

In 1893, Urban G. Iles of Wellston, Missouri patented a punched-card voting system that included a ballot tabulating machine. [493] Where Monaghan's or Dougan's machines simply tore holes in the ballot, the punch for Iles' machine was a positive-action paper punch, as shown in Figure 11. Iles' machine used pre-printed ballot cards, so voters could easily verify their ballots. Additionally, a pair of ballots identical to those used by voters could be used as labels, one on the face of the voting machine and one for the counters on the tabulating machine. Iles

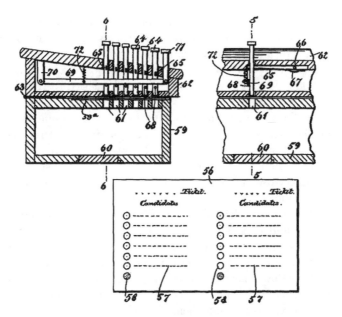

FIGURE 11 Urban G. Iles' punched-card voting machine, top, and an example ballot card, bottom. Voters pushed the buttons, 64 in the upper left figure, to vote against candidates, or pushed the straight-party button, 71, to vote against all candidates in one column. From U.S. Patent 500,001.

intended his tabulator to be a precinct-count device, and he described polling-place procedures in which each ballot was tabulated immediately, in the voter's presence, before it was dropped in the ballot box. In retrospect, the only odd feature of this machine is that it required voters to punch the names of all candidates they wished to oppose. While voting against candidates might confuse modern voters, in the 1890s, many voters were accustomed to scratching out the names of candidates they opposed on partisan paper ballots.

A voter using Dougan's or Iles' mechanisms had no protection against making an overvote, that is, voting for too many candidates in one race. Harris' machine had a new and simple interlock mechanism to prevent overvotes: When pressed to cast a vote, each punch locked down, stretching a piece of string threaded through the punch shafts. The amount of slack in the string determined the total number of votes permitted in each race. Dougan's machine had no provision for straight-party voting, a defect that Iles' and Harris' machines corrected.

The idea of using punched-card ballots to record votes was revived by Fred M. Carroll of IBM. In 1940, Carroll was granted a patent for a voting machine that recorded votes on punched cards using a mechanism as massive and expensive as a classic lever machine.[148] IBM's prototype allowed for 30 distinct vote-for-one races on the ballot. The machine prevented overvoting in vote-for-one races, but it was unable to handle races in which the voter was entitled to vote for more than one candidate.

IBM's punched-card tabulators were big expensive machines, so it was expected that each county would have a single centrally located punched-card tabulator to count the ballots. This forced a shift to central-count tabulation. With such a system, ballot boxes are sealed when the polls close and are taken to a central tabulation center. This exposes the ballots to potential manipulation or substitution in transit.

In the years that followed, many other patents would be granted for elaborate and expensive voting machines that recorded votes on punched cards, but most of these machines went nowhere. George Rathbun of Manhattan, Kansas obtained patents in 1944 on a punched-card voting system that allowed each polling place to have just one expensive punch mechanism to record the votes from many removable "ballot parts" used by voters to input their selections.[835,836] Cothburn O'Neal of Arlington, Texas obtained a series of patents that continued into the 1970s on extraordinarily complex but compact mechanical ballot punches.[795,797]

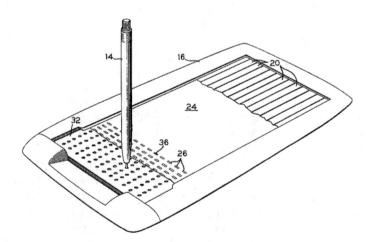

FIGURE 12 The IBM Portapunch, The stylus (14) is being used to punch a punched-card (24) held in the holder (16) through a template (32). The card is pre-scored in every possible punch position (26).
From U.S. Patent 3,007,620.

Punched cards would come into their own as a vote recording medium as a result of a different line of development. Many of the punched-card data processing applications of the first half of the 20th century required keypunch clerks to transcribe handwritten notes onto punched cards. The process was expensive, and for many years IBM had been investigating ways to eliminate the clerical step and allow workers in the field to record data directly in machine readable form. In the mid 1950s, this led Charles Holovka Jr. to develop and patent a portable hand-held punch for pre-scored punched-cards. [465] Conventional punched cards require a punch and die to make a clean hole. In contrast, Holovka's system used cards on which most of the perimeter of each punching position was pre-scored. As a result, the hole could be cleanly punched with a hand-held stylus working against a resilient backing. After refinements patented by Carl Abissi, Guy Laframboise and Merle Prater, the system came to market as the IBM Portapunch, as shown in Figure 12. [3,356]

The Portapunch was a pocket-sized handheld device that allowed a worker in the field to record data directly onto pre-scored punched cards by pressing a stylus through holes in a template over the card. With no moving parts, aside from the handheld stylus and the resilient rubber backing strips behind the card, Portapunches cost only a few dollars each. When a student called Joseph Harris's attention to the Portapunch, he very quickly saw the possibility of adapting it to voting. At the time, Harris was on the faculty of the University of California at Berkeley. Working with William Rouverol, a mechanical engineering professor, Harris transformed the Portapunch into what became the Votomatic. [732] Harris received his first Votomatic patent in 1965, [437] and a patent on a refined machine in 1966. [438] The former is shown in Figure 13.

In converting the Portapunch into a voting system, Harris and Rouverol incorporated the mechanism that had been a hand-held clerical device into the table-top of a lightweight voting booth, added a registration system to help align the ballot card for punching, and, most significantly, developed a way to pack the text of a complete general election onto a label that would fit over IBM's standard 3 1/4 by 7 3/8 inch punched card ballot. The trick was to arrange the ballot label as a booklet. Opening the booklet to any page exposed one of the 12 columns of the punched card in the space between two pages of the booklet. Those two pages could then be used to describe up to 40 punching positions in that column, although most ballots used far fewer than this maximum.

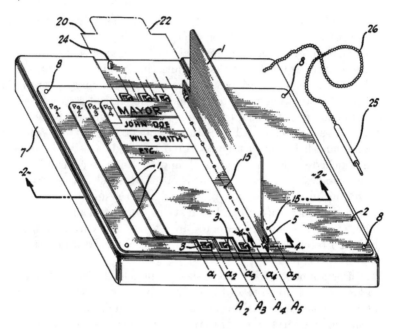

FIGURE 13 The Votomatic. The central part of the machine is a Portapunch mechanism, almost completely obscured by the pages of the ballot label (1). Prior to voting, the voter slides the ballot (20) into the machine from the top. The punching stylus (25) is chained to the machine on the right. Later patents covered improved hinges for the ballot pages, improved alignment of the ballot for punching, and better styluses. From U.S. Patent 3,201,038.

3.5 The Trouble With Chad

One weakness of the Portapunch was discovered very early. In their Portapunch patent granted in 1961, Guy Laframboise and Merle Prater wrote that "precautions should be taken to insure that all of the chips punched from the card are expelled from the resilient die strips* and that none of these chips will remain caught in the grip of the resilient strips after the punching tool is withdrawn. If chips[†] are permitted to accumulate between the resilient die strips, this can interfere with the punching operations, and occasionally it has been observed that a partially punched chip was left clinging to a card[‡] after the punch was withdrawn because the card-supporting surface of the punch board had

---

*In the Portapunch and Votomatic, the card is supported from behind by parallel die strips. Punching the card pushes the displaced chad between the die strips.

†IBM terminology for what others knew as chad.

‡Later called hanging chad.

become so clogged with chips as to prevent a clean punching operation. Incompletely punched cards can cause serious errors to occur in data processing operations utilizing such cards." [356]

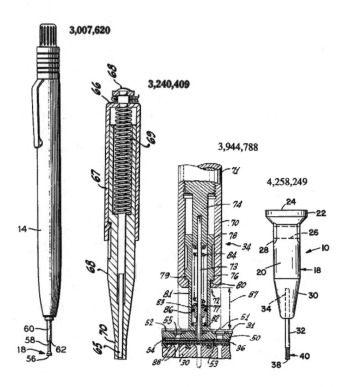

FIGURE 14 Various Portapunch and Votomatic punches, all designed to reduce the likelihood of hanging or dimpled chad.
From the indicated U.S. Patents.

Laframboise and Prater's warning was prophetic, and in the years that followed, patent after patent attempted to reduce the likelihood of this problem with improved stylus designs. Laframboise and Prater included one in their patent. [356] Harris included yet another in his second patent. [438] Several subsequent patents offered new alternatives. Stylus designs incorporating roughened shanks, needle points and various spring-loading mechanisms were all tried, as shown in Figure 14. [181,18] Unfortunately, while each of these styluses may have offered some improvement, none of them addressed the root problem that Laframboise and Prater had identified: poor maintenance.

A year after election 2000, at the suggestion of one of us, Douglas Jones, the Palm Beach Post examined the 4,867 test ballots from the 531 polling places in the county.[316] Pollworkers had been instructed to punch one test ballot on each voting machine before the polls opened on November 7. In theory, the pollworkers should have noticed if there was a problem punching one of these test ballots, and where problems were noticed, the machine in question should have been pulled from service.

In fact, over 11% of the test ballots showed problems, either in the testing itself or in the state of the machine. 65 test ballots contained no evidence of a vote for any presidential candidate, where each test ballot was supposed to be punched for all of them. Three percent of the test ballots had dimples or other incomplete punching suggestive of the problems Laframboise and Prater had warned about. Unfortunately, not one voting machine was pulled from service as a result of these tests.

It turns out that Palm Beach County had been using two different types of punched card voting machines that were, in theory, interchangeable. 455 precincts used Votomatic machines, while 76 precincts used DataPunch machines. The county followed the recommended cleaning instructions for each. In the case of the Votomatic, this involved unscrewing the back of the machine and using a vacuum cleaner to suck out the chad. In the case of the DataPunch machines, the instructions embossed on each machine say "SHAKE WELL TO REMOVE CHADS," so that is what was done. Our experiments with the DataPunch machine show that following these instructions removes only a small fraction of the accumulated chad, and that chad buildups can indeed prevent effective punching on these machines.

3.6   The Success of the Votomatic

The Votomatic had three things going for it. First, it was cheap. Lever voting machines could cost thousands of dollars, but IBM sold the injection-molded Votomatic for only $185 in 1965. It was inexpensive to store and transport as well. Lever voting machines could weigh close to a half ton, but a Votomatic machine weighed only 6 pounds.[480]

The second advantage was one of technology. Voting on punched cards brought elections into the computer era. Unlike lever voting machines, if there was doubt about the integrity of an election, the ballots could be recounted. Ballots were separate, so there was no record of the order in which votes were cast, and vote counting was done by fast objective machinery, so ballot handling was minimized. To many observers in the 1960s and 1970s, the Votomatic system really did appear to be close to ideal.

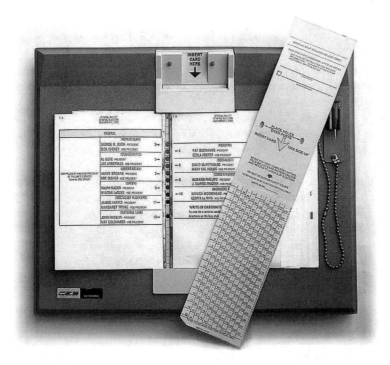

FIGURE 15 A commercial Votomatic and a Votomatic punched-card ballot. The machine is fitted with a replica of the Palm Beach County ballot label from November 7, 2000, open to the Presidential race to show the *butterfly* arrangement of the candidates. When the ballot stub is torn from the ballot, what remains is a standard punched card. Photo by Douglas Jones.

The third advantage was one of accessibility. Short voters and those confined to wheelchairs had significant problems reaching the top rows of levers on mechanical lever voting machines. Some jurisdictions provided step stools for short voters, but this was hardly an inviting accommodation. In contrast, the Votomatic voting machine could be used while seated, and the holes in the template over the ballot were helpful for voters with motor problems. Holding a pencil-shaped punch was difficult for some voters, but in 1987 John Ahmann received a patent application for a modified votomatic stylus that was well adapted for the needs of those suffering from multiple sclerosis, cerebral palsy, arthritis, Parkinson's disease and similar motor disorders.[19] This was one of the first patents to directly address the problem of providing accessibility for voters with disabilities.

After developing their original prototypes, Harris and Rouverol took them to the state fair in Oregon, where about 5000 fairgoers cast ballots on them. This real-world experience was very important, forcing the inventors to deal with wear and tear on the machinery as it was used by real people. After this trial, Monterey and San Joaquin counties in California, as well as Fulton and DeKalb counties in Georgia, used Votomatics on a trial basis during the 1964 general election. Harris and Rouverol raised a quarter of a million dollars to cover their initial work, but many counties were hesitant to buy into the new system until IBM joined the venture on March 19, 1965. [732]

The Votomatic looked like an obvious product line for IBM. This was not simply because IBM owned the Portapunch patents and had the manufacturing and sales force necessary to support such a product. Rather, IBM understood very well that sales of machines such as the Votomatic and the Portapunch was only the start. The profit was in the supplies that were required for each election. IBM was the major vendor of punched cards and could easily provide punched-card ballots and ballot labels printed on a similar grade of paper. In addition, IBM would profit from the leasing of tabulating machines needed to count the punched-card ballots.

It did not take IBM long to discover that the voting system business had a serious downside. Whenever a candidate lost an election that involved new voting technology, it was natural to try to pin the blame on the technology. Furthermore, as we have discussed above, established voting machine vendors were not averse to engaging in illegal tactics in order to sell their systems in the face of the very real price advantage of the Votomatic. As a result, IBM left the voting systems market, spinning off Computer Election Systems in 1968. Harris sold his interest in the Votomatic shortly afterward. [732]

With its high-tech appeal and low price, the Votomatic became the single most widely used voting system in the United States. Several states adopted the system statewide, among them Illinois, and it was very popular in large urban areas such as Miami and Los Angeles. By 1980, over 29% of U.S. voters were voting on Votomatic-style punched-card ballots, using systems provided by almost a dozen vendors. [305] By 1992, the Votomatic system was the dominant voting system in the United States, used by 27% more voters than used mechanical lever voting machines. By this time, newer electronic voting technologies were becoming strong competitors, but they represented a much smaller market share. [306]

A noteworthy consequence of the shift from lever machines to the Votomatic system was a shift from precinct-count to central-count ballot tabulation. With lever machines, the totals for each precinct could be announced and recorded by election observers at the precinct immediately after the polls closed, while with the Votomatic, no results were known until the ballots had been transported to the counting center and tabulated.

3.7 What's Wrong with the Votomatic

In many ways, the Votomatic was a very good design. After inserting a ballot in the Votomatic punching fixture, the voter can pull out the ballot and inspect it in order to see if the ballot, as punched, accurately reflects the voter's intent. This voter-verification step is one of the central attributes of the best voting systems. On standard votomatic ballots, each punching position is clearly marked, and after voting there should either be a punched hole or no hole in each punching position. What could be easier?

There are two problems. First, for voters to verify Votomatic ballots, they must decode the relationship between the numbers on the ballot cards and the candidate names. There is no intuitive connection between the number four, for example, and Pat Buchanan, the candidate assigned to position four on the Palm Beach County ballot from November 2000. Ballot labels on the Votomatic always included position numbers by each candidate name, so alert voters could figure out how to verify their ballots. Unfortunately, not all voters were that alert, and the decoding was just hard enough that most voters did not do so.

The second problem with the Votomatic ballot is that there are not just two possible states for each voting position. The bit of chad in each position may be unpunched or cleanly punched, but it may also be partially punched. The obscure terminology of "chadology" includes such evocative terms as trapdoor chad, dangling chad, dimpled chad, pregnant chad and pinhole chad. Some of these are illustrated in Figure 16. These terms can be precisely defined, and the physical conditions that produce each can be clearly identified, but the law on hand-recounts of Votomatic ballots rarely rests on such an understanding.

The most common objective rules for interpreting partially detached chad determine whether the chad may be removed prior to machine tabulation or counted as a vote in a hand recount, depending on how many corners of the chad remain attached to the ballot. Variations of this have been used, for example, in Arizona, Michigan, Nevada, Ohio, and Texas. [735] Unfortunately, the number of detached corners is poor evidence of voter intent.

FIGURE 16 Close-up of the back of a Votomatic punched-card ballot
showing hanging chad, trap-door chad, pregnant and dimpled chad.
Photo by Douglas Jones.

Brit Williams noted in 2000 that a partially detached piece of chad
could have many causes: "The voter may have meant to vote for that
candidate, or was [the voter] just resting the stylus near that candidate's
name while studying the ballot?" [1036] While counting the loose corners
on the chad cannot answer this question, it turns out that the chad does
record something very important: how hard the voter pressed the voting
stylus against that piece of chad.

It takes about 12 ounces of force to cast a vote on a well-maintained
Votomatic voting machine, punching the bit of chad loose from the
ballot and through the space between the elastomeric strips behind the
ballot. [536] If the strips have hardened with age, or if an obstruction
blocks the punch, it can take considerably more force to punch out the
chad. To evaluate voter intent on a partially punched bit of chad, it
would seem reasonable to ask: "Did the voter press hard enough to
punch out the chad on a well regulated voting machine?"

One of us, Douglas Jones, tested the Votomatic shown in Figure
15 to see how the mark produced on the card depended on how hard
the stylus was pressed. The stylus used in these tests resembled the
rightmost one in Figure 14, with a pyramidal needle 0.005 inches high
in the center of the 0.04 inch diameter flat face of the stylus.

In these tests, the needle began to dimple the surface of the card at
a force of about 4 ounces. As the pressure approached 20 ounces, the
circular face of the stylus began to imprint itself on the ballot. Since
20 ounces is significantly more than the force required to punch out

the chad on a well maintained machine, it would seem reasonable to conclude that any chad on which the round stylus face is partially imprinted ought to be counted as an intended vote, regardless of whether it is partially dislodged from the card. Similarly, in cases where chad is partially dislodged from the card without a dimple from the needle on the stylus tip, it was probably punched outside the context of the votomatic machine.

Another problem Jones found with the Votomatic ballot was that dimpled chad, trapdoor chad and dangling chad may easily be forced back into the card by burnishing the ballot card with a fingernail against a hard surface such as a desktop. This takes only a second, and only microscopic examination of the card surface will reveal torn fibers at the corners of the bit of chad and the faint dimple made by the needle tip in the center of the stylus. Unfortunately, hand counting rules that require the use of microscopes to search the card for loose fibers, microscopic dimples, and the faint impression of the voting stylus are not practical. So far as we are aware, such criteria have never been used in practice.

Loose chad in areas where ballots were handled was not just a theoretical possibility. An observer at a simulated recount in the San Francisco area in the late 1970s was amazed to see chad falling to the floor during the count, with more pieces escaping whenever the ballots were run through the machinery. Election workers responding to his questions about this said "Oh, we'd never have an election so close that a few chad pieces would effect the outcome." [675]

The public outcry after the election of 2000 led Florida and several other states to abandon Votomatic technology, but it remained in use in Ohio, Illinois and several other states until the Help America Vote Act of 2002 (HAVA) effectively banned pre-scored punched card ballots. [191] As we discuss in Chapter 6, HAVA was passed after serious problems with newer electronic voting systems cropped up in Florida's August 2002 primaries. Among other things, HAVA gave the states 4 years to replace all lever and punched-card voting machines with newer equipment.

4

Filling in the Bubble: Optical Mark-Sense Ballots

The selection of the appropriate marking device improves the efficiency of ballot tabulation and decreases the impact of marginal marks. ... Making the appropriate device available or communicating it to those who will be participating in early or absentee voting is as important as the selection.

ES&S Model 650 Best Practices Manual [310]

By the middle of the 20th century, paperless mechanical voting machines were the dominant election technology in the United States. As we saw in Chapter 3, the Votomatic punched-card voting system was the first new technology to successfully challenge lever voting machines. But there was another technology waiting in the wings—optical mark-sense scanners. As with punched cards, optical scanning was not originally developed for voting. The first mark-sense scanners were designed for scoring standardized tests.

Scoring a multiple-choice standardized test is a tedious job, so in 1932, Reynold Johnson set out to automate the job. Johnson, a high-school teacher in Michigan, knew that graphite pencil lead is somewhat conductive, and he built a test-scoring machine that used this fact to detect which choices the student had marked. IBM eventually hired him and underwrote the patenting and commercial development of his idea. [517,343] IBM trademarked the term *mark sense* to refer specifically to Johnson's mark-sensing technology, and introduced a line of mark-sense data processing equipment, starting in 1938 with the Model 805 Automatic Test Scoring Machine. [479]

The IBM 805 was quickly put to use for scoring a wide variety of tests. The machine was tested by comparing machine and hand-scoring of the same test papers. In general, machine and hand scores differed on only 2.6 percent of test papers, and on 0.15% of test items. [361] This was good enough that within two years after it was introduced, one commentator wrote: "Every school should investigate the possibilities inherent in the electrical test-scoring machine of the International Business Machines Corporation." [965]

As use of machine-scored standardized tests spread, several inventors noticed the possibility of applying the same technology to elections. Hiram Keith of Ventura, California filed for the first patent on a crude mark-sense voting system in 1953. The primary problem with Keith's machine was it could only sense marks made with special conductive ink or metallic crayons.

These early systems sensed marks on the page by detecting the conductivity of the mark. IBM sought alternatives to this from the very start. As early as 1932, IBM's Richard Warren filed for a patent on a mark-sense test-scoring machine that used reflected light to sense marks on student answer sheets. [995] The problem with electrical mark-sense machines is that they judge an invisible attribute of the mark. In contrast, optical mark-sense scanners have the potential to judge marks based on attributes that most people can see.

IBM continued work on optical mark sensing, but it was Everet Lindquist of the University of Iowa who pushed optical mark-sense scanning into production. In 1955, he filed a patent on a test scoring machine. [603] Lindquist was one of the developers of the ACT college entrance exam, and he was not satisfied with the IBM 805, the only commercial offering at the time. The enormous volume of paperwork involved in processing the ACT and SAT exams remained a major force in the development of new mark-sensing technologies for several decades.

In 1959, under the leadership of Frank Preston, the Norden Division of United Aircraft began developing the Norden Electronic Vote Tallying System. Los Angeles County commissioned the development of this system, at a cost of one million dollars. Where the IBM and Lindquist scanners used visible and infrared light, the Norden system used ultraviolet light. This required voters to mark their ballots using fluorescent ink applied with special rubber stamps.

The Norden system was immense, weighing 15,000 pounds and requiring a 1,200 square foot computer room. It had a core memory with a capacity of 600 17-bit words, and it contained around 3800 transistors. The air compressor, vacuum pump, and fans consumed a tremendous amount of power. Despite being comparable in size to many of the general-purpose computers of the era, it was not a computer. It could do just one thing, count votes. [1001]

The state of California certified the Norden system in 1961, and Orange County immediately purchased the prototype. Orange County used the Norden system until 1986, but only two other California counties tried it: Kern County and Contra Costa County used the system in the 1964 general election, and Kern County kept it through the 1966 primaries. By mid-1962, Coleman Engineering had acquired the Norden system, where it became the Model 2902 Coleman VTS vote tabulation system. Gyrex Corporation purchased the the product line in 1971 and invested significant effort in modernizing the system by replacing Norden's special purpose control units with off-the-shelf 16-bit minicomputers. [58] Even with these modernizations, the Gyrex system remained expensive, selling for a whopping 1.15 million dollars. By 1975, the Gyrex system was in use in only three counties nationally: Multnomah County, Oregon; Hamilton County, Ohio; and Orange County, California. [716]

Aside from cost and size, the biggest drawback of the Norden-Coleman-Gyrex machine was the requirement that voters use special fluorescent ink. Providing special markers for absentee voters was impractical, and even in the controlled environment of a voting booth, it is difficult to ensure that voters use the marker provided, instead of their own pens or pencils. By the time the Norden VTS came to market, machines in the educational testing arena had been scanning ordinary graphite pencil marks for 20 years. This technology was so pervasive that for many Americans the instruction to "fill in the bubble by your answer with a number-2 soft lead pencil" was a central symbol of educational testing.

In 1964, Gerold Holzer, Norman Walker, and Harry Wilcock filed their patent for the Votronic, the first practical* vote tabulator designed to sense regular pencil marks. [472] Their optical mark-sense system read marks using the reflection of ordinary white light bulbs off the ballot and onto the photosensor, as shown in Figure 17. Note that the photosensors used on the Votronic and many other early mark-sense scanners were more sensitive to infrared light than to visible light. A metal mask helped guide the paper and provided a hole defining the area of the page to be scanned. The Votronic was small enough to be considered somewhat portable—at least as portable as a lever voting machine.

---

*In 1957, James L. Fechter and Everett E. Stallard filed for a patent, granted in 1960, for an optical mark-sense voting machine. [325] Although they solved several important problems, programming their machine for a particular ballot style required rewiring, using a plugboard, and we have found no evidence that this machine was ever used.

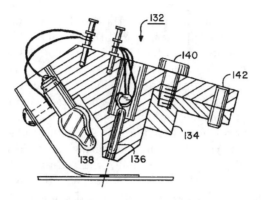

FIGURE 17 Cross section of the mark-sensing mechanism of the Votronic. Lightbulb 138 illuminates the ballot, bottom. The curved metal shoe, on the left, holds the ballot flat and blocks the view of irrelevant parts of the ballot. Photodiode 136 measures the reflected light to sense marks. From U.S. Patent 3,218,439.

The Votronic model 23PB, made by Votronics Inc. of San Diego, was certified for use in California early in 1964. San Diego County was the first to adopt the system, using it in the 1964 general election. By 1965, Cubic Industrial Corp. had taken over and obtained Ohio certification. [1015] Cubic's Votronic Model 5-62 remained in production at least until 1975, by which time accessories such as printers had been added to the machine. [58] By the 1968 general election, nine California counties were using the Votronic. [59]

The Votronic machine was designed to be small, inexpensive, and simple enough to use at individual precincts for counting votes on Election Day. Immediately after the polls closed, officials could open the ballot box and count the ballots electronically, on the spot. The machine was easy to reprogram to count ballots from a different precinct, so a county that could not afford one machine for each precinct could use Votronics in their central tabulating center.

The Votronic ballot was limited to four columns, each holding up to 100 *voting targets*, that is, spaces voters could mark to cast votes. This forced the use of an office-block ballot layout, since there were too few columns to permit either a party-row or a party-column format. As with mechanical lever voting machines, where the interlocking mechanisms forced the use of party-row or party-column ballot layouts, the ballot layout used with the Votronic was forced by the technology, not by political considerations.

Programming the Votronic to tabulate ballots was remarkably fast and elegant. After setting a control switch to program mode, two or three ballots were fed through the machine. The first was marked in every potential voting position to indicate which targets on the ballot were to be counted. The second programming ballot indicated the number of votes permitted in each race simply by voting for the maximum number of permitted candidates. A third programming ballot was necessary only when the right to vote in a race was contingent on how the voter had responded in the immediately preceding race. This complex feature was needed to support California's recall rules, which specify that a vote for a recall confers the right to vote for a replacement candidate on the same ballot.

There were two drawbacks to the Votronic as it was initially designed: The Votronic display could show the total for only one candidate at a time, and the machine had no printer. As a result, a poll worker had to transcribe the totals from the machine's display after the votes were counted. The machine had a clever scheme to help avoid clerical errors: Sliding a mechanical cursor over a blank ballot selected which vote total the machine displayed, so that writing the total by the cursor automatically put each total adjacent to the corresponding candidate's name.

By the end of the 1960s, the appeal of optical mark-sense vote tabulation was growing rapidly, but the technology was far from perfect. The biggest problem was that the machines could only reliably count properly made marks. Voters who used the wrong type of pen or who did not make a dark enough mark were at risk of having their votes ignored, while there was also a possibility that some smudges or accidental marks would be counted. Nonetheless, mark-sense ballots could easily be recounted if there was any question about an election, and unlike punched cards, a hand count of mark-sense ballots does not involve the obscure issue of chad interpretation. Furthermore, the price of computer technology was falling rapidly. The optical mark-sense voting systems of the 1960s were designed in an era when computer hardware was expensive, bulky, and slow. Around 1970, mass-produced minicomputers became available for under $10,000, and just a few years later single-chip microprocessors, such as the Intel 8080 and the Motorola 6800, forced prices even lower. By the middle of the 1970s, small computer systems could be built for under $1000.

With mark-sense readers, the integration of microprocessors took two distinct directions. One was to develop high-performance systems to compete with large machines like the Norden/Coleman VTS. The priority here was high-speed scanning without misfeeds and jams. Reliable high-capacity machines were perfect for election officials who wanted to maintain a central-count system, one where votes would be counted in a few large, central counting areas after the polls closed. Given that central counting could be done with only a few machines per county, the machines could be large and expensive, but they had to be fast. Central counting had the advantage that all tabulation takes place in one location where election monitors can easily observe the process. However, the disadvantage is that transporting ballots introduces the opportunity for post-election ballot tampering or even outright substitution.

The other direction of development followed naturally from the design of the Votronic machine. These systems were low-speed ballot tabulators robust enough to install in each precinct on Election Day. Such small, portable precinct-count systems had no need for high-speed paper processing. Ballots could be fed into the machine individually by the voters themselves when they cast their ballot or by poll workers immediately after the polls closed. By counting ballots immediately, the opportunities for post-election ballot fraud were reduced, but at the cost of trusting each precinct to conduct an honest count. Clearly, monitoring the proper use of high-tech tabulating machines at hundreds of precincts is more difficult than monitoring the count at a single central location. It was not immediately obvious which of these two systems was better.

4.1 Central-Count Machines

In 1969, Westinghouse Learning Corporation acquired the rights to Lindquist's mark-sense work. This made Westinghouse the primary vendor for machines to count the Iowa Test of Basic Skills, the Iowa Test of Educational Development, and the ACT exam.[810] In October 1974, Robert Urosevich of the Klopp Printing Company in Omaha approached John McMillin of Westinghouse to ask if Westinghouse scanners could be used to count ballots. Klopp had been in the ballot printing business for many years, and Urosevitch knew many election officials and understood the problems they faced.[677]

Robert Urosevich and his brother Todd, an IBM salesman, formed Data Mark Systems to act as the marketing, sales, and service agent for the new Westinghouse voting products. The startup capital came from the Newlin Foundation, a charity associated with Pioneer Hy-Bred. Aside from the ballot tabulation software, the Westinghouse ballot scanners were essentially standard test scanning machines. To demonstrate the capabilities of their new system, Westinghouse created the

Scan-A-Van, a truck loaded with several of their scanners and the mini-computer needed to run them. The new system saw its first test during the May 11, 1976 primary in Douglas County, Nebraska, under the glare of television lights. The test was deemed a success, and Douglas County became the first Data Mark customer. That November, Douglas County ballots were counted on three W600B scanners interfaced to a Hewlett-Packard 2100-series minicomputer and a line printer.

The W600B scanner could handle 600 pages per hour, and it had an automatic sorting mechanism that placed scanned pages into one of three output hoppers. Ballots that scanned normally went into a large hopper, while ballots containing write-in votes, timing and index marks in abnormal places, or overvotes were sorted into two smaller hoppers. In the central-count context, the ability to read ballots from many different precincts was important. Westinghouse understood this from the start, and designed ballots with a pair of code-tracks along the left edge that could be used to encode information such as precinct numbers. In effect, the code tracks were long skinny bar codes designed to be read by exactly the same kind of read heads that were used to read the votes on the ballots.

Even with their public success, sales of the Data Mark system were slow. Although they obtained California certification in 1976, [60] their only customers four years later were Douglas and Sarpy Counties in Nebraska and Jefferson County, Missouri. [677] Rock Island, Illinois, which used a Westinghouse ballot scanner for about six elections in 1981 and 1982, dealt directly with Westinghouse instead of going through Data Mark. [676] From the corporate perspective of a large company like Westinghouse, educational testing was a small business, and ballot scanners were insignificant. With no immediate prospect of significant return on investment, there was little reason for Westinghouse to remain in the market.

For a small startup like Data Mark Systems, the story was quite different. Ballot scanners were their only business, and the lack of support from Westinghouse was frustrating. As Westinghouse backed out of the business, the Urosevich brothers and several key Westinghouse staffers formed a new company named American Information Systems to pursue the ballot scanner market. Their first product was the eccentrically numbered AIS 315 ballot scanner.

The AIS 315 was developed largely by Jim Lane, a former Westinghouse employee. The 315 was in many ways a simplified successor to the W600 scanner. [97] Weighing just under 300 pounds, the AIS 315 was the size of a small photocopier and designed to sit on a tabletop or on a heavy-wheeled cart. It could handle two-sided ballots printed on

Figure 18 The ES&S 650, successor to the AIS 315 scanner. Alongside the scanner is a jogger to square up ballot stacks. Under the scanner on the same cart are the printers. Photo by Douglas Jones.

80-pound legal-sized paper. The smaller and slower AIS 115 followed quickly in the marketplace. [482]

AIS ballot scanners were certified for use in Ohio in 1982, [1015] New Jersey in 1983, [782] Kansas in 1984, [540] and Washington in 1985. [723] These scanners and their successors have proven very durable. In Mississippi, for example, 12 counties purchased AIS scanners in 1987 and 1988 that were still in use in 2000. [169]

The ES&S Model 650 scanner shown in Figure 18 is typical of the AIS family of scanners. This scanner is the direct descendant of the AIS 550 and the earlier 315. It uses essentially the same mechanism, but with updated electronics. In 1998, ES&S offered Model 550 scanners to Dallas, Texas at a price of $44,750 each. [249] Unlike the Westinghouse scanner with its multiple output hoppers, the AIS scanners feature extremely simple paper paths. When the scanner detects a misfeed or a ballot containing an overvote or a write-in vote it simply halts, displaying an explanation for the operator. It is up to the operator to pick up the problem ballot and deal with it appropriately.

4.2 Precinct-Count Machines

While the American Information Systems line of central-count scanners was being born, James Narey, who had worked at Coleman Engineering, and William Saylor set about designing a better precinct-count scanner. [246] Their patent, filed in 1975, describes "a multi-functional 'ballot box' which not only receives the ballots as fed in by the voters, but tallies the votes cast so as to give a complete printout of all the ballots entered, showing subtotals for the various candidates or propositions, and the grand totals as desired." The patent required a custom-built, programmable processor, along with read-only and read-write semiconductor memories, cutting edge technology at the time. [730]

As built, an off-the-shelf microprocessor was substituted for the custom processor. The machine was marketed by Gyrex Corporation as the MTB-1 ballot scanner, and approved for use in California in 1975. [58] This machine scanned a long narrow single-column ballot about 3 inches wide, as shown in Figure 19. Voters directly inserted their ballots into the scanner at the precinct, and the scanner would immediately scan the ballot and drop it into the attached ballot box. When the polls closed, the machine would print out the precinct totals on a built-in printer. The entire machine with integrated printer and ballot box weighed 63 pounds and cost around $3,500 when discounted for multiple units. [716] Later, it was modified to scan two-sided ballots and support a "multi-precinct ballot tabulation configuration," which meant it could process more than one ballot style, using a rudimentary bar code to identify the ballot style. Valtec took over the MTB-1 in 1977, and in 1979, Major Data Concepts took over Valtec. By then, the machine that could process two-sided ballots was known as the MTB-2.

Other companies were interested in the ballot-scanner market. When IBM dropped the Votomatic punch card system, a Berkeley, California company called Computer Election Systems Incorporated was formed to take over the product license. [732] CESI was dominant in the Votomatic market, and it was only natural that the company would be looking at new ways to expand its product line. CESI's first entry into the precinct-ballot-count market was the PBC punched-card tabulator, a $950 tabulator for Votomatic ballots introduced in 1974. [60,716] This machine, originally built around an Intel 4040 microprocessor, is almost certainly the first voting machine to use a microprocessor. It remained in use in some jurisdictions until the end of the punched-card era.

CESI acted as a dealer for the MTB-2 in the early 1980s, marketing it as the CESI Tally II precinct-count tabulator. Linn County, Iowa replaced its aging lever voting machines in 1981 with 77 Tally II scanners at a cost of $3740 each. Despite a fire that delayed full deployment of the Tally II scanners, voter response to the new system was very positive. Although no new machines were manufactured after 1984, Linn County continued using these machines well into the 1990s. [582]

Even with their widespread adoption, the Tally I and II precinct-count tabulators had significant shortcomings, chief among them the long skinny ballot format. Charles Fogg and others, working for CESI, addressed this issue with the Optech I, patented in 1984. [353] The Optech ballot was two-sided, with two 5-inch-wide columns per side,

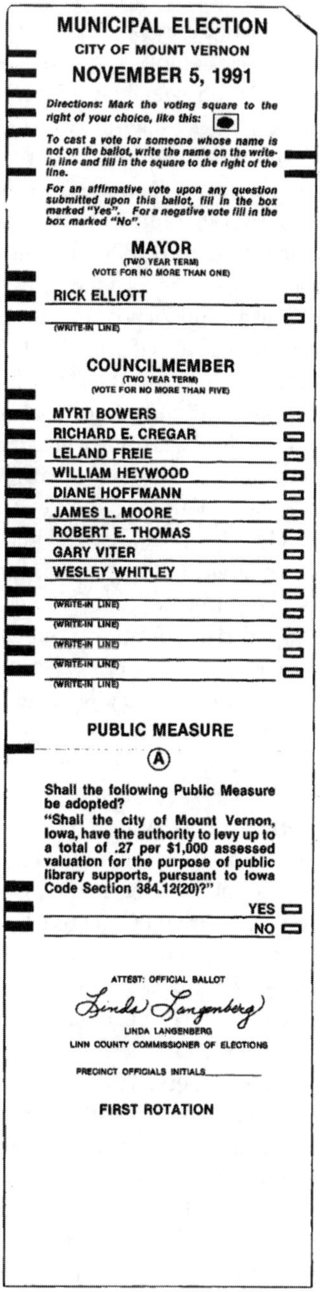

Figure 19 A Ballot for the MTB-2/CESI Tally II scanner from Mount Vernon, Iowa. Timing marks along the left side of the ballot allow the scanner to locate the voting targets on the right. The extra timing marks at the top right of the ballot are a rudimentary bar code for the ballot style or precinct number. Ballot provided by Linda Langenberg.

MUNICIPAL ELECTION
CITY OF MOUNT VERNON
NOVEMBER 5, 1991

Directions: Mark the voting square to the right of your choice, like this: ◉

To cast a vote for someone whose name is not on the ballot, write the name on the write-in line and fill in the square to the right of the line.

For an affirmative vote upon any question submitted upon this ballot, fill in the box marked "Yes".   For a negative vote fill in the box marked "No".

MAYOR
(TWO YEAR TERM)
(VOTE FOR NO MORE THAN ONE)

RICK ELLIOTT

(WRITE-IN LINE)

COUNCILMEMBER
(TWO YEAR TERM)
(VOTE FOR NO MORE THAN FIVE)

MYRT BOWERS
RICHARD E. CREGAR
LELAND FREIE
WILLIAM HEYWOOD
DIANE HOFFMANN
JAMES L. MOORE
ROBERT E. THOMAS
GARY VITER
WESLEY WHITLEY

(WRITE-IN LINE)
(WRITE-IN LINE)
(WRITE-IN LINE)
(WRITE-IN LINE)
(WRITE-IN LINE)

PUBLIC MEASURE
Ⓐ

Shall the following Public Measure be adopted?
"Shall the city of Mount Vernon, Iowa, have the authority to levy up to a total of .27 per $1,000 assessed valuation for the purpose of public library supports, pursuant to Iowa Code Section 384.12(20)?"

YES ▭
NO ▭

ATTEST: OFFICIAL BALLOT

Linda Langenberg
LINDA LANGENBERG
LINN COUNTY COMMISSIONER OF ELECTIONS

PRECINCT OFFICIALS INITIALS_____

FIRST ROTATION

and could be up to 24 inches long, with timing marks down the center of the card. In effect, the ballot was two Tally II ballots side-by-side with the index marks down the center.

The Optech scanner was approved for use in California and Pennsylvania in mid 1983. [60,811] It used a classic 8-bit microprocessor, the Intel 8085, and had only 2 kilobytes of read-write memory plus 32 kilobytes of read-only memory to hold the firmware.* One innovation introduced on this machine was a removable memory pack about the size of a pack of cigarettes containing both the preprogrammed read-only memory holding the election configuration and the programmable read-only memory the machine used to store ballot data as each ballot was scanned. The design was such that all information specific to a particular election was in the memory pack. At the close of the polls, the memory pack was designed to be removed and taken to the election headquarters, so that the results could be electronically incorporated into the canvass of the jurisdiction.

An important feature of the Optech scanner was that it included a diverter, allowing it to sort ballots into either of two canvas ballot bags. Typically, ballots with write-in votes were separated from the others for hand tabulation. The earlier Tally II had included an automatic ballot marker that could flag such ballots with a red stripe, but this left the poll workers with the annoying job of manually sorting through all of the ballots to find the flagged ones.

Johnson County Iowa purchased 55 Optech scanners in 1984 for $2750 each. Unfortunately, ballots tended to hang up on the weave of the canvas ballot bags, and in a high turnout general election the ballots sometimes backed up enough to jam the machine. The solution was a steel ballot box to replace the lightweight canvas. The combination of an Optech scanner on a steel box was dubbed the Optech II. Johnson County bought 59 of these at $3,800 each. [920]

The Optech scanner could reverse its feed motor. While this feature may have been introduced to allow the machine to clear jams and misfeeds, it also allowed the machine to reject overvoted ballots and ballots that scanned as blank. The earlier Tally II simply marked problem ballots for manual processing after the polls closed. Returning problem ballots to the voter for correction, as the Optech could do, seems more likely to give the right result than turning them over to a resolution board for interpretation. This "second-chance" feature has become one of the most important advantages of precinct count scanning.

---

*The term *firmware* generally refers to computer programs that are delivered as part of a computerized mechanism and are seen as a fixed part of the mechanism by its users.

In 1985, CESI was acquired by Texas-based Cronus Industries, Inc., and folded into their voting equipment subsidiary, Business Records Corporation (BRC).[112] The Optech precinct-count systems were quickly certified across the country, and some election officials even used them as central count systems, primarily for absentee ballots. Cronus spun off BRC in 1990, by which time it had made several acquisitions, including the former Gyrex product line.[247]

While BRC continued to develop the Optech line, James Narey briefly flirted with launching a competing product, the Megascan.[246] The Megascan had two important new features that improved the usability of ballot formats. One was a system of markings that allowed the scanner to operate correctly, no matter how the ballot was inserted into the machine. This made it much easier for voters to insert their own ballots directly into the scanner.

The second feature was a new form of self-clocking voting target along with new marking instructions, as shown on the example ballot in Figure 20. Earlier mark-sense forms had used index marks along the edge to identify the locations of the voting targets. The self-clocking target used two closely-spaced index marks with a gap between them. Each pair of index marks was printed in the form of a broken arrow pointing to a candidate's name, and voters are instructed to "connect the arrow" in order to vote for a particular candidate. Connecting the index marks with a straight line darkens the target region between them, exactly where the scanner looks for votes.

This new form of target had several advantages. First, it encouraged the voter to use a horizontal line connecting the head and tail of the arrow. A scanner that moves the page vertically is more likely to sense a horizontal line than other marks. Second, placing the timing marks adjacent to the target reduced the system's sensitivity to paper shrinkage and small printing misalignments. Of course, with millions of people trained by various educational tests to "fill in the bubble," this new target design posed human-factors problems simply by being different. Well written instructions should have eliminated such problems, but poor explanations are common on all government forms, including ballots.

By 1989, when the U.S. government issued a patent for Narey's new ballot arrangement, he had sold the Megascan idea to BRC.[729] It appears that the BRC Optech III scanner was, for all intents and purposes, the Megascan. BRC understood that large jurisdictions which used precinct-count scanners also needed central-count scanners to process absentee ballots, so they developed the Optech IV-C high-speed central-count scanner shown in Figure 21. The Optech IV-C patent,

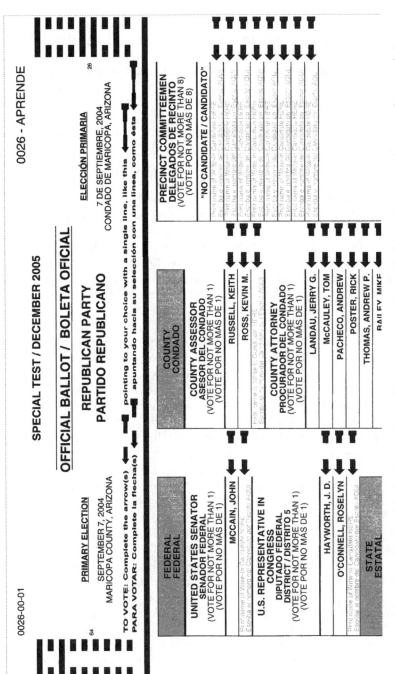

FIGURE 20 A bilingual ballot for the Optech III and IV-C scanners, from the 2004 primary in Maricopa County, Arizona. The marks to the left and right of the ballot header are primitive bar codes identifying this as a Republican ballot from Precinct 26. These codes and additional small marks at the ballot foot (not shown) identify the ballot orientation. The head and tail of each "connect the arrow" voting target are the index marks used to locate that target. Ballot from Douglas Jones' collection.

granted in 1993, clearly states the value of scanning mark-sense voting targets with visible light instead of the infrared light used by most earlier scanners. [946]

In late 1996, BRC agreed to sell its election business to AIS, which was by then the dominant manufacturer of central-count mark-sense voting systems. The Antitrust Division of the U.S. Department of Justice intervened, delaying the merger while they found a way to prevent the merged companies from forming an effective monopoly. The merger was finalized in 1997 after BRC sold the rights to the technology behind the Optech line of scanners to another vendor, Sequoia Pacific Systems. [113] After this sale, the merged companies were reorganized as Election Systems and Software (ES&S). As a result of the agreement with the Justice Department, both ES&S and Sequoia supported the Optech scanner line, although Sequoia changed the product names to the Optech 300-P and Optech 400-C. Aside from the name change, the ES&S and Sequoia systems were essentially identical. ES&S, however, continued development of their own precinct-count scanner, because they were forbidden to sell Optech scanners to new customers by their agreement with the Justice Department.

The origin of Sequoia Pacific traces back to the packaging division of Diamond National, a company best known for its near monopoly on kitchen matches. In early 1968, Diamond acquired rights to a punched-card voting system from Mathematical Systems and underwrote a patent application by James C. Fielder. Why was a match company interested in voting? Because their packaging division owned cardboard and paper mills, and punched cards are cardboard.

A noteworthy feature of Fielder's system was that it used cards with candidate names and issues printed on the card. With the Votomatic, by contrast, each punch position was numbered and the candidate names appeared only on the ballot labels. [339] Fielder's voting system eventually evolved into the Datavote system, a modestly successful competitor to the Votomatic. [58]

By the early 1980s, Diamond was a bloated conglomerate, a ripe target for a corporate raid. Sir James Goldsmith bought the company and set about breaking it up. In 1983, the packaging division, was sold to Jefferson Smurfit Group, an Irish cardboard company. [396] Smurfit renamed the company Sequoia Pacific, and within a year the new company purchased the voting machine business of AVM corporation. [895] By that time, AVM had diversified to the point that its primary business was lockers and office furniture. The value of AVM's mechanical voting technology may not have been great, but AVM had two valuable assets: an experienced sales force with established relation-

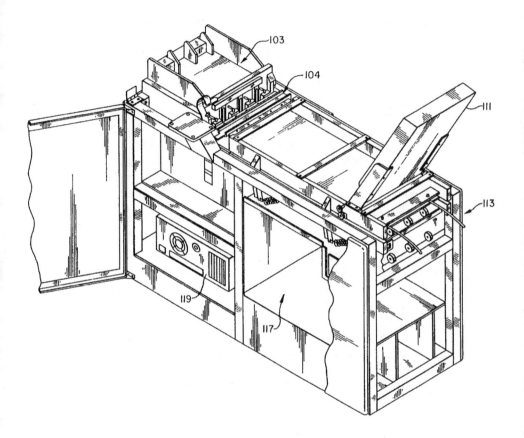

FIGURE 21 The Optech IV-C high-speed central-count scanner. The feed hopper is at the upper left, 103. After passing the scan head, 104, most ballots fly out to the right into a box (not shown). Overvoted and problem ballots are diverted into tray at the top right, 111. Ballots holding write-in votes are diverted into the hopper at the lower right, 117. Operation is controlled by a personal computer hidden inside at the lower left, 119. From U.S. Patent 5,248,872.

ships with state and county election offices across the United States, and a portfolio of patents for direct-recording electronic voting machines.

In the spring of 1989, another precinct-count voting system emerged in the marketplace, the Unisys ES-2000. This was built under license from Data Information Management Systems of Ventura, California. DIMS held a patent granted to Kenneth D. Webb for a precinct-count voting system similar to the MTB-2 in that it used a long narrow single-column ballot. [1000] The ES-2000 was a vast improvement on Webb's system in that it used standard-sized paper with a very flexible layout of rows and columns.

Unisys Corporation was the result of the merger of two old computer giants, Burroughs and Sperry-Univac. The Unisys press release announcing the ES-2000 emphasized that voters could insert their ballots directly into the scanner and that, at the end of the day, the scanner would automatically upload the results into a Unix-based server at election headquarters. [971]

By the Spring of 1990, Anoka County Minnesota had permission to use the ES-2000 in their primary and general elections that year. Unisys was now selling the ES-2000 under the trade-name Accu-Vote. The scanner was listed by Unisys at a price of $7225, including the ballot box, battery backup, carrying case and memory card, although a 30% discount was available to jurisdictions adopting the scanner before 1991. [614]

The ES-2000 was actually developed by another company, North American Professional Technologies. NAPT was founded by Clinton H. Rickards in 1983, and began development of the ES-2000 in 1986. Development of a new voting system is expensive, and by the time the ES-2000 came to market, NAPT was a subsidiary of Macrotrends International Ventures Inc. of Vancouver. [624,391] Macrotrends was a venture capital firm with a sometimes questionable reputation. [429] How did Unisys get involved? The answer is simple: marketing and service. Unisys computer systems were still widely used by governments at all levels in the 1980s, so the Unisys sales and service organization had good connections with people who might be willing to try a new computerized voting system.

The relationship with Unisys did not last. In late 1991, NAPT merged with Macrotrends to form Global Election Systems Inc. The corporation was technically Canadian, but the executive offices were in McKinney, Texas. Global immediately purchased a share in the patent rights of Data Information Management Systems. [391] Through the decade of the 1990s, Global would grow to become a major force in the election equipment marketplace, largely on the strength of the AccuVote ES-2000.*

In 2002, Diebold Inc., a well established manufacturer of bank vaults, automatic teller machines and other security-related products, bought Global to create Diebold Election Systems Inc. Global and Diebold continued to make the Accuvote ES-2000, although the name changed to the Accuvote OS, standing for Optical Scan, to distinguish it from the Accuvote TS, the touch-screen voting system that Global acquired with the purchase of I-Mark Systems. Diebold Election Systems was for a few years in the early 21st century one of the largest and most important voting system companies. The story of Diebold's meteoric rise and fall is intimately tied to the story of the Diebold TS and therefore is properly the subject of Chapters 5 and 7.

4.3   Mark-Sense Machines in Action

Mark-sense ballots are superior to punched-card ballots, because voters can easily verify that their ballots are marked as intended. This is partly because the candidate names and issues are printed directly on the ballot, but also because most people have years of experience interpreting pen and pencil marks on paper, while very few have experience interpreting irregular bits of chad. Nonetheless, mark-sense ballots are not foolproof. Different ballots scanners vary in their sensitivity, and absentee ballots can cause numerous problems.

On September 7, 2004 John McComish, Anton Orlich, and the others shown in Figure 22, ran in the Republican primary for Arizona's 20th state-house district in Maricopa County, Arizona. The 20th district was one of many in the County, which is one of the largest local election jurisdictions in the United States. In the 2004 primary, county officials handled 331,691 ballots.

McComish and Orlich came very close to a tie for second place in a vote-for-two race, with 5,529 votes for McComish and 5,533 votes for Orlich, giving Orlich a four-vote margin.[55] The narrow margin of victory triggered an automatic recount.[56] In the recount, McComish got 5,633 votes to 5,620 votes for Orlich, a gain of close to 100 votes for each candidate that allowed McComish to win by a 13-vote margin. Overall, the recount picked up 489 new votes, 464 of which were found on absentee ballots. The new votes were distributed across all the candidates. This means that new votes were found on 2.9% of

---

*Curiously, Global abandoned its attempt to register the AccuVote trademark. A small Dallas company, Accuvote International Inc., had developed a voting system patented by Cothburn O'Neal in the early 1970s.[795,796]

Figure 22 The state legislative races from the September 7, 2004 primary election in Arizona State House District 20. The blank lines with illegible instructions are for write-in votes. From the same ballot shown in Figure 20.

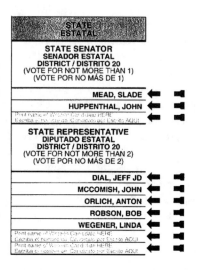

the 17,029 ballots cast in the District 20 primary.[604,605] Was it possible that the scanners used for the first count had missed close to 3% of all votes cast in this race? Since the number of ballots hadn't changed, it was clear that the increase was due either to changes to the ballots themselves or to a change in how those ballots were counted.

Maricopa County used Optech ballots with self-clocking targets, as shown in Figures 20 and 22. The instructions printed on each ballot ask voters to "complete the arrow(s) pointing to your choice with a single line." Ballots were counted in individual precincts on the day of the primary using Optech III-P Eagle tabulators. Absentee ballots were tabulated centrally on Optech IV-C tabulators that the county acquired in 1995. In the recount all ballots were counted on the Optech IV-C tabulators.[633]

When a recount gives a different result from the first count, the obvious question is "Where did the difference come from?" Either 489 ballots were changed, the tabulating mechanism was changed, or some combination thereof.

Altering the ballots themselves would be a classic example of election fraud. To prevent alteration, officials need to establish a reliable chain of custody from the moment the voter marks each ballot until the ballots are removed from storage for any post-election investigation or recount. In Maricopa County, there was no clear record of who had access to the ballots between the primary and the recount. Arizona law required that the ballots be stored in the county treasurer's vault, but it eventually emerged that the ballots were stored in a secure rented warehouse somewhere near the Phoenix Airport. [282,159]

There was also the issue of how ballots were sorted, counted, and recounted. For a recount, the county could either count all 331,691 ballots, including absentee ballots, or they could sort out the relevant ballots by hand, in this case just the Republican ballots from the 20th state-house district. The county opted to sort, which took several days. Whenever ballots are handled, there is a risk that they will be mishandled or altered. The traditional way to control this risk is to invite observers from the opposing sides to be present when ballots are handled. Unfortunately, the county notified only the Republican Party, not the individual primary candidates who were entitled to observe the ballot sorting. Orlich, considered a party outsider, questioned the impartiality of observers solely representing the party organization. [633]

On election day, ballots cast by voters at the precincts had been counted on Optech III-P Eagle precinct-count scanners, while the recount was done using the much faster Optech IV-C scanners in the election office. These ballots contributed only 25 of the 489 new votes picked up in the recount. In contrast, 464 of the 489 new votes were picked up from absentee ballots that were both counted and recounted on Optech IV-C central-count scanners.

Six Optech IV-C scanners were used for the first count of the 7,906 Republican District 20 absentee and provisional ballots. The ballots were scanned at random, mixed in with all the other absentee ballots from the election. For the recount, since the ballots were sorted, all of the District 20 Republican absentee ballots were scanned on one machine, machine number five. [633]

Genuinely identical machines would be expected to scan identically, but real machines are never identical. As a consequence, the hypothesis that the ballots were altered between the first count and the recount must be balanced against the hypothesis that the different machines had differing sensitivities. Specifically, it is possible that machine number five was so sensitive that it counted 464 marks during the recount that had been missed by the other scanners.

Finding 464 new votes on 7,906 absentee and provisional ballots implies that 5.9% of the ballots, more than 1 in 20, contained marks that were not seen on the first count. Karen Osborne, director of elections for Maricopa County, explained that absentee voters frequently cast votes using crayon, glitter pen, or other ballot markers for which the vote tabulator was not designed. Furthermore, she noted that when ballots are folded for mailing, some marks will smudge onto other parts of the ballot. In sum, she said that she wouldn't be surprised to find that 20% of absentee ballots were miscounted. [633] It is not reassuring to hear such a low accuracy estimate from a respected election official.

Do scanners of the same make and model have markedly different sensing thresholds? Karen Osborne said she knew that the Optech IV-C machines were definitely more sensitive than the Optech III Eagle, but she said that these machines were all calibrated to industry standards approved through national testing laboratories. In fact, all of Maricopa County's scanners had been approved under the 1990 Federal Election Commission Voluntary Voting System Standards. These standards require that scanners be able to accurately distinguish perfectly marked voting targets from unmarked targets, but they say nothing about sensitivity thresholds for less-than-perfect marks. [326]

A year after the Maricopa County primary, the Arizona Senate Government Accountability and Reform Committee was still interested in what had happened in District 20. Senator Jack Harper, committee chair, contacted one of us, Douglas Jones, in November 2005 asking for help in the investigation. On December 20, with legislative subpoenas provided by Senator Harper, Jones was able to run tests on the six operational Optech IV-C scanners in the Maricopa County Election Department.

Jones tested the scanners with sixteen different kinds of markers, ranging from the classic number-2 soft-lead pencil to a variety of pens and even glitter pen. He tested black, red, blue and violet inks, felt-tip pens, ballpoint pens, and gel pens. Some of his findings were expected. The Optech IV-C scanner is largely insensitive to red ink. It does not matter whether it is red ink from a felt-tip marker, a ballpoint pen or a glitter pen. This is not surprising, since the Optech IV-C uses red LEDs to illuminate the voting targets, and red ink is almost invisible under red light. [946]

What was more disturbing was the variation in scanner sensitivity to marks made with different pens. Two months before Jones' tests, Karen Osborne, Maricopa County's director of elections, recommended using Bic Round Stic™ ballpoint pens and warned against using Sanford Sharpie® markers. [633,860] Jones found that the Optech IV-C was extraordinarily sensitive to pencil lead and almost as sensitive to blue glitter pen and Sharpie markers. With a Bic pen, the scanner could easily pick up a dark scribble in the voting target, but if a voter made a single pen stroke, the mark was not reliably detected. [531]

Jones also found significant differences in sensitivity from sensor to sensor on the scanners. Some of this is unavoidable, since no matter how carefully the sensors are adjusted, it is impossible to adjust them to be precisely identical. As a result, there will always be some marginal marks, that is, marks that are read as votes by one sensor and ignored by another. In an ideal scanner, with a well designed ballot and good instructions, voters should hardly ever make such marks. Unfortunately, with the scanners used in Maricopa County, marks made with a black Bic pen by exactly following the ballot marking instructions were marginal.

Each Optech 400-C has eight sensors for tabulating votes, four for the front of the ballot and four for for the back, plus additional sensors for index marks. Technicians from the vendor had just tested and adjusted the calibration of the sensors before the tests Jones ran, but one in eight sensors could not reliably sense a single stroke with a black Bic pen across the voting target. Several other conventional ballpoint pens were just as bad. Given that the recommended ballot marker was a ballpoint pen and that the voting instructions said to vote with "a single line," this is not good.

Was the calibration problem in Maricopa County a likely cause of the extra votes found in the recount? Absentee ballots were scanned at random on any of six machines on the first count. If we assume that one in eight of the sensors had difficulty sensing single strokes of a ballpoint pen during the first count and that all of these strokes were counted on the recount, the 6% gain in the recount of absentee and provisional ballots implies that almost half of the ballots counted must have been voted with single pen strokes.

The obvious question is, if the directions ask voters to make a single line, how many will stop at a single pen stroke, and how many will carefully darken that line? An examination of the actual ballots could have answered that question, but a legislative subpoena granting access to the ballots was not sufficient. Maricopa County successfully fought the subpoena and blocked access to the ballots. Furthermore, there was no public data available on how actual voters mark ballots. Shortly after Jones released the results of his investigation, the ballots were impounded by Federal authorities. [754] The Federal investigation was eventually dropped, reaching no firm conclusion about what had happened and releasing no information about the actual ballot markings they found. [159]

There is no reason to believe that the Optech IV-C scanners used in Maricopa County were unusual. They had been freshly re-calibrated by technicians from ES&S prior to the election, and again prior to the testing requested by the Arizona Senate. Furthermore, the Federal voting system standards to which the Optech IV-C and its competitors were tested did not address scanner calibration. As a result, only those local election officials who make the effort to carefully monitor how their machines are calibrated are safe from such difficulties.

4.4 What is a Vote?

Many different inventors were involved in developing mark-sense ballot scanners, so it is natural that there are different methods for distinguishing marks intended as votes from other marks. The 1990 and subsequent Federal voting system standards largely ignore this issue, at least in part because the question of what marks on a ballot constitute a legal vote has traditionally been left to the states. Section 301(a)6 of HAVA, the Help America Vote Act of 2002, explicitly leaves this issue to the states, while 301(a)5 defines accuracy in a way that explicitly excludes anything attributable to an act of the voter. [191] In response to HAVA, states enacted rules defining which marks count as votes, but these rules rarely touch directly on the question of how to set scanner sensing thresholds. Instead, determining scanner thresholds is generally left to the vendors. Fortunately, while there are not uniform standards, all of the scanners are generally sensible, and the vast majority of marks voters actually make are easily classified.

Even if the standards were rigorous and the machines uniformly tested to those standards, we would still expect a few votes to be miscounted—for reasons that are human, technical and legal. While engineers and political scientists may view the human and technical issues as paramount, regulators and courts look first to the law. Broadly speaking, laws regulating the interpretation of marks on machine-countable ballots follow one of two models: One model focuses on voter intent, while the other focuses on the machine. This distinction was first clearly articulated in the court arguments following the Florida recounts after the 2000 election. [961]

Many states have long honored voter intent, at least when ballots are counted by hand. Michigan law, for example, states that: "If an electronic voting system requires that the elector place a mark in a predefined area on the ballot in order to cast a vote, the vote shall not be considered valid unless there is a mark within the predefined area and it is clearly evident that the intent of the voter was to cast a vote. In determining intent of the voter, the board of canvassers or election official shall compare the mark with other marks appearing on the ballot." [705] This text required only slight modification after the election of 2000. [706]

A key issue in the Florida presidential recount was the lack of a clear statewide standard for interpreting problematic ballots. As a result,

Florida enacted administrative rules in 2002. These rules were basically a catalog of the eccentric markings noticed during the recount, with the additional requirement that eccentric marks would be counted only if they were used consistently. [345] Later revisions added illustrations, but retained the same basic structure. [346]

Florida's recount statute allows human counting only of ballots flagged as overvoted or undervoted by the scanner. [347] As such, Florida law is a hybrid of the machine and voter-intent models. The machine dominates this model, because under normal circumstances the scanner used in a recount is the final judge of which ballots should be seen by a person. A scanner that misinterprets ballots cannot be challenged, because it is improper to look at ballots that have not been flagged as overvotes. Several other states follow this path. In Idaho, for example, when ballots are scanned on the first count, they must be scanned for the recount. [481] In addition, Idaho's rules for interpreting voter intent require that the ballot be marked in "a pre-defined area on the ballot in order to" be counted, and require manual interpretation only of ballots that scan as blank. [483]

On the other side, there are many states where voter intent is central. In 1965, shortly after California permitted use of computer software to tabulate punched-card ballots, California enacted a law requiring a "one percent manual tally" as part of the canvass of each election "to verify the accuracy of the automated count." [134]* Because the manual tally of the votes is independent of the tabulating machine, the count sets a standard by which the machine can be judged. Few other states followed California's lead until the 21st century. Then, as we will see in Chapter 5, the shortcomings of direct recording electronic voting machines lead to increased interest in election auditing.

4.5 The Human Element

Whenever humans mark ballots, there is an inevitably possibility of marks that a scanner cannot correctly classify. It is up to the voter to fill in the voting target, whether it is an oval or the gap between halves of the broken arrow. A typical ballot designed to be scanned by the AIS/ES&S family of scanners is shown in Figure 23. Note the instructions "to vote, you must blacken the oval completely next to the candidate of your choice, using only the pencil provided." The instructions give the prescribed mark, and provide an illustration, but real people rarely duplicate the prescribed mark, exactly filling in the oval voting target. Most people trying to make the prescribed mark will

---

*For additional discussion of California's voting system legislation, see Chapter 8.

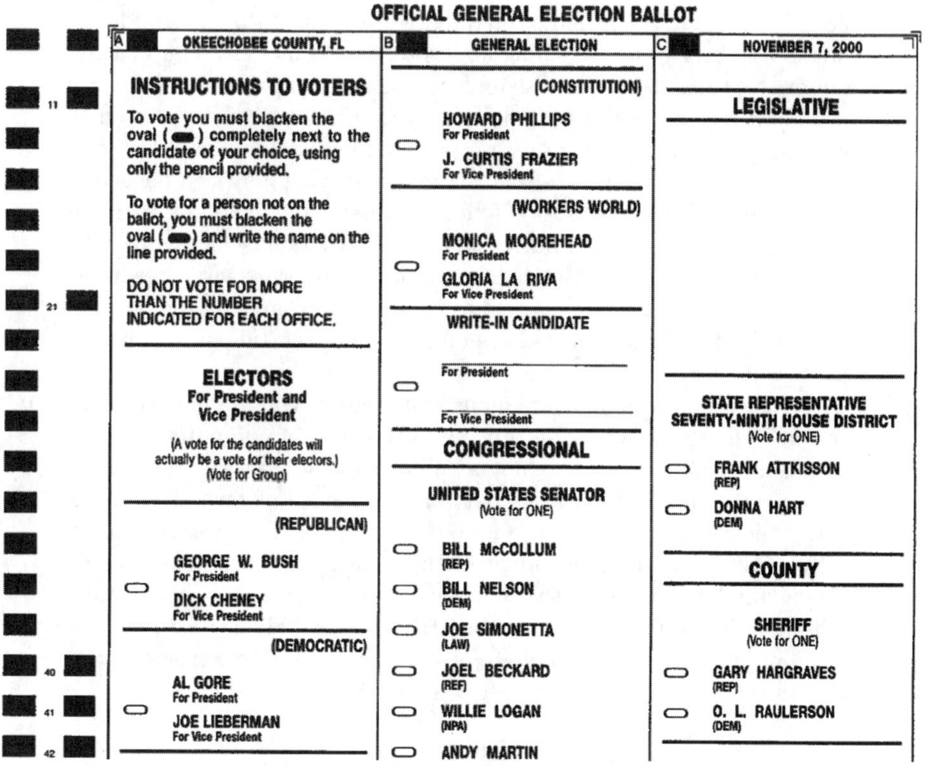

OFFICIAL GENERAL ELECTION BALLOT

A OKEECHOBEE COUNTY, FL | B GENERAL ELECTION | C NOVEMBER 7, 2000

11

INSTRUCTIONS TO VOTERS

To vote you must blacken the oval ( ) completely next to the candidate of your choice, using only the pencil provided.

To vote for a person not on the ballot, you must blacken the oval ( ) and write the name on the line provided.

21

DO NOT VOTE FOR MORE THAN THE NUMBER INDICATED FOR EACH OFFICE.

ELECTORS
For President and Vice President

(A vote for the candidates will actually be a vote for their electors.)
(Vote for Group)

(REPUBLICAN)
GEORGE W. BUSH
For President
DICK CHENEY
For Vice President

(DEMOCRATIC)

40

AL GORE
For President

41

JOE LIEBERMAN
For Vice President

42

(CONSTITUTION)
HOWARD PHILLIPS
For President
J. CURTIS FRAZIER
For Vice President

(WORKERS WORLD)
MONICA MOOREHEAD
For President
GLORIA LA RIVA
For Vice President

WRITE-IN CANDIDATE
For President
For Vice President

CONGRESSIONAL

UNITED STATES SENATOR
(Vote for ONE)
BILL McCOLLUM
(REP)
BILL NELSON
(DEM)
JOE SIMONETTA
(LAW)
JOEL BECKARD
(REF)
WILLIE LOGAN
(NPA)
ANDY MARTIN

LEGISLATIVE

STATE REPRESENTATIVE
SEVENTY-NINTH HOUSE DISTRICT
(Vote for ONE)
FRANK ATTKISSON
(REP)
DONNA HART
(DEM)

COUNTY

SHERIFF
(Vote for ONE)
GARY HARGRAVES
(REP)
O. L. RAULERSON
(DEM)

FIGURE 23 A ballot from Okeechobee County, Florida from the 2000 general election, designed to be scanned on an ES&S scanner. The leftmost column of marks are index marks. The marks immediately to the right of these are a primitive bar code for the precinct number and ballot style. There are many problems with the design of this ballot that are discussed in the text. Ballot image from Okeechobee County public records.

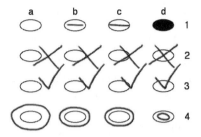

Figure 24 Pencil marks used in a 2004 test of an AIS/ES&S model 650 ballot scanner. The scanner ignored the marks in columns a and b while it counted those in c and d.

leave some white space in the oval or will go outside the lines. Some voters will even make X marks or checkmarks in the oval, and some will leave hesitation marks.

Hesitation marks are typically the result of the voter resting the tip of the ballot marker or pencil on the page while reading the associated text. An accidental hesitation mark made in a voting target by one voter could easily be as dark as a deliberate checkmark made by another. Short of looking at the entire ballot to determine what kinds of marks the voter habitually makes, there is no way to distinguish one voter's accidental hesitation marks from marks another voter makes deliberately. Things become even more complex if voters attempt erasures or other forms of correction on the ballot.

Most optical mark-sense scanners designed prior to the 1990s used infrared light to sense marks. Unfortunately, people cannot see if the ballot marker they used is visible under infrared. Graphite pencil lead is equally black by visible light and infrared, but as the Optech IV patent notes, "most common pens do not use ink that absorbs infrared light. Therefore, special pens with infrared absorbing ink must be used to mark the ballot." [946]

This raises an issue that is both human and technical. When precincts use infrared scanners, they typically provide officially approved pens or pencils. Nonetheless, voters sometimes use their own pens or pencils, particularly when the polling place is crowded and the pen or pencil in the voting booth is missing, dull or out of ink. When absentee ballots are mailed to voters, many jurisdictions include miniature pens or pencils with the ballot. These are frequently uncomfortably small to use, so again, many voters ignore them and reach for whatever is convenient.

In 2004, one of us, Douglas Jones, tested the ES&S 650 scanners used by Miami-Dade County, He used a variety of check marks, lines, and circles through and around an oval target, and with several different pens and pencils. [526] The ES&S 650 could easily sense a variety of marks, including straight lines, check marks and x's in the voting target. What was somewhat surprising was that the machine sensed some marks made outside the boundary of the oval voting targets. The machine does not simply evaluate the darkness of the mark. Rather, the sensitivity of the machine is highest near the center of the voting target and declines toward the edge of the sensing region. A single pencil stroke within the sensitive area would be counted, but it takes a considerably bigger mark outside the oval target to trigger the machine.

The marks voters make on ballots depend on the marker, the voter, and the ballot, including the ballot layout and the way the voting instructions are worded. The layout of the ballot and the wording of the instructions are typically a matter of state law, and sometimes that law is misleading. Consider, for example, the instructions found on Florida's ballots in the 2000 general election. In most races, the voter was instructed to "vote for one," but in the presidential race, where presidential and vice presidential candidates run together, voters were instructed to "vote for group," as can be seen in Figure 23. This seems like an invitation to voters to overvote, invalidating their presidential vote.

In Charlotte and Liberty Counties, election offices changed the wording to "vote for one group," probably in violation of Florida regulations. The results were something of a natural experiment in human factors. When one of us, Douglas Jones, analyzed the overvote rates in the presidential race for Florida voters using centrally-counted mark-sense ballots, he found that of the 99,000 voters instructed to "vote for group," 7.4% cast overvotes. Of the 72,000 voters instructed to "vote for one group," 4.3% cast overvotes. [522]

All of the Florida ballots discussed above were counted on ES&S Model 150 or 550 central-count scanners. Furthermore, on all of these ballots, the presidential race was split across two columns of the ballot, as shown in Figure 23. The first eight candidates were listed in one column, while the final two candidates and the write-in blanks were at the top of the next column. In Lake County, a county that also used ES&S central-count tabulators, the typography was different, allowing the 11 choices in the presidential race to be presented in one column. Lake County also changed the instructions to "vote for one group." On the 92,000 ballots cast in Lake County, the presidential overvote rate was just 3.4%.

The problems with the two-column ballot layout were widely recognized. Election Systems and Software strongly advised against it, and shortly after the election of 2000, an analysis of the overvotes on two column ballots by the Orlando Sentinel showed that the two-column design probably cost Al Gore 2,416 votes and George Bush 1,852 votes.

Thus, eliminating this one ballot design error could have changed the outcome of the presidential election. [575]

Natural experiments are messy, relying as they do on chance and accident to control the variables being studied. As such, the numbers coming from the election of 2000 should be viewed with a grain of salt. The variation between individual counties is extreme. For example, Charlotte County had an overvote rate of about 4.2%, while Gadsden County had an overvote rate of over 11%, yet both counties had ballots that were identical to the Okeechobee County ballot shown in Figure 23. The demographics of these counties are quite different. Nonetheless, the results of this natural experiment strongly suggest that poor ballot design is very dangerous and that very small changes in ballot design can have effects large enough to change the outcome of an election.

4.6   Image-Based Mark Sensing

The early optical mark-sense scanners all used one or sometimes two photosensors to scan each column of marks on the ballot. Some used analog mark-sensing, where the threshold for sensitivity was set by analog circuitry. Others converted the raw photosensor output to digital form prior to deciding whether or not to count a mark. Some used sensors physically adjacent to the paper, while others sensed the ballot from a distance by means of lenses or fiber optics. This variety has been used to draw marketing distinctions, but for practical purposes, it makes very little difference. None of these mark-sensing technologies recognize the shape of a mark, so from the scanner's perspective, there is no difference between a checkmark, an X or a partially marked voting target. All these machines did is evaluate the overall darkness of the mark and, in some cases, the presence of edges perpendicular to the direction of the scanning track.

The late 1970s heralded a new era in semiconductors as integrated circuit chips grew considerably more complex. Among these new chips were those that could sense images. The first of these were charge-coupled device sensors, known as CCD sensors, designed with a single line of 1024 sensors. Each sensor on such a device senses the brightness of one point or pixel along the line. Before leaving Westinghouse Learning Corporation for Data Mark Systems, John McMillin had already applied for a patent using these types of image sensors for scanning mark sense forms. [674] His system used a 1024 pixel CCD and a lens to scan the width of the page, giving a resolution of more than 100 pixels per inch.

Figure 25 A pixelated view of a
marked voting target as seen by an
ES&S model 100 precinct-count
ballot scanner.
From U.S. Patent 6,854,644.

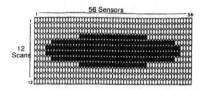

Today, we take large integrated-circuit image sensors for granted in such things as digital cameras. In the 1980s, the advent of simple one-dimensional sensors spawned a revolution in such applications as fax machines and page scanners. The first machine to incorporate this technology into a ballot tabulator was the American Information Systems PBC 100 scanner, later known as the Model 100. The system, which came on the market just as AIS was reorganized into ES&S, uses an Intel 80386 microprocessor to process the data from the image sensor. [54] It reads the election configuration from a PCMCIA memory card* before opening the polls. When the polls close, it records the results to the memory card and optionally transmits them by modem to the election office. [722] As such, the PCMCIA card serves the same purposes as the memory pack used on the Optech I scanner. In 1998, ES&S offered Model 100 scanners to Dallas, Texas at a price of $5,500 each. [249]

Fidlar and Chambers (later Fidlar Doubleday) was the next vendor to explore pixel-based mark sensing. In this case, their principal product was a touch-screen machine designed for use in the precinct. Fidlar was a printing company from Rock Island, Illinois that had been printing ballots for a century and had moved into sales and service for punched-card voting systems. Naturally, when they developed a touch-screen voting machine, they paired it with punched-cards for absentee voters. [506]

In late 1999, however, Fidlar and Chambers offered a new alternative, the AbScan-T absentee ballot scanner. This was nothing more than an off-the-shelf Fujitsu flat-bed scanner, equipped with Fujitsu's optional automatic document feeder attachment, and connected with a personal computer running Fidlar's ballot image analysis software. [508] Another innovative aspect of the system was that Fidlar supported ballot-on-demand printing, using a laser printer, so it was unnecessary to print absentee ballots in bulk before an election. Instead, ballots could be printed as needed, in response to individual requests from absentee voters. [338]

---

*PCMCIA cards or PC cards are about the size of a calling card. Many laptop computers have used PCMCIA cards for wireless modems, but the standard was originally developed for memory cards.

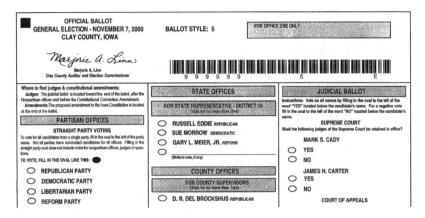

FIGURE 26   A ballot from Clay County, Iowa from the 2000 general election, designed for use with the Fidlar and Chambers AbScan-T system. Note the elimination of index marks and the use of a conventional bar code to encode the ballot style and other information.
Ballot from Douglas Jones' collection.

Surry County, North Carolina and Clay County, Iowa both used the Fidlar system for the 2000 general election. The ballot used in Clay County, shown in Figure 26, illustrates some additional innovations in the Fidlar system. Where earlier ballots and mark-sense test forms had index marks along the edges, or cleverly disguised as part of the voting target in the Optech system, the Fidlar ballot had just two square black fiducial marks. The term *fiducial mark* is used in image analysis and printing to refer to marks used as reference points for measurements in an image, or for aligning one image with another. Fidlar's fiducial marks were black squares, one in the upper left corner of the ballot, the other in the lower right. These allowed Fidlar's ballot analysis software to triangulate the location of individual voting targets despite changes in ballot size due to humidity or variations in printing, and despite changes in ballot orientation due to careless feeding of ballots into the scanner.

Finally, note that the Fidlar ballot shown in Figure 26 uses a conventional-looking bar code to encode the ballot style and other information. Much more information can be encoded in this bar code than could be encoded in the primitive codes illustrated in Figures 19, 20 and 23.

In the years since 2000, several other vendors have come out with vote scanners comparable to the ES&S Model 100 and the Fidlar AbScan-T. The Hart Intercivic eScan precinct-count scanner and Ballot Now central-count scanner are conceptually descended from the ES&S Model 100 and Fidlar AbScan-T. [444,837] The Dominion CF200 precinct-count scanner and CF500 central-count scanners are also comparable. [790] Dominion Voting Systems, a Canadian company, partnered with Sequoia Voting Systems to market the technology in the United States, and in 2010 Dominion bought Sequoia. [279]

These more recent systems typically digitize images of all ballots scanned. This allows write-in votes and problematic ballot markings to be processed using the digitized images, so that once the ballots are scanned, they need not be handled except in the event of a recount or audit.

Neither AIS, ES&S nor Fidlar filed patents on pixel-based scanning at the time they came to market with their products. Another vendor, Avante International Technology, Inc., pursued patents aggressively. On October 1, 2001, Kevin Chung and Victor Dong filed a provisional patent application for an optical-scan voting system. Over the next year, after filing a number of other provisional applications, they filed for a patent that was granted on May 17, 2005 and a second patent on July 18, 2006. [165,166] On June 28, 2006, Avante sued Diebold, ES&S and Sequoia for patent infringement. [916]

There is no evidence that anyone associated with Avante had done any work on election technology prior to Election 2000. Avante's patent claims included such ideas as capturing digital images of ballots using a commercial off-the-shelf scanner, detecting ballot orientation and scale using fiducial marks, and encoding precinct and ballot style using a bar code. Given that the Fidlar AbScan-T system had been on the market in 2000, the patent clearly was granted in error. Unfortunately, while Fidlar patented their touch-screen voting system, they never patented their mark-sense system, and it was never widely enough used to attract much notice. In the case of ES&S, it was only after Avante had filed its provisional patents that ES&S finally filed for a patent on the Model 100. [98]

On March 17, 2009, Judge Thomas C. Mummert III declared the key claims of Avante's patents to be invalid. [721] Only Premier Election Solutions (the former Diebold Election Systems) and Sequoia hung on until the end, and this may not have been a wise choice. The victory in this court case left both companies cash poor, and within a year, Election Systems and Software had purchased Premier, while Dominion Voting Systems had purchased Sequoia. The cost of defending their products against Avante's lawsuit was probably not the cause of the downfall of these companies, but it was an expense they could not easily afford.

4.7 New Directions

The ES&S patent was an important step forward. All of the early pixel-based mark-sense scanners had sensed marks based on simple threshold algorithms. What ES&S eventually did with the Model 100 scanner was to develop mark recognition algorithms that were sensitive to the shape of the mark. They used the catchphrase *intelligent mark recognition* to describe their new approach. [54,98] Given that the Model 100 is based on a relatively slow microprocessor, the Intel 386, it should be possible to do much better, but even today the majority of new scanners still evaluate marks based on very simplistic criteria.

Image-based scanners ought to be able to distinguish smudges and erasures from deliberate marks. Smudges and erasures generally have indistinct edges, while deliberately made marks have sharp edges. It also ought to be possible to classify marks according to shape, distinguishing checkmarks, x-marks, filled voting targets and circled voting targets. This would allow the identification of consistent use of non-standard marks, a common legal criterion for acceptable use of such marks.

It is reasonable to expect scanners to compare the image of each ballot scanned with the image of the corresponding blank ballot in order to locate all added marks, whether or not those marks are in designated voting areas. Such comparison would eliminate the need for conventional timing marks or fiducial marks by using all of the print on the ballot as a background against which to locate voting targets. Once all markings on the ballot have been identified, a scanner could automatically reject ballots containing stray marks, or refer them to the resolution board.

As things currently stand, two different jurisdictions using ballots that look similar might classify the same ballot marking differently, one counting it as a vote and the other discounting it. While there are marginal marks for which such discrepancies are unavoidable, we can work to reduce the range of problem marks. Some of the differences today are the result of differing state laws about which marks are legal votes, while other differences are the result of vendors designing machines to significantly different conceptions as to which marks ought to be counted. Better federal voting system standards would clearly help, as would a commitment from the states to bring their laws into some kind of uniformity.

5

Trusting in Technology:
Direct-Recording Electronic Voting

Q: Can we have a recount?

A: Yes, of course, but the system will give the same result. This is one of the main features of the system. Any vote in the system is a good vote. The in-built security within the system ensures the accuracy and integrity of the data.

Nedap Powervote System promotional material [744]

After the embarrassment of Election 2000, the state of Florida moved to replace its Votomatic punched card voting machines and mechanical lever voting machines with new equipment. The Florida Election Reform Act of 2001 required use of either precinct-count optical mark-sense ballot scanners or touch-screen voting machines. While permitting older electronic voting technologies, the act repeatedly uses the word "touchscreen." [349,351]

In 2002, Sarasota County opted to replace its Votomatic punched card system with the iVotronic voting system made by Election Systems and Software of Omaha Nebraska. This machine, shown in Figure 27, is an example of a direct-recording electronic or DRE voting machine. Like many other DRE voting machines, it uses a flat panel display to present the ballot to the voter with a touch-panel overlaying the display for voter input. As with mechanical lever voting machines, cast votes are directly recorded without producing any tangible intermediate document that could be described as a ballot. Such machines are often described as touch-screen voting systems, even though there are many DRE voting machines that do not use touch screens.

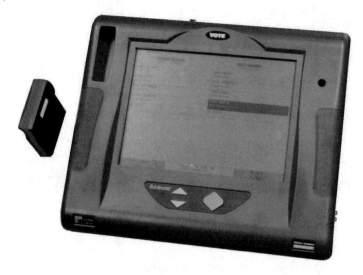

FIGURE 27   The ES&S iVotronic, a touch-screen direct-recording electronic voting machine. The PEB cartridge to the left can be inserted in the slot on the upper left of the machine to upload and download data. It is also used to unlock the machine before each voter is allowed to vote.
Photo by Douglas Jones.

Sarasota did many things right. Sarasota's new machines saw their first use in a single-issue referendum in March 2002, so many voters and poll workers had some experience with the new machines before their first major test—the September primary election. The March 2002 election was also a first for ES&S. It was the first county-wide use of the iVotronic, although the machine had seen trial use since 1999.[309] In the September primary, voting the full ballot required the voter to wade through 13 to 14 screenfuls of candidates and ballot questions.[88] Poll-worker training in Sarasota was also taken very seriously. A minimum of 6 hours of training was required, and some workers were required to take 12 hours of training and pass a test.[114] As a result, while other Florida counties faced problems with the new technology, Sarasota did fairly well, at least initially.

The first hint of a problem was hidden in obscure statistics coming out of the March 2002 election. A symptom of trouble in the 2000 presidential election was the high rate of undervotes in some counties. One of the promises of the new touch-screen voting machines was that they would reduce the undervote rate by reducing the difficulty of voting. When the undervote rate for the March election was examined, however, it was not significantly different from the historical undervote rate seen on paper ballots in a similar election, 1.19% versus the previous 1.37%. [89]

In the following general elections, the undervote rates for Sarasota's iVotronic users continued to be in the same range that they had been with older voting technology. Looking at the top race on the ticket each year, the rates were 2.4% in the 2002 Congressional race, 0.4% in the 2004 Presidential race, and 1.2% in the 2006 Senatorial race. Unfortunately, in 2006 something was seriously wrong. The undervote rate in Sarasota County in the 2006 Congressional race was 12.9%. [348]

The effort to determine the cause of the extraordinary undervote rate in the 2006 Congressional election in Sarasota would continue for years, but the lack of an immediate explanation was itself significant. In 2007, just 4 months after the general election, Governor Charlie Crist (R) proposed a ban on DRE voting machines in Florida, except to serve the needs of voters with disabilities. [17,350] As a result, Florida moved to the use of optical mark-sense scanning state wide. We will return to this story, but first we need to explore the origins and development of direct-recording electronic voting in order to understand what it does and does not do.

5.1 Voting by Electricity

With the advent of time-sharing systems and minicomputers in the mid 1960s, the idea of voting by computer was in the air. As discussed in Chapters 3 and 4, computer technology was already being used to count paper punched-card and mark-sense ballots. The first computer networks were coming into their own, and it seemed obvious that the new technology could directly accept and tabulate votes, with no need for a paper document. Some saw the integration of computerized voting with communications networks as forming the basis for a system of direct democracy. [558,1039] However, as early as 1964, others were lampooning the idea. [368]

The first practical direct-recording electronic voting machines came on the marketplace in the 1970s, but it is possible to identify precursors from as far back as the 19th century. The elimination of paper ballots, the direct counting of votes, and the removal of all questions of ballot interpretation were important goals of the early developers of mechanical lever voting machines, as we describe in Chapter 2. The parallel between DRE voting machines and lever voting machines is sufficiently strong that we can refer to the latter as direct-recording mechanical voting machines.

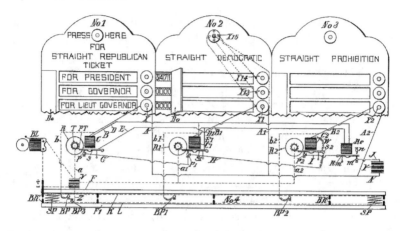

FIGURE 28 Wood's direct recording electrical voting machine. A front view of the push-button voting panel is shown across the top, while the wiring diagram for one office (LIEUT GOVERNOR) is given in the middle. The bottom portion of the drawing shows the foot switch used to prevent the machine from being operated except when someone was standing in front of it. From U.S. Patent 616,174.

The dream of recording votes by electricity is also quite old. Henderson and Edison patented electrical voting machines for use in legislative chambers.[290,455] Frank Wood of Boston patented the first direct-recording electric voting machine suitable for general elections in 1898.[1019] Where modern DRE machines use electronics and computer technology, Wood's machine used relays and electromechanical counters, cutting-edge technology for the day. As can be seen in Figure 28, this push-button voting machine even had logic to prevent overvoting, and a person had to physically stand at the machine before it would register a vote. By the early 20th century, the rise of mechanical machines eclipsed these early electrical systems, and the idea of electrical vote recording was largely forgotten.

It was not until the 1960s that the idea of electromechanical vote recording re-emerged. In 1960, Aaron Aronson filed a patent application for a push-button voting machine. Unlike the mechanical voting machines of the era, where programming for a particular election was done by adding and removing linkages behind the face of the machine, Aronson's machine used a massive plug-board for programming. In 1961, Horace Railsback and Harold Stewart filed a large patent application for an electromechanical voting system that included voting machines, magnetic-tape result cartridges, and a central election results tabulation system. [833]

The above proposals were all electromechanical, but AVM Corporation was already thinking in terms of modern electronics. In 1959, Anatolijus Jazbutis of AVM filed for a patent on a transistorized DRE voting machine. An interesting feature of the patent was the proposal to use a single central "registering device" for each precinct to accumulate the votes cast on a number of separate "voting panels," one in each voting booth. The registering device would eliminate an annoying clerical job required with mechanical voting machines: Adding up the totals from each machine to compute the precinct-wide totals for each candidate. [513]

While AVM's first electronic voting machine used the newest technology, programming the machine for an election was decidedly awkward. The face of each voting panel was composed of numerous modules, one per candidate plus one per straight party lever and one per write-in option. Since different module types were used to enforce each voting rule, the face of the panel had to be rebuilt for each election by plugging in the appropriate modules. There were also jumpers and switches to be set. Were it not for the jumpers and switches behind the face of the machine, the plug-in programming model used for this machine would have had one very positive aspect—an election observer could easily inspect the programming by simply noting which types of modules were in use.

Others pursued modular electronic voting machines into the 1970s, notably Roy Martin and Clarence Pittman of Atlanta, who were granted a patent in 1974. [637] AVM, meanwhile, appears to have dropped the idea of plugboard programming as they began to understand the possibility of embedding small computers in their machines in order to reduce their size and price. In 1974, for example, a group at AVM led by Michael Moldovan was granted a patent on a compact voting machine where most of the logic was implemented by a small embedded minicomputer that they designed. [715]*

From Wood's direct-recording electrical voting machine in the 1890s to AVM's efforts in the 1970s, all the machine designs attempted to imitate the look and feel of mechanical voting machines. They all displayed the full ballot as an array of voting positions, either in party row or party column format. While DRE voting machines offering such a full-face ballot display eventually came to market, the first successful DRE voting systems took a different approach.

---

*Between 1965 and 1975, small cheap minicomputers were used in growing numbers of computerized machines, paving the way for the microprocessor revolution of the next decade.

5.2 The First Generation at the Polls

The first direct-recording electronic voting machine to see significant use was the Video Voter, developed by a team at the Frank Thornber Company in Chicago, headed by Richard McKay, the company's owner. During the period that Thornber developed the Video Voter, the Thornber company grew to the point that a large majority of Illinois counties were using its services. [217]

The development of the Video Voter is documented in a pair of patents issued in 1974 and 1977. [665,664] The basic idea was to display just a portion of the ballot on the screen. Any voting machine displaying only one or a few races at a time is forced to use an office-block style of ballot presentation. McKay's original design used rear projection microfilm to display each page of the ballot. Nonetheless, the machine was named in anticipation of the eventual use of a video display.

As with the machine designed by Jazbutis for AVM a decade earlier, the Video Voter relied on a single computerized "data center" at each precinct with up to eight "vote heads," one per voting booth. The 1975 version of the data center weighed 80 pounds and cost $2,450, while each vote head weighed 90 pounds and cost $1,600. The carrying case for each vote head could be converted into a voting booth. The data center was designed to be programmed for each election using a magnetic-tape cartridge, and it would record the election results on the same cartridge after the polls were closed. [716] Early microprocessors were available at the time the Video Voter was designed, but they were not fast enough, so the data center incorporated a small custom-designed processor, effectively a minicomputer, that executed firmware from a read-only memory. [248]

In 1974, the Video Voter was first used on a trial basis in two Chicago suburbs, Streamwood, in Cook County and Woodstock, in McHenry County, making the Video Voter the first direct-recording electronic voting system to reach the market. Eventually, the Video Voter was used in four small Illinois counties, Coles, McDonough, Warren and Livingston, although none used it after 1980. [248,924] The Frank Thornber Company was acquired by Business Records Corporation in 1985. [217]

5.2.1 Microvote

The Video Voter was ahead of its time. It was a decade before other DRE machines, using the much simpler technology of print on paper, came on the market. In 1985, William Carson of Indianapolis filed for a patent on an electronic voting machine built by Carson Manufac-

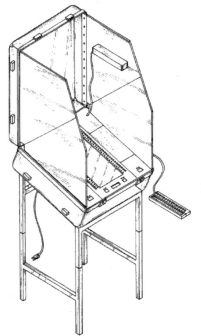

Figure 29 The Microvote MV-464
direct-recording electronic voting
machine. The entire machine folds
into a suitcase, with enough room
under the lid to hold the legs,
pollworker control panel and voting
booth lights. From U.S. Patent
4,649,264.

turing Company and marketed by a new company, Microvote General
Corporation of Carmel, Indiana.[149]

Carson's MV-464 voting machine, shown in Figure 29, featured a
display window with a row of 32 push buttons on each side. The ballot
displayed on the window was printed on paper. For small elections
involving fewer than 64 candidates, a single page behind the window
would have sufficed. But because general elections are frequently quite
complex, the paper was mounted on rollers, one under each column of
push buttons, so that the paper could be scrolled from side to side to
display successive pages of ballot issues.

Most previous direct-recording voting systems shared a common
weakness: The vote total for each candidate was stored in just one
place, either a mechanical counter or a memory location in a computer.
Any failure in that storage mechanism meant that the corresponding
vote record would be lost. The MV-464 addressed this weakness by
storing vote records redundantly, one copy in an electronic record, and
another copy printed on a roll of adding-machine tape inside the machine. In the event of any question about the integrity of the electronic records in the machine, the paper record could be recounted by
hand.

Carson was aware of the threat to voter privacy resulting from printing votes sequentially, so he randomized somewhat the order of printing. The machine did not print any vote records until 4 records had been accumulated. From this point on, each time a voter used the machine, it printed one of the 4 records in its memory, selected at "random." The exact mechanism used for randomization was not disclosed, but even weak randomization offers greater ballot secrecy than simple sequential recording. The price for the randomization was that in the event of a failure in the electronics, the last 4 votes cast would be lost.

In 1990, when Microvote offered the MV-464 system to Dubuque County, Iowa, they quoted a price of $3,323 each, a price that probably included the central computer system to support the 130 machines the county needed. [512]

5.2.2   The Shouptronic

Microvote had competition. In 1984, Robert J. Boram filed for patents on behalf of the R.F. Shoup Corporation for a new voting machine that would be marketed as the Shouptronic. [101,102] Shoup was AVM's single surviving competitor in the mechanical voting system arena. The Shouptronic was a full-face machine, using an array of push buttons behind a paper ballot label protected by a clear plastic sheet. As with Microvote's machine, the Shouptronic maintained a running vote count in its internal memory and included a printer to print the vote totals after the polls closed.

The Shouptronic featured a memory cartridge similar to that used on the Optech I mark-sense ballot scanner, a machine that had come on the market only a year earlier. The cartridges of both machines used programmable read-only memory chips to hold election configuration information. Where the Optech I used battery-backed read-write memory to hold election results, the Shouptronic used a second programmable read-only memory chip.

The key property of programmable read-only memory or PROM is that once data is written to PROM, the data is difficult or impossible to erase.* In contrast, data in read-write memory can be written, erased, and changed arbitrarily. In effect, the programmable read-only memory used in the Shouptronic cartridge has properties similar to the paper ballots retained by the Optech scanner or to the printed paper record of the Microvote machine. All of these machines maintained redundant but more vulnerable records in read-write memory. On the Optech ma-

---

*The difficulty of erasure varies with the type of PROM; UVPROMS can be erased by exposure to ultraviolet light while EEPROMS can be erased electrically.

chine, the read-write memory was in the memory cartridge, while on the Microvote and Shouptronic machines the read-write memory was a permanent part of the machine itself.

The Shouptronic was approved for sale in Pennsylvania in 1984, and the first sales were made that year. By 1993, 11,000 Shouptronic machines had been sold. [811,359] The Shouptronic was significantly more expensive than the Microvote system. In early 1990, Microvote offered MV-464 machines to Trimble County, Kentucky at $3000 each, while the offer for Shouptronic machines was $4975 each. [451] It is apparent that Shoup, with its established sales and service organization, could charge significantly more per machine than a relatively young start-up company.

While Boram's basic design for the Shouptronic has survived essentially unchanged over the years, the corporation that designed the machine is long gone. In 1989, Danaher Corporation acquired Guardian Voting, which had the rights to the Shouptronic. [221] By 1999, the machine was being marketed by Danaher Controls as the ELECTronic 1242 voting machine. [811]

5.2.3   Sequoia and Nedap

Two other first-generation electronic voting machines have seen significant use. Both are very similar to the Shouptronic with full-face ballot displays based on an array of push-button switches behind a printed copy of the ballot issues. The Sequoia AVC Advantage and the Nedap ES3B both record votes redundantly in electronic memories, using hand carried results cartridges to deliver the results to a tabulation center after the polls close.

The Sequoia AVC Advantage, shown in Figure 30, was introduced in 1990. Much of the design of this machine was contracted out, producing one of the most elegant looking of the first generation DRE voting machines. James Bleck led the design team that filed design patents on the machine in 1988. [94,95] One commentator described the machine as being "svelte," and *Business Week* credited it with turning the company around. [92,787]

Sequoia had purchased the voting machine division of AVM Corporation in 1984, as discussed in Chapter 3. With that purchase, Sequoia acquired not only a portfolio of patents for electronic voting machines, but also the AVM Automatic Voting Computer, a machine that had been certified for use in New Jersey and Pennsylvania in 1982. [782,811] The machine appears to have been based on AVM's final patent for an electronic voting machine, granted to Thomas De Phillipo in 1977, and is an obvious predecessor of the Sequoia AVC Advantage. [818] None of

Figure 30 The Sequoia AVC Advantage unfolded for voting. In its folded format, the privacy panels fold down to cover the face of the machine and the face folds down parallel to the electronics cabinet.
From U.S. Patent D319,459.

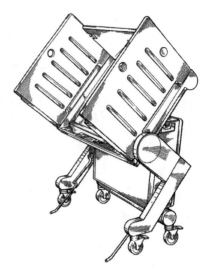

the AVM patents demonstrates the sophistication in physical design of the AVC Advantage.

Sequoia's AVC Advantage was certified for use in Kansas in 1986 and in New Jersey in 1987. [539,782] The machine was far lighter than AVM's earlier mechanical voting machines, but at 260 pounds, it was still quite heavy. It was not cheap. In 1992, Sequoia offered AVC Advantages to Denver for $5500 each. [92] Despite the price, the Advantage saw widespread use over the next two decades.

The Dutch Nedap voting system, introduced in the Netherlands in the early 1990s, was used by 90% of the Dutch electorate by 2006. [801] Nedap, more properly N.V. Nederlandsche Apparatenfabriek, produced items such as electronic ID cards and door locks. In 2003, Liberty Election Systems began marketing the Nedap system in the United States. Their web page from 2003 to 2005 made their focus clear, proclaiming "Libertyvote NEDAP, The Future of New York State Election Technology." [599]

New York, the first state to use mechanical voting machines, was also the last to move to any form of electronic voting. In 1984, New York City, a long-time user of Shoup's mechanical voting systems, began investigating a move to electronic voting machines. The city started carefully, contracting with SRI International to evaluate the potential bidders. In 1988, SRI delivered its report, concluding that none of the vendors had machines that met New York's requirements, but that Sequoia had the greatest probability of successfully implementing a system to meet those requirements. [697]

1988 was a pivotal time in the history of electronic voting. That August, Roy Saltman at the National Bureau of Standards issued a major report on computerized voting systems. [869] In November, Ronnie Dugger published a groundbreaking essay on electronic voting in *The New Yorker*. [287] Both of these efforts documented numerous failures in computerized vote counting, raising questions not only about established technologies such as the Votomatic, but also about the newer emerging electronic voting technologies. That year, just 2.7% of U.S. voters used DRE voting machines, and another 7.5% used mark-sense ballots. In contrast, over 40% of voters used Votomatic punched card ballots.

New York did not move quickly, and by mid 1990 only two vendors remained, Shoup and Sequoia. [76] There was some doubt that the new system would be available in time for the 1992 general election, but by the end of the year a contract had been awarded to Sequoia. [77] Sample machines were delivered, and as the evaluation process continued, skepticism about the machines continued to mount. Some computer scientists, such as Rebecca Mercuri and Peter Neumann, expressed serious concerns about the new technology. [697,698] Ultimately, the effort to replace New York's old Shoup machines would languish for another two decades, at which time Nedap, partnering with Liberty Election Systems would go head-to-head with Sequoia, offering machines that were little changed from their offerings in the 1990s. [714,600]

5.3 Second Generation DRE Voting Systems

In 1990, Orville Smith, commenting on the bids for new voting machines in Trimble County, Kentucky, said "we might as well get the cheaper one, because it'll be obsolete in 10 years." [451] What Smith recognized was that microcomputer technology was advancing so fast that it was easy to envision building a voting machine based on personal-computer technology and a video display screen.

A group at Texas Instruments, led by Julien Anno, patented one of the first voting systems using laptop computer technology in 1993. [51] The system incorporated an electronic pollbook, that is a computerized version of the book at the polling place containing the list of registered voters. On signing in to vote, the electronic pollbook would issue the voter a card. Inserting the card in the voting machine authorized the machine to present a ballot to the voter. Information on each voter's card ensured that the machine delivered the correct ballot to that voter. In Anno's original design, the voter authorization card was printed with a bar code on thermal printer paper. Anno was Belgian, and the two electronic voting systems that have been widely used in Belgium since 1995 strongly resemble Anno's basic idea, except that they use magnetic-stripe cards, instead of Anno's original bar-coded tickets. [800]

5.3.1 The Votronic

The second generation of DRE voting machines reached the marketplace with the Votronic. Shelby Thomas, president of a small Virginia election services company Election Products Inc., had the idea for the machine in the early 1990's. He took his idea to a local engineering consulting firm, ILJ Corporation, of Richmond. [358] By 1993, John Davis, president of ILJ, had delivered a prototype, and Davis and Thomas applied for a patent* the next year. [229,997]

Unrelated to the mark-sense system by the same name from the 1960's, the Votronic used the combination of a flat panel liquid crystal display and touch screen that has come to define electronic voting machines in the minds of many. One commentator described the Votronic as resembling a "child's Magna Doodle." [997] The Votronic fit comfortably in a suitcase-sized carrying case and could be carried to cars of voters with disabilities that prevented their getting from their cars into the polling place, making curbside voting possible. [358]

The Votronic included an innovative new cartridge, the Personal Electronic Ballot (PEB), used to communicate setup information to the machine before the election and to accumulate results at the close of the polls. The PEB was not a passive memory device; rather, it was a small computer system, not much larger than a pack of cigarettes, containing a battery, a microcontroller†, and non-volatile memory. When inserted in its dock on the front of the Votronic, the PEB used infrared light to establish a very short-range network connection with the machine.

The developers thought of the PEB as the electronic analog of a ballot; they viewed the machine in the voting booth as the electronic analog of a pencil for marking the ballot. The inventors intended the poll workers to hand PEBs to voters as they signed into the polling place. In practice, pollworkers usually escorted each voter to the machine and used the PEB to activate the machine, before turning it over to the voter. Other voting system developers would later pursue the idea of using an electronic medium that actually carries a voter's individual ballot, most notably in Kazakhstan. [532]

---

*The Votronic patent incorrectly lists the engineering consulting firm as ILT Corp.

†Microcontrollers combine a very small microprocessor with read-only memory for a very small program and a very small amount of memory (RAM) to store temporary variables.

The Votronic was first used in Georgetown County, South Carolina in the March 1996 primary. [997] Within the year Pasquotank County, North Carolina bought 63 machines. The machine was also certified for use in Texas. With just 11 employees and all production of the $3,295 Votronic outsourced, Election Products was in desperate need of a distribution network. [358]

Shortly after Election Systems and Software (ES&S) was formed by the merger of American Information Systems and Business Records Corporation, ES&S acquired the rights to the Votronic. With its national sales and marketing force, ES&S gained immediate traction selling the system, and it began to invest in updating the design, redesigning the packaging, and adding features supporting broader access for voters with disabilities. The new system was sold as the iVotronic, but in dealings with states that had already certified the Votronic, ES&S emphasized that the changes were cosmetic. [496] New Jersey did not even require recertification of the new package. [782]

While the Votronic and iVotronic hardware were typical of laptop computer technology in the early 1990s, they did not use any commodity operating system such as Linux, MacOS or Windows. Instead, they ran firmware from read-only memory that was specifically written for the voting application. Like many of the personal computers of the 1980s, the iVotronic had ugly typography, as illustrated in Figure 31 which shows the ballot used in Sarasota in the 2006 general election. This crude graphical style was one contributor to problems in that election.

The demand for foreign language support led ES&S to seek a fast road to supporting a large number of fonts. Had the iVotronic used a commodity operating system, it could have used the large font libraries and rendering tools of the host system. The Votronic and iVotronic firmware, however, was limited to just 256 printable characters, with boldface and large print characters counting toward the limit. Because it did not use a standard operating system, ES&S had to find an alternative for the iVotronic. Their solution was to use a larger computer at the election office to compute or render the images of the ballot content and then download these pre-rendered images into the voting machine before the election. ES&S referred to ballots displayed this way as "bitmap" ballots. This allowed the very simple firmware within the voting machine to display ballots with arbitrary text and graphics, since all the details of type fonts and character layout were handled by the computer in the election office long before the polls open. Unfortunately, as we will see in Chapter 6, opening the polls on early versions of the iVotronic with pre-rendered ballots was extraor-

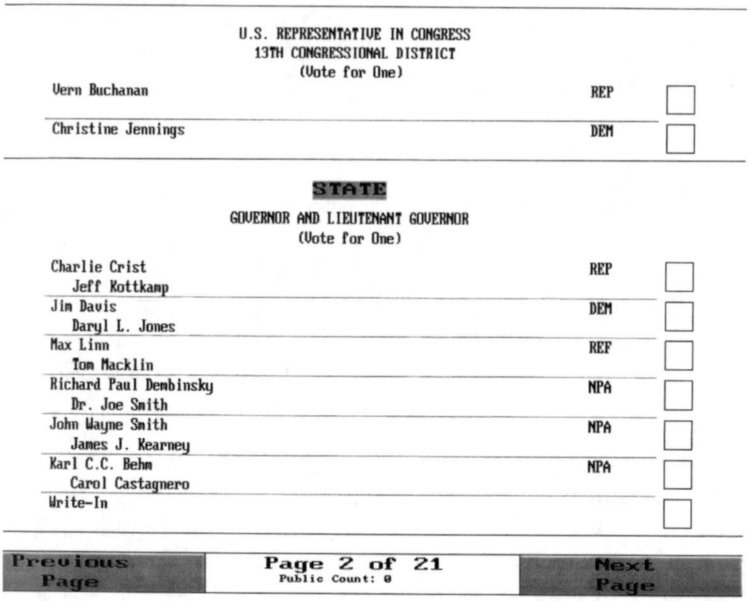

U.S. REPRESENTATIVE IN CONGRESS
13TH CONGRESSIONAL DISTRICT
(Vote for One)

Vern Buchanan	REP	☐
Christine Jennings	DEM	☐

STATE

GOVERNOR AND LIEUTENANT GOVERNOR
(Vote for One)

Charlie Crist Jeff Kottkamp	REP	☐
Jim Davis Daryl L. Jones	DEM	☐
Max Linn Tom Macklin	REF	☐
Richard Paul Dembinsky Dr. Joe Smith	NPA	☐
John Wayne Smith James J. Kearney	NPA	☐
Karl C.C. Behm Carol Castagnero	NPA	☐
Write-In		☐

Previous Page	Page 2 of 21 Public Count: 0	Next Page

FIGURE 31 The ballot presented by the ES&S iVotronic in the 2006 election in Sarasota, Florida. Sarasota County public records.

dinarily slow, leading to serious problems in Miami-Dade County in 2002.[526]

In the case of the iVotronic, pre-rendering came as an afterthought. In 2006, Ka-Ping Yee and a group at the University of California at Berkeley showed that designing a voting system from scratch around the idea of pre-rendering can lead to remarkable reductions in the size of the firmware resident in the voting machine.[1024]

5.3.2 Fidlar and Chambers

As personal computer operating systems grew more powerful, the easiest way to develop new voting systems was to build on top of a standard PC platform. This approach was followed twice in the late 1990s to develop a pair of notable voting systems. In both cases, the initial prototypes were based on Microsoft's Windows 95 operating system, and both assumed that voters would be issued smart voter ID cards. A smart card is a card the size of a commonplace credit card with a small microprocessor and flash memory embedded in it. Smart cards are potentially very secure, but the security depends entirely on how the microprocessor is programmed.

Fidlar was a long established election services company in western Illinois and a major rival of the Frank Thornber Company, the developer of the Video Voter in the 1970s. [217] In late 1996, Fidlar and Chambers demonstrated a new touch-screen voting system, the EV 2000, and in 1998, Moutaz Kotob and a team of Fidlar employees filed a patent application for this voting system. [502,572] Aside from the use of a touch screen, laptop computer technology, and smart cards, the distinctive feature of the new machine was that all the machines in each precinct were intended to be connected in a local area network. Ohio certified the system in late 1997. [1015] It was adopted by Surry County, North Carolina and Clay County, Iowa in time for the 2000 general election. [338,780]

Fidlar's innovation, networking all of the machines in the polling place, was put to two uses. First, at the close of the polls, the network allowed the results for the entire polling place to be automatically consolidated. The second use was more innovative. When EV 2000 voting machines were networked in a polling place, all votes cast on each machine are stored both in that machine and in others. This approach to redundant vote storage gave some hope that votes would not be lost, even if one voting machine is completely destroyed during an election. A decade after Fidlar first explored networked redundant vote storage, Daniel Sandler and Dan Wallach at Rice University showed that if the data from all of the machines in the local network are cryptographically entangled,* each machine on the local network can serve as a witness to the integrity of all of the others. Furthermore, if just one machine survives from a precinct, all of the results from that precinct can be reconstructed. [874]

Although Fidlar and Chambers was an established election services company with its own sales and support network, it did not have the resources needed to achieve significant market penetration. A fresh infusion of capital came in 1999 when John Elliott bought Fidlar and Chambers and merged it with Doubleday, a publishing company he owned, to create Fidlar Doubleday. [583] While Fidlar continued to support the EV 2000, the system never achieved the market penetration necessary to justify the upgrades needed to meet the requirements of the Help America Vote Act of 2002. Fidlar Doubleday still exists, but it is difficult to find evidence that it was once a developer of innovative voting systems.

---

*Cryptographic entanglement creates a situation where making an undetectable change in the data on one machine requires cracking the security of all of the machines.

5.3.3 The path from I-Mark to Diebold

I-Mark Systems developed the second machine that came to market based on Microsoft Windows 95. This machine was a far greater success than the Fidlar EV 2000. Bob Urosevich, former president of American Information Systems, left AIS in 1995 to form I-Mark Systems. The new startup's goal was to develop a voting kiosk that could be placed in shopping malls or other public places, with a "vote anywhere" model that eliminated the need for voters to go to their assigned polling places and had the potential to eliminate the need for pollworkers.[391]

Urosevich envisioned a system in which voters would be issued smart-cards as their voter IDs. When a voter inserted a voter-ID in the voting kiosk, the machine would administer the appropriate ballot, just as with Anno's bar-coded card. In addition, as the voter finished voting and before the kiosk returned the voter's ID card, the kiosk would record on the card that the voter had cast a ballot in that election. Urosevich suggested that if the ID card was not sufficient as a proof of identity, the kiosk could be modified to include what various company publications described as "biometric encryption authorization technology."[389,391] Later developments would make it clear that this term had no well-defined meaning.

The prototype I-Mark kiosk enclosed an IBM PC and its CRT video monitor in a laminate-covered pedestal. Input was done with a light pen (a wand the voter could touch to the screen to make selections). The PC ran Microsoft Windows 95. After the prototype had been demonstrated and certified for use in Kansas in mid 1997, a second version of the Electronic Ballot Station was built. The bulky desktop PC inside the kiosk was replaced with what was essentially laptop computer technology, a flat-panel display with a touch-screen hinged to the top of a lightweight base that incorporated the computer and smart-card reader. It was marketed as the EBS model 100, and was certified for use in Kentucky in the fall of 1997.[538,552]

I-Mark Systems was built following a standard business model: raise capital to develop a system, and then sell out to a larger company that can provide the sales and support network needed to push the prototype to market. In this case, I-Mark was acquired by Global Election Systems in 1997. As part of the acquisition, Bob Urosevich was appointed Vice President of Sales and Marketing at Global.[391] Since Global already had significant market penetration with its Accuvote precinct-count ballot scanner, it was natural to rename the re-packaged EBS Model 100 the AccuVote-TS (for touchscreen), while the precinct-count scanner became the AccuVote OS (for optical scan).

The AccuVote TS was officially announced on November 7, 2000, simultaneously with its first use in Mahoning County, Ohio.[390] The announcement repeated Bob Urosevich's vision of eventually migrating to the vote-anywhere model, while at the same time making clear that the AccuVote TS was fully functional as a stand-alone voting machine for precinct use. The Accuvote TS went on to become the center of controversy and a symbol of the problems with electronic voting, but we shall defer that story until Chapter 7.

5.3.4 Alternatives to Touch Screens

The link between electronic voting and touch-screen technology is so strong that some people use the phrase *touch-screen voting machine* as if it were a synonym for a direct-recording electronic voting system. In Florida, for example, the Election Reform Act of 2001 explicitly authorizes use of "touchscreen systems," rather than the broader class of DRE voting machines.[349,351] Two second-generation systems, the Microvote Infinity and the Hart eSlate, illustrate that touch-screens are not the central feature of modern direct-recording electronic voting machines.

Since the scrolling paper display mechanism of the Microvote MV-464 looked increasingly archaic, Carson Manufacturing and Microvote set out to develop a second generation machine, which they named the Microvote Infinity.[150] This machine retained the essential user-interface elements of the original machine, a central screen flanked by two columns of push buttons for entering votes. By replacing the scrolling paper display of the MV-464 with a flat-panel display in their new Infinity, they were able to produce a lightweight and accessible voting machine that could be substituted for the original with minimal need for voter instruction or for rethinking the way ballots are format-ted. The Infinity was publicly demonstrated in late 2001 and approved for use in Indiana in early 2002.[497,498] It remains in widespread use today in Indiana and Tennessee.[499,957]

In 1997, Neil McClure and Kermit Lohry filed a patent application for a new networked voting machine.[653] In conception, the network-based aspects of the machine were not very different from the Fidlar ES 2000, but it was a full-face push-button machine. Initially, the de-velopers founded their own company, Worldwide Election Systems, to market the machine they named *The Elector*.[413] As with I-mark, when it came time to market their system, they needed a partner. Hart In-formation Services, an established Texas ballot printer, bought several small election companies in the late 1990s, including Worldwide, before reorganizing as Hart Intercivic.[445]

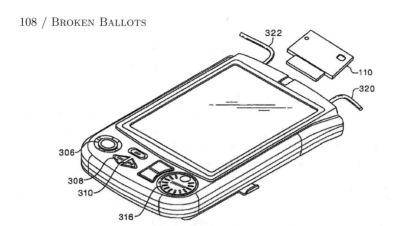

FIGURE 32 The Hart Intercivic eSlate voting terminal. The network cables, 320 and 322, and the disability access unit, 110, plug into the back. The round knob on the right front, 316, is used to dial in candidate selections, the triangular buttons 308 and 310 are for navigating through the ballot, and the left button, 306, is for casting the voted ballot.
From U.S. Patent 7,032,821.

With support from Hart, McClure and his associates redesigned their system using a flat-panel display, producing the machine they dubbed the eSlate, shown in Figure 32. The eSlate saw successful use in the 2000 presidential election in Tarrant County, Texas and several other counties. It attracted significant attention with its features supporting the needs of voters with disabilities.[918] A few months later, the inventors applied for a patent for the eSlate.[654]

Where the Votronic had been described as looking like a Magna Doodle, one writer described the eSlate as looking like "a Palm Pilot on steroids."[72] It might have been more accurate to describe it as an Etch-a-Sketch, since instead of a touch screen, the eSlate had a knob or dial that voters turned to make their candidate selections. While the knob interface was unexpected and unfamiliar, leading to slow voting and significant voter dissatisfaction, it actually works rather well, at least in vote-for-one races.[456] When comparing human factors issues in voting system user interfaces, it is clear that the devil is in the details. Replacing a touch screen with a dial may be less significant than how users correct errors and how they navigate from page to page in the ballot.

5.4 What's Wrong with DRE Voting?

Even before direct recording electronic voting machines were a significant factor in the marketplace, computerized voting systems had begun to attract attention. Roy Saltman's 1975 report on computerized vote tallying documented an uncomfortable status quo in which election officials used computers without any real control over the software, which remains the proprietary property of an election contractor. [868] Saltman's 1988 report itemized numerous threats posed by software, ranging from the accidental to the malicious. [869] By 1988, the issue started to attract a larger audience with Ronnie Dugger's *New Yorker* article, based in significant part on Saltman's work. [287]

There were no secrets with mechanical voting machines. How they worked was a matter of public record, well documented in patents. With the shift to computerized voting systems, the software was generally treated as a trade secret, the private property of the voting system vendor and not available for inspection by anyone.

Michael Shamos, who served for many years as a voting system examiner in Pennsylvania, commented that "the manufacturers of voting equipment claim that their software is a trade secret and go to extraordinary lengths to preserve that myth." He went on to say that after over 20 years of examining voting systems, he had yet to find any significant differences "except possibly for the number of bugs they contain." [899] While keeping bugs secret may prevent malicious exploitation of those bugs, it does not allow the public to assess the quality of the voting equipment or the competence of the public officials who have spent public money on that equipment.

In 1975, Roy Saltman recognized that operating systems pose a special threat. He noted that complex operating systems are never fully debugged, so they can never be expected to withstand an assault by a determined attacker. Some bugs have no security consequences, but others provide potential attackers with the tools they need to break into computer systems and take control. In the light of this, Saltman recommended that the best operating system for a voting application is "the least complex operating system that provides the capabilities required." He went on to suggest that all voting system software should be subject to what he called "the principle of least complexity," so that source code audits and other measures would be practical. [868]

Most discussions of software-based threats to voting integrity focus on outside hackers somehow breaking into the system, but accidents can be as dangerous as malice. This was demonstrated by an accidental attack Douglas Jones, one of the authors, discovered in early 1998. Fidlar and Chambers had brought their new EV-2000 voting machine before the Iowa Board of Examiners for Voting Machines and Electronic Voting Systems. Serving as an examiner, Jones was casting a sequence of test ballots, when he noticed that each time a list of candidates was presented, the check box by one candidate was slightly emphasized. The emphasis was subtle, but after several test ballots, a pattern emerged: The candidate emphasized was always the one that had received the vote on the previous ballot. In effect, the machine was showing each voter the selections made by the previous voter. [507]

Clearly, Fidlar and Chambers had not designed the EV 2000 to violate voter privacy rights. Eventually, Fidlar's representatives at the voting machine examination figured out what had happened. Microsoft had just released a new version of the Windows 95 operating system, and Fidlar had dutifully installed the new release on their voting machine. Microsoft had advertised the new version as containing bug fixes and cosmetic enhancements, emphasizing that application programs that worked under the previous version would operate with no changes under the upgrade. One of Microsoft's cosmetic change was a slight highlight to the most recently selected item in a menu display. This example clearly illustrates the risk of violating Saltman's principle of least complexity. In the context of filling out forms or similar office applications, slightly highlighting the most recently selected menu item might have been useful, but this function has no place in the context of a voting system.

Saltman proposed his principle of least complexity in part to make it feasible to audit the software in a voting system. His principle raises a serious research question. How small can the security-critical component of a voting system be made, and is this small enough that reading the code can be expected to reveal any security problems in the code?

After observing that the main program for the AccuVote TS consisted of over 31,000 lines of code, Ka-Ping Yee and a group at the University of California at Berkeley decided to write a new voting system following the principle of least complexity. The result of their work was a touch-screen electronic voting machine in which the entire program was under 300 lines of code. [1024] They cheated by using a remarkably flexible programming language, Python. But even if they had restricted themselves to a less expressive language, their code would still have been very small, in significant part because it relied on pre-rendered graphics. Extending their voting system to make it accessible for voters with disabilities expanded the program to 460 lines of Python code. [1023]

Having produced such a small voting system, Ka-Ping Yee deliberately hid three bugs in the source code, and then brought in five computer scientists to do an intensive security review of the software. The bugs were deliberately crafted to create subtle security flaws that would permit attacks on the integrity of an election. Between the five reviewers, only 2 of the 3 planted bugs were found, and no new bugs were uncovered. The Berkeley experiment demonstrated that reviewing source code of systems with thousands of lines of code is a very weak defense. While tiny software systems may be more trustworthy than large ones, even the smallest systems are big enough to hide dangerous bugs.

5.5 Voter Verifiability

Long before Ka-Ping Yee's work, many critics understood that a complete review of the workings of a direct-recording voting system is impossible. If this is so, how can such a system be audited? Just because voters can see their selections correctly displayed on the screen of a direct-recording electronic voting machine or on the face of a mechanical voting machine does not mean that the machine has recorded their votes correctly. As Horatio Rogers said in 1897, a voter on such a voting machine "has no knowledge through his senses" that he has voted, but rather, must trust that "the machine has worked as intended . . . ". [853]

As long ago as 1889, Jacob Myers anticipated this objection to direct-recording voting systems. The solution he patented was a voting machine that retained a physical record of each vote cast in the form of a metal token. [725] In 1899, Joseph Gray patented a mechanical voting machine that both counted the votes and recorded them by punching a paper ballot that the voter could inspect before dropping it in the ballot box. [401] Gray's patent explains the purpose of the paper records, saying "in this manner we have a mechanical check for the tickets [paper records], while the ticket is also a check upon the [mechanical] register."

While losing candidates in most states have long had the right to demand some kind of recount, the idea of auditing elections is relatively new. With the introduction of the Votomatic, computer programs replaced people and relatively simple mechanisms as vote counters. Distrust of mechanisms as complex and inscrutable as computer software is natural and justified. California's response, in 1965, was to pass a law requiring routine post-election auditing of 1% of the precincts, randomly selected. The ballots from those precincts are then hand counted. [134] The California audit law worked well with punched-card and optical mark-sense ballots, but there were obvious issues about how the law should be applied when DRE voting machines were introduced, as discussed in Chapter 8.

Despite over 40 years of positive experience with routine post election auditing in California and frequent post-election recounts in several other states, some election officials have resisted proposals to conduct routine auditing. The most common objection is that auditing costs money that they do not have. We suspect that those objecting to audits significantly overestimate the costs. We discuss alternative auditing methods and their costs in Chapter 13. A second and less worthy concern may be behind some of the objections to auditing. If auditing does reveal problems in an election, this could be very uncomfortable for the election officials and candidates involved.

In 1992, Rebecca Mercuri reinvented Gray's idea, suggesting that "the only reasonable method of auditing a DRE election would involve printing each ballot before the voter exited the machine. The voter would then examine the ballot for correctness and insert it into a ballot box." [699] Others have proposed similar mechanisms. Mercuri combined several ideas in her 2002 description of a "better ballot box," merging a DRE voting machine with paper ballots printed behind glass and automatically deposited in a ballot box only if the voters confirm that they are accurate. [700] Mercuri became such a champion of this idea that it frequently was referred to as the *Mercuri Method* in the early 21st century. There has been some debate about the proper name for this idea. Some have called the paper records generated by such a system a *voter-verifiable paper trail* or VVPT, but Mercuri argued for *voter-verified physical audit trail* or VVPAT. [701] The latter name emphasizes two things: First, we want more than verifiability, we want the voter to actually verify, and second, it is not the use of paper that matters here, but the use of a physical medium.

Some of us are convinced that the audit requirements of the Help America Vote Act of 2002 (HAVA), Section 301(a)(2), were intended to be read as requiring a voter-verifable paper trail. [191] Unfortunately, after HAVA was passed, the operative interpretation was significantly weaker. Instead of requiring a VVPAT, HAVA has been interpreted as requiring first that voters be able to verify their ballots and second that a paper record be printed for the purpose of recounts. These two requirements have come to be read as separate requirements, permitting systems in which a paper record need not be seen by the voter or even printed contemporaneously with the casting of the vote.

Shortly after the election of 2000, Kevin Chung filed for a patent which was the basis of the Avante Vote Trakker, first used in Sacramento in the 2002 general election. [166] Avante's system in its early form resembled a rather ugly and boxy DRE voting machine. Before committing each ballot to the machine's internal electronic ballot box, Avante printed the voter's choices on a long narrow strip of paper. In a general election, the paper record could be so long that it reached the floor. After allowing time for the voter to inspect the paper copy, the paper was sucked back into the machine. [70]

In early 2003, Santa Clara County, California, home of Silicon Valley and Stanford University, was preparing to spend $20 million on new Sequoia Voting Systems AVC Edge touch-screen voting machines (see Chapter 8). To the surprise of many, David Dill, a computer scientist at Stanford, and one of the authors, Barbara Simons, along with several others, testified against DRE machines at a January meeting of the County Supervisors. Dill, who would go on to found the Verified Voting Foundation, began circulating the Resolution on Electronic Voting, a petition now signed by thousands of computer science professionals, attorneys, politicians, voting rights experts, and citizens. The cornerstone of this campaign was a demand that all direct-recording electronic voting machines be equipped with a voter-verified paper trail. [205,274,273]

Spurred by the events in Santa Clara County, Sequoia Voting Systems was the first major vendor to produce a VVPAT retrofit for their touch-screen voting machine, the Sequoia AVC Edge. A team led by John Homewood filed for a provisional application in the Spring of 2003 and a full patent application in early 2004. [473]

The Sequoia system uses a thermal printer and a roll of cash-register receipt tape. After each voter completes a ballot on the display screen, the printed choices are displayed behind a glass window for voter approval, and then rolled onto a take-up reel before the next voter enters the voting booth. Unlike the Avante Vote Trakker, the tape is not cut after each ballot is printed.

In late 2003, the state of Nevada required that all voting equipment in that state be equipped to produce voter-verified paper records. Sequoia's new VeriVote printer for the AVC Edge was adopted statewide. [892] As these new machines came into use in 2004, critics quickly noticed several problems. Among the most obvious were that it was hard to read the thermal printer tape through the plastic cover, that many voters did not bother to check the paper record, and that the printers themselves sometimes jammed. Michael Shamos at Carnegie-Mellon University was the most articulate observer of these flaws. [899]

One flaw that Shamos pointed out has particular relevance to Sequoia's VeriVote and all other VVPAT systems that follow that model: recording votes sequentially on a reel of paper is a potential violation of a voter's right to a secret ballot. Shamos was not the first to notice this problem. In 1893, John McTammany wrote that a sequential vote record allows an observer or dishonest official to note the order in which people vote on a machine and then use that information to connect voters to their ballots. [684]

Whether or not a sequential ordering is considered a violation of a voter's right to a secret ballot depends on exactly how a secret ballot is defined. As discussed in Chapter 2, there are two distinct approaches to defining ballot secrecy. Under the British model, the state retains the connection between the voter and the cast ballot, but guards that information as a secret. Under the absolute model, it is illegal to retain any information that might connect a voter to a cast ballot. Retaining a sequential record of the votes might be permissible under the British model, but it must be forbidden under the absolute model.

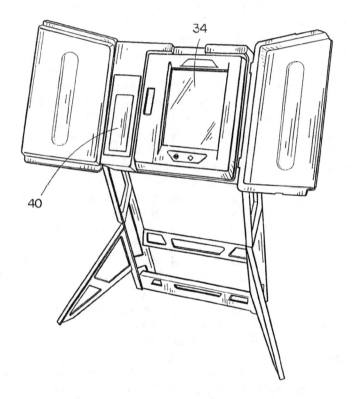

FIGURE 33 The ES&S iVotronic (34) mounted in a voting booth to the right of the ES&S real-time audit log printer (40).
From U.S. Patent 7,387,244.

As interest in voter-verifiable paper trails increased, both Diebold and ES&S came to market with VVPAT retrofits for their touch-screen machines. Both deployed printers on cash-register tape using reel-to-reel recording. Diebold's AccuView printer, announced in early 2005, was generally comparable to Sequoia's design. [695] ES&S, in contrast, took an innovative but controversial approach. In 2005, Steve Bolton and his associates at ES&S filed a patent application for what they called a "voter-verifiable real-time audit log" or RTAL. [99] An iVotronic with an RTAL is shown in Figure 33

While all other voter-verifiable paper trail schemes wait to print the paper record until the voter had completed the entire ballot, the ES&S RTAL prints each selection at the time it is made. Thus, whenever a voter touches the screen to select a candidate, the printer immediately prints that selection. The advantage is immediate feedback to the voter, if the voter happens to watch the printout. The disadvantage is that in the event the voter makes any changes, all the voter's previous selections have been retained. In a recount or audit of the paper records, only the last vote recorded for each office should be counted. The inclusion of prior selections can make ballot verification of RTALs challenging for voters, and manual counting of RTALs even more difficult for election officials.

Other smaller vendors tried to enter the market with systems that, like Avante, produced each ballot on a separate sheet of paper. In 2003, Sanford Morganstein filed for a patent on a voting system where the touch-screen voting machine was used entirely to record and print a paper ballot that the voter would then hand-carry to a ballot box that included a scanner. [720] Morganstein founded Populex Corporation to sell his machine. The same year, Eugene Cummings, who had developed a conceptually similar machine, filed for a patent on a machine he called the Automark. [219] The key difference between these two machines was that after a voter makes his or her selections on an Automark, it prints marks to fill in the voting targets on a pre-printed optical mark-sense ballot form. Therefore, it can be used with any existing precinct-count optical mark-sense scanner. In contrast, the Populex system prints ballots in a unique style incorporating a bar code, requiring a specialized ballot scanner. In effect, both machines could be described as behaving like very expensive pencils, but the Automark addresses an important niche market, that of providing for voters with disabilities in jurisdictions using optical mark-sense scanners.

5.5.1 Alternatives to Paper?

Several interesting alternatives have been suggested that could eliminate some of the problems of voter-verified paper audit trails. One proposal is to replace the printer and paper record with an electronic recorder incorporating a second display device. David Chaum coined the term *votemeter* for this idea, although the idea is sometimes ascribed to Eric Fischer, because his report is one of the first to clearly describe the idea. [160,341] A votemeter could be much simpler than the voting machine to which it is connected. With a standard interface specification, votemeters and all of their component parts could be produced independently from any component of the voting machine. Unfortunately, we do not know how to assure the integrity of a national supply of honest votemeters. A dishonest supplier could build votemeters that pass all likely tests but that could be rigged to record one thing while displaying something else to the voter. Furthermore, any question about whether voters will take the time to verify their ballots could just as easily apply to a votemeter display as it does to a VVPAT.

The idea of pulling randomly selected voting machines from polling places on the day of the election and subjecting them to intensive tests may have occurred independently to several people around the same time. This is usually called *parallel testing*, a term due to Michael Shamos, but it has also been called parallel monitoring. [578,899] The first trial of parallel testing was during the California primary in 2004, but as with many of the parallel tests done since, that effort involved various compromises. In practice, most parallel tests have involved selecting machines for testing well in advance of the election, and testing them with carefully constructed test scripts. A malicious voting machine could easily detect the use of such a test script and behave honestly when it recognizes that it is being tested. More realistic models of parallel testing make it harder for a voting machine to detect the test, but such models are generally more disruptive, and therefore unacceptable to election officials. [526]

In 2004, Ted Selker at MIT suggested what he called a voter-verified audio transcript. [890] Instead of using a printer to create a paper record that the voter had to look at to verify, voters would wear headphones and listen to audio reports of their selections as they made them. When Selker tested this idea, one surprising result was that many voters caught errors that they missed when the audio feedback was not offered.

Yet another alternative has emerged independently in several different places. In 2007, a group at Auburn University led by Juan Gilbert developed the Prime III voting system. This system included what the developers called a voter-verified video audit trail; it included a video recorder to record the output to the display screen along with the audio output to the headphones. [216] Barring some serious hardware hacking, Prime III should record what the voter actually sees and hears. In 2008, Arel Cordero at the University of California at Berkeley suggested using what he called replayable voting machine audit logs to capture voter intent. In its crudest form, a camera would record the voter's view of the screen while the voter voted; the refined version digitally captured a sequence of screen shots and touch coordinates from within the voting system software. [207]

As with the ES&S real time audit log, both the audio log and schemes that transcribe the sequence of screenshots pose several problems. Cordero and Selker attempted to overcome the problems with reel-to-reel recording by keeping sequential recordings of the actions of each voter, while randomizing the order in which the records were stored. Selker did this using a very low-tech approach, randomly picking a cassette tape from a basket to record each voter's session, while Cordero used high powered cryptography.

A second problem with these alternatives is the difficulty of actually conducting an audit. In 2008, a group based at Rice and Auburn Universities reported on experiments comparing hand counting of "fill in the bubble" ballots designed for optical mark-sense scanning with spools of VVPAT tape and the Prime III video audit trail. They found that accurate hand counting is difficult, even with conventional paper ballots. In that case, 35% of the people performing the count made errors, and the average error rate was 0.9%. A cash-register-tape VVPAT is significantly harder to hand count, and video transcripts are still more difficult. [392] The error rate reported by the Rice-Auburn study for hand-counted paper ballots does not agree with the reports we have heard from election officials who routinely conduct audits or recounts by hand. We speculate that the accuracy depends on how the tellers are trained for the counting, and the procedures they use.

Parallel testing is no easier. A representative of one voting machine vendor in the late 1990s quipped that "you cannot expect to do a realistic test of a DRE system by entering votes by hand. It is so hard to do this that if you enter a realistic number of ballots, you will make so many mistakes that your test is useless." [522] Entering one ballot accurately is fairly easy, but testers tend to start making mistakes after they have entered several. Effective testing require measures such as two person teams, one to enter votes and another to proofread the entry, or video cameras to record the entire process in order to allow diagnosis of errors in data entry. [526]

5.6 Experimental Studies

There are two central premises behind the idea of the voter-verifiable paper audit trail. First, that voters will take the time to verify that what is printed represents their choice, and second that recounting the printed record on the paper is an effective way to audit or re-count an election. There have been several experimental studies of these premises, and the results are not encouraging.

When Nevada deployed Sequoia AVC Edge machines with a voter-verifiable paper audit trail for the November 2, 2004 general election, the Lombardo Consulting Group conducted a public opinion survey asking how voters liked the new system. Their first question was "Did you know why there was a roll of paper scrolling next to the voting screen?" Although pollworkers had been instructed to explain the purpose of the attached printer, a quarter of the voters did not know the answer. Only about 1/3 of the voters claimed to have checked the paper record for all the votes they cast, while 1/5 of the voters claimed to have checked most of their votes. [613]

In 2007, Sarah Everett reported on a series of experiments she had done at Rice University, testing how voters interacted with different types of voting machines. She found that the rate at which voters made errors in expressing their intent did not depend significantly on previous experience with the technology used, with the level of computer expertise, or with the actual voting technology. Overall, 27% of the ballots cast contained at least one error—defined as a vote in a race that differed from the voter's intent. [323]

The experimental DRE voting machine Everett used was a touch-screen machine that administered ballots as a series of pages or screens, imitating the style of most touch-screen voting machines. At the end of each voting session, the machine displayed a review screen showing all of the choices a voter had made. The voter's final confirmation of the review screen resulted in the official act of casting the ballot. Everett's most startling discovery was that when she deliberately programmed her machine to omit or alter votes on the review screen, only about 1/3 of her subjects noticed the change. In her words, "voters simply breezed past the review screen and submitted the corrupted ballots." This is fully consistent with the Lombardo survey in Nevada, if we assume that Nevada voters over-reported the accuracy of their proof-reading. Follow-up work at Rice done by Bryan Campbell showed that better review-screen design increased the effectiveness, but even with his best designs, half of the test subjects did not notice review-screen anomalies. [145]

The work at Rice used fictional candidate names. In followup work done in 2009 by one of us, Douglas Jones and his students at the University of Iowa, we used the general election ballot from 2008 on our experimental voting machine. Our test of a dishonest summary screen involved flipping the two presidential candidates, McCain and Obama.

Vote flipping is a term that has come to describe the experience of a voter who sees one candidate's name on the review screen, while having intended to vote for some other candidate. All of our experimental subjects had voted in the 2008 election, so name recognition for the candidates was very high, and the presidential race is the most prominent on the ballot. Nonetheless, only 2/3 of the subjects noticed the change. [639]

A central idea underlying the design of most second-generation DRE voting machines is that after voting, the voter is presented with a review screen. The legal act of casting a ballot on such a machine comes when the voter presses the "cast ballot" button while viewing this screen. The studies discussed above raise serious doubt on the soundness of the review screen idea. Numerous studies show that voters make mistakes using all types of ballots, and that forgetting to vote in a race, undervoting, is frequently less common than selecting a candidate other than the one the voter intended. [145,323,456] Merely adding a review screen or asking voters to proofread their ballots is not an effective way to deal with such errors.

5.7   What Happened in Sarasota?

Even before the polls opened on Election Day in 2006, both of the authors received email reports from concerned Sarasota voters reporting on problems they were having at the polls. In fact, three days before the election the Sarasota Herald Tribune ran an editorial on the subject. [875] The most common complaint we heard was that vote flipping had occurred. Unfortunately, vote flipping describes a symptom and not a cause. What voters reported to us after casting ballots in early voting was that they were sure that they had cast votes in the House race, yet the review screen showed that they had not. We also heard voter complaints that it was difficult to get the touch screen to register their touches; eventually, we learned of a memo from ES&S acknowledging the problem. [82]

As the extraordinary undervote rate in Sarasota came to light, various hypotheses to explain the vote flipping were suggested, but there was very little evidence. Among the hypotheses were rigged or defective machines that had deliberately undercounted the Democratic votes, poor ballot design in Sarasota county that had misled Sarasota voters into skipping the Congressional race, and touch-screen calibration problems that had caused voters to select one candidate when they intended to select another. The one suggestion that was ruled out very early was that the undervote rate was the result of voter disgust with negative campaigning.

Statistical analysis of voting patterns in Florida's 13th district provided strong evidence that something went wrong. This analysis points squarely at Sarasota's voting machines as the probable cause of the undervotes, since voters in other counties in the district and voters voting on paper had much lower undervote rates. While such work cannot explain what it was about the machines that caused the undervotes, it strongly supports the hypothesis that the high undervote in Sarasota actually changed the election outcome. [61]

The immediate investigation of the problem by the Florida Department of Elections focused on rigged or defective machines. Specifically, the question the audit team asked was: Had the iVotronic machines used in Sarasota "accurately recorded voters' selections and votes cast and tabulated the results ...." The auditors conducted a source-code review of the iVotronic firmware that focused on the accuracy question. They also performed what they called parallel tests, although it is difficult to describe a post-election test as being parallel to the election. The result of the study was that there was "no evidence to suggest or conclude that the official certified election results did not reflect the actual votes cast" and there was "no evidence of election procedural error ...." [350]

The charge to the Florida investigators was narrow, and it was interpreted narrowly. In asking if the voting machines were able to "accurately record voters' selections," the investigators took the review screen as ground truth for what the voter had selected. The investigation did not ask whether voters had difficulty making selections. From the point of view of the investigators, voters who did not closely proofread their review screens were careless.

The official Florida report was subject to strong criticism. David Dill at Stanford and Dan Wallach at Rice quickly identified the narrow focus of the official investigation and recommended a number of other areas to investigate. [275]

Ted Selker at MIT conducted a series of small experiments showing that 16% of voters missed the congressional race when they used a ballot that imitated the Sarasota ballot, shown in Figure 31. Furthermore, he demonstrated that changes to the layout of the ballot could eliminate the large undervote. [889] The specific problem with the ballot layout Selker identified was that the two-candidate congressional race was at the screen top above a color-highlighted headline. Unfortunately, we are trained by conventional typography to ignore text above the headline. That is where newspapers put meaningless slogans and teasers for content inside the paper, and that is where many web sites put banner advertisements. Web page designers refer to this as *banner blindness*.

It is clear that a conventional voter-verifiable paper audit trail would not have helped in Sarasota. If large numbers of voters did not examine the review screen to see if their votes had been registered, it is highly unlikely that they would have examined a printed copy of the same information. Had Florida opted to require a VVPAT, Sarasota would have used the ES&S real-time audit log printer for the iVotronic. Curiously, this might have helped.

The iVotronic, like all DRE voting machines designed since the mid 1990s, maintains an internal *event log*, a sequential record containing event notices and the times at which those events occurred. The events recorded include the time the polls opened, the time the polls closed, and the time at which each voter finished with the review screen. Thus, an audit of the event log can check that no ballots were cast before the time the polls were supposed to open, and it can reconcile the number of events reporting the casting of ballots with the number of electronic ballot records retained in the machine's ballot box. Unfortunately, the event logs maintained on conventional DRE machines do not record anything about the voter's experience during a voting session.

With ES&S's real-time audit log, however, as with the experimental video audit logs discussed earlier, most voter actions are recorded. The event log would reveal if voters systematically missed some race and only voted in that race after going back to it from the review screen. One of the authors, Douglas Jones, along with his students at the University of Iowa, set out to design an audit log that would record enough information to diagnose user interface problems, without violating voters' rights to a secret ballot.[639] We then tested this with a voting machine that deliberately exhibited many of the flaws that people had suggested were responsible for the outcome of the election in Sarasota.

One result we did not expect was the impact of touch-screen insensitivity on the likelihood that voters would proofread their ballots. Under normal circumstances, a significant fraction of voters not only proofread their ballots but also go back and visit pages of their ballot from the review screen to make sure that their choices are correct. When voters noticed that we had flipped their votes, the review activity went way up. When we rigged the experimental voting machine to have an insensitive touch screen, to mimic the behavior reported by some Sarasota voters and acknowledged by an ES&S memo, we found that voter review activity plummeted. That is, when touch screens fail to respond promptly to normal pressure, voters actively flee the system as the voting session comes to an end, instead of taking the time to review their work.

Kristen Greene, also working at Rice, conducted additional experiments to study the impact of the Sarasota ballot layout.[403] Her work was significantly more rigorous than Selkers, but it confirmed his basic conclusion that the Sarasota ballot layout caused many voters to skip the congressional race. 27 of Greene's 137 experimental subjects skipped over the congressional race on their first pass through the ballot. Greene studied the effect of the highlighted STATE banner dividing the congressional race from the gurbernatorial race (see Figure 31). She found that removing the color highlighting had little effect, but that adding a second race to the first page on the ballot significantly reduced the number of people who missed the congressional race on the second page. This suggests that the phrase *banner blindness* offers a misleading explanation of what happened.

Ted Selker and Kristen Greene's work on the Sarasota ballot layout, Sarah Everett's work on review screens and our observations on the impact of an insensitive touch screen, when combined, provide a convincing explanation of what happened in Sarasota. The fact that it took four years after the election to understand what probably happened reflects badly on the state of election administration and on the direct-recording electronic voting machines currently on the market.

6

Establishing a Standard: Regulating Voting Systems

The vendor's not going to want a report that has something negative in it, so they will retest and retest and retest and retest until they make it right, until we get everything in there that is done to the standard. Then we write a report.

Shawn Southworth, Cyber Labs [174]

Any system of elections requires regulation, regardless of the technology. An effective legal framework determines who can vote and when and how the votes are counted. Winners are often determined though runoffs, recounts, or other complexities, the rules for which must be legislated in advance. Since the early days of democracy, legislatures have made adjustments to the basic rules of elections, as technology has evolved from paper ballots to mechanical voting machines to direct-recording electronic devices.

When an election is disputed, there must be some final arbitrator, and for legislative elections, the legislature itself frequently serves in this role. Contested Congressional elections, for example, are decided by Congress. This happened with the 2006 election in Florida's 13th Congressional district, discussed in Chapter 5. Having a legislature resolve disputes involving the reelection of its own members clearly tempts the ruling party to ignore the facts and decide disputes on a purely partisan basis. How legislatures deal with this temptation is one of the great tests of any democracy.

In the early 20th century, mechanical voting systems posed new regulatory challenges. As counties and states prepared to buy new machines, election authorities needed standards to determine what these machines were supposed to do. Prior to the late 20th century, this task was largely delegated to the states. Each state was free to adopt its own rules, but states frequently copied large parts of their statutes from other states. The 1972 Mississippi statute is typical.[713] It listed the following requirements of a voting machine:

- It shall secure to the voter secrecy in the act of voting;
- it shall provide facilities for voting for all candidates of as many political parties or organizations as may make nominations, and for or against as many questions as submitted;
- it shall, except at primary elections, permit the voter to vote for all the candidates of one party or in the part for the candidates of one or more other parties;
- it shall permit the voter to vote for as many persons for an office as he is lawfully entitled to vote for, but not more;
- it shall prevent the voter from voting for the same person more than once for the same office;
- it shall permit the voter to vote for or against any question he may have the right to vote on, but no other;
- if used in primary elections, it shall be so equipped that the election officials can lock out all rows except those of the voter's party by a single adjustment on the outside of the machine;
- it shall correctly register or record and accurately count all votes cast for any and all persons and for or against any and all questions;
- it shall be provided with a "protective counter" or "protective device" whereby any operation of the machine before or after the election will be detected;
- it shall be provided with a counter which shall show at all times during an election how many persons have voted;
- it shall be provided with a mechanical model, illustrating the manner of voting on the machine, suitable for the instruction of voters;
- it may also be provided with one (1) device for each party, for voting for all the presidential electors of that party by one (1) operation, and a ballot therefor containing only the words "Presidential Electors For" preceded by the name of that party and followed by the names of the candidates thereof for the offices of President and Vice-President, and a registering device therefor which shall register the vote cast for said electors when thus voted collectively; provided, however, that means shall be furnished whereby the voter can cast a vote for individual electors when permitted to do so by law.

This Mississippi law mixes a variety of different types of requirements in a single list. There are requirements about the nature of the ballot—multiple candidates from multiple parties for multiple offices with the option of straight party voting; there are requirements for different types of elections—general and primary; there are requirements for voter instruction—a demonstration model; and there are requirements for security—the secret ballot and the protective counter. This mixing of unrelated requirements makes the list difficult to assess and gives evidence that the list was not the result of any kind of intelligent design, but rather was the result of an evolutionary process.

Some of the requirements are vague. There is no specific statement of how many parties, how many offices, or how many candidates the machine must support. Others are very specific. Instead of specifying the problem of providing voter training, the law requires use of a model machine. By mandating the ability to lock out all rows except the row belonging to the voter's party in a primary election, the law effectively requires a party-row ballot layout.

In his 1934 book, *Election Administration in the United States*, Joseph P. Harris said "laws authorizing the use of voting machines are practically identical in the several states, due, no doubt, to the fact that they were enacted at the instigation of the manufacturers." [432] Voting technology was sufficiently complex in the 1920's that state legislators looked for experts to assist with developing regulations. In most cases, the experts they found were the vendors.

The situation Harris described is a classic example of *regulatory capture*, a term that describes what happens when the industry being regulated gains control of the regulatory process. [579] Whoever can "capture" the regulatory process can reap immense benefits. As states investigated new technology such as punched-card, mark-sense and then DRE voting systems, helpful vendors were deeply involved in developing regulations for these systems, while simultaneously trying to lock in their technology and lock out their competitors'.

This is not a new story. As we saw in Chapter 2, the first legislation in New York permitting the use of voting machines was written by the inventors of those systems. By 1897, the New York legislature, tired of facing direct lobbying from the vendors, created the New York Board of Voting Machine Commissioners to act as a buffer. [620] This was the first regulatory board for voting machines, and many states followed New York's example.

As Harris observed in 1934, these state boards were typically financed by fees paid by voting system vendors. The statutory fee varied "from a flat $450 in New York State to ten dollars per day for each examiner in the state of Washington." [432] If the fee had not been set by law, the exact same payment from a voting machine vendor to the state examiner would have been considered a bribe. Sixty years later, one of us, Douglas Jones, was appointed to the Iowa Board of Examiners for Voting Machines and Electronic Voting Systems. Despite the recent reorganization of the board, the fee structure for the Iowa board remained at the level Harris reported in 1934, $450 split between the three examiners.

The Iowa Board of Examiners is typical of a working oversight board. Created when Iowa first moved to mechanical lever voting machines in the 1920s, the members of the Board of Examiners were originally gubernatorial appointees with no statutory qualifications for membership. In the early 1990s, the Board was placed under the Secretary of State, and specific qualifications were enacted for membership on the Board: "At least one of the examiners shall have been trained in computer programming and operations. The other two members shall be directly involved in the administration of elections . . . ." [509] Typically, the "other two members" in Iowa are county auditors, the elected county office holders in charge of elections. The number and qualifications of the examiners varies from state to state. Some states do not have a standing board of examiners, and instead appoint examiners or hire consultants whenever the state receives a vendor proposal.

As originally envisioned in New York and as still practiced in many states, any vendor wishing to sell a particular voting machine in a state must first convince that state's board of examiners that the machine meets the requirements set by that state. Only after the board has determined that a machine meets requirements may counties purchase that particular voting machine. In some states, notably Georgia and Maryland, the state has opted to use a single uniform voting system statewide, so counties are not free to make independent purchase decisions.

Regardless of how voting equipment is purchased, the actual elections are largely run by local election offices. In some states these officials are elected; in others they are appointed. The local election officers are responsible for carrying out the law, but final authority rests with the state election office, typically under the authority of the secretary of state. The federal role historically has been primarily advisory, except where there was evidence of crime or violations of civil rights.

6.1 The Press for Standards

The Federal Election Campaign Act of 1971 (FECA) provided for the federal government to monitor the conduct of elections. [196] Amendments to FECA passed in 1974 created the Federal Election Commission. [198] While the legislation was primarily concerned with campaign finance, the law also created the Clearinghouse on Election Administration, originally placed under the General Accounting Office until the FEC was organized.

Shortly after the Clearinghouse was organized, its director, Gary Greenhalgh, began working with Roy G. Saltman of the National Bureau of Standards to plan a review of the use of "automatic digital processing equipment in the vote-tallying process," including the "methods currently being employed ... to detect and prevent computer vote fraud." Saltman's first report on this subject was issued in 1975. [868,1008,870] Many of Saltman's findings mirrored what Harris had said 40 years earlier. Saltman concluded that election administrators were ill-equipped to handle the new technology and that most states lacked a clear list of machine requirements. No one tested these new systems to see if they did what they were supposed to do, or if they were secure. Without uniform standards, there could be no way to ensure that elections were free and fair across many state and local jurisdictions.

Saltman recommended a coordinated research program, training for election administrators, exploration of standards for election auditing, and the creation of a national election systems standards laboratory. The laboratory would be responsible for setting national minimum standards for election procedures and equipment.

A year after Saltman completed his report, the Federal Election Commission convened a 17-member panel to advise the Clearinghouse on Election Administration. Panelists considered evaluation of voting equipment a major problem, noting that some states do not even require testing of new types of equipment. One panelist quipped that under the circumstances, "the voters and the candidates become guinea pigs for new products." [925]

A few years later, the federal government responded to Saltman's report with Section 302 of the 1980 amendments to FECA. Section 302 directed the FEC, with technical support from the National Bureau of Standards, to "conduct a preliminary study with respect to the future development of voluntary engineering and procedural performance standards for voting systems used in the United States." [199]

Saltman released a second report in 1988, *Accuracy, Integrity, and Security in Computerized Vote Tallying,* probably the most important report on voting published in the second half of the 20th century. [869] By that time, Votomatic and optical mark-sense systems had been in use for over two decades and direct-recording electronic voting systems were coming onto the market.

Saltman concluded that many of the failures of computerized voting systems were due to procedural and administrative errors. These errors were becoming a major problem as the technical complexity of voting systems moved well beyond the level that typical election officials were capable of handling. A number of Saltman's procedural recommendations were eventually incorporated into many states' election laws, including requirements for pre-election testing, manual inspection of any ballots that tabulating machines could not interpret, and post-election auditing. Unfortunately, states vary considerably in the extent to which they have adopted these ideas.

Saltman's second report strongly endorsed the idea of a federal role in voting system standards, but he also wanted to raise the level of professionalism among election officials. He had observed in his first report that "there is no organized technical information collection and exchange program among election administrators."

In fact, there was some exchange. The *International Association of Clerks, Recorders, Election Officials and Treasurers* (IACREOT), founded in 1971, is open to local election officials, as well as other county-level officials.[373] The *National Association of Secretaries of State*, (NASS) which dates to 1904, brings together the chief election officials of most states.[998]* IACREOT and NASS were not enough. For both organizations, elections were submerged in a much larger set of issues.

Saltman's second report put considerable weight on the founding of the Election Center in 1984 to provide "organized technical information collection and exchange program among election administrators." The Election Center grew out of a series of regional workshops convened by the Federal Election Commission's Clearinghouse on Election Administration, organized by clearinghouse director Gary Greenhalgh.[1011]

Greenhalgh quit his job at the FEC in 1985 to run the Election Center, and then sold the Election Center to the Academy for State and Local Government in 1986.[405] He continued as executive director for less than a year before taking a position at Shoup.[923] Greenhalgh's term at Shoup ended in early 1989 when he formed an election sales and service company to represent Microvote. By his own account, however, Greenhalgh continued his close association with the Election Center until 1997, by which time the Election Center was deeply involved in voting system certification.

---

*There are states, notably New York, where the secretary of state is not the chief election official.

In 1989, the Election Center helped launch the *National Association of State Election Directors* (NASED). [304] Both the Election Center and NASED have the potential to provide needed support for elections officials across the country, but there are serious questions about the role of the Election Center. How much of the training it offers to election officials is covert marketing and lobbying support for the vendors?

When Greenhalgh took his job at Shoup in 1987, he noted that there could be areas where his new role "would conflict with the objectives of the Center." [404] Given Greenhalgh's role in shaping those objectives, and the Center's growing involvement in voting system certification in the 1990s, the potential for conflict of interest was significant. The formal relationship between the Election Center and NASED continued until at least 2003. During that time the Election Center served as the NASED Voting Systems Secretariat, providing administrative support for NASED's involvement in voting system certification. As we shall see, there were times when the Election Center and NASED appeared to have greater concern for the interests of the vendors than for their nominal constituencies.

6.2   The 1990 Voting System Standards

After years of study, the FEC contracted with Robert Naegele to develop the initial drafts of what would become the 1990 standards, under the direction of a Voting System Standards Committee that included Thomas R. Wilkey and Britain J. Williams. Naegele had served as a voting system examiner to the State of California since the 1970s. In addition to examining voting systems for several other states, he had helped New York City draft requirements for electronic voting systems to support their unsuccessful move to DRE voting in the 1980s. [1011] Wilkey had begun working as an elections clerk in 1968 and joined the New York State Board of Elections in 1979. [1009,1010] Brit Williams began consulting for the Clearinghouse on Election Administration in 1984. In 1986 he joined the NASED voting systems board and also began testing and certifying voting systems for the state of Georgia. [1012] In 1990, he joined the faculty of Kennesaw State College (now Kennesaw State University). [551]

In 1990, the Federal Election Commission released *Performance and Test Standards for Marksense, Punchcard and Direct Recording Electronic Voting Systems*. [326] The FEC had no authority to enforce these standards, so from a federal standpoint they were voluntary. Because there was no formal process to certify compliance, acceptance of the standards was slow.[1009] In 1994, NASED stepped in and created a testing process. Once a process was in place, states began to enact the 1990 standards into law. By early 2001, 37 states had done so, making the standards effectively mandatory from the perspective of voting system vendors.[944]

6.2.1 Independent Testing Authorities

The process NASED developed for certifying voting equipment was similar to the approach many other industries took for product certification. Voting equipment vendors presented their machinery to an approved *independent testing authority*, or ITA, and paid the ITA for testing. If the ITA found a system adequate, NASED then certified that the system met federal standards and gave the equipment a NASED approval number.

Independent testing authorities have been around for a long time. One of the best known, Underwriters' Laboratories (UL), was founded by the National Board of Fire Underwriters in the 1890s to test electrical products for fire safety. For UL approval, the manufacturer submits its product to UL or a UL affiliate, and pays all of the costs of testing and certification.[970] The FCC handles testing for compliance with radio frequency interference regulations in a similar way, allowing the actual tests to be done by private independent testing labs.

Since vendors pay for their own testing and certification, there is a potential conflict of interest that could lead testers to certify substandard equipment. In the case of product safety certifications, testers would face extraordinary liability if a certified product were found to have failed due to flaws that violated standards. When it comes to accidents and fires, insurance investigators act on behalf of the insurer and policyholders, which is to say, on behalf of the accident victims, not the manufacturers.

With elections, it is difficult to create a system of checks and balances for independent testing authorities. Election directors frequently depend on vendors for the maintenance of complex voting systems, and public officials have a strong vested interest in discouraging public disclosure or discussion of flaws in systems acquired under their leadership. Furthermore, disclosure of voting system failures endangers public confidence in elections, posing a threat to the legitimacy of government. In the elections domain, there is nothing analogous to insurers acting on behalf of policy holders to investigate failures.

In theory, under the system established to support the FEC voting system standards, ITAs were accountable to the NASED laboratory accreditation board. In fact, the only serious accountability was to the vendors, the companies who paid the ITAs to certify their products. It was never clear to what extent the NASED laboratory accreditation board, or indeed anyone at the Election Center, was competent to evaluate any of the ITAs.

In 1994, Wyle Laboratories in Huntsville, Alabama, was accredited as an ITA for voting systems, and remained the only accredited lab until 2001. [370] Wyle is a large testing laboratory with a long track record of testing both aviation and consumer products. [1022] In the years immediately prior to their accreditation by NASED, Wyle had tested voting system for several states.

Very early in the process, Wyle had begun to subcontract the software examinations required by the FEC standards. In 1996, one of the authors, Douglas Jones, found a fax heading on a page of a Wyle report submitted to the state of Iowa indicating the involvement of Rheyn Technologies, Inc. in the firmware evaluation for a new voting machine. Rheyn appears to have been an unaccredited subcontractor, although no explanation of their role was ever offered to the state of Iowa. In 2001, R. Doug Lewis, speaking for the Election Center in its role as the manager of the NASED voting systems testing program, publicly disclosed the involvement of two other subcontractors, Nichols Research Labs and PSINet. [597]

Many discussions of election technology hinge on the distinction between *software* and *firmware*. The glossary to the 1990 standards define firmware in much the same way as the rest of the computer industry: "computer programs (software) stored in read-only memory (ROM) devices imbedded in the system and not capable of being altered during system operation." [326] In section 8.2, the standard implies a very different definition: "software (central count) and firmware (precinct count)." Unfortunately, this second definition has become entrenched in the voting system industry. It is now common to refer to all programming that runs in the precinct as firmware, even when it is loaded from disk or flash memory and therefore easily altered at any time.

The result of the drift in the definition of firmware is that numerous voting systems have been developed where the so-called firmware is easy to alter. Among the voting systems discussed in Chapter 5, several were developed based on Microsoft Windows 95, among them the Fidlar and Chambers EV 2000 and the I-Mark EBS model 100 (the prototype for what was later marketed as the AccuVote TS). Neither Windows 95 nor any application operating under Windows 95 can fairly be called firmware under the conventional definition, since that version of Windows could not run from read-only memory, and Windows applications can be altered during system operation.*

Despite its shortcomings, the ITA process was a clear improvement over nothing. Developing a voting system knowing that someone else will look at the details distinctly changes the development process, and even weak standards have an influence. By the late 1990s, the ITA process was finding and forcing the repair of problems that might otherwise have caused serious trouble. With the ITA process in place, states began to require compliance with the FEC standards. By 2001, 33 states plus the District of Columbia required full conformity with the 1990 standards, and another 4 required partial conformity. [370] States remained free to set additional requirements before jurisdictions could make purchases, so many states retained their existing voting system approval or state certification processes.

6.2.2   Accomplishments of the 1990 Standards

There were several aspects of the 1990 FEC standards that were quite good. The standards acknowledged that election equipment was more like military equipment than consumer electronics. Election machinery is frequently stored for months in a warehouse, and then pulled out for use in a situation where failure is unacceptable. On Election Day, voting equipment must work from the time the polls open to the time the polls close. In contrast, with consumer electronics, retailers frequently assume that roughly one machine in six will be returned under the terms of the manufacturer's warrantee.

Because it is not simple to replace a failed voting machine on Election Day, the FEC standards included many requirements for what technology testers call "shake and bake" tests. A voting machine must survive the vibration of being trucked to the polls, storage in a hot or cold warehouse, and being dropped by a careless worker. ITAs routinely shake, bake, freeze, and drop machines to test the machines' durability.

The 1990 standards required that voting machines provide at least some support for auditing. As discussed in Chapter 2, developers of mechanical voting machines had understood the need for a public counter in the 19th century. Recording the value of this counter before and after the election allowed auditors to check that ballots were not added or subtracted from the ballot box. Section 4.8 of the 1990 standards extended this requirement by stipulating that each machine record an "audit trail" or "audit log," by which the standards meant a record of

---

*Windows CE, developed later, comes much closer to the standard definition of firmware, but even it relies heavily on dynamic linkage, allowing components to be replaced while the system is running.

Votronic	PEB#	Type	Date	Time	Event
5114909	123196	SUP	08/10/2004	14:29:31	01 Terminal clear and test
	131898	SUP	08/13/2004	08:34:25	09 Terminal open
			08/13/2004	09:51:10	13 Print zero tape
			08/13/2004	09:52:35	13 Print zero tape
			08/13/2004	12:25:58	20 Normal ballot cast
			08/13/2004	16:43:04	20 Normal ballot cast
			08/13/2004	16:44:56	20 Normal ballot cast
			08/13/2004	16:46:14	20 Normal ballot cast
			08/13/2004	16:47:47	20 Normal ballot cast
			08/13/2004	16:49:29	20 Normal ballot cast
			08/13/2004	16:51:21	20 Normal ballot cast
			08/13/2004	16:54:13	20 Normal ballot cast
			08/13/2004	18:42:59	27 Override
			08/13/2004	18:43:00	10 Terminal close
			08/13/2004	18:44:41	12 Audit upload
			08/13/2004	18:47:18	14 Print Precinct results
			08/13/2004	18:48:43	14 Print Precinct results
			08/13/2004	18:50:09	14 Print Precinct results
	128025	SUP	08/14/2004	11:18:18	04 Enter service menu
			08/14/2004	11:18:32	06 Enter ECA menu

FIGURE 34 An "audit log" recorded by an ES&S iVotronic DRE voting machine serial number 5,114,909 during pre-election testing before the 2004 primary in Miami-Dade County, Florida. 8 test ballots were cast on this machine. From Miami-Dade County public records.

the time at which each significant event in the voting system occurred. Elsewhere in the computer industry, the proper term for such a log is an "event log," a term that was eventually adopted in later standards.

The standards were somewhat vague about exactly what events should be logged, but typical voting machines built to satisfy the 1990 standards recorded the time the polls were opened, the time the polls were closed, the times at which ballots were cast, and the times of events such as power failures, low battery alarms, etc. This information, illustrated in Figure 34, has proven to be of significant value to some election auditors, even though it is not sufficient to permit even partial reconstruction of election results. While some auditors have made extensive use of data from event logs, most jurisdictions never use the data, and some appear to be unaware that it even exists. David Wagner concluded in his 2010 report on audit logs that there were numerous barriers to effective use of the logs maintained by current voting systems, and that one of the most important was a lack of standards governing both what is logged and the format of those logs. [989]

Section 2.3.2 of the 1990 standards required that voting machines incorporate redundant storage of vote records. Ballot scanners were acknowledged to met the requirement by retaining the original paper record along with the data scanned from that record. [326] The idea that voting machines should store data redundantly is an old one. As mentioned in Chapter 5, Jacob Myers patented a voting machine that stored metal tokens in a hopper for each candidate as it counted the votes. Myers explained the need for redundancy, saying "... votes are counted as they are cast [so] the total number can be ascertained rapidly and accurately at the close of the polls without the necessity of counting by hand ..., though this may be done as a check or verification should it be necessary or desirable." [725] If, for example, the mechanical counting mechanism had broken, the tokens could be manually counted, while if one of the bins for collecting the tokens broke and spilled them inside the machine, the counter would still register the correct sum.

Myers did not pursue his idea of redundant storage, but as computerized systems were developed, the need for redundancy became more acute. When a voting machine maintains data in the main memory of a computer, even the briefest interruption of the electric supply can corrupt the data. The Shouptronic and Microvote systems discussed in Chapter 5 met the redundant memory requirement half a decade before the FEC finalized the 1990 standards, and all subsequent machines sold in the United states have continued to meet this requirement.

6.2.3   Shortcomings of the 1990 Standards

The software standards from 1990 were far less successful. They were brief, only nine pages in Chapter 4, augmented by ten-pages in Appendix E. Much of the material was non-binding or advisory in nature. These standards governed the form and structure of the software more than its function. In many cases, requirements that started out appearing to be objective ended up being merely advisory. Consider the requirement that "the system shall" monitor data quality using mechanisms to "be determined by the vendor." The standards provided nothing to help an ITA determine whether the vendor used appropriate mechanisms to meet this requirement.

The security section, Chapter 5 of the 1990 standards, was even briefer, only five pages. As with the software standards, these "requirements" frequently boiled down to mere advice. For example, the standard provided helpful suggestions about both access control policies and their enforcement mechanisms, but offered a minimal guideline: "The general features and capabilities of the access policy shall be specified by the vendor." The vendor was then required to provide "access control measures" to enforce the unspecified policy. The standard continued, "the vendor shall provide a penetration analysis" to assess the security of the resulting system, but then "for security reasons, such penetration analysis shall not be distributed to user jurisdictions." A penetration analysis is a study of how the security of the system can be circumvented. Given the analysis, a state might be able to design procedures to defend against known weaknesses of the system, while without such analysis, states can determine neither if a system is reasonably secure nor whether the procedural defenses are useful.

The 1990 security requirements focused in large part on procedural and policy issues, while giving advice to jurisdictions using the voting system. The standards asked that the system owner develop a security plan, maintain the equipment securely, and install software and firmware correctly. As a consequence, the standards largely exempted system designers from dealing with important security issues. The fact is that a vast majority of election officials do not have a meaningful security plan, nor do they have sufficient knowledge of computer security to design and implement one. When one of us, Douglas Jones, conducted a court-ordered assessment of the voting system acquisition process in Colorado, he observed that "The state has demonstrated . . . no understanding of which documents are and are not security critical. In its assessment of the Diebold and Sequoia voting systems, the state has overlooked significant security problems that ought to have been addressed prior to any decision to permit use of these machines . . . ." [530] Andrew Appel at Princeton University reached similar conclusions in his assessment of state mandated procedures for use of adhesive security seals on New Jersey voting machines. [52]

In the time Jones spent as a voting system examiner in Iowa during the 1990s, he never saw a penetration analysis. Furthermore, the reports from ITAs that he read did not suggest that the ITAs were very competent at assessing software. By 2000, he was speaking in public about the general shortcomings of the 1990 standards. [519] In 2001, he disclosed specific examples that illustrated how the ITAs had failed in their security assessments of several voting systems. [521]

On January 29, 2003, activist Bev Harris discovered the source code for Diebold's AccuVote TS voting machine on a public server. She downloaded a total of 40,000 files that she eventually uploaded to a server in New Zealand. [430] Harris contacted David Dill at Stanford University, who passed on the news to Aviel Rubin, director of the Information Security Institute at Johns Hopkins University, and several others. [858] As described in Chapter 7, this set off a chain of events that thrust the integrity of electronic voting squarely into the public eye. Among the consequences was confirmation, in what became known as the Hopkins-Rice Report, that defects Jones had reported to Global Election Systems in 1997, and described in congressional testimony four years later, remained unchanged six years later. [565,858]

Immediately following the release of the Hopkins-Rice Report, Maryland commissioned followup studies. [831,884] Ohio was also concerned and asked for additional studies. [184,501] California's response, although delayed, was a top-to-bottom review of all voting systems used in California, as discussed in Chapter 8. The studies confirmed the conclusions of the Hopkins-Rice Report. Furthermore, the studies done by Ohio and California demonstrated that serious problems were in no way limited to the AccuVote TS. All of the widely used electronic voting systems, both DRE and optical mark-sense, were found to suffer from major security flaws.

Designers of secure computer systems are always advised to design for *defense in depth*, an old military term for a layered defense based on the assumption that since the enemy might break through any particular defensive line, each line should have a fall-back position. Layering security to contain a failure or breach is a fundamental concept in computer security, as well as warfare. [737] Merely adding multiple security layers is not enough. Each layer must contain effective mechanisms. At the same time, the mechanisms themselves must support the security policy. For example, Diebold's public response to the Hopkins-Rice Report asserted that "Checks and balances in elections equipment and procedures prevent alleged fraud scenarios." [267] Unfortunately, we have not found effective procedural defenses in any state we have examined. Instead, what we have observed is frequently best described as security theater, complex and difficult procedures that accomplish very little. This was clearly demonstrated in Andrew Appel's study of the use of security seals in New Jersey. [52]

Another major failing of the 1990 standards is an enormous loophole in Section 7.1.2. This section allows systems to incorporate unexamined *commercial off-the-shelf* (COTS) components. [326] In both hardware and software domains, the use of COTS instead of custom-designed components can significantly reduce overall system costs. This is particularly true in the software domain, where a major issue since the 1970s has been the *software crisis*. [581] Simply put, while the cost of computer hardware has been falling decade by decade, the same is not true of software. For many applications, it costs as much to develop software for the least expensive microprocessors of today as it did for the large mainframe computers of the 1960s. Some of today's software is inexpensive, but that is largely because the economics of mass markets spreads the high development costs over many users.

The use of COTS components has a second benefit beyond cost. COTS components are usually more reliable than custom-made parts because they have a larger user community. More users translates to a higher likelihood that bugs will be found, reported, and fixed. To gain these benefits, the 1990 voting system standards encouraged use of COTS components by waiving many of the testing requirements for those parts of voting systems that involved unmodified COTS components. In the case of COTS software, the standards waived the requirements for source code examination and design review.

At first glance, writing software standards to encourage use of standard COTS components instead of custom developed one-of-a-kind parts seems like a useful way to address the software crisis in the voting domain. Unfortunately, the rules included in the 1990 standards to encourage the use of COTS created problems.

The incident involving the Fidlar and Chambers EV 2000 touchscreen voting machine discussed in Chapter 5 illustrates some of the problems posed by COTS software. Recall that Fidlar brought a machine before the Iowa Board of Examiners on January 9, 1998, expecting things to go well. Their machine had gone into production over a year previously, and it had been approved for use in Ohio the previous July. [1015]

The Fidlar EV 2000 was a second generation DRE voting system designed to the 1990 federal voting system standards. While testing the EV 2000 for Iowa, one of us, Douglas Jones, noted that the machine was disclosing each voter's selections to the next voter by a slight highlighting of the the the check-boxes of the most recently selected candidate names. [507] The cause of this highlighting was eventually attributed to a change in Microsoft Windows.

According to Fidlar's representative at the Iowa tests, Fidlar had submitted their system to Wyle Laboratories for testing, but the tests had not yet been completed. Between the time that Fidlar submitted the software and the Iowa tests, Microsoft had released a new version of Windows. Wyle Labs told Fidlar that, since the new version of Windows was COTS software with nothing but bug fixes and cosmetic changes, there was no need to include it in their testing. More specifically, since Microsoft's changes had not involved any change to what Microsoft calls the *applications programmer interface* or API of the operating system, and since Fidlar had not had to change any elements of their own voting software to work with the updated version of Windows, no retesting would be needed. Fidlar opted to upgrade to the newest version of Windows before coming to Iowa.

Had Fidlar been required to go through a complete re-testing of their system after any change to a COTS component, there could have been several undesirable outcomes. First, had Fidlar continued using Windows, there would have been a strong incentive to avoid installing patches and bug fixes, since each would require a new test. As a result, they would not install security upgrades on a regular basis, leading to a situation in which each release of security upgrades by Microsoft would constitute an advertisement of another security flaw in Fidlar's system. The alternative would be to forgo the use of a commercial operating system and other reusable components, significantly driving up the cost of system development.

Note that when Fidlar's system was examined in Iowa, there were three examiners involved in testing the machine, but only one of them noticed the problem. When a flaw is this subtle, it might go unobserved through many election cycles. Voters might never have noticed the highlighting flaw, but a voter who did notice would be in a position to buy or coerce the vote of the person ahead of him at the polling place. Unlike the natural checks and balances set up in product liability testing, a voter would have little recourse. In theory, a voter could sue the county for violating his civil rights, and the county could sue the vendor, but with no intent to defraud, such suits would likely fail. With no financial incentive for enforcement, and no consequence to the vendor, there is little reason for voters or election officials to find or report errors.

6.2.4 Records Retention

In one problematic area, the 1990 standards mixed reasonable requirements with a muddled division of responsibility and a fumbled followthrough. Section 301 of the Civil Rights Act of 1960 required that "every officer of election shall retain and preserve, for a period of twenty-two months from the date of any ... [federal] election ... all records and papers which come into his possession relating to any ... act requisite to voting in such election." [195] Appendix C of the 1990 FEC standards quotes Section 301 and explains that "the purpose of this law is to assist the federal government in discharging its law enforcement responsibilities in connection with civil rights and election crimes .... As such, all documentation that may be relevant to the detection and prosecution of federal civil rights or election crimes are required to be maintained." [326]

Appendix C continues to give the Justice Department's interpretation of what must be saved. The focus is on paper documents, ranging from voter registration forms to absentee ballot envelopes to tally sheets and canvass reports, but it also singles out "all computer programs utilized to tabulate votes electronically." Finally, the Justice Department held that the act "requires the retention of the ballots themselves, at least in those jurisdictions where" paper or punched card ballots are used.

The Appendix goes on to give general rules for retention of data, but the standards do not provide anything specific with regard to electronic systems. Instead, they require that the vendors pass sufficient information through the Federal Election Commission to the Justice Department that the latter can rule, for each voting system, on what "specific data and document items" are to be retained, and in what form.

For the document retention component of the 1990 standards to be effective, the Justice Department's rulings for each voting system should have been widely disseminated. Every jurisdiction using an electronic voting system should have seen a copy of the records retention ruling for that system. Unfortunately, in our years of involvement with electronic voting, we have never seen or heard of such a ruling, so we suspect that the procedures outlined in Appendix C were never properly put into practice.

6.3   2002 and Interim Standards

Even prior to the election of 2000, it was clear that the original 1990 standards were inadequate. In 1997, just three years after the voting systems testing program began, NASED informed the Federal Election Commission that the 1990 standards needed revision. In 1999, before the 2000 election cast a spotlight on voting technology, the revision process was underway. The 18 member Voting System Standards Committee overseeing the revision included Thomas Wilkey, Brit Williams, and Robert Naegele, all of whom were involved in the 1990 standards, as well additional election officials and technical experts. Rounding out the committee were ex-officio members, representative of both the Federal Election Commission and the three accredited independent testing authorities, and Stephen Berger, chair of the Institute for Electrical and Electronic Engineers (IEEE) working group on voting system standards. [328]

The revised FEC standard was adopted in the summer of 2002 shortly before passage of the Help America Vote Act. The new standards still contained a number of admitted weaknesses. The standards overview singled out five major areas where the revised standards fail to address known issues:

• Administrative and managerial practices,

- Linkage between voting systems and voter registration databases,
- Regulation of commercial off-the-shelf components,
- Internet voting, and
- Errors that are a consequence of voter actions.

Another source of significant trouble was in the area of reliability requirements. Reliability is frequently measured in terms of *mean time between failures*, that is, the average interval between system failures or breakdowns. Section 3.4.3 of the 2002 standards require a mean time between failures of 163 hours. [329] If a polling place is open from 6 AM to 9 PM for a total of 15 hours, this failure rate implies that each machine has about a 1 in 11 chance of failing during the election. If a polling place is opened 10 hours, then each machine has about a 1 in 17 a chance of failure.

While the reliability constraints are weak, the accuracy requirements given in Section 3.2.1 of the 2002 standards are bizarre. "The system shall achieve a target error rate of no more than one in 10,000,000 ballot positions, with a maximum acceptable error rate in the test process of one in 500,000 ballot positions." [329] Appendix C.5 of volume II of the standards concludes that a voting machine must process 1,549,700 voting positions without error. [330] Note that the reference is not to errors per ballot, but rather to errors per voting position. The ballot from Clay County, Iowa shown in Figure 26, has 68 voting positions, so the standard permits misreading one ballot in 22,789. The presidential race on the Clay County ballot has 10 voting positions, so this permits misreading one vote in 154,970 presidential votes. The biggest problem, acknowledged in the standards, is that the accuracy requirement ignores voter errors caused by poor usability of the voter interface, a human factors issue. There is ample evidence that error rates made by real voters are from 10 to 1000 times higher than the rates set by the standard, making the standard almost irrelevant. [145,323,456]

The 2002 standards significantly altered the records retention requirements. Section 2.2.11 summarizes the legal basis for requiring records retention, explaining that the law "does not require that election officials generate any specific type or classification of election record," but that if any record is generated, the law requires "the appropriate authority to retain the records for 22 months." The requirement that the Justice Department rule on what must be retained for each machine was replaced by a general statement of the Justice Department's understanding of the requirements.

The result was a very specific statement of the requirement that "all audit trail information ... shall be retained in its original format," whether machine-generated electronic or human created paper records. Unfortunately, that was the end of the specific requirements. The standard went on to recommend retention, but permit deletion of electronic records of machine configuration data "if there is an official, authenticatable printed copy of all final database information." This confusion was compounded by what followed, which stated that the same applied to "electronic records of the aggregate data for each device" and "to vote results generated by each precinct device or system." There was no standard for what constitutes an authenticatable paper record. In many cases, the translation from internal electronic records to paper records is far from trivial, and wherever software is involved in translation between data formats, that software is potentially suspect.

It is fair to ask what the Justice Department did not understand about the phrase "all records" in the Civil Rights Act of 1960. The requirement that the software used in a jurisdiction be retained has been abandoned, thwarting investigation of whether improper software might have been used. While the standards continue to require that voting systems maintain redundant records of cast ballots, nothing was said about preserving the redundant copies, impeding investigation of any differences that might emerge. Regrettably, this appears to be the Justice Department's last word on the issue of records retention, since the same material has been preserved in subsequent revisions.

With the passage of the Help America Vote Act of 2002, the FEC no longer had authority to promulgate voting system standards.[191] Nonetheless, the 2002 standards remained in effect until 2007, when the 2005 Voluntary Voting Systems Guidelines, developed by the Election Assistance Commission, finally took effect.[295]

6.4   The Help America Vote Act of 2002

After the election of 2000 shook the country, there was widespread public pressure to do something, but there was little consensus about what to do. Florida's Election Reform Act of 2001 banned the use of punched-card voting machines, requiring that they be replaced with either precinct-count mark-sense machines or direct-recording electronic voting machines. The law required counties to have new systems in place for the September 2002 primaries.[349,351]

Eliminating punched cards was a natural reaction to what had happened, but it did not address the underlying problem. While the Votomatic system had many flaws, the first problem to focus national attention on the Votomatic was Palm Beach County's *butterfly ballot*, shown in Figure 35. The butterfly ballot was a human-factors prob-

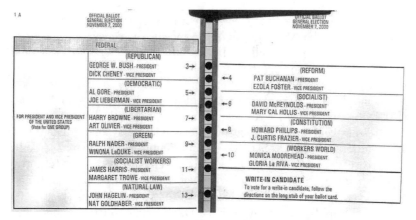

FIGURE 35 The "butterfly ballot" used in Palm Beach County, Florida in the November 2002 general election. Photo by Douglas Jones.

lem, but it was not the fault of the Votomatic. Poor ballot design in the 2000 presidential election probably cost thousands of votes, though estimating the exact number is difficult. There is no doubt, however, that bad ballot design was as prevalent among Florida counties using optical mark-sense ballots as among those using the Votomatic.[522]

There were two root problems in Florida, neither inherently tied to the voting technology. First, Florida's ballot access laws were the most permissive in the country, so Florida had more presidential candidates on the ballot than any other state. Second, the state election office had insufficient resources and inadequate control over ballot layout. Counties that tried to solve the first problem creatively inadvertently violated voters' civil rights, since the likelihood of a person's vote being valid ended up depending on the voter's county of residence.

The Florida legislature wasn't alone in attempting to force reform. Hoping to avoid another fiasco, the U.S. Congress also took action. Representatives Robert Ney (R-Ohio) and Steny Hoyer(D-Md.) responded by introducing the Help America Vote Act of 2001 (HR 3295).[776] This act, informally called HAVA, offered significant funding to states wanting to upgrade their voting systems in exchange for mandatory compliance with the FEC voting system standards. It also created a new agency, the Election Assistance Commission (EAC), charged with overseeing the disbursement of money and the development of new voting system standards.

Opposition to the Ney-Hoyer bill was widespread. In testimony before the House Judicial Committee, representatives of The League of

Women Voters and the American Association of People with Disabilities (the AAPD) opposed it. At a December 5, 2001 hearing before the House Judiciary Committee, Jim Dickson of the AAPD argued forcefully for the voting rights of people with disabilities, but complained that the proposed legislation was too weak to be of much use.[253] At the same hearing, Lloyd Leonard of the League of Women Voters stated that in many ways the proposed law was a step backward, and furthermore "it fails to create minimum Federal standards for America's voting systems." [593]

One of the most significant problems with the Ney-Hoyer bill is that it forced states to spend money on new voting systems before updated standards could possibly be put in place. With the public exposure of the problems in Florida, politicians wanted to take action. None wanted to hear the reality of technical development, namely that standards should come first. In speaking with members of Congress and their staff, we have concluded that many did not understand that once new standards were approved, it could take up to four years for companies to develop, test, and certify new equipment to meet those standards. As Jones observed in 2001, a reasonable schedule for bringing new standards to the polling place would proceed as follows: [520]

In year one, the vendor has time to develop technology that meets the requirements of the new standards. However, unless the changes required by the standards are trivial, most vendor efforts prior to adopting the new standards will have focused on lobbying against them. Only when that battle is lost can we expect vendors to make any serious efforts to comply.

Year two allows time for voting system testing and certification. Software inspection, in particular, is a labor intensive task that should not be rushed. Furthermore, a meaningful testing and certification schedule must allow for the possibility that vendors will be forced to make significant redesigns.

Year three allows for contract negotiation and manufacturing. Negotiating for a system that is not yet certified is dangerous, so jurisdictions should not be under pressure to negotiate with vendors before their products are complete and certified. Competitive bidding should not be rushed, particularly when millions of taxpayer dollars are involved.

Year four allows for preliminary use. New voting equipment should not see its first use in a high-stakes national election. The first uses should be in local elections with low turnout and low pressure. Only after pollworkers and significant numbers of voters have used the system should the equipment be deployed in a high stakes, high pressure general election.

Unfortunately, with its short re-election cycle, Congress rarely seems to think about long term implications. A cynic might say that HAVA was drafted more to show that Congress could act quickly than to actually benefit the voter.

The second major problem with the Ney-Hoyer bill was the extraordinary complex administrative structure it created. The EAC it envisioned was governed by a 25-member Board of Advisors representing the following groups:

- The United States Commission on Civil Rights
- The Architectural and Transportation Barrier Compliance Board
- The National Governors Association
- The National Conference of State Legislatures
- The National Association of Secretaries of State
- The National Association of Election Directors
- The National Association of Counties
- The National Association of County Recorders, Election Administrators, and Clerks
- The United States Conference of Mayors
- The Election Center
- "professionals in the field of science and technology"
- The chief of the Office of Public Integrity of the Department of Justice

The EAC was also required to consult with a Standards Board consisting of two representatives of each state, including one representing the state election office and one representing local election officials. The Ney-Hoyer bill placed the actual drafting of standards in the hands of a 15-member Technical Standards Development Committee. This committee included representatives of the National Institute of Standards and Technology (NIST, the former National Bureau of Standards) the American National Standards Institute (ANSI), the Standards Board, the Board of Advisors, the Architectural and Transportation Barrier Compliance Board, and an unspecified number of "other individuals with technical and scientific expertise relating to voting systems and voting equipment."

After circulating in draft form for months, the Ney-Hoyer bill was passed by the House just a month after its formal introduction in November 2001. The House leadership limited debate to only one hour and refused to permit amendments, except for one from the Committee on House Administration. The Senate version passed in April 2002 and went to conference committee with the House version. By midsummer, many of us expected the bill to die quietly in conference, barring a miracle. It seemed that no compromise was possible between the House and Senate versions, and furthermore, it seemed that nobody really cared enough about the bill to push for such a compromise. [1011]

6.4.1 Disaster in Miami

On September 10, 2002 Florida held a primary for the midterm election. It was the first major test in Miami-Dade County of the new iVotronic touch-screen voting machines that replaced the Votomatic systems used in 2000. The disaster that day in Miami was the miracle that was needed to force the passage of the Help America Vote Act.

In Florida, the legislature forced replacement of punch-card equipment in May 2001, creating a timetable of only 16 months for the purchase of new equipment before Fall 2002. Miami's situation was more complex than many jurisdictions because, while much of Florida requires English-Spanish bilingual ballots, Miami is trilingual, requiring ballots in English, Spanish and Haitian Creole. Multilingual ballots pose a serious challenge when printed on paper. Printing three languages on a single ballot detracts from readability, while the alternative, printing separate bilingual ballots for each minority language, leads to a proliferation of ballot styles. Miami opted to avoid these problems by using a touch-screen voting system, the ES&S iVotronic.

From Miami's point of view, the iVotronic looked like a safe bet. While the machine was relatively new, having been introduced in 1999, it was basically a repackaged version of the Votronic, a machine that had been in use in North and South Carolina as early as March 1996. It was reasonable to expect that this new system would be a mature product with few problems.

Since Haitian Creole, Spanish and English all use the Roman alphabet, few foresaw that trilingual ballots would pose any difficulty. Unfortunately, the limited built-in character set of the iVotronic could not handle the wide variety of accent marks used in Haitian Creole. This forced the use of pre-rendering or what ES&S called a "bitmap ballot display", as discussed in Chapter 5.

Miami was the first ES&S customer to need pre-rendering, and the downside of this new technology quickly became apparent. Where the election configuration files for the older textual ballot display were compact and easily loaded into the iVotronic, the pre-rendered ballot was loaded into the machine as a large album of screen images. As anyone familiar with digital cameras knows, image files are typically much larger than text files. A new approach to loading the election configuration was required, because the PEB, the memory device formerly used to load the election configuration, did not have a large enough memory. To solve this problem, ES&S incorporated a compact flash card socket into the iVotronic.

Like Palm Beach County, Miami used their new iVotronic machines in several small elections before their September primary, but small elections do not test the response of a system to large amounts of data. When pollworkers attempted to start Miami's iVotronic voting machines on the morning of the election, they were dismayed by how long it took to open the polls. Many polling places opened late, and voters were turned away. [251] The Miami office of Inspector General issued a preliminary report on the debacle ten days later, and an additional report the next May. [650,651] The reports covered all aspects of the relationship between ES&S and the county.

A major concern of the reports was the slow start-up time of the iVotronic. When one of us, Douglas Jones was asked by the county to conduct an additional investigation, he discovered that when the iVotronic was started in "bitmap mode", it checked that it could read each image file on the compact flash card, leading to a delay of from 8 to 70 minutes per machine. [527]* If the pollworkers waited for each machine to complete the start-up before starting the next machine, opening the polls in a polling place equipped with 10 machines took over 2 hours instead of the one hour typically allowed. The Inspector General described the outcome as a debacle; the ACLU described it as a fiasco. [32,651]

Of course, Miami-Dade county ought to have had backup procedures in place in the event of trouble, and they did. The procedures in the pollworker manual would have allowed voters to begin voting as soon as any machines were operational, but some pollworkers refused to open their precincts until all machines were ready. [650] Consequently, in addition to the technical problems, a combination of inadequate pollworker training and machinery that was too complex for the average pollworker contributed to the problem.

6.4.2 Congress Responds

The Congressional response to the news out of Florida was swift. Between September 18 and October 10, the House issued numerous instructions to the conference committee that had been sitting on the Help America Vote Act. The revised bill was introduced in the House late on the 10th, and it was passed immediately by a roll-call vote of

---

*The longer time was for machines equipped with audio ballots, typically one per polling place.

357 to 48. The Senate considered the Act on October 15 and 16, and the President signed the bill into law on October 29. [191]

The text of the Help America Vote Act of 2002 differed in some interesting ways from the original draft legislation. The new text referred to voluntary voting system guidelines instead of the voting system standards that were in the original version. Federal officials had been bending over backwards to emphasize that compliance with the 1990 voting system standards was entirely voluntary, even though the majority of states required conformance with those standards. The changed wording in HAVA was a similar attempt to sugar coat the legislation, so that opponents of government regulation would vote for it.

Another curious change was the addition of one statutory member to the Technical Guidelines Development Committee (TGDC), originally called the Technical Standards Development Committee. Section 221(c)(1)(C) of the final draft gave a statutory seat on the committee to a representative of the Institute for Electrical and Electronic Engineers (IEEE). On May 24, Judith Gorman, managing director of the IEEE Standards Association, had sent a letter to the members of the House-Senate conference committee responsible for HAVA, asking that the organization be given a statutory seat on the Technical Standards Development Committee. [399] The IEEE has a long record in developing industrial standards and had created the P1583 Voting System Standards working group. To an outsider the offer of technical support was extraordinarily attractive, promising significant expertise to a standards development process that lacked technical depth. Unfortunately, as we will see, there were times when significant factions within the IEEE seemed more concerned with protecting vendor interests than with providing unbiased technical expertise.

HAVA required the new Election Assistance Commission (EAC) to be in place by February 2003, but actual appointments were delayed until December 13, 2003. Statutory positions required for full operation of the Commission, including the staff director, general counsel, and inspector general, remained vacant at the end of that year. Only $1.2 million had been appropriated for the fiscal 2004 operating budget, making hiring difficult. There wasn't even enough money to lease office space. [292] DeForest B. Soaries, chair of the new EAC, begged Congress for a $10 million operating budget for fiscal 2005 budget. [927] Congress responded by appropriating a total budget of $13.8 million, including almost $2.8 million earmarked for launching the Technical Guidelines Development Committee and $3.7 million for an operating budget. [299] This was an improvement, but far short of what the EAC needed to carry out its mandate.

6.5   The IEEE steps in

The IEEE is the largest technical society in the world, with over 400,000 members internationally. Among its activities, it sets standards in many areas of the electrical and computer industry. After the election of 2000 many electrical engineers wondered how they could help solve the technical problems raised by the election. It seemed natural for IEEE to form a voting system standards committee and to volunteer their expertise to the FEC and the newly formed EAC.[84] The story of the IEEE standards effort illustrates some of the hostility that developed between vendor representatives and technologists concerned about the security of electronic voting machines.

There were several grassroots attempts to do something about voting within the IEEE in the immediate aftermath of the 2000 election, including both an effort in the New York section to design a voting machine and an effort in the Committee on Communication and Information Policy. Stanley Klein, an active member of the latter committee, circulated a proposal for what became the IEEE voting system standards effort in early 2001.[563,702]

The IEEE Standards Board accepted the proposal and chartered Project 1583, with Stephen Berger as chair. P1583 held its first meeting, an hour-long conference call, on August 7, 2001, with 5 members, including the chair. Aside from updates on current events, the major issues on the agenda were a roadmap outlining 6 different areas the standards could address and a discussion of the need for a standard coordinating committee.[487] The membership was very small, and in September the committee decided to invite voting equipment manufacturers to join.[486] Through the remainder of 2001, as the membership grew, the primary business was orientation, both to the existing voting system standards and to the ground rules for standards development.[485,488]

One of us, Douglas Jones, attended a meeting where Berger spoke in early 2002. He said that he knew little about voting technology, and that the reason he was appointed chair of P1583 was his extensive experience with the standards process. Berger's prior work with IEEE standards was primarily in the area of electromagnetic compatibility.[83] His initial involvement with voting machines appears to have involved evaluating hearing-aid compatability of accessible DRE voting machines.

In early 2002, one of the first orders of business for the new committee was a briefing by Brit Williams and Tom Wilkey, two long-time members of the FEC's Voting System Standards Committee.[489] As

P1583 evolved, its agenda was shaped to a significant extent by the question of how the FEC 2002 Voting Equipment Standards should be revised, the same question that would confront the EAC's Technical Guidelines Development Committee, once it finally came into operation.

Most IEEE standards are developed by and for the electronics industry. Typical standards committees are dominated by representatives of the companies that have the most to gain from developing those standards. This structure comes with a serious risk of regulatory capture. Anti-trust experts have long known that established vendors can easily use industrial standards to create barriers to entry for new competitors. The American National Standards Institute, ANSI, sets strict rules for standards committees to help control this risk, and the IEEE Standards Committee is accredited under these rules.

ANSI rules do not prevent vendor involvement. Rather, they force accredited standards organizations to hear opposing points of view and to open their decision making process to all participants. The rules adopted by P1583 opened membership to "everyone willing to actively participate," with individual membership open to anyone who can "demonstrate professional experience or relevant technical expertise." Membership did not depend on being physically present at meetings, but could be maintained by "participating by correspondence." Voting by proxy was permitted. [484]

Given the experience vendors have with both current products and the marketplace, their participation is the standards process can be essential. However, when vendors and other representatives of the status quo work to shut others out, the standards process can break down. This is what happened with P1583.

In May 2003 Stanley Klein sent an email to several colleagues urging them to get involved to counter vendor assertions that providing a "reasonable" level of security would be too costly. A number of computer scientists, including David Dill and Barbara Simons, responded by joining P1583. Others, such as Rebecca Mercuri, David Chaum, and Vince Lipsio were already members. The P1583 committee did not formally seat these new members until September, after the release of the Hopkins-Rice Report had focused public attention on voting technology.

In late 2001, Standards Coordinating Committee 38 was organized by IEEE to coordinate the developments of any standard put forth by P1583. Initially, Stephen Berger chaired both SCC38 and P1583, but in late 2003 Herb Deutsch replaced Berger as P1583 chair. Deutsch was a software product manager at ES&S with roots in the voting industry dating back to the Video Voter.[248,491] Whereas there had been little vendor involvement in P1583 during 2001, things had changed by mid 2003. By then, much of the leadership came from the vendor community. There had been an effort by non-vendor members to require all committee members to provide conflict of interest statements, but it had been rebuffed. The committee's secretary/technical editor, Doug Fletcher, served as Chief Technology Officer of Pivot International, an ES&S subcontractor;[202] the committee's project manager, Neil McClure, invented the Hart E-Slate, and served as vice-president and general manager of Hart Intercivic;[653,654] and the accessibility subcommittee chair, Ian Piper, was product manager for Diebold Election Systems.[490]

In August 2003 Fletcher announced that a draft standard was to be voted on shortly by the members of P1583. The announcement upset members of P1583 who were concerned about security, because the draft made no mention of voter-verified ballots. When people complained about the rush to vote, they were told that HAVA required new standards to be in place by January, 2004. At this point the first EAC commissioners had not even been appointed.

In an effort to prevent a standard from being bulldozed through the committee, several committee members approached the Electronic Frontier Foundation (EFF), a major civil rights organization in the area of of technology and society, asking for help. On August 28, Cindy Cohn, the EFF's Legal Director, wrote a letter to the IEEE and P1583 leadership summarizing a number of procedural irregularities in the conduct of committee business, including failure to distribute comments on the draft standard to committee members, failure to post meeting agendas to the project web site, and failure to give notice to all committee members of conference calls where important business was transacted.[175]

On September 16 a conference call was held in response to some questions raised by the opponents of the draft standards. With only 15 members present on the call, plus two proxies, the applicants for new memberships were in a position to derail the motion to approve the draft IEEE voting system standard. To protect their draft from the new members, the meeting began with a motion to defer admission of new members until the vote on the draft standard. When the new members were finally accepted, the meeting was abruptly adjourned to prevent any vote to reconsider.[492]

Because of a lack of response to her previous letter, together with the conference call shenanigans, Cindy Cohn sent a follow-up letter on September 18 summarizing even more irregularities, including conducting business without a quorum and restricting members' voting rights.[176] EFF also issued a press release urging that balloting on the draft standards be stopped.

Although supporters of verified voting were unable to stop the balloting, to their amazement they learned on September 24 that the draft standard had been defeated 6 to 13. No one quite understood why, but one conjecture was that the outcome was a result of negative publicity that had not been anticipated by the ballot supporters. For example, there was an article in Salon.com in September that reflected some of the bitterness of the fight:

> Advocates of the audit-trail requirement claim that the IEEE standards group has been hijacked by a "cabal" representing the voting equipment industry; this industry coalition has systematically attempted to "disenfranchise" its critics by abusing technicalities in the meeting bylaws, these activists charge.[628]

In addition, R. Doug Lewis, executive director of The Election Center and administrator for the NASED voting system certification program, had helped organize a conference call in August between representatives of the major voting system vendors and the Information Technology Association of America, a major lobbying group. The goal of the call was to establish a public relations campaign to counter questions about voting systems being raised by security researchers and opponents of electronic voting, a reference to the Hopkins-Rice Report that had just come out.[27,922] There had been prior suspicions of a connection between NASED and industry lobbyists, but coverage of the August conference call by at least one reporter and one activist made this connection a matter of public record.

In November, Stan Klein, an opponent of the vendor faction, sent email to P1583, saying "As far as NASED [is concerned], I believe their integrity is severely compromised, and I would give no more weight to their recommendations than I would give to those of a lobbyist for the voting machine industry." Klein's message was apparently suppressed by the committee leadership, because he had to resend it to the individual committee members before he got a response.[562]

On December 10 and 11, 2003, the National Institute of Standards and Technology sponsored a workshop entitled *Building Trust and Confidence in Voting Systems*.[736] This event brought together most of the participants in the national debate over voting technology. Both opponents and defenders of the status quo spoke, including several P1583 members. While the workshop helped clarify the issues surrounding voting systems, it did little to build trust and confidence. In fact, as the conference ended, one of us, Douglas Jones, witnessed a loud argument between two P1583 members, Klein and Vern Williams. Williams, chair of the P1583 security subcommittee, objected to security requirements that would add to the cost of voting machine testing. Klein claimed that leadership had tried to suppress participation in P1583 by preventing discussion of comments on the draft standard, rescheduling meetings, and tinkering with agendas, all threatening the legitimacy and accreditation of the entire IEEE standards effort.

The committee continued to put forth drafts into 2004 and 2005, but has accomplished little since then. At the crux of the breakdown was the issue of voter-verified paper trails. Some members wanted a mandate that direct-recording electronic voting machines incorporate a voter-verified paper trail, and others, primarily vendor representatives and their allies, wanted to write rules that discouraged the use of paper-based technologies.

In spite of the dissension over voting machine security, some of the P1583 subcommittees conducted vital work, especially the usability group. Given that the 2002 FEC standard was almost entirely silent about usability, the work of the subcommittee provided some important input into the later standards promulgated by the EAC.

6.6 Continuing Developments

The EAC was crippled by a lack of funds and by Congressional disinterest, but by mid 2004 it finally managed to convene the Technical Guidelines Development Committee (TGDC) mandated by HAVA. The initial membership included several old hands, such as Brit Williams, who had worked on both prior FEC standards, and Steven Berger from IEEE P1583. The most interesting of the new appointments were Ronald Rivest, one of the world's greatest cryptographers, and Whitney Quesenbery, a prominent usability consultant. [296]

On December 13, 2005, more than three years after the passage of the Help America Vote Act, the EAC adopted its first set of Voluntary Voting System Guidelines. [295] Even though they are called "guidelines" and not "standards", the majority of states had legislation requiring some level of conformance to the standards. Vendors were given two years to make their systems compliant before the standards went into effect in December of 2007.

While an improvement over the 1990 standards, there were still issues with the the 2005 guidelines. Volume II, Section 5.2 of the guidelines maintain the generous exemption for commercial off-the-shelf components. [298] The software guidelines, contained in Volume I, Section

5.2.6 and Volume II, Section 5.4.2, remain weak. The material in the standards has a very strong bias toward the C programming language, but the guidelines also invite the vendor to use "published, reviewed, and industry accepted coding conventions," instead of the weak conventions in the guidelines. [297,298] This permits vendors to make very good choices, but it provides no mechanism to reject a vendor who uses a published but widely lampooned set of coding conventions. The largest loophole in the guidelines is found in Volume II, Appendix B.6: "any uncorrected deficiency that does not involve the loss or corruption of voting data shall not necessarily be cause for rejection." [298] In effect, the guidelines are purely advisory unless data is actually lost or corrupted during testing.

On August 31, 2007, less than two years after the passage of the new guidelines, the TGDC released a complete rewrite. Where the 2005 guidelines had largely carried forward the structure of the 2002 and 1990 FEC standards, the new document was completely reorganized. [956] This version of the guidelines was never approved by the EAC, in part because of opposition from the EAC Board of Advisors and Standards Board to software independence (see below). Nonetheless, the 2007 guidelines incorporated a number of important features. A key contribution was a refinement of the taxonomy of voting systems. Where prior standards had distinguished primarily between optical mark-sense technology and direct-recording technology, Section 2.5 of the 2007 proposed guidelines distinguished between a much wider variety of voting systems.

Perhaps the most significant innovation of the 2007 guidelines is the concept of "software independence," defined in Section 2.4. In a software-independent voting system, "an undetected error or fault in the voting system's software is not capable of causing an undetectable change in election results." This idea was largely due to Ronald Rivest, with significant input from John Wack. [851] The 2007 proposed guidelines required that all conforming voting systems must be software independent, and it identified a variety of existing ways to achieve this goal, including optical mark-sense scanners, used with manually or machine-marked paper ballots, and DREs with voter-verified paper audit trails. While all of the currently available approaches to software independence are paper-based, the definition does not exclude other technologies.

The definition of software independence accepted by the 2007 guidelines is weak—it only requires that it be possible to detect that the software has altered the election results. With machine-counted paper ballots or a voter-verified paper trail, it is possible not only to detect improper results but also to correct them by a hand count. Rivest and Wack described this as strong software independence.

The primary objection to software independence is simple. No paperless direct-recording electronic voting machine is software independent. As we will discuss in Chapter 9, some factions of the disability-rights community see paperless DRE voting systems as the ultimate solution to voting system accessibility. Any voting system where voters are asked to handle paper ballots or view paper records is seen as unacceptable to this faction, because such systems impose dexterity or vision requirements on voters.

On June 13, 2007, the EAC took another extraordinary step, revoking the interim accreditation of Cyber Labs, the independent testing authority that had certified much of the software used on America's voting machines.[300] In August, Cyber had replaced Shawn Southworth as project director in charge of voting system examination, but failed to report the change to the EAC until October. The notification failure was considered the nominal reason for the company's decertification, but there had been other problems. Cyber's reports on voting systems, when compared with reports from Wyle Labs and Systest, the other two independent testing authorities with long involvement in voting system testing, were the least informative. No reason was ever given for replacing Southworth, but he had become controversial after making it clear in an interview published in 2006 that he would never produce a negative report for a voting system vendor, even though that report was confidential.[174] By this point, the entire ITA process for voting system certification had fallen into such disrepute that the EAC emphasized that the new Voting Systems Testing Labs or VSTLs were not ITAs.

While other states rushed to conform to HAVA requirements, New York did nothing. New York's voters seemed to have an inordinate trust in the mechanical lever voting technology that had been invented in that state over a century ago, and New York's voting officials were not convinced that the new electronic voting systems on the market offered any improvement. New York was under threat of legal action by the Justice Department for failing to comply with HAVA by the time New York issued draft voting system standards in late 2005.[752] One of us, Douglas Jones, commented extensively on the 2005 and successive standards drafts. Consequently, he was able to contribute significantly to the law that was eventually passed in New York.[529,528] In the spring of 2006, the Justice Department filed suit against New York for failing to comply with HAVA[240] (see Chapter 9). It was not until the 2010 primary that new optical mark-sense voting systems finally replaced

New York's mechanical lever machines. The introduction did not go smoothly, and the public responded angrily.[446]

In the years since the passage of HAVA, both of the authors have been appointed to positions connected to the Election Assistance Commission. In 2008, Barbara Simons was appointed to the EAC Board of Advisors, and in 2009, Douglas Jones was appointed to the Technical Guidelines Development Committee.[302,303]

Unfortunately, while the TGDC continues to work on developing new draft standards for possible release, there has been backlash against the entire process. In 2005 and again in 2010, the National Association of Secretaries of State recommended to Congress that the EAC be dissolved, returning the authority over voting system regulation to the states.[734] In early 2011, Representative Kevin Brady of Texas introduced the *Cut Unsustainable and Top-Heavy Spending Act of 2011*. Section 38 of this act proposed to eliminate the EAC.[193] A month later, Representative Gregg Harper of Mississippi introduced a more narrowly targeted bill *To Terminate the Election Assistance Commission* ....[194] The former act included no provisions to transfer any current EAC activities to other agencies, while the latter would re-establish the status quo from the 1990's with the FEC in charge. Shortly before this book went to press, Harper's bill was passed by the U.S. House on a party-line vote.

6.7 International Standards

The United States is not the only nation to experiment with electronic voting systems. Brazil, India, and the Netherlands have all used direct-recording electronic voting systems for a number of years.[801,834] As a consequence, there have been serious efforts at crafting voting system standards in other parts of the world.

The most important of these is an effort by the Council of Europe.[211] As in the United States, the European standards are nonbinding recommendations. They also are very brief because they are at a much higher level. For example: "15. The e-voting system shall prevent the changing of a vote once that vote has been cast." The Council of Europe standards rarely suggest how a problem should be solved. Rather, they simply require that it be solved. The standards also extend outside the voting booth, covering voter registration and a significant number of audit requirements.

The Council of Europe standards are weakened by their multinational nature. Elections in the United States are fairly uniform nationwide, despite the fact that they are conducted largely under state law. In contrast, elections in Europe vary immensely between countries, and the variation forces the standards to back away from many issues. In addition, the standards suggest a patronizing view of voters and frequently assume that "the competent authorities" are trustworthy. [525,662]

The broadest class of multinational voting standards stems directly from international law. Which standards apply to a country depend in part on what treaties that country has ratified. Most international law applying to elections in the United States follows from treaties connected with the Organization of American States and the Organization for Security and Cooperation in Europe. While treaty obligations rarely mention voting technology, technical constraints can be inferred from treaty language. Consider the *Inter-American Democratic Charter of 2001*, which says that "the peoples of the Americas have a right to democracy," (Article 1) and "periodic, free and fair elections based on secret balloting and universal suffrage" (Article 3). [803] From this, one can conclude that signatories of this charter should not use electronic voting systems that do not offer a secret ballot or that limit suffrage through some element of their design. Accessibility for voters with disabilities follows naturally from this.

The *Charter of Paris for a New Europe* offers more detail. [188] The annex to the charter quotes paragraphs 6 through 8 of the Copenhagen Document. [189] In just one page of text, these paragraphs require that the signatory nations "hold free elections at reasonable intervals," and that the signatory nations "guarantee universal and equal suffrage to adult citizens." In addition, signatories must "ensure that votes are cast by secret ballot or by equivalent free voting procedure, and that they are counted and reported honestly with the official results made public." The secret ballot requirement is further strengthened by the requirement that signatories ensure that voters may cast their vote "free of fear or retribution." The requirement for honest counting and reporting leads naturally to a requirement for transparency, since there is no way to determine the honesty of a count conducted behind closed doors.

The United States signed these international agreements to put pressure on emerging democracies in Latin America and Eastern Europe. As endorsers of these charters, we have a moral obligation to adhere to them. Failure to do so clearly weakens any authority the United States may have when urging other nations to live up to their human rights commitments. Furthermore, international election observers will evaluate elections in the United States according to these standards.

There are several legal arguments in the United States against allowing international treaties to take precedence over domestic law. [974]

Nonetheless, it was very odd to see the Justice Department in 2005 arguing against the very same treaties that the State Department has so strongly endorsed, as happened in the case of Gregorio Igartúa-de la Rosa v. United States of America. [547] This case challenged the limited voting rights of Puerto Rico's citizens, citing the Inter-American Democratic Charter.

7

The Problems with Diebold: The Myth of Trade-Secret Software

We're not idiots, though we may act from time to time as not the smartest.

Diebold Elections System CEO Robert J. Urosevich speaking to California regulators [883]

In the summer of 2003, Wired News announced that an unknown hacker had broken into the Diebold staff website. [691] The hacker provided Wired News with a large archive of Diebold internal emails dating from January 1999 to March 2003. Diebold refused to acknowledge that the emails were authentic.

Nonetheless, when the emails were posted on voting activist Bev Harris' BlackBoxVoting.org website, Diebold forced the ISP hosting the Harris website to remove all links to the material, because of alleged copyright violations. After the emails on Harris' website were made inaccessible, they started appearing on other websites, resulting in additional Diebold letters and takedown notices.

In October 2003 a group of Swarthmore College students, called the Swarthmore Coalition for the Digital Commons, posted the emails on the Swarthmore College website. [951] After receiving a takedown demand from Diebold, the College removed the Diebold emails. The resulting publicity led students from at least 50 universities and colleges, and even two high schools, to post the Diebold emails or links to them.

The next month the Swarthmore students announced that the Electronic Frontier Foundation would be suing Diebold on their behalf for abusing copyright law and that Swarthmore was supporting their legal effort. On December 1 Diebold stated it was withdrawing the complaints against those who had posted the Diebold emails on websites. [313] Around the same time Rep. Dennis Kucinich (D) posted links to the Diebold emails on his House of Representatives website to protest what Kucinich's website said were Diebold's "coercive legal claims." [573]

The students received a favorable ruling from the United States District Court for the Northern District of California in October 2004, thereby providing Diebold with the dubious distinction of being the first company to be held liable for violating a key section of the Digital Millennium Copyright Act (DMCA). The court held that emails discussing technical problems with Diebold's voting machines were not protected by copyright. The court also found that "The fact that Diebold never actually brought suit against any alleged infringers suggests strongly that Diebold sought to use the DMCA's safe harbor provision . . . as a sword to suppress publication of embarrassing content rather than as a shield to protect its intellectual property." [352] Diebold was subsequently ordered to pay $125,000 in damages and fees.

To see why Diebold attempted to prevent the public from viewing the emails, here are some excerpts. [950]

- "Elections are not rocket science. Why is it so hard to get things right! I have never been at any other company that has been so miss [sic] managed."
- In response to a question about a presentation in El Paso County, Colorado: "For a demonstration I suggest you fake it."
- "I have become increasingly concerned about the apparent lack of concern over the practice of writing contracts to provide products and services which do not exist and then attempting to build these items on an unreasonable timetable with no written plan, little to no time for testing, and minimal resources. It also seems to be an accepted practice to exaggerate our progress and functionality to our customers and ourselves then make excuses at delivery time when these products and services do not meet expectations."
- "I need some answers! Our department is being audited by the County. I have been waiting for someone to give me an explanation as to why Precinct 216 gave Al Gore a minus 16022 when it was uploaded. Will someone please explain this so that I have the information to give the auditor instead of standing here 'looking dumb.'"

7.1 Overview

Why are we devoting an entire chapter to one voting machine vendor? The answer is that Diebold's major role, incompetence, and bad luck caused Diebold to become the poster child of much that is wrong with

DREs. Since Diebold was the first voting system vendor to have software security vulnerabilities revealed by independent computer security experts, Diebold has been subjected to considerable scrutiny. Diebold often responded by attacking its critics and claiming that problems had been fixed, even though subsequent reports and studies showed that many of those vulnerabilities had not been corrected. Regrettably, Diebold was far from unique. Other vendors have had major engineering and security vulnerabilities—as has been repeatedly revealed, for example in testing commissioned by the Secretaries of State of California and Ohio.

Founded in 1859 by Charles Diebold, Diebold initially produced safes and bank vaults. [266] In the 1970s Diebold started selling ATMs, eventually becoming the largest ATM vendor in the U.S. As discussed in Chapter 5, Diebold's involvement with voting machines began when it acquired Global Election Systems (GES) in January 2002. GES was renamed Diebold Election Systems (DES), and Robert Urosevich, who had been President of GES, became the CEO of DES. [391] At the time Robert Urosevich's brother Todd was a Vice-President at voting machine vendor ES&S, co-founded by the two brothers in the 1980s.

FIGURE 36 A smart-card for the Global AccuTouch before it was renamed the Diebold Accuvote TS. The oval on the left side is the contact pad for the chip embedded in the card. Photo by Douglas Jones

In the 2004 presidential election, Diebold and ES&S together tabulated the votes of over 3000 of the roughly 4000 local election jurisdictions that provided that information to the Election Assistance Commission (EAC). [294] (There are about 9000 local election jurisdictions in the United States). [342] Perhaps because of controversy surrounding the role of the Urosevich brothers, Thomas W. Swidarski replaced Robert Urosevich at Diebold in August 2004, and Todd Urosevich later stepped down from his Vice-President position at ES&S. [462] Swidarski became Diebold CEO when Walden O'Dell resigned on December 12, 2005. [64]

Diebold's financial rating was downgraded on August 13, 2007, because of problems with the voting portion of the business. [554] After unsuccessful efforts to sell the election systems subsidiary, Diebold Election System's name was changed to Premier Election Solutions, and Premier was made somewhat independent of Diebold. [825]

On September 3, 2009 Diebold made the electrifying announcement that the company had sold its election system business to ES&S for only $5 million. [270] There was an immediate outcry, because the sale would have given ES&S control over more than 75% of the voting machine market. Sen. Charles Schumer (D) urged the Justice Department to probe the sale, warning that "Competition is needed to reduce chances of widespread election fraud." [881] About a week after the announced sale, Hart Intercivic filed a lawsuit against Diebold and ES&S, claiming that the sale posed an "imminent threat of irreparable harm to other vendors like Hart." [443]

On March 8, 2010 the Department of Justice announced that it was requiring ES&S "to divest voting equipment systems assets it purchased in September 2009 from Premier Election Solutions Inc. in order to restore competition." [243] Dominion Voting Systems, which purchased the assets that ES&S was forced to sell, subsequently purchased Sequoia Voting Systems. [279] It remains to be seen if Dominion will be in a position to compete against ES&S.

Since most of the events discussed in this chapter occurred before the name change, the name "Diebold" will be used, where appropriate.

7.2 Early Events

7.2.1 The O'Dell Letter

Diebold's involvement with voting machines received significant national press when then Diebold CEO Walden O'Dell stated in an August 14, 2003 letter to Central Ohio Republicans that he was "committed to helping Ohio deliver its electoral votes to the President next year." [926] It was subsequently revealed that O'Dell and other Diebold executives had made sizable campaign contributions, almost all of them to the Republican Party. From 2003 to the fall of 2004, Diebold also paid $275,000 to Greenberg Traurig, LLP, the lobbying firm of Jack Abramoff, for lobbying in New York State. [182]

The O'Dell letter, the Diebold political contributions, and the fact that at one point the Urosevich brothers collectively controlled the machine that counted the majority of votes cast in the U.S. set off alarms. The lack of solid evidence did not prevent conspiracy theorists from having a field day. Undocumented claims that the Urosevich brothers had rigged elections played into the hands of supporters of paperless DREs. For example, the Information Technology & Innovation Foundation ignored the key role played by computer scientists in fighting insecure computerized voting systems by painting almost all opponents of DRE voting systems with the same brush—as Luddites, conspiracy theorists, and fear mongers:

> Many opponents of electronic voting machines are motivated by a distrust of technology, anger at election results, and conspiracy theories about voting companies.... They scare voters and election officials into demanding something they do understand: paper. [153]

FIGURE 37 A Diebold voting machine from early 2003.
Photo by Douglas Jones

7.2.2 Georgia

The fallout from O'Dell's statement and the accompanying PR problems pale in comparison to the impact of the security breach uncovered by Bev Harris. [427] In February 2003 she announced that she had discovered Diebold voting machine software on an insecure website. The website contained files with names like "rob-georgia.zip," as well as large parts of GEMS (the Global Election Management System), which is the centralized ballot tabulation software used for Diebold DREs and optical scan systems. While many people initially assumed the worst about the "rob-georgia" file, it turned out that "rob" was not a verb, but rather the first name of Rob Behler, a programmer employed by a company doing consulting work for Diebold on voting software for the state of Georgia.

In an interview with Harris, Behler explained the use of the web-site. [428] He said that corrections for the voting machine software (software patches) were being written by a Canadian named Talbot Iredale. Iredale would post new patches on the website, and Behler and his colleagues would download the patches and install them directly on the voting machines. According to Behler, the patches were never examined by an Independent Testing Authority (ITA).

Behler summarized his views about the accuracy of Diebold machines used in the Georgia 2002 election by saying, "If you were to ask me to tell you how accurate I thought the vote count was, I'd have to say 'no comment' because after what I saw, I have an inherent distrust of the machines. I was absolutely astounded that they functioned at all in the election."

Nonetheless, officials in Georgia insisted that their systems were secure. Shortly after Harris' discovery came to light, Britain Williams, who had conducted certification evaluations of computer-based voting systems for the State of Georgia since 1986, assured voters that all voting system software used by the state came from an ITA that had conducted the appropriate NASED (National Association of State Election Directors) tests on the software. [1013] Williams chaired NASED's Voting Systems Board Technical Committee at the time. Behler's comments about software patches were in direct conflict with Williams' claim.

7.2.3   The Hopkins-Rice Report

After analyzing some of the software obtained by Harris, Johns Hopkins Professor Aviel Rubin, Rice Professor Dan Wallach, and students Tadayoshi Kohno and Adam Stubblefield published a security analysis in a Johns Hopkins University research report. [565] The computer science researchers found that it would be relatively simple for someone with the right access to insert a malicious worm or virus into the system. They also discovered other serious problems, including programming errors and the improper use of cryptography.

Cryptography is the mathematical study of encoding (*encrypting*) information and decoding (*decrypting*) encrypted information. A simple example of encryption reassigns letters: if "k" stands for "h", "r" for "e", "t" for "l", and "n" for "o", "krttn" is an encoding of "hello." The table giving the letter reassignments is called the *key*.

One of the more shocking revelations was that Diebold used a single key to encrypt all of the data on every storage device. It was as if General Motors had used the identical ignition key for each car. An attacker who knew the key, possibly by copying it from the source code, and had access to the storage device would have had the ability to modify voting and auditing records. *Source code* is the software written by computer programmers using a programming language such as C or Java. The encryption key was an eight character string embedded in the text of the program: F2654hD4. Since Diebold's programmers used the same key in every machine, the entire system was compromised.

Even more surprising, Diebold had known of the key vulnerability since at least 1997. That was when Douglas Jones, then a member of the Iowa Board of Examiners for Voting Machines and Electronic Voting Equipment, found this error and warned Urosevich of the risk to the entire product line if someone were to obtain the key by getting a machine on the surplus market or out of the trash. [523]

The New York Times broke the story of the Hopkins-Rice Report on July 24, 2003. [882] Reaction was widespread and swift, both from scientists, who were shocked by the findings, and from a number of election officials who defended their purchasing decisions.

Diebold initially denied that the software examined by the computer scientists had ever been deployed in an election. [564] Yet, in an August 4 Wired News article, Mike Jacobsen, a spokesman for Diebold, confirmed that the software had been used in November 2002 general elections in Georgia and Maryland, and in counties in California and Kansas." [1016]

Diebold responded to the Hopkins-Rice Report, saying that the claim that malicious software could be inserted into the system was baseless. [267] Nonetheless, the problem still hadn't been fixed three years later, when a team at Princeton University did precisely what Diebold said could not be done (see Section 7.4.3).

For the next few months Rubin, who received considerable media attention, was frequently attacked. For example, Britain Williams contacted the Director of the Information Security Institute at Johns Hopkins, where Rubin worked. According to Rubin's book *Brave New Ballot*, Williams "demanded that I be 'reprimanded' for my irresponsible report and suggested that Hopkins consider firing me." [858] At the time, Rubin was unaware of Williams' involvement with certifying Georgia's Diebold voting machines. Rubin subsequently learned that Williams was on the faculty at Kennesaw State University in Georgia, where he also ran the Center for Election systems. The Center tested and evaluated the paperless Diebold DREs first used in Georgia in the 2002 election, an election that generated controversy because of victories by

Republican gubernatorial and Senate candidates who had been trailing in the pre-election polls. [173]

Even the President of Johns Hopkins was contacted about Rubin, this time by Stephen Berger. Berger, who subsequently represented the IEEE (Institute of Electrical and Electronic Engineers) on the Technical Guidelines Development Committee (TGDC, see Chapter 5), asked in a letter if the Hopkins-Rice Report had been peer reviewed or published in a refereed journal. According to Rubin, Berger requested a full accounting of the 'nature and extent' of that review process. [858] The Hopkins-Rice report was accepted a few months later in the highly respected peer reviewed IEEE Symposium on Security and Privacy.

Diebold sent the authors warning letters threatening legal action and demanding that the authors "cease and desist all uses of the Code." [858] ("Code" is another term for "software"). The threat was quashed by a strong response from Johns Hopkins' legal staff.

7.2.4   Diebold posts partial election results on-line

Around the same time, questions were being raised about Diebold's claim that the voting machines were never connected to the Internet. In September 2003, voting activist Jim March announced that a file from the original insecure Diebold website dated March 5, 2002 appeared to contain ballot images and an actual tally of votes midway through the San Luis Obispo County, California primary election. The votes were most likely absentee and "postal precinct" votes tallied at the county offices during the day. [631] While tabulation may legally begin when the polls open, no totals may be released until after the polls close.

Just how Diebold came to have election data on its website during an actual election was not explained. The password March found for the file, Sophia, suggests the possible identity of its creator, since a Diebold employee named Sophia was involved with on-site support during the election. Diebold acknowledged the incident and said it was investigating. [568]

March's discovery brought into question Diebold's repeated assertion that the security loopholes in their voting systems are of no importance, because procedural safeguards provide protection. It appears that such procedural safeguards were not in place in San Luis Obispo County, despite the presence of on-site supervision by a Diebold employee. Somehow, the Diebold system used to accumulate absentee and postal ballots was connected to the Internet.

Furthermore, email from Diebold technician Robert Chen, dated October 28, 2002 and subsequently leaked by an insider to Bev Harris, claimed that the GEMS system (the tabulation software used by

Diebold) in Alameda County, California was on-line, reachable directly from the outside world. [630]

7.2.5 Convicted Felons

Diebold continued to generate press. In December 2003, Bev Harris and Andy Stephenson announced that Diebold employed at least five convicted felons in key positions, including programmer and former GES senior vice-president Jeffrey W. Dean, who had been found guilty of manipulating computer files to steal money. [567] Diebold responded that the company performs background checks on potential employees. Diebold also stated that several of the named individuals had worked for GES, and that many of the GES employees, including Dean, had left when the company was purchased by Diebold. However, according to Harris, Dean was subsequently retained by Diebold as a consultant. [426]

7.3 Early State Diebold Studies

7.3.1 The SAIC Report

Because of security issues raised in the Hopkins paper, the State of Maryland, which had just committed to purchasing Diebold DREs, commissioned a study of Diebold machines by Science Applications International Corporation (SAIC).

When the SAIC report was publicly released in September 2003, about 2/3 of it, including the entire risk assessments section, was redacted by the State of Maryland. [884] Even the name of the operating system was redacted, which seemed rather odd since it was known, thanks to publicly released internal Diebold emails, that Diebold was running Windows CE 3.0.

Why, one might ask, would anyone feel the need to redact the name of the Windows operating system? A likely explanation is that Windows CE is intended to be modified by the purchaser. Consequently, just as with vendor-written software, risks of election related malicious code exist with Windows CE. Yet, because the certification process treated Windows CE as if it were a non-modified operating system, the actual code was never examined by the ITAs.

The limited amount of information initially released was surprisingly damning. For example, the redacted version stated that the Diebold system was so complicated that even if all of the problems were fixed, there still could be security risks because of poorly trained election officials. In addition, the final paragraph of the executive summary warned that the system as implemented was "at high risk of compromise," though it also said that the recommendations included in the report would reduce the risks to the system. The report observed that

"Any computerized voting system implemented using the present set of policies and procedures would require these same mitigations." Since Maryland's election related policies and procedures are not unusual, there is good reason to suspect that the election procedures of many other states would have been similarly judged, had they been subjected to the same risk assessment.

In spite of the fact that the redacted version of the SAIC report was highly critical of Diebold and supported the Hopkins-Rice Report on most issues, both the State of Maryland and Diebold claimed that the SAIC report vindicated the purchase of Diebold machines.

7.3.2   How the Unredacted Version Got Released

It was not until early November 2006 that the unredacted version of the SAIC report was leaked to ABC News Producer Rebecca Abrahams, though an earlier unsuccessful attempt to obtain the unredacted report had been made by Maryland attorney Ken Fox. [5] Abrahams shared the unredacted report with Stephen Spoonamore, CEO of Cybrinth, a cybersecurity company. Spoonamore was so alarmed by the report that he sent sealed envelopes containing copies of the report, together with his analysis, to five trusted individuals, along with directions to open the envelopes 72 hours after his upcoming meeting with the Maryland Board of Elections (BoE), unless he instructed otherwise.

Spoonamore brought the leaked copy to a public hearing of the BoE. After State Administrator of Elections Linda Lamone (D) and Diebold reassured the BoE about the security of the upcoming election, Spoonamore spoke, stating that the unredacted SAIC report documented that Diebold machines could not be secured for an election. [935] He also said that the full report, which he believed had never been shown to the BoE, had been edited to reverse or hide its conclusions. He added that he had a complete copy of the SAIC report with him and offered to provide further analysis. The meeting was immediately ended, and the BoE was advised by Lamone not to accept a copy of the complete report.

Two board members spoke with Spoonamore afterwards and invited him to talk with them about his concerns after the upcoming election. According to Spoonamore, when he followed up to schedule a meeting, he was informed by Linda Lamone's office that the General Council to the BoE had advised Board members not to meet with him. [934]

One of the people to whom a copy was sent was Brad Friedman, publisher of Brad Blog. Abrahams wrote the story that accompanied the release of the unredacted report on BradBlog. [4]

Why the Redactions?

Had the explicit and implicit recommendations of the SAIC report been implemented, almost none of the redacted revelations would have threatened the security of the voting system. It appears that a key motivation for many, if not most, of the redactions was that both Diebold and the State of Maryland could thus avoid admitting the existence of some serious security problems and then fixing them. Multiple redacted portions support that conclusion, as well as a comment by SAIC study leader Frank Schugar to Aviel Rubin that the redactions had been made by Maryland officials. [858]

7.3.3 The Ohio Reports

The State of Ohio, home of Diebold headquarters, had been considering the purchase of Diebold DREs for the entire state. After the release of the Hopkins-Rice Report, Ohio hired Compuware to test Diebold hardware and software, and InfoSentry to conduct a security assessment. On December 2, 2003, Ohio Secretary of State J. Kenneth Blackwell (R) released the reports. He also stated that Ohio would request a HAVA deadline extension to allow manufacturers time to correct security problems uncovered in the reports.

The InfoSENTRY Report

The summary report from InfoSentry Services said very little about the voting systems, while focusing instead on issues of certification and security planning. [501] As was the case with the SAIC report, however, some of the InfoSentry recommendations disclosed huge flaws in state election procedures. The report also recommended that the Secretary of State create a statewide system to track voting system security incidents, and consider creating a similar system to track defects and repairs.

In Ohio, as with most other states, incidents that suggest potential problems in voting systems generally go unreported, are not uniformly reported, or are reported to people who have no obligation to act on those reports. Existing reports are not stored in a uniform fashion. Consequently, major flaws could occur repeatedly throughout the country without raising any serious questions about the voting systems.

The Compuware Report

The Compuware report provided some technical details that were redacted in the SAIC report and revealed some surprising security weaknesses, for example the lack of password protection for supervisory functions. [184] The investigators also found yet another insecure password in the Diebold voting system, this time for the supervisor smart card used to start up each voting machine on Election Day, as well as to terminate the voting process at the end of the day. When that card is inserted into the DRE, the election official must enter the correct PIN for use of that card. Someone who obtained or counterfeited a supervisor card would be able to undermine an election by prematurely halting the voting machines, thereby denying some voters the opportunity to vote. The PIN was a four-digit number, and the team guessed it on the third attempt, thereby gaining access to the supervisor functions on the AccuVote TS. The PIN was 1111 for all machines.

While the table of "requirements tested and test results" given in the Compuware report was somewhat superficial, it confirmed many of the security weaknesses identified by the Hopkins-Rice Report and validated by the SAIC report. Unfortunately, the Compuware report appears to conclude that since the authors were unsuccessful in carrying out an attack, then the safeguards were adequate—a risky and unrealistic assumption at best.

7.3.4   The RABA Report

In November 2003, the Maryland Department of Legislative Services commissioned RABA Technologies to conduct a "red team" effort to hack into the Diebold AccuVote TS and GEMS system. (A "red team" consists of good guys who try to break into systems in order to detect security holes that bad guys could exploit, so that those holes can be fixed.) The system that was examined utilized Maryland's security action plans, formulated in response to the SAIC report.

After studying Diebold's source code for about a week, the red team was able to hack into the Diebold system on January 19, 2004.[831] Once they had broken into the voting system, the team had the ability to modify election results.

The team found many security problems. Software to protect against the Blaster worm, a serious worm that had spread like wildfire six months previously, had not been installed—thereby making GEMS vulnerable to a remote attack. Numerous vulnerabilities resulted from "poor physical security coupled with software that fails to use robust encryption and authentication." For example, an attacker could install malicious code using a memory card. The report also revealed the use of identical physical keys on security panels covering the memory card slot, as well as locks that could be picked in a few seconds.

The RABA report concluded: "DIEBOLD software reflects a layered approach to security." In other words, Diebold simply added patches as new problems were identified. However, the report observed, true security can come only from using established security models and appropriate software engineering processes. The authors recommended a "pervasive code rewrite" to eliminate the risks they had identified, adding that their analysis "lacked the time and resources to determine if DIEBOLD has the expertise to accomplish this task."

With so much bad news, Diebold announced in December 2003 that it was restructuring its compliance and certification process, to be overseen by a compliance and certification officer, a new position.[268] The announcement could be seen as a direct response to the SAIC, Compuware, and InfoSENTRY reports, all of which implied that states should have demanded a greater emphasis on security from Diebold and other voting system vendors.

In spite of the negative reports, Maryland, under the leadership of Linda Lamone, proceeded with the commitment to purchase 16,000 Diebold DREs at the end of 2003 for a cost of about $55.6 million.[879]

These early studies repeatedly demonstrated the vast array of security issues that might confront election officials, ranging from simple concerns, such as turning off the voting machines prematurely, to malicious tampering. Someone wanting to affect election results might gain access to the physically locked panel and insert a virus or worm using a flash drive. An individual with the right knowledge and access, possibly an insider, could tamper with results or change a number of other steps in the process. While physical and procedural programs can lower risks, there were good reasons to wonder if county election officials were capable of keeping these machines safe without considerable assistance.

But the news continued to get worse.

7.4   Demonstrations of Election Rigging

It's one thing to downplay an abstract report about security vulnerabilities, and quite another to try to dismiss real life demonstrations of vote manipulation. The first such demonstration was led by Finnish computer security expert Harri Hursti, who was involved with two separate investigations. Both investigations uncovered vulnerabilities, one especially grave, in two different Diebold voting systems. And in both cases the election officials who had the temerity to allow the examination of a Diebold voting system by an independent computer security expert suffered retribution. One, Ion Sancho (No Party Affiliation), almost lost his job; the other, Bruce Funk (R), actually did lose his job. Both Sancho and Funk were attacked by Diebold and state or local officials.

It is no wonder that independent examination of voting systems on the local level remains relatively rare. Election officials saw what happened to Sancho and Funk.

7.4.1 The First Hursti Investigation

In early 2005 Ion Sancho, Election Supervisor of Leon County, Florida, invited computer security experts Harri Hursti and Herbert Thompson to test the security of a Diebold precinct-based optical scan voting system. Bev Harris provided source code files, program files, some software (a compiler), and user manuals, all of which had been downloaded from a Diebold website in 2003.

The researchers discovered that a removable memory card that had been thought to contain only static information about the current election also contained software that could be executed. This software controlled how result reports were printed and could be changed by anyone with brief access to the memory card. [476] In December, Hursti returned to Leon County, where he conducted a physical election simulation in which he was able to: 1) falsify election result reports so that they did not match the actual vote; 2) remove information about pre-loaded votes that can be used to rig an election; and 3) conceal the malicious behavior so that it would not show up during pre-election testing.

Since Hursti's attack falsifies the reported results, but not the paper ballots, his attack would not be caught by pre-election testing. While some states conduct a post-election comparison of the results produced locally by the optical scan machine ("poll tapes") with those produced by the central tabulator, such minimal audits would completely miss a Hursti-style attack. However, his attack **would** be detected if a manual audit of the paper ballots were conducted (see Chapter 13). Regrettably, most states do not routinely conduct such audits.

Standard programming techniques (such as a digital signature or even a checksum) that would have made the Hursti attack difficult to impossible were not implemented by Diebold. In his report Hursti compared the security vulnerability to "a house with an unlockable revolving door."

Hursti's attack exploits the fact that computers count the same way that automobile odometers track mileage. Since most odometers cannot store a 7 digit number, if the number on an odometer is 999,999, the next time a mile is driven the odometer will "roll over" to zero. The same thing happens with a computer. For the machines Hursti tested, the equivalent of 999,999 is the number 65,535. Just as in a car $999,999 + 1 = 1,000,000 = 0$, so too in a Diebold machine $65,535 + 1 = 65,536 = 0$. This is called an integer overflow. It would be possible to prevent such an attack if the machines checked for integer overflow, but the Diebold machines did not.

So, if someone wants to pre-load 100 votes for candidate B, all he need do is to give candidate A an initial tally of $65,536 - 50 = 65,486$, while giving candidate B a starting tally of 50 votes, instead of 0. After candidate A had received 50 votes, his tally would roll over to 0, thereby depriving him of the initial 50 votes. Furthermore, because candidate B started with 50 votes, the total number of votes cast would be correct, even though the individual vote tallies would be rigged.

Diebold was not happy that Sancho had tested their machine. In June Diebold accused Sancho of undermining the public's confidence in their systems and warned that the Leon County system had been compromised due to Sancho's negligence. Diebold spokesman David Bear complained that Hursti's results were unfounded, because no responsible election official would allow a hacker to have "complete unfettered access" to voting machines. [394] Bear's response flies in the face of reality. There are many opportunities for malicious software to be installed by an insider, an election official, a poll worker, a delivery person, a custodian, or anyone who has a few minutes of unobserved time with a machine. For example, voting machines are often delivered to workers' homes prior to Election Day, a practice colloquially known as "sleep-overs."

After repeated requests to get the most recent software upgrade installed, as required by the Leon County service agreement with Diebold, Sancho was told that Diebold would not honor its contract. Instead, Diebold demanded that Sancho sign a new contract prohibiting the combination of Diebold machines with the Automark, a voting system for people with disabilities that Sancho had wanted to purchase from ES&S, the company marketing the Automark.

Sancho refused to sign a new Diebold contract and instead attempted to purchase all of his machines from ES&S. Although Sancho had been in touch with high-ranking officials at ES&S and had even been quoted a price of approximately $1.8 million, in late December Sancho received a message on his cell phone saying that the sale could not go through, because ES&S was overcommitted. However, ES&S subsequently signed a contract with neighboring Volusia County. They also notified the state of Maryland that they would be able to supply the entire state with machines for the '06 elections.

Sancho next approached Sequoia, the last remaining vendor of a voting system certified by Florida that could be used by voters with disabilities. (Ballot printing and marking systems were not then certified by Florida). Sequoia initially agreed to deliver a contract, but they backed out in early March 2006, claiming that they were at capacity and were not taking new orders for 2006.

Here is how Sancho describes what happened.

> Unknown to me, Kathy Dent (Supervisor of Elections, Sarasota County), an ES&S client and one of the our state's biggest proponents of DREs, contacted Aldo Tesi, the head of ES&S, and urged him not to sell Leon County this equipment. In late December the Florida sales rep for ES&S nervously gave me a call at my home and dropped that bombshell on me. Now, Leon County could be in potential violation of HAVA, as well as the Florida variant of the Federal law. I was contacted by the Florida rep of Sequoia, who offered to sell me his company's machines, which I was forced to pursue. But this sale was vetoed by his corporate boss, thus none of the three vendors certified to sell equipment in Florida would sell me the equipment needed to comply with Sec. 301 of HAVA. That's when the coordinated political attacks started. [872]

According to Susan Pynchon of the Florida Fair Elections Coalition, Diebold also attempted to get Sancho fired:

> At a Leon County Commission meeting on February 28, 2006, county staff revealed that Chuck Owen, Division Counsel for Diebold Election Systems, met with county staff behind closed doors on February 27. According to staff, Owen stated that Diebold would sell its touch-screen voting machines to the county if, and only if, the county removed Supervisor Sancho from office. [830]

Because no vendor would sell machines to Sancho, Leon County was forced to return the HAVA funds it had received. Rather than question the blackballing of Leon County by the vendors, on March 3, 2006 Secretary of State Sue Cobb (R) sent Sancho a letter acknowledging the receipt of the returned $564.421.95 of HAVA money and threatening legal action if voting systems were not delivered to Leon County by May 1, 2006. [172] On March 8, 2006 Sancho notified Diebold of his intent to sue for breach of contract.

Meanwhile, in February 2006 a technical committee of the California Secretary of State not only validated Hursti's findings—thereby vindicating Sancho and probably saving his job—but also detected additional security problems (see Chapter 8).

Although Florida did not act on the California findings, the Florida legislature restored Leon County's lost funds in May, the Diebold machines arrived in June, and Leon County conducted a successful election in September, 2006.

7.4.2   The Second Hursti Investigation

While Ion Sancho was able to hold onto his job, long time county clerk Bruce Funk of Emery County, Utah was not so fortunate. After finding numerous problems with Emery County's Diebold DREs, Funk invited Hursti to test them.

As a result of the testing, in May 2006 Hursti announced that there was a second Diebold security vulnerability that was so serious that both Hursti and the computer security experts who were told of the vulnerability refused initially to reveal the details publicly. [477] Basically, Diebold had included a "back door" in its software, allowing anyone to change or modify the software by inserting malicious code using the removable memory card. There were no technical safeguards in place to ensure that only authorized people could make changes. Hursti also demonstrated how to access the memory card easily by simply removing five standard Phillips screws from the case of the machine.

In an early response to the back door vulnerability, Diebold spokesman David Bear said, "It's only a vulnerability to those who would commit a felony [tampering with an election]." [993] Diebold also accused both Sancho and Funk of breach of contract for allowing unauthorized third parties to inspect the machines. [566]

Michael Shamos, a computer scientist and voting system examiner in Pennsylvania, was quoted in the New York Times as saying, "It's the most severe security flaw ever discovered in a voting system." [223] The same article contained another quote from Bear: "For there to be a problem here, you're basically assuming a premise where you have some evil and nefarious election officials who would sneak in and introduce a piece of software. I don't believe these evil elections people exist."

When Funk's actions became known, he was pressured by county commissioners to resign. Although Funk verbally agreed to resign, within hours he changed his mind, saying that he was elected by the people of Emery County, and only they could tell him to go. Nonetheless, the commissioners claimed that he had resigned, changed the locks on his office, and appointed a replacement. [993]

Later that year Ed Felten and his students at Princeton used the back door uncovered by Hursti to demonstrate how to infect Diebold DREs with a virus that could spread from machine to machine.

7.4.3   The Princeton Virus

Princeton Professor Ed Felten, together with students Ari Feldman and Alex Halderman, conducted a four-month study of a Diebold Accu-Vote TS DRE machine provided by former Diebold contractor Chris Hood. Their security analysis, released in September 2006, applied to a machine that was going to be heavily deployed in the 2006 midterm elections. [335] More than 10% of the US population in more than 17% of all precincts nationwide, including all of Maryland and Georgia, would be voting on Diebold AccuVote machines. [307]

The Princeton group exploited a physical vulnerability in Diebold DREs, pointed out by both the redacted SAIC report and the RABA report, to create a computer virus that could be spread from an infected machine to an uninfected one via removable memory cards.

The vulnerability is disarmingly simple. The Diebold AccuVote TS stores a removable memory card behind a locked door on the side of the machine. An identical key is used to unlock the doors on all AccuVote machines. Furthermore, the key can be purchased over the Internet and is widely used in office furniture and hotel minibars. The lock is so insecure that it is easily picked; one member of the Princeton group could do so in less than 10 seconds. After gaining access by opening the unlocked door or by removing some screws and lifting off the top of the machine, it was possible to remove the original memory card, insert a memory card containing malicious software, reboot the machine, and then replace the original memory card—all within about a minute.

Once a virus is installed, it spreads by hitching a ride on an infected removable memory card, much as viruses used to be spread by infected floppy disks. If a technician, who is using a memory card to upgrade or perform maintenance on a set of machines, inserts an uninfected memory card into a contaminated machine, the memory card becomes infected. The newly contaminated card then spreads the virus to every other machine into which it is inserted. Alternatively, the virus could be spread at the end of an election, if one of the machines is selected to tally all the votes. Each of the memory cards, including the infected card, is fed into the tallying machine. Once the tallying machine is infected by the memory card, it will infect all subsequently inserted memory cards. Finally, the virus can be spread before an election— when election definition files are transferred from machine to machine— via an infected memory card.

The virus could rig an election, corrupt results, or cause machines to behave slowly or erratically (denial of service attack) in areas that are known to favor an opposing candidate. In all cases the malicious behavior could be impossible to detect. Since Diebold TS DREs do not have paper audit trails, there would be no possibility of an audit or recount.

Diebold issued a response in which they argued that the software examined by the researchers was old, normal security procedures were ignored, the machines are never attached to a network, and "proper procedures and adequate testing assure an accurate voting process." [128] The Princeton group replied that they used a version of the software that had been deployed in national elections, they had never claimed that the machines were attached to a network, and they had focused on security procedures. [336] They concluded, "If Diebold really believes its latest systems are secure, it should allow third parties like us to evaluate them." Diebold did not take them up on their offer.

It is clear from the Princeton report that a virus could be transmitted from machine to machine via the memory card. But rather than address that risk, Diebold reacted as if the Princeton team had assumed that the machines had been networked together, which the Princeton group clearly had not done. Out of touch answers to critics had become so common that many experts wondered if anyone at Diebold truly understood the technology, if they simply weren't reading the reports, or if they were trying to distract the public by raising irrelevant threats and then pointing out that those threats didn't apply.

7.5 Some Later State Diebold Studies

7.5.1 Cuyahoga County, Ohio

Cuyahoga County, home of Cleveland, was the center of controversy for several years.

The 2004 Election

Problems started in 2004, when a close presidential election race triggered a recount in Cuyahoga County. Under Ohio law, officials are instructed to recount a random sample totaling one percent of the votes. If there are discrepancies, then a full recount is conducted. In order to avoid the cost of a full recount, some Cuyahoga County elections officials pre-counted several precincts in advance, looking for those precincts where the machine and hand counts matched. They then "randomly" selected the matching precincts for the hand recount.

In April 2006 the special prosecutor, who had been appointed to investigate the recount, indicted three people working in the election office, charging them with misdemeanor and felony violations of state law. [652] In January 2007 one election worker was found not guilty and the other two received felony convictions and 18-month prison sentences for illegally rigging the 2004 presidential recount. However, in August 2007 the convicted election workers were given a new trial that ended with a no contest plea agreement, resulting in only six months' probation with no convictions. [778]

The 2006 Primary Report

Shortly after the 2004 election, Michael Vu, hired by the Cuyahoga County Board of Elections (CCBOE) as Election Director in 2003, replaced the county's punch card voting machines with Diebold AccuVote TSx DREs with Voter Verified Paper Audit Trails (VVPATs). When Ohio used the Diebold machines for the first time in the May 2, 2006 primaries, disaster struck. Precincts opened late, some ballots omitted certain races, memory cards were misplaced or lost, some machines stopped working, VVPATs failed, and confusion reigned. [372] By May 6 the CCBOE had established the Cuyahoga Election Review Panel to investigate the May 2 primary. The panel was charged with identifying the problems, ascertaining the causes, and providing a set of recommendations.

The final panel report, released on July 20, 2006, criticized the manner in which the primary was conducted. [15] The report found that a number of DREs "crashed, froze, or malfunctioned during boot-up or use on Election Day, an unknown number of which were returned to service without further investigation." Furthermore, 51 days after the May primary, 12 memory cards were still missing, though it was possible to count the votes by collecting the vote data from the relevant DREs. Memory cards were not treated with the necessary care, could be tampered with, and were overpriced. Disturbing in light of the missing cards, the report found that poll workers sometimes placed memory cards in the wrong DREs. As with previous studies, the panel noted the security risk of using an identical key for all machines to open the door for the memory card.

Poll workers had problems loading the VVPAT thermal paper, which they sometimes loaded backwards, thereby eliminating the paper trail. Thermal VVPAT paper used for the Accuvote is similar to gas station receipts. The thermal printer works on only one side of the paper; furthermore, paper rolls need to be stored properly to avoid fading.

Many voters did not check their VVPATs, because the VVPAT printer had an opaque cover that had to be opened to see the VVPAT. To add insult to injury, the VVPAT was difficult to read because of the font size and the magnifying plastic cover.

Perhaps the most stunning finding dealt with the manner in which the CCBOE processed the 18,000 mail-in optical scan paper ballots. Rather than count those ballots manually or with a scanner, the ballots were manually transcribed into the DREs. The Secretary of State had instructed the CCBOE not to permit the DREs to print paper receipts during the transcription. Since the printing couldn't be turned off manually, workers intentionally loaded the paper backwards when processing mail-in ballots, so that the printers could not print. The lack of a paper trail eliminated a check on the accuracy of the manual transcriptions.

The 2006 Election Report

Because of continued concerns about the quality of Cuyahoga County elections, the CCBOE commissioned another audit, this one of the November 2006 election. The Cuyahoga County Audit report, issued in April 2007, stated that hundreds of votes were lost, and some were counted twice. [178] The report also found indications of possible database corruption, probably related to the most crucial revelation from the audit report, namely that Diebold used the Microsoft Jet database for storing ballot information. Jet is an old database that is known to be insecure and unreliable, as Microsoft readily acknowledges. [167] Microsoft has been selling databases that are more secure and reliable than Jet for a long time.

There is no excuse for Diebold to have used such an inadequate database. Yet, according to the New York Times, a Diebold spokesman responded by saying that "whatever problems there were with the system had been corrected. In some instances, he said, there were no problems at all: the committee had simply misunderstood the system." [285]

Michael Vu resigned from his position as Director of the CCBOE in February 2007. [67] Less than two months later he was hired as assistant registrar of voters by San Diego County at an annual salary of $130,000. [186]

7.5.2   The University of Connecticut Study

In July 2007 the University of Connecticut's VoTeR Center announced that it had uncovered previously undetected security problems with the VVPAT equipped Diebold DRE (AccuVote TSx). [556] Since Connecticut had required voting machine vendors to provide machines for testing by the state, the Connecticut Secretary of State had given the Center, which has received funding from the state for its voting machine work, two Diebold terminals for testing. The team was in a situation similar to that of an attacker who has access only to the machine: the team had none of the system's internal documents, internal machine specifications, or source code.

The university group was able to hack into the machines and under certain conditions to swap votes between two candidates. They also were able to delete a candidate's name from the DRE screen by slightly modifying the name, for example by changing a "C" to a "D." Because the Diebold software detected an inconsistency in the name, the name would not be displayed. Instead there was a blank space where the candidate's name should have been. (If a voter voted the blank space as if the name were there, the candidate whose name had been deleted would receive a vote). The authors conjectured that Diebold engineers added software to protect the data and to check the data integrity in the system, but that this software was incomplete and provided only partial security.

In order to execute the attacks, the team first had to gain access to the removable memory card, just as the Princeton group had done. The physical key for opening the the AccuVote TSx was difficult to copy, an improvement over the AccuVote TS, but it was still not adequately protected. As had been observed in Cuyahoga County, every polling place was sent a copy of the key, additional keys were not numbered, and no record was kept of which key was assigned to which polling place. Once the memory card had been removed from the Diebold terminal, the card was easily modified using a standard notebook PC. As with several other potential attacks, the UConn attack could be executed by any of the many people who have time alone, even just a few minutes, with a Diebold terminal.

7.5.3   The California Top-to-Bottom Review

In 2007 the State of California conducted the most thorough study of voting systems that had yet been done. Unlike prior ITA code reviews, California's Top-to-Bottom review examined a wide range of issues, including accessibility, documentation, source code, and security (see Chapter 8 for more details). California Secretary of State Bowen (D) contracted out the testing to the University of California, which hired experts for the significantly expanded scope of testing. Much testing was done that presumably had not been done by the ITAs, such as hiring red teams to try to break into the systems. The overall results were made public, though information about particularly sensitive vulnerabilities was withheld. In this chapter we discuss only Diebold security issues.

The red team analyzing the Diebold machines could break into the system. The team also could introduce malicious code into the TSx that would reinitialize an election, thereby deleting all electronic records of ballots, including backup records, cast on the system up to that point. They even devised a simple attack that used a "common household substance" (they did not reveal the substance in the public document) that could destroy not only those VVPATs that had already been printed, but also potentially those that would be printed following the attack. [1]

Of course such an attack would be discovered at the end of the election, but the damage would have been done.

A public hearing was held shortly after the release of the red teams' reports, all of which were negative. [140] In a written response Diebold stated that many of the problems uncovered by the red team had been fixed in a more recent version of the software. Since that software had not yet been certified in California, it was not analyzed. However, Diebold's claim rings hollow, given that the source code review team confirmed that many vulnerabilities detected by previous studies had not been fixed in the software they reviewed.

A few days after the hearing, the source code reviews were released. The source code team's Diebold report supported the red team's analysis and, if anything, was even more negative. [131] Uncovered threats included vulnerability to malicious software, susceptibility to viruses, failure to protect ballot secrecy, and vulnerability to malicious insiders.

The executive summary of the report on Diebold's source code formally stated what industry experts and computer programmers had suspected: many of the serious security risks identified in previous studies had not been repaired. While the source code team's study uncovered a number of previously unpublished vulnerabilities, it also reinforced warnings from several prior studies. Noting that many of the vulnerabilities resulted from deep architectural flaws in the design of the systems, which in turn caused "weakness-in-depth" in the security of the systems, the report observed that the security of Diebold's systems rested almost solely on the effectiveness of election procedures. The report concluded that a major re-engineering of the software to make it secure by design would be the safest way to repair the system.

Bowen decertified all tested systems and then conditionally recertified them.

7.5.4   The Ohio EVEREST Study

Shortly after taking office in January 2007, Ohio Secretary of State Jennifer Brunner (D) announced that Ohio would also conduct a thorough review of its voting systems, which included the Diebold AccuVote TSx DRE. [1005] The $1.9 million study was conducted by university computer security researchers and SysTest Labs, one of the ITAs.

Not surprisingly, the study, which was released in December, 2007, uncovered serious security exposures. [322] Not only did EVEREST (Evaluation & Validation of Election-Related Equipment, Standards & Testing) confirm the findings of the Top-to-Bottom Review, but it uncovered still more vulnerabilities.

As a result of the study, Brunner issued her findings, in which she stated that "Ohio's electronic voting systems have 'critical security failures' which could impact the integrity of elections. . . . To put it in everyday terms, the tools needed to compromise an accurate vote count could be as simple as tampering with the paper audit trail connector or using a magnet and a personal digital assistant." After observing that the results underscored the need for fundamental change, Brunner recommended that all voting systems, including all DREs, should be replaced by optical scan systems, with Automark machines provided for voters with disabilities. [124]

7.6 Linda Lamone and Maryland

Some members of both major parties have devoted themselves to making our elections more secure, reliable, and transparent, while others have refused to acknowledge systemic risks, even when they are spelled out for them. Maryland is an interesting example.

7.6.1 Lamone and Computer Scientists

The Maryland story did not end in 2003 with the statewide purchase of Diebold AccuVote TS paperless DREs. After the publication of the Hopkins-Rice Report, Linda Lamone became extremely vocal in her defense of paperless DREs and condemnation of computer security experts. A November 2003 article quoted Lamone as saying "I think they [Aviel Rubin and other computer scientists] are doing a great disservice to democracy, frankly." [237] Like Diebold, she complained that those raising security issues about voting machines were undermining voter trust in the system.

Lamone's concerns about the writings and statements of computer scientists were not limited to press interviews. On July 18, 2004 Douglas Jones posted on his University of Iowa website a response to a document defending paperless DREs produced by the Maryland State Board of Elections. [524,638] Lamone reacted by attempting to censor Jones' webpage. On August 10 Jones received a note saying that Lamone had written to the President of the University of Iowa requesting that Jones' document be removed from the website so that her office could be "provided the opportunity to correct several incorrect and misleading statements contained in Dr. Jones' response." Jones never saw the Lamone letter—only the official university response denying her request.

Rather than confront Diebold about the major security problems uncovered by computer security experts, Lamone seems to have focused on justifying the millions of dollars spent on the purchase of Diebold machines. She attempted to discredit computer scientists, especially Maryland resident Aviel Rubin, and she suppressed or misrepresented negative analyses to make them seem positive, as she had done previously with the SAIC report.

7.6.2 Maryland Politics

Despite Lamone's efforts to minimize DRE security concerns, a number of voters demanded and were given provisional paper ballots in the March 2004 primary as an alternative to voting on paperless Diebold DREs. About 100 of these voters were angry to learn after the primary that their votes were not going to be counted. [214] One of the disenfranchised voters, 76-year-old Helen K. Kolbe of Howard County, organized a group of twenty other Howard county residents to argue before the State Board of Elections that their votes should be counted. Kolbe was quoted as saying "I did not vote with the intention of not voting." [819] Nonetheless, all of the paper ballots were discarded. Hearings officer Nicole Trella said that since the attempt to vote on paper ballots was merely a protest against the electronic machines, the complainant must bear the consequences. [560]

In April 2004 voting activists sued Maryland to decertify the paperless DREs as illegal under Maryland law that required the ability to recount an election. [214] They also filed a motion for a preliminary injunction to try to get paper ballots for the 2004 General Election. The motion was dismissed in June, shortly before Maryland residents learned that they had recently voted on Diebold models that had not been federally certified. [898] The dismissal was appealed, but in September Circuit Court Judge Joseph P. Manck ruled against the plaintiffs, saying that concerns that electronic machines might be vulnerable to tampering were "a very real fear," but that Maryland officials had "taken all reasonable steps to protect the integrity of the voting process." [847] The case to decertify paperless DREs is still pending, but it might be rendered moot by later developments.

In light of the favorable court ruling, many people were surprised to learn in early September 2004 that Lamone had been placed on paid leave and that the state board was considering removing her for "incompetence, misconduct or other good cause." [366] Democrats claimed that the effort to remove Lamone was motivated by Republican Governor Robert L. Ehrlich Jr.'s wish to have a member of his own party in Lamone's position. A judge subsequently reinstated Lamone, and her support for Diebold and paperless DREs continued unabated.

In March 2005 TrueVoteMD, a group of voting activists, announced that according to Montgomery County sources there had been a "lock-

down" of all Diebold voting machines since the November presidential
elections, including 12 machines in Montgomery County, because of
statewide machine failures. [66] In the same month Montgomery County
produced a report entitled *2004 Presidential General Election Review—
Lessons Learned.* [719] According to the report, "189 voting units (7%)
of units deployed failed on Election Day. An additional 122 voting units
(or 5%) were suspect based on number of votes captured."

Subsequent testing revealed that of 148 voting units examined, 35
failed. Internal Diebold emails dating from 2002 and memos dated December 3, 2002 (see Figure 38) and March 28, 2004 reveal that Diebold
knew that a defective motherboard in the DREs used in Maryland
and Georgia could cause the screen freezes observed in Montgomery
County. [458] Yet, the defective motherboards were not replaced until
2005, after the 2004 Presidential election, in what Maryland officials
referred to as a "technology refresh." [78]

Despite ongoing problems with Diebold machines in Maryland and
issues about Diebold machines being raised in California, in late August
2005 the Maryland Board of Public Works announced that the state
would spend $7.9 million to purchase Diebold machines for Baltimore,
$2.3 million for machines for Prince George's, Montgomery, and Bal-
timore counties, and $6.1 million for a maintenance and management
services contract. [65]

After having defended paperless DREs for a couple of years, in February 2006 Governor Ehrlich released a letter in which he said that he
no longer had "confidence in the State Board of Elections' ability to
conduct fair and accurate elections in 2006." [291] He went on to call for
a voter verified paper trail and lambasted the State Board of Elections
for major cost overruns. Both Lamone and Diebold responded. Lamone protested that the state had spent a significant amount of money
on the system and change would be "a catastrophe." [634] Mark Radke,
director of Diebold's election systems, claimed that the Diebold system
in Maryland was the most accurate in the country and that the state
was making decisions based on false information.

A few days after Ehrlich's letter, the Washington Post observed in
an editorial that some Democratic leaders who earlier had been calling
for a paper trail had started belittling the problem of paperless voting
machines. [996] Efforts to legislate an end to Maryland's paperless DREs
continued, as did Lamone's opposition to any kind of paper trail. Lamone was quoted as saying at a Maryland state hearing, "Simply adding
paper [to a voting system] does not make it secure." [122] The same

From: GEORGIA
To
DIEBOLD RE Problems
WITH VOTING UNITS

12/3/02

ATTACHMENT___

Punch List

	Issue/Item	Source	Solution Desired by State	Supporting Document
1	Voting System shall be certified pursuant to national and state standards	RFP S 2.4.1	Confirmation that statewide uniform voting system is appropriately certified	
2	TS unit screen "freeze"	RFP S 2.5.3; Proposal V. p.12 – State & County experience	Confirmation via verifiable testing data that screen freeze problem is corrected and repair does not generate additional problems.	
3	Inoperable "Charging" function on TS units	RFP S 2.5.3; Proposal V. p.12 – State Notified Diebold of Problem following Installation of patch on VEC demo unit	Charging function repaired with confirmation via verifiable testing data that screen freeze problem is corrected and repair does not generate additional problems.	
4	TS unit Error message "Memory Critically Low" or similar message	RFP S 2.5.3; Proposal V. p.12 – State experienced on General Election Day – No prior notice of problem provided by Diebold	Memory problem corrected with confirmation via verifiable testing data that screen freeze problem is corrected and repair does not generate additional problems.	

FIGURE 38 A memo from Georgia mentioning the screen freeze problem, December 2002

article quoted Prof. Michael Shamos, one of the few computer scientists who has defended paperless DREs, as supporting Lamone:

> "I think that the old adage, 'If it ain't broke, don't fix it,' applies here," said Shamos who has analyzed voting systems since 1980. "There is nothing demonstrably wrong with the Maryland voting system."

In spite of Lamone's opposition, on May 17, 2007 Maryland Governor Martin O'Malley (D) signed the Voter-Verifiable Paper Records bill, SB 392. The bill called for Maryland's paperless DREs to be replaced before the 2010 elections. The legislation was conditional on the provision of funding to replace the DREs.

Lamone's enthusiasm for Diebold reached a new high when she allowed the company to include her endorsement of Diebold's electronic poll book, a device used for statewide databases of registered voters, in their sales brochure. [1033] The brochure contained a color photo of Lamone sitting at a desk with the Maryland state flag in the background, and included her quote: "Our election judges just love this product, and so do I. We in Maryland are extremely pleased with the performance of the system during the general election." Lamone, who said she was not compensated by Diebold, defended her endorsement, saying that she had made similar statements in testimony and news releases. [838]

Her testimonial, however, seemed inappropriate, especially since there had been serious problems with the Diebold poll books in Maryland's September 2006 primaries (see Chapter 10). Governor O'Malley, state legislators, and others supported calls from voting rights advocates to have the endorsement reviewed by the state ethics commission. In response to a request from the Governor, two days after the story broke Lamone sent a letter to Diebold requesting that the sales brochure be withdrawn. [580] A day later Diebold agreed to the withdrawal.

In January 2008 Governor O'Malley announced that he was including funding for replacement optical scan voting systems in his budget proposal. An optical scan system was selected and approved by the State Board of Elections (SBE) in December 2009. However, in January 2010 O'Malley did not include funding to purchase the new voting system, based on cost projections prepared by the SBE showing that transitioning to op-scan would cost $13 million more than continuing to use the existing touch-screen voting equipment during the 2010 elections. [878]

SAVE our Votes, a Maryland election integrity organization, prepared a detailed analysis showing that SBE had inflated some costs of op-scan, while greatly understating the costs of operating the DREs.[878] Indeed, after it was too late to purchase the new op-scan system, the

SBE requested nearly $10 million in additional funds to operate the existing touch-screen system during the 2010 elections.[794] A subsequent cost study mandated by the General Assembly and conducted by RTI International showed that Maryland would save money by switching to optical scan.[857]

7.7 What Can We Learn from Diebold?

The demise of Diebold Election Systems was probably due at least in part to the large amount of unfavorable press that Diebold received. The Diebold story illustrates the importance of having the press actively monitoring all aspects of elections, including voting system testing, security, reliability, and accuracy; voting system vendors; and election officials.

As was mentioned at the beginning of this chapter, many of the Diebold problems that were publicly exposed, such as the serious security vulnerabilities, also exist in other vendors' systems. The red teams working for California's Top-to-Bottom Review were able to break into all of the systems they tested, not just the Diebold system.

One of the key distinguishing features of the Diebold story is that Diebold software was downloaded by Bev Harris back in 2003. Years before independent computer scientists analyzed and tested voting system software for California's Top-to-Botttom Review and Ohio's EVEREST Study, computer scientists could examine Diebold software. We can only conjecture as to what might have happened if ES&S, Sequoia, and Hart Intercivic software had also been made available for examination by independent computer security experts. It is little wonder that DRE vendors have insisted that their software is proprietary, and strenuously resisted independent inspection of their software and voting systems by computer security experts.

8

The California Soap Opera

I was shocked. Everyone seemed to be in bed with everyone else. You had these so-called independent testing authorities floating out there in an undefined pseudo-public, pseudo-private status whose source of income is the vendors themselves.

Former California Secretary of State Kevin Shelley (D)
May 30, 2004 [9]

Congress enacted the Help America Vote Act, which pushed many counties into buying electronic systems that—as we've seen for some time and we saw again in the independent UC [Univ. of California] review—were not properly reviewed or tested to ensure that they protected the integrity of the vote.

California Secretary of State Debra Bowen (D)
August 4, 2007 [105]

Computerized voting equipment is inherently subject to programming error, equipment malfunction, and malicious tampering. [274] So begins the Resolution on Electronic Voting, posted in early 2003 by Stanford computer science professor David Dill, and eventually signed by over 2000 technologists, including many prominent representatives of academia and industry. The petition marked the beginning of what has become widespread resistance to insecure computerized voting systems by computer scientists.* The birthplace of the resistance was Silicon Valley, the center of many computer-related industries.

Shortly after posting the petition, Dill learned that Santa Clara County (the heart of Silicon Valley) was planning to purchase paperless DRE voting machines. Shocked that such insecure devices were being considered, several computer scientists tried to convince the Santa

---

*While a number of computer scientists, such as Peter Neumann and Rebecca Mercuri, had been warning of the risks of paperless voting systems for several years, the involvement of large numbers of computer scientists started with the petition.

Clara County Supervisors not to purchase the machines. Instead of meeting with the critics to try to understand their concerns, the response of Santa Clara County registrar of voters Jesse Durazo was hostile: "These scientific smart people have not worked in an election, but they've created this whole UFO effect." [387]

The computer scientists' effort was an exercise in frustration. At public Board of Supervisors meetings, when vendor marketing representatives typically were allocated a significant amount of time to make presentations, prominent computer scientists would be given only a couple of minutes each. In spite of the petition, letters to the editor, articles and editorials in the San Jose Mercury News, meetings, phone calls, and even national press attention,* the Supervisors voted 3–2 in February 2003 to purchase Sequoia paperless DRE machines. However, because of political pressure and uncertainties as to the outcome of a recently created state task force, the Supervisors insisted that Sequoia agree to cover the cost of "whatever equipment, process and use requirements that the State may establish for a voter-verified paper ballot audit trail." [663] The Associated Press erroneously reported that Santa Clara was "the first county in the nation to purchase the so-called voter-verified paper backup system." [62] While the AP misunderstood the outcome of the meeting, the county subsequently was saved the cost of retrofitting or replacing the paperless DREs.

As a result of the Santa Clara controversy, California became a key state in the battle for secure voting machines. When former Secretary of State Kevin Shelley challenged voting machine vendors over the security and accuracy of their machines, several election officials who had already purchased paperless DRE systems sued him. When current Secretary of State Bowen instituted strong reforms, they sued her as well. Throw in Election Day meltdowns, legislation, lawsuits, and conflicts of interest, and we have the lively story of California's voting machine struggles.

8.1   Some Early Events

In 1965 California passed the first election laws requiring a manual post-election ballot audit of 1% of all precincts, randomly selected. [134,25] As a result, California became the first of what is now a small number of states to conduct routine post-election audits, although there is pressure nationally and in other states to make post-election ballot audits mandatory.

---

*Andy Bowers of National Public Radio attended the final Supervisors' meeting and reported on the outcome.

8.1.1 An Early ACLU Court Case

In response to the problems in the 2000 presidential election, the ACLU of Southern California, together with the AFL-CIO, Common Cause, the Southern Christian Leadership Conference, and the Chicano Federation of San Diego County, filed a lawsuit in April 2001 calling for the elimination of punch card voting systems in California (*Common Cause v. Jones*). Dan Tokaji, then staff attorney at the ACLU of Southern California, observed that punch card systems in California had a disproportionately high uncounted vote rate and that minorities were more likely to reside in counties using such systems. [962] He warned, "unless the state takes action, California could become the next Florida." [11]

In April 2001 U.S. District Judge Stephen V. Wilson denied the state's motion to throw out the ACLU lawsuit, and in September 2001 California Secretary of State Bill Jones (R) decertified punch card machines, effective July 2005. Not satisfied with Jones' 2005 deadline, the ACLU and its associates, including the Southwest Voter Registration and Education Project, returned to court in an effort to require that the decertification take effect before the 2004 presidential elections. On February 13 Wilson ruled in favor of the ACLU. [1002] A pleased Tokaji said that Californians would be able to "go to the polls in 2004 with confidence that their votes will actually be counted." [704]

8.1.2 Proposition 41

Following the court decision, Californians passed Proposition 41, the "Voting Modernization Bond Act," in March 2002. [826] Prop. 41, authored by then Majority Leader Kevin Shelley (D) and Speaker Robert Hertzberg (D), provided $200 million to modernize voting systems. It also stated, "Any voting system purchased using bond funds that does not require a voter to directly mark on the ballot must produce, at the time the voter votes his or her ballot or at the time the polls are closed, a paper version or representation of the voter ballot or of all the ballots cast on a unit of the voting system."

Unfortunately, the inclusion of "or at the time the polls are closed" in the text allowed election officials to justify using DRE ballot images printed at the end of Election Day for the 1% manual audit. Since it is impossible for voters to verify printouts that they never see, Prop. 41 seriously undermined the value of the post-election audit. Shelley has since acknowledged that he did not have major concerns about electronic voting at the time. "It wasn't until after I took office [as Secretary of State] in 2003 that I became aware of the risks of electronic voting as a result of my first meeting with David Dill." [908]

8.2 Shelley Battles Vendors & Election Officials

8.2.1 The Ad Hoc Touch Screen Task Force

On February 6, 2003 Shelley met with Dill to discuss paperless voting machines. Shelley reflected that "upon first hearing David Dill's concerns, I thought he was 'way out there.' I soon came to realize just how on the money he was." [908] The next day Shelley announced that he was forming a task force to study voting machine issues. The San Jose Mercury News quoted Shelley as saying, "We need to get these scientists together because they're scaring the crap out of Santa Clara County, and the board of supervisors is saying, 'We don't know what to do.' We have a political problem as well as a technology problem that's going to happen in county after county, and we need to address it right now." [206]

The Ad Hoc Touch Screen Task Force created by Shelley and chaired by Undersecretary of State Mark Kyle included computer scientists, local election officials, and a disability rights advocate.* The diversity reflected Shelley's wish to have a wide range of interests represented. Shelley required the task force to hold public hearings around the state and he attended two out of the four hearings.

The task force released its report in July 2003. [578] Dill complained that two of the three Independent Testing Authorities (ITA) failed to answer even the simplest questions. He also said that while the voting machine vendors were more cooperative, they refused to provide information that would allow the panel to evaluate the security of the machines. [272] Consequently, the report advocated periodic reviews of voting systems, federal testing that is open to citizen observation, and substantial improvements in federal testing to enhance voting equipment security. The report also recommended that the state obtain copies of all material that the vendors provide to federal testers, including source code and documentation, and that the blanket exemption from inspection or testing of Commercial Off-the-Shelf software for systems without voter verification be eliminated. They further suggested creating a national database for documenting election system

---

*The task force members were Mark Kyle, Undersecretary of State (Chair), Marc Carrel, Assistant Secretary of State for Policy & Planning (Co-Chair), Kim Alexander, Founder and President of the California Voter Foundation, David Dill, Professor of Computer Science, Stanford University, David Jefferson, Computer Scientist, Lawrence Livermore National Laboratory, Robert Naegele, President, Granite Creek Technology, Inc., Shawn Casey O'Brien, former Executive Director, Unique People's Voting Project, Mischelle Townsend, Registrar of Voters, Riverside County, Charlie Wallis, Department IT Coordinator, San Diego County Registrar's Office, and Jim Wisley, Office of Assembly Speaker Herb Wesson.

problems, as well as a state Technical Oversight Committee of technical experts. Many of the Task Force's common-sense recommendations have also been proposed at the federal level, where they have met with significant opposition.

While there was no consensus about the need for a Voter-Verified Paper Audit Trail (VVPAT), a minority of the task force called for a state ban on future purchases of paperless DREs. If an immediate ban were not an option, they wanted a VVPAT requirement by January 2007, with a possible extension for DREs currently in use until 2010. Ultimately Shelley, disagreeing with his own staff, acknowledged the minority's security concerns. "I read every word of the report and every piece of written testimony that was submitted at each hearing, and deliberated considerably prior to coming to my final recommendations. The evidence that there were major security concerns was so overwhelming for me at least that I deemed it time to act—and act soon." [908]

8.2.2 Certification

Because of "disconcerting information" that Diebold may have installed uncertified software on its Alameda County machines, on November 3, 2003 Assistant Secretary of State Marc Carrel announced that Shelley had halted the state certification process for new voting machines manufactured by Diebold. [1027] Nine days later Shelley ordered an audit of all California voting systems to check for uncertified software. [367] By this time, it was known that Diebold had installed uncertified software in the machines Alameda County had used in the October 7, 2003 gubernatorial recall and November 4, 2003 elections.

State law requires that the Secretary of State certify all voting machine software, including changes and last minute patches. Yet, around the time that uncertified Diebold software was becoming an issue, the Los Angeles Times quoted Conny McCormack (D), Registrar of Voters of Los Angeles County, as saying: "All of us have made changes to our software—even major changes—and none of us have gone back to the Secretary of State. But it was no secret we've been doing this all along." [459] Her comment made clear that election procedures, as carried out in practice, often did not follow state law. Shelley has since said, "I was deeply troubled to learn that Ms. McCormack was correct and that the Secretary of State's office historically had not always enforced the various certification laws. There was too much of a 'go along to get along' practice by the Secretary of State's office as it applied to the local election officials." [908]

The audit determined that all 17 California counties using Diebold software were deploying software or firmware versions that had not been certified by the Secretary of State.* Shelley observed, "Rarely do you find anyone batting zero, but Diebold indeed had achieved that dubious distinction." [908] Three of the counties were also running versions that had not yet been certified at the federal level. [1028]

8.2.3 Paper

On November 21, 2003, Shelley announced that as of July 2005 no California county would be allowed to purchase a DRE that did not produce an accessible voter-verified paper audit trail, and that by July 2006 all voting machines used in California must provide an accessible voter-verified paper audit trail. [905]

The California Association of Clerks and Election Officials responded with a press release saying, "Despite opposition by the California Association of Clerks and Election Officials, the League of Women Voters, numerous disability Rights organizations and other organizations, Shelley has not consulted with county election officials about the merits or demerits of a paper trail, but is instead responding to a select few academicians with no election experience." The statement also denounced Shelley's decisions as "a major defeat for the disabled community, as well as the minority language communities" and referred to the "theoretical and hypothetical doomsday scenarios posited by scientists, commentators and others with no elections administration experience." [136]

Shelley told us that he "found the clerk and election officials comments disingenuous, since I had indeed created a task force that included local election officials and I reviewed their recommendations. While the clerks may deem that I didn't 'consult' with them, the fact is that I did consult; I just didn't agree. That was what they found unforgivable." [908]

Partially in response to the recently released RABA report (see Chapter 7), on February 6, 2004 Shelley ordered counties to implement additional security measures. He also ordered Diebold to provide his office with its source code, so that the code could be reviewed by independent experts.[†] A few days later, registrars from ten counties that used paperless DREs claimed in a strongly worded letter that Shelley did not have the authority to issue the security directives.[‡]

---

*The latest version of Diebold's GEMS software certified in California was 117.17; the audit found that the versions in use in the state were 117.20, 117.22, 117.23, 118.18, and 118.18.02.

[†]This order was not implemented until the 2007 Top-to-Bottom Review ordered by Secretary of State Bowen.

[‡]The counties were Kern, Los Angeles, Napa, Plumas, Riverside, San Diego, San Joaquin, San Bernardino, Santa Clara, and Shasta.

When a legal effort to prohibit the use of paperless voting machines in an upcoming California election was thrown out by the courts, some DRE opponents urged voters to use absentee paper ballots. In response, Riverside County Registrar of Voters Mischelle Townsend (R), whose county was the first in California to purchase DREs, together with San Bernardino County Registrar of Voters Scott Konopasek, published an opinion piece in the Press Enterprise.[964] They complained that "These recommendations cross the line of civil discourse and pose a real threat to the democratic process they purport to defend ... To actively attempt to discredit, in the minds of voters, the certified, reliable and time-tested voting technology on the eve of an election for the purposes of promoting personal agendas is dangerous, dishonest and destructive. To accuse or imply that local elections officials lack a concern for the security and integrity of our elections is untrue and libelous."

8.2.4 The March 2004 Primary: Diebold Malfunctions

The March 2004 primary, which took place just three days after the publication of the Townsend/Konopasek article, had significant problems.

The opening of the polls in San Diego and Alameda counties was delayed as much as several hours because of Diebold machine problems. It turned out that Diebold had deployed a device for encoding voter-access cards that had not been adequately tested. According to an article by reporter Ian Hoffman:

> At 1:45 p.m. Tuesday, technicians and poll workers had restarted electronic voting at most of 200 affected precincts in Alameda County. News reporters were clamoring for an explanation of the breakdowns. A Diebold public relations officer approached Brad Clark, the county's registrar of voters, and suggested he put off attributing the problems to her company's encoders. Clark nodded his agreement that the full magnitude of the encoder problem wasn't absolutely clear. "Is there any other way in which I can support you today?" Diebold's Ann Sinclair asked. As Sinclair walked away, a reporter asked whether she was with Diebold. "No," she said. "I'm just here to help Brad out." She begged off further conversation, saying she had a cold. It's not clear to e-voting skeptics what exactly Sinclair and other Diebold PR staff in California are helping—the integrity of elections or Diebold's bottom line.[461]

Prior to the March primary, Diebold had sought to have a piece of equipment certified in time for the primary. Shelley agreed, but only on condition that Diebold receive federal certification of the same equipment. As a precaution, Shelley called the ITA that was reviewing Diebold equipment to determine if the certification would be completed in time. "I was told by the ITA representative that they could not give me that information, because it was proprietary, given their contractual relationship with the vendor, Diebold. This is when I realized that our so-called independent testing authorities were really no more than tools of the vendors themselves." [908]

Shelley learned after the March primary that Diebold had defied his mandate and instead had asked the ITA to certify an entirely different piece of equipment. Shelley felt that Diebold had engaged in "duplicitous and deceitful conduct." [908] As a result, a conference call was set up between senior staff members of Shelley's office and senior officials at Diebold. [909] Shelley described the meeting: "I sat in the room unbeknownst to Diebold listening to the back and forth between my staff and Diebold. At some point I was so appalled at the capricious arrogance displayed by the Diebold officials towards my staff—literally making light of the fact that they had lied to us—that I made my presence known." [908]

Chief Counsel to the Secretary of State Randy Riddle, who was present for the call, observed that "Kevin made clear that . . . if it were up to him, the company would not be doing election business in California. My own personal opinion is that the company made a lot of promises . . . in order to sell its equipment, and when it turned out that it did not have the ability to keep those promises, it then felt compelled to be less than forthright about that fact so that it would not lose business in the biggest market in the country." [849]

In April 2004 San Diego County announced that Diebold machines miscounted 2,821 absentee ballots in the Democratic presidential and Republican Senate primaries. [718] Most of the miscounts occurred in the Democratic primary and resulted in Kerry votes being incorrectly awarded to Gephardt. Because the absentee ballots were paper, the problem was uncovered in the audit and was fixed by a recount. The county claimed that the large number of ballots and candidates overwhelmed the tabulation system, and demanded that Diebold fix the problems before the November election. [718]

There was no independent investigation of the problem in San Diego County, nor any clarification as to why the tabulation systems should have been overwhelmed. A more likely explanation is that a software bug or mislabeling caused a machine to incorrectly credit Kerry votes to Gephardt. Had the same problem happened with a paperless voting system, it is highly improbable that the mistake would have been corrected.

Also in April the Oakland Tribune revealed that memos from Diebold's law firm, Jones Day, had warned Diebold that the use of uncertified software in the March primary would be a violation of California's election law.[460] The memos suggested that Diebold refer to new uncertified voting software as "experimental." The Tribune also charged that state officials were being presented with "sweeping" confidentiality agreements "designed to hide flaws in Diebold software as much as its intellectual property."

A few days later Jones Day, claiming that the leaked memos were protected by client-attorney privilege, sued the Oakland Tribune.[799] Jones Day eventually dropped the lawsuit, and the Tribune brought an anti-SLAPP (Strategic Lawsuit Against Public Participation) suit against Jones Day to recover legal fees. However, after several court proceedings, the Tribune dropped its lawsuit.[545]

8.2.5 The March 2004 Primary: Controversy in Riverside

Linda Soubirous, who ran in the March 2004 Republican primary for a seat on the Riverside County Board of Supervisors and who missed forcing a November runoff by 45 votes, demanded that Registrar of Voters Townsend conduct a recount. Her demand was triggered in part by the halting of election night updates for more than an hour, during which time Art Cassel, a Soubirous supporter, observed two Sequoia employees typing on a computer terminal linked to the ballot tabulation software for the county's Sequoia machines. Sequoia claimed that the employees were providing "legally authorized technical support."[692] When the updates resumed, Soubirous opponent's lead had increased from about 47% of the vote to above the 50% threshold needed to avoid a runoff.[569]

Townsend was put on the defensive at the end of March when Cassel filed a complaint claiming that she had illegally received travel and lodgings worth $1080 from Sequoia Voting Systems, the company running the Riverside elections, in violation of the county's $340 gift limit.[693] The complaint also accused Townsend of failing to file conflict-of-interest forms for 1998, 1999, 2001, and 2002.[209] Townsend responded that the complaint was political and that Cassel was associated with Soubirous.[209] The Los Angeles Times subsequently revealed that O'Reilly Public Relations, a company retained by Sequoia, was supporting Townsend in letters sent to reporters.[694]

In April the Riverside recount was completed. The manual recount of the absentee voters' paper ballots increased the final vote count for all the candidates and narrowed the number required for Soubirous to qualify for a run-off election to 35 votes.[210] Because the DRE voting machines were paperless, the recount of the DRE results simply compared the vote totals from the ballot cartridges of each DRE to the result stored on the centralized tabulating system. Referring to the electronic recount, Gregory Luke, Soubirous' attorney, said, "We were subjected to a reprint, not a recount." He called it "an empty formality suitable only for banana republics or dictatorships." [414]

Soubirous, together with VerifiedVoting.org and three Riverside County voters, filed a lawsuit against Townsend and Riverside County. The suit requested materials pertaining to the recount, all of which Townsend had refused to provide. [932] In September 2004 California Superior Court Judge James S. Hawkins ruled in favor of Riverside County, saying that they did not have to provide the material requested in the lawsuit. [571] Soubirous appealed, but on February 8, 2006 the state appellate court affirmed the lower court's ruling, saying that Soubirous had not proven that having access to the records would change the outcome of the election, and in any case it was too late for another recount. [233]

8.2.6   Shelley's Decertification Orders

In early April 2004 an analysis of the problems of the March primaries was completed by the Voting Systems and Procedures Panel (VSPP). The VSPP, like the Ad Hoc Touch Screen Task Force, was chaired by Undersecretary of State Mark Kyle and reported to Shelley. On April 22 the VSPP made the startling recommendations that not only should the Secretary of State decertify the Diebold TSx DRE, but he also should consider bringing criminal and civil charges against Diebold for violating California election code. [139] Assistant Secretary of State Marc Carrel accused Diebold of "bait-and-switch" tactics, adding, "I keep hearing apologies. I keep hearing misleading statements. I feel like Bill Murray in Groundhog Day—it keeps repeating and repeating and repeating. I'm disgusted by the actions of this company." [1030] The VSPP subsequently recommended that the state's other DREs be allowed to be used, if voters were also provided with a paper ballot option.

A few days later Shelley adopted the VSPP recommendations by decertifying all DRE systems used in California and conditionally recertifying all except the Diebold TSx. [906] Shelley said that he "came real close" to decertifying all of the DRE systems outright, but instead decided to allow other companies' machines to be used in the November elections, so long as the counties provided a paper ballot alternative and satisfied a list of other conditions. [883] Shelley also publicly asked the Attorney General to pursue criminal and civil actions against Diebold. "They broke the law. Their conduct was absolutely reprehensible. Their conduct should never be tolerated from anyone doing business again with the state of California." [815] With prescience he added, "I suspect I will face criticisms from county election officials who have resisted my crackdown on electronic voting systems as well as by some activists who want to ban outright all the touch-screen systems." [921]

One of the most important components of Shelley's recertification order was the requirement that vendors must, upon demand of the Secretary of State, provide the following documentation: a) all source code that could be disclosed by the vendor (i.e. code written by the vendor, as opposed to COTS), b) all documents submitted during the federal qualification process, c) complete documentation of each hardware and software version used for any component of the voting system, and d) complete documentation regarding the development process. Shelley's order provided a legal foundation for similar demands made by Secretary of State Bowen a few years later.

The ban on Diebold TSx machines meant that about two million voters in San Diego, San Joaquin, Solano, and Kern Counties would be required to use paper ballots instead of Diebold DRE machines for the 2004 presidential election. As Shelley anticipated, election officials in counties that had purchased DRE systems objected strongly to his decision. Townsend accused Shelley of not listening "to the people who are conducting the elections and instead to people putting forth what-if scenarios that have never occurred." [814] She even claimed in a press release that Shelley's orders were a "disaster for California that will jeopardize the integrity of the November election." [850]

On May 6 the Riverside County Board of Supervisors joined the Benavidez case (*AAPD v Shelley*), a suit against Shelley that had been brought in March by eleven voters with disabilities, the American Association of People with Disabilities (AAPD), the California Council of the Blind, and the California Foundation for Independent Living Centers (see Chapter 9). The revised lawsuit sought a temporary restraining order against Shelley because of his decertification orders. The plaintiffs demanded touch screen voting machines, arguing that Shelley's decision "strips hundreds of thousands of people with disabilities of their constitutional and statutory voting rights." [850]

Riverside joined, according to Board of Supervisors Chair Roy Wilson, because of Shelley's "assault on the touch-screen voting system pioneered by Riverside County." [232] Kern, Plumas, and San Bernardino counties were later added to the lawsuit.

Other counties dealt with Shelley's decision in a different fashion. San Joaquin County got Diebold to pay for the cost of paper ballots, while Solano County cancelled its contract with Diebold (see below).

In June 2004, before the lawsuit against Shelley was decided, Townsend announced that she was retiring for family reasons, effective July 17.[542] In the same month Shelley released the first set of standards for an Accessible Voter-Verified Paper Audit Trail (AVVPAT).[1032] Previously, no standards existed for any kind of voter-verified paper system, accessible or otherwise.

On July 6, 2004 U.S. District Court Judge Florence-Marie Cooper not only denied the restraining order but also strongly defended Shelley's right to decertify DREs.[203] Part of her decision stated that "the Secretary [of State] is, therefore, not only authorized, but expressly directed to withdraw his approval of any voting system found to be defective or unacceptable." She also discounted the argument that eliminating DRE systems discriminates against the visually or manually impaired, saying that the evidence does not support that claim. The case was subsequently dropped.[985] Judge Cooper's decision is currently the controlling federal law and was later cited in a similar lawsuit against Secretary of State Bowen.

In September 2004 California joined a lawsuit against Diebold that had been filed the previous November by Bev Harris and Jim March. California Attorney General Bill Lockyer (D) claimed that Diebold had deceived California by making false claims about its products. Although Shelley had felt that Diebold had also engaged in criminal behavior, Lockyer decided not to pursue criminal charges.[816] In the same month, and in spite of opposition from many county registrars, bipartisan legislation that essentially codified Shelley's orders and mandated a voter-verified paper record for all voting machines by the 2006 primary was signed into law by Governor Schwarzenegger (R).

Around the end of a very eventful 2004, Diebold settled with the State of California for $2.6 million, with another $100,000 going to Alameda County.[103] Diebold also announced in January 2005 that its AccuVote TSx DRE would be produced with an optional voter-verified paper trail.[410]

8.2.7 Shelley Resigns

In early February 2005 Shelley announced his resignation, effective March 1.[839] He had been under attack for allegedly misspending federal election funds, and had become embroiled in a controversy over illegal contributions to his campaign by donor Julie Lee. Lee pleaded guilty to grand theft, embezzlement, and forgery in July 2008, but Shelley was never found personally responsible for any wrongdoing or misuse of federal funds.[888] In April 2005, Attorney General Lockyer exonerated Shelley in the Julie Lee case, saying that Shelley was "absolutely innocent of any personal involvement in the crimes that Julie Lee committed." [2] Shelley commented to us, "Clearly my aggressive stance on voting integrity issues fiercely alienated some influential people and interests who wanted me out. But I have no regrets for having stood proudly for some very fundamental principles of democracy: that every vote counts, and just as importantly, that each vote is counted just as it was intended when cast." [907]

Shelley was replaced by Bruce McPherson (R) in March. McPherson, who did not share Shelley's concerns about voter-verified paper trails, joined with the California Association of Clerks and Elections Officials in opposing VVPAT legislation proposed by then State Senator Debra Bowen (D). [463] Bowen's legislation also required that the VVPATs be used for the mandated 1% manual recount, and in the event of a total recount, the results from the paper records would be the official results. McPherson's opposition was largely in response to concerns of some disability rights advocates, who complained that blind voters could not see the VVPAT and therefore the VVPATs should not be the ballot of record. The fact that sighted voters could verify their ballots and hopefully detect software bugs or malicious code—which would benefit all voters—seemed of secondary importance. In spite of the opposition, Governor Schwarzenegger signed Bowen's legislation into law on October 7, 2005. [142]

8.3 California's Revolving Door

Some key California players were election officials who subsequently accepted positions with voting machine vendors. While the revolving door phenomenon is hardly unique to California, California provides a window into the practice.

8.3.1 Sequoia Hires and Lobbies

The most prominent California election official to take advantage of the revolving door was former Secretary of State Bill Jones (R). After having decertified punch card voting machines, Jones joined then Assembly Majority Leader Shelley, Common Cause, the California League of Women Voters, and other public interest organizations in lobbying for Prop. 41, the bond issue that provided $200 million for the purchase of new voting machines. [910] The pro-Prop. 41 campaign also received substantial vendor contributions, including $100,000 from Sequoia and $50,000 from ES&S. [840]

Shortly after Jones' term as Secretary of State ended in early January 2003, he sent letters to the members of the Santa Clara County Board of Supervisors in which he said, "The touch-screen system Santa

Clara is considering purchasing has been successfully used in Riverside County since 1999." [8] A month later Jones became a paid consultant for Sequoia, the company that produced Riverside County's machines. According to the San Jose Mercury News, Jones, who claimed that his compensation was not linked to sales, received $10,000 a month from March to August 2003. [8] The paper quoted Jones: "I talked to people who called me. I was not interested in selling." However, an article in the Los Angeles Times stated that Jones lobbied San Bernardino County supervisors before they gave final approval to the purchase of Sequoia machines. [840]

Jones was preceded at Sequoia in 2002 by his former Assistant Secretary of State Alfie Charles (R). After taking his new job, Charles also lobbied Santa Clara County to buy Sequoia machines. [840] Earlier in 2002 Sequoia had hired another California election official, Santa Clara County's Registrar Kathryn Ferguson, as Vice President of Governmental Relations and Public Affairs. [893] Ferguson did not stay long, moving in 2003 to the job of Voter Registration/Election Management Product Manager at Hart Intercivic. [441]

8.3.2 Dedier's Controversial Move to ES&S

The rush to hire California election officials was not limited to Sequoia and Hart Intercivic. On October 15, 2002, shortly after Charles went to Sequoia but before Jones followed him there, ES&S announced that Lou Dedier, California's Deputy Secretary of State, had been named an ES&S vice president and general manager of California operations. [308] The part of the press release that drew the most attention was this quote from Dedier: "I've evaluated several election management vendors over the years, and ES&S clearly has by far the best election systems and support."

Because of Dedier's previous role with California's certification of voting systems, his new position at ES&S generated considerable controversy. Jones, who publicly accused Dedier of undermining the creditability of the certification process, asked the state Fair Political Practices Commission to investigate. [840]

Highlighting Dedier's comment about evaluating election management vendors, Avante International, Hart Intercivic, and Diebold expressed concerned that Dedier would make unfair use of his knowledge of their voting systems. Dedier responded that he was "shocked at the idea of anything being said of inappropriate behavior." Dedier claimed that the press release quote was just for PR, and he had handled only public documents. [344] However, Dedier also had had access to confidential ITA reports.

Shortly before taking his new job, Dedier had recommended deferral of statewide certification for Avante International. Although he also recommended conditionally certifying Avante for a pilot election in Sacramento, Avante complained that Dedier's pending job move had created a significant conflict-of-interest in his evaluation of their voting system. [840]

8.3.3 Seiler's Impressive Career

Also protesting Dedier's move because of ethical and conflict of interest issues was Deborah Seiler, who at the time was head of West Coast sales for Diebold. [840,225] Seiler had been Assistant to the California Secretary of State for Elections and Political Reform, assistant Chief of Elections, a Commissioner on the California Fair Political Practices Commission, and chief consultant to the State Assembly Elections, Reapportionment and Constitutional Amendments Committee. [871] After serving in the Secretary of State's office, Seiler spent eight years at Sequoia as government relations director, before moving to Diebold.

Seiler's complaints about Dedier's ethics seem somewhat hypocritical, given that just two months earlier she had convinced Solano County to purchase almost 1200 Diebold TSx DRE voting systems that were not federally or state certified. [63,929] According to a local paper, Seiler had told Solano supervisors that the Diebold machines had already received certification, though she had been unable to produce documentation of certification. [1031]

Solano County eventually paid Diebold more than $400,000 for the privilege of canceling its $4.1 million contract in April 2004. Despite the loss, Solano County hired Seiler as Assistant Registrar of Voters in September 2004. In June 2007 Seiler moved again, this time to San Diego County as Registrar of Voters. [871] Seiler replaced Mischelle Townsend, who had been hired as interim registrar by San Diego County in April 2007. [187] Seiler also had sold San Diego its paperless Diebold TSx DREs at a cost of $31 million.

When Secretary of State Debra Bowen subsequently decertified and then conditionally recertified Diebold machines because of the multitude of vulnerabilities and flaws uncovered by the Top-To-Bottom Review (see Section 8.5), Seiler defended the machines, repeating many of the vendor arguments. After stating that election officials had long known about the machine vulnerabilities, Seiler claimed that it was nearly impossible for someone to tamper with the machines and not get caught, as if that were the only problem uncovered by the reviews. [417] Seiler also suggested that Bowen's decisions were politically motivated and claimed that the testing conditions were unrealistic. [185]

8.4   More Diebold Revelations

8.4.1   96 Diebold Machines

Because of paper jams in two out of three Diebold AccuView printers in earlier tests, on July 21, 2005 California conducted what may have been the first test of a DRE voting machine to simulate real Election Day conditions. In slightly over five hours about one hundred votes were cast according to a script on each of 96 Diebold TSx machines with AccuView printers, resulting in fourteen printer problems and twenty software crashes. In October 2005, California's Voting Systems Technology Assessment Advisory Board, which oversaw and analyzed the test results, issued a report. [91] The report estimated "the Mean Time Between Failures (MTBF) of these machines to be approximately 15 hours under the conditions experienced during volume testing." Since the observed failure rate was more than ten times higher than permitted by federal standards, the report opined that "the federal qualification process is apparently inadequate to ensure that voting machines will be reliable enough for use in elections."

A week after the tests, Secretary of State McPherson announced that he was turning down Diebold's certification application for the Diebold TSx. [23] Because the testers had not anticipated widespread software failures, initial reports mentioned a roughly 10% printer failure. In fact, much to the astonishment of the technical team, roughly 20% of the tested machines experienced a variety of software failures. The testers were concerned that the unexpectedly large number of detected software failures might be just the tip of the iceberg and that there could be a large number of undetected software defects. They urged the Secretary of State to demand access to the source code and binary executables for all electronic voting machines. They also suggested that California require vendors to provide the state with "a comprehensive itemized accounting of the cause of each software failure, complete with enough technical details that independent technical experts can confirm the vendor's account for each. Even with such an accounting, ... there is no way to know whether the defects have been fixed satisfactorily (as opposed to just hidden), or whether they represent symptoms of more serious architectural flaws, without access to the source." [91]

It was subsequently determined that when the voter's finger slid out of the button area in the final cast ballot action, system errors occurred that would require the voting machine to be restarted (rebooted). [360] The errors were insidious and difficult to find with conventional testing. Once the cause of the bug was determined, Diebold fixed the software.

A very worrisome implication of the sliding finger bug is that there is no way to know if selections made by voters who encountered the bug in previous elections—in any state in which the Diebold TSx was used—were properly recorded.

McPherson announced in August that voting machine vendors applying for certification in California would be required to state in writing that their machines meet all HAVA requirements and that they would cover any costs associated with modifications, upgrades, or improvements required to make machines HAVA compliant.[678] In October McPherson expanded his requirements by announcing that all voting machine vendors wishing to have their machines certified in California would be required to agree to volume testing that simulated Election Day use.[24]

As a result of McPherson's decision to deny certification, San Joaquin County, which had already purchased Diebold TSx machines, decided to use paper ballots, paid for by Diebold, in the November 2005 special election.[537]

8.4.2 A Second Diebold Study

Because of the issues raised by the first Hursti attack (see Chapter 7), McPherson commissioned the Voting Systems Technology Assessment Advisory Board to examine a portion of the Diebold source code for the Diebold AccuVote OS optical scanner and the Diebold AccuVote-TSx touch screen voting machine.*

Although the study examined only a small portion of the Diebold code, the researchers stated in their February 2006 report that there were some serious vulnerabilities with the code and architecture.[987] The authors felt, however, that the vulnerabilities were manageable in the short term, i.e. for the upcoming special election to replace Congressman Cunningham in early April. The report included some long-term recommendations such as changing the machine architecture so that no code is stored on removable memory cards. The authors observed that there still were known, and possibly unknown, vulnerabilities in portions of the code that they did not examine. Their work was made needlessly difficult because they did not have any manuals or other documentation (aside from comments included in the code), and they did not have access to an actual system. Moreover, they had less than a month to review the source code.

Since the study concluded that the detected flaws in Diebold software and architecture could be mitigated by a variety of short-term se-

---

*The study examined only the Accubasic interpreter and related code; the version numbers for the AccuVote OS and TSx respectively were 1.96.6 and 4.6.4.

curity measures, McPherson conditionally recertified the machines. [679]
He also asked Diebold to fix the security flaws uncovered by the report.
The researchers expected that the bugs would be fixed before the June
elections, and that they would be asked to verify those fixes. Neither
happened. While some of the bugs ultimately were fixed, others that
had been uncovered by the California study were still in software that
was examined for the State of Florida by Florida State University in
mid-2007. [365] Consequently, the entire 2006 election season was conducted with dangerous known bugs in place. The McPherson administration did not require that the bugs be fixed quickly, even in the face
of the far more consequential Hursti II evelations (see Chapter 7).

The two Diebold reports have several disturbing implications that
were obvious at the time and were reinforced by the very serious revelations from the ensuing "Top-To-Bottom Review" ordered by Secretary
of State Bowen.

1. It was clear that the ITA testing had been totally inadequate;
   there is circumstantial evidence that strongly suggests that the
   ITAs did not detect the vulnerabilities uncovered by the panel.
   For example, Ciber, one of the ITAs, had been retained by
   Diebold to conduct a security review. Ciber discovered hardly
   any of the security vulnerabilities uncovered by the study commissioned by McPherson. The Ciber executive summary said,
   "The TSx interpreter inspected appears to be ready for an election." [168]

2. At the time there was no way to know if more serious vulnerabilities existed in the code that was not examined, or if serious
   vulnerabilities in the examined code escaped detection by the
   panel. We have since learned that there were even more serious
   vulnerabilities in the unexamined code.

3. The panel made several recommendations for how counties might
   deal with the problems in the short run, but at the time the report
   was released, it was impossible to know if the counties would
   follow those recommendations or the extent, if any, to which the
   Secretary of State would exercise oversight of those counties.

4. Since most counties had already purchased equipment by the time
   the reports were released, there was a question as to whether the
   counties should use equipment they had already purchased that
   had known vulnerabilities. Localities throughout the country that
   had not yet purchased equipment should not have been buying
   machines until at a minimum the long-term corrections recommended in the report were implemented.

8.4.3   June 6, 2006: The Primary and Special Election

The June 6, 2006 California primary was the first statewide election in which all DRE systems were required to have VVPAT printers. Because some of the Diebold DRE voter access cards (cards used by voters in casting their ballots) provided to a number of Kern County polling places were not working, backlogs developed as soon as the polls opened. With Kern County officials urging voters not to go to the polls until after 10 am, backup paper ballots ran out, and at least one poll worker ended up photocopying blank ballots for use by voters. Some voters were encouraged to vote on the sample voter ballots from their voter pamphlets.[952] The situation could have been even worse had not the county Sheriff's department made emergency deliveries of working cards via helicopter. The chief elections official, Ann Barnett, later complained that Diebold had not informed county officials of the procedures needed to update the cards.[464]

8.5   The Top to Bottom Review

In November 2006 Debra Bowen (D) defeated McPherson in the race for Secretary of State. Bowen, who ran on a platform of reforming the voting system in California, had said she would conduct a Top-To-Bottom Review (TTBR) of voting systems used in California. On March 26, 2007, Bowen's office notified vendors of the upcoming TTBR and requested working models of the voting machines selected for testing, as well as copies of the software, hardware, and documentation. Bowen also contracted with the University of California to assemble red teams, source code review teams, a document review team, and an accessibility review team.

Bowen could require vendors to provide systems and documentation for testing at least in part because of agreements that former Secretary of State Shelley had demanded of vendors as a condition for re-certification. After some foot dragging, Diebold, Sequoia, and Hart Intercivic eventually complied with Bowen's request. ES&S, however, did not provide the material until June 26.

Since the California legislature had moved the primaries up to February 2008, any decertification orders had to be announced no later than August 3, 2007, six months prior to the next election. This deadline created enormous time pressure for all of the review teams and for Bowen's office. The reviewers felt that they did not have sufficient time for a thorough examination.[90]

8.5.1 TTBR Reports and Recertification Requirements

On July 27, Bowen started releasing the TTBR reports.[141] Negative results produced during such a very short period of time raised serious questions about the quality of the testing done by the ITA and about whether results of those tests were ever acted upon.

The reports produced by the red teams and source code teams were devastating. The red teams were able to break into every tested machine, and the source code teams found major security holes in all the machines. To avoid providing a road map for subverting elections, each machine report had both a public and a confidential portion. Nonetheless, all of the public source code reports, which at that time were the result of the most extensive and comprehensive review of voting systems ever conducted, revealed significant, widespread, and elementary vulnerabilities and failures. The other reports were also quite negative. The accessibility report concluded that "the three tested voting systems are all substantially noncompliant when assessed against the requirements of the HAVA"[863] (see Chapter 9). The documentation researchers, noting that the testing laboratories had not conducted a number of required system tests, also criticized documentation usability, which varied greatly among the vendors.

Election officials and vendors immediately attacked Bowen. Although all of the reports were negative, most of the attacks focused on the red team reports.

At a public hearing held by Bowen on July 30, 2007, John Tuteur, Napa County Registrar of Voters claimed: "There's never been any question about the accuracy or security of the touch screen results for the five statewide elections that we have conducted [using the machines]." He then denounced both the studies and Bowen, accusing her of wasting almost $1 million and of eroding the public's confidence in the election process for "crass political purposes."[968]

Despite this opposition, on August 3, 2007, Bowen made the dramatic announcement that she was decertifying all electronic voting systems tested in the TTBR, as well as the ES&S InkaVote system that was submitted too late for testing. She conditionally recertified all except the InkaVote.[141] Each recertification order contained a long list of detected problems and a still longer list of conditions, some quite arduous, that the tested vendors would have to satisfy to be recertified. Here is a small sample:

- Only one DRE machine could be used per polling location on Election Day or during early voting (Diebold and Sequoia); this restriction did not apply to the Hart Intercivic machines.

- If any voter with a disability voted on a DRE system, at least 4 other votes had to be cast on that machine to protect the voter's privacy.

- All votes cast on DREs had to be manually counted, using the voter-verified paper audit trails. If the difference between the two top candidates was less than 0.5%, then 10% of all precincts randomly selected were to be manually recounted. [106]

- Jurisdictions were required to reinstall all software and firmware on all machines.

- Any post-election auditing costs were to be paid for by the vendor.

In addition, Bowen required all the vendors to produce plans for "hardening" their equipment to protect against the security vulnerabilities detected by the TTBR. There were other general requirements, as well as specific requirements for individual vendors.

Because of the missed submission deadline, InkaVote, an optical scan paper-based system, was tested after the other systems. Security vulnerabilities were uncovered and the system was found to have "accessibility barriers for all categories of disabilities." Nonetheless, on January 2, 2008, the InkaVote system was conditionally recertified.

8.5.2 Vendors and Election Officials Respond

The decertification orders and recertification conditions shocked the voting establishment, and the attacks against Bowen continued. On August 6, 2007 a San Francisco radio station reported that Napa County Registrar Tuteur was planning to find a way to overturn Bowen's decision. [544] Other election officials jumped to the defense of the voting machines. San Bernardino County Registrar Kari Verjil was quoted as saying that, "Voting equipment is always secure." She also claimed that no one has the type of long-term access to the machines that the security-testing teams did. [966] Riverside County Supervisor Jeff Stone said, "I think it's a knee jerk reaction to a lab situation." He also asserted that electronic voting machines are safer from tampering than paper ballots.

Perhaps the most bizarre complaint came from Conny McCormack, Los Angeles County Registrar. Apparently more concerned about vendor profits than election security, she told the Board of Supervisors that because a recount could cost ES&S, manufacturer of the InkaVote, $400,000, "they [ES&S] wouldn't have any profit at all." [424] Los Angeles is the only place in California using InkaVote.

The vendors joined the chorus. It is difficult to imagine that automobile manufacturers would respond to negative crash test results by arguing that their cars would not crash because traffic lights, speed limits, and safe drivers or good road conditions would prevent such crashes. Yet that is precisely the kind of argument made by voting machine vendors.

Diebold stated, "Secretary Bowen's top-to-bottom review was designed to ignore security procedures and protocols that are used during every election. Her team of hackers was given unfettered access to the equipment, the source code, and all other information on security features provided by DESI to the Secretary of State's office. And she refused to include in the review the current version of DESI's touch screen software with enhanced security features.* Local election officials in California have put in place proper policies and procedures which complement the security features of DESI's voting solutions. We will continue to work with them to ensure that on Election Day every vote cast on DESI voting solutions is safe, secure and accurate." [269]

Sounding a similar theme, Sequoia complained that the TTBR was not conducted in "a true election environment" and that the security evaluation was "an unrealistic worst case scenario." Ignoring the many situations in which individuals have unsupervised access to voting machines, Sequoia added, "The methodology used implies that election authority 'insiders' have unlimited access to equipment, with no surveillance of their activities through automated methods. This is untrue." [894]

Hart Intercivic echoed the other vendors' complaints. "Putting isolated technology in the hands of computer experts in order to engage in unrestricted, calculated, advanced and malicious attacks is highly improbable in a real-world election ... Hart Intercivic's Voting Systems are secure, accurate, reliable and accessible for all voters." [442]

Matt Blaze, leader of the group that analyzed Sequoia's source code, addressed some of the negative comments made by election officials and vendors:

> We found significant, deeply-rooted security weaknesses in all three vendors' software ... It should now be clear that the red teams were successful not because they somehow "cheated," but rather because the built-in security mechanisms they were up against simply don't work properly. Reliably protecting these systems under operational conditions will likely be very hard. The problems we found in the code were far more pervasive, and much more easily exploitable, than I had

---

*The version referred to by Diebold had not been certified by California. As Diebold knew, the TTBR examined only California-certified systems, all of which had been used in previous elections and likely would have been used in upcoming elections, had the TTBR not occurred.

ever imagined they would be ... I was especially struck by the utter banality of most of the flaws we discovered. Exploitable vulnerabilities arose not so much from esoteric weaknesses that taxed our ingenuity, but rather from the garden-variety design and implementation blunders that plague any system not built with security as a central requirement. There was a pervasive lack of good security engineering across all three systems, and I'm at a loss to explain how any of them survived whatever process certified them as secure in the first place. Our hard work notwithstanding, unearthing exploitable deficiencies was surprisingly—and disturbingly—easy.

...

Unfortunately, while finding many of the vulnerabilities may have been straightforward enough, fixing them won't be ... [The voting systems] need to be re-engineered from the ground up. No code review can ever hope to identify every bug, and so we can never be sure that the last one has been fixed. A high assurance of security requires robust designs where we don't need to find every bug, where the security doesn't depend on the quixotic goal of creating perfect software everywhere.

In the short term, election administrators will likely be looking for ways to salvage their equipment with beefed up physical security and procedural controls. That's a natural response, but I wish I could be more optimistic about their chances for success. Without radical changes to the software and architecture, it's not clear that a practical strategy that provides acceptable security even exists. There's just not a lot to work with.

I don't envy the officials who need to run elections next year. [93]

8.5.3 Election Officials Sue Bowen

Following the pattern established with Secretary of State Shelley, in December 2007 the county of San Diego, led by Registrar of Voters Deborah Seiler, sued Secretary of State Bowen over the post-election manual audit requirements. [873] Riverside, Kern, and San Bernardino subsequently joined the lawsuit. On January 22, 2008 Judge Patricia Y. Cowett sided with Bowen, as a different judge had done three and a half years earlier with Shelley. [212] The ruling stated, "If the SOS discovers, as she has, serious security flaws in a voting machine, the SOS has an express obligation to remedy the situation."

However, on August 29, 2008 California's Fourth Appellate District Court ruled that Bowen had failed to follow public notice guidelines when she required a 10% manual audit for very close elections. The court rejected Bowen's claim that the audit requirement applied only to those voting systems that had been shown by the TTBR to be vulnerable. Consequently, in the 2008 presidential election California's manual audit reverted to the old 1% requirement.

8.6 Conclusion

There are many factors that have contributed to the tension between election officials and critics of the new voting systems. With the passage of HAVA, election officials had to make major purchases of complex technologies. They were dependent on vendor claims that the voting machines were reliable, accurate, and secure—claims that were supported by a governmental stamp of approval.

Unfortunately, that stamp of approval had little value. During the first few years after the passage of HAVA, national voting system standards were abysmally inadequate, as was the testing. It is hardly surprising that, after investing large sums of money in what they thought were state-of-the-art systems, election officials were resentful of criticisms of voting system testing and of the voting systems themselves. The last thing they wanted to hear was that their new systems might have security and accuracy problems.

Furthermore, the complexity of the new voting systems has made election officials dependent on vendors for maintenance and upgrades to their equipment. Compounding the dependence problem, election officials, having seen what happened to colleagues who stood up to vendors, are probably reluctant to place themselves in similar situations (see Chapter 7).

After investing millions of taxpayer dollars in computerized voting machines, many election officials resist acknowledging, possibly even to themselves, that the money might have been spent unwisely. Finally, most election officials, as well as declared winners, do not want the outcome of an election to be questioned by the public.

The combination of dependence, fear, and reluctance to admit the possibility of mistakes has generated opposition to reform and hostility towards computer scientists, election integrity advocates, and reforming secretaries of state.

We need to modernize the way we run elections by holding voting systems and election officials to high standards of accountability. Such accountability can be achieved only by mandating that all voting systems used for national, state, and local elections allow effective post-election ballot audits (see Chapter 13). These audits, and total recounts when necessary, must be required by law.

So long as voting systems are sold as indivisible units, with service available from just one vendor, counties will be locked in with their chosen vendor for the life of whatever voting system they buy. This is not a healthy situation; it puts the vendor in a position of power over the county. We therefore must find a way to ensure that voting machine maintenance and service contracts are competitive. As things currently stand, vendors can use the claim that all technical information about their machines is proprietary to prevent any competition in the maintenance and service arena.

Legislation and regulations will be of little use unless we also provide election officials with the financial and human resources required to run secure elections and to conduct post-election ballot audits.

9

Voters with Disabilities: Manipulating the Grass Roots

I am particularly offended by the reoccurring claim that people with disabilities are disenfranchised. This is highly inflammatory rhetoric, ignoring the definition of enfranchisement, which is a person's right to vote. When I turned 18, I became enfranchised. Not having the ability to vote without another human being's assistance is the reality that I deal with, but does not make me disenfranchised. . . . Other disability rights advocates claim that decertification [of DREs] would be a step back, treating people with disabilities as second class citizens. I argue that requiring California voters to use dangerously flawed DREs will be forcing second rate technology on us all.

Testimony of Natalie Wormeli, Submitted to a California Senate Committee, May 5, 2004 [1021]

This year, my total voting time was an hour and five minutes, which appears to be typical for audio voting on these machines with long California ballots. Thankfully, my wife was also voting at the same time and was able to assist the pollworkers and me, so I could vote 'independently'."

Noel Runyan, describing his voting experience in the 2010 midterm election—the 10th time he attempted to vote on a DRE

9.1 A Story

We start with two stories that illustrate some of the issues involving voters with disabilities. Our first story was provided by a blind voter, Noel Runyan. Runyan had attempted to vote on an "accessible" Sequoia DRE in March 2004, without success. Here, he describes his first marginally successful use of such a machine that November.

My own voting experience started at 7 in the morning. I had to keep my Braille reading fingers in my pocket to make sure they would be warm enough for reading my Braille notes. Even so, the polling place was so cold that my fingers were having a lot of trouble reading Braille near the end of my time at the voting machine. After signing in, and getting my voter smart card, I had to wait 8 minutes for them to reboot the audio voting machine. They had been using it for touch screen voting, as there was a very long line and just 5 voting machines for our combined 2-precinct site.

The volume control on the front of the key pad was not working well, and was resulting in scratchy and intermittent sound. By the time I got the volume set to where I could understand it, the introduction message had already finished the English instructions and was off into other languages. I was not sure what I should do, so I finally gave up and pressed the select button. This eventually got me to the language menu, where I was able to select English and get started with my ballot.

It took me 30 minutes to work my way through the ballot and make my selections. After that, I had quite a bit of trouble getting into the review mode, to get a full list of all my selections. When I did, it went on and on, for 23 minutes, like a long uncontrolled drink from a firehose. The review function read each item, and then, at the very end, said what my selection was for that item. It even threw in the details of what the fiscal impact would be, and took forever. This is completely backwards. When I did find that I had made a mistake in my selections, I had to wait until the end of the whole review process to correct it, instead of being able to stop, make the change, and then continue with the review where I left off.

I did not want to abort the ballot verification review to make a correction, and then have to start the 23 minute review all over again. When I later attempted to change one of my selections from "no" to "yes", the machine would not let me just select "yes", until I had first gone to the "no" entry and deselected it. This was very awkward and confusing.

At one point, as I was nearing the end of the ballot, I was dumped back into the language selection menu. I was being very careful to not push the "help" button, so I don't know why this language menu popped up. For a scary minute, I was afraid I had just lost my ballot and was having to start all over. I re-selected "English" and fortunately was returned to my previous location in the ballot.

An additional frustration was that the volume on some of the messages was so much lower than the rest of the messages that I had to fiddle with turning up the volume, repeating the message, and then turning the volume back down before proceeding.

From the time I signed in and got my voter smart card, it took 8 minutes to reboot the machine as an audio voting machine, 30 minutes to make my choices, 23 minutes to review and verify, and another 4 minutes to make a correction and record my vote. Not counting the hour waiting in line, it took me about 65 minutes to mark and record my ballot.

It would have taken even longer if I had been willing to wait, as prompted, until the end of each message to push the "select" button. The messages mislead some folks because they say something like, "...at the end of this message, you can press the ...". This implies that you are supposed to wait until the speech message finishes. [861]

As we quoted at the start of this chapter, Noel Runyan's more recent experience shows no significant improvement. It still takes him over an hour to cast a ballot on these machines.

9.2   A Second Story

VOTING IS OUR CIVIL RIGHT!!
VOTING IS OUR CIVIL RIGHT!!

Those words rang out from the back of a room where computer scientists, election integrity advocates, election officials, and vendor representatives were listening to a presentation at a July 2003 workshop. As all heads turned, the workshop attendees saw a group of people with disabilities led by Jim Dickson, vice-president of the American Association of People with Disabilities (AAPD).

The gathering was an informal workshop on Voter-Verifiable Election Technology, organized on short notice and attended by both authors. [976] An announcement encouraging people to submit proposals for presentations had been posted on the web and sent to a variety of mailing lists and individuals. [975] When several usability experts registered for the workshop, a usability panel was added; it would have been straightforward to include accessibility issues, had Dickson contacted the organizers.*

The chanting interrupted a presentation by a representative of Accupoll, a vendor that produced a touch screen voting machine with a paper trail. As the group proceeded down the aisle, several attendees responded to the chanting: "They were talking about accessibility when you interrupted." Ignoring comments from the audience, Dick-

---

*The workshop, proposed by cryptographer David Chaum in June 2003, was sponsored by the U.S. Public Policy Committee of USACM (USACM). It was planned to coincide with the July 2003 annual meeting of the International Association of Clerks, Recorders, Election Officials, and Treasurers (IACREOT).

son, who is blind, called out for David Dill, who identified himself. (Dill co-chaired the workshop with Barbara Simons).

After being given the microphone, Dickson began by saying "We are appalled and flatly oppose this paper ballot scam which is going to deny us our civil right to vote." He asked Dill first to blindfold himself, using what appeared to be a hotel napkin, and then to read what was written on a piece of paper, which Dickson referred to as a ballot. Dill said that he was unable to read the paper. Immediately, Al Kolwicz, a systems architect and businessman, jumped up and said that he would emulate a text to speech scanner, so that Dill would know what the ballot said.

Kolwicz's response took some of the steam out of the demonstration. The attendees invited the demonstrators to remain and participate in the rest of the workshop. In addition, the schedule was modified so that Dickson and a colleague could debate Dill and Rebecca Mercuri at the end of the workshop.

During the debate, Dickson accused advocates of verifiable ballots of "fear mongering" and claimed that "All of these hot air ideas that we can make it [voter verified paper ballots] accessible means I and my colleagues and 37 million voting age disabled Americans have to wait to get a secret ballot."

Dill and Mercuri presented overviews of security problems with paperless DREs. Together with the other attendees, they pleaded with Dickson and the demonstrators to join them in advocating for systems that are both accessible and secure. As this chapter documents, Dickson chose to ignore their pleas. The security and accessibility of our elections almost certainly would have been greatly improved, had he decided otherwise.

Afterwards, the Accupoll representative invited the demonstrators to try out their machine; there were reports that several people were pleased with it.

9.3 Many Voices

While Dickson has continued advocating for paperless DREs, several disability rights groups have been neutral or modified previous opposition to voter verified paper ballots. Still others have long understood that both accessibility and security of voting systems are crucial intertwined goals.

For example, in March 2004 Dawn Wilcox, President of the Silicon Valley Council of the Blind, asked people to send her stories about their experiences using Sequoia DREs in the March 2004 primary.[1007] More than fifty people responded, of whom only two said that the machines had functioned smoothly. Wilcox observed that the study was "important because some disabled rights advocates claim that electronic voting machines are more reliable and easier to use for disabled persons than voting machines that have a paper trail." She also wrote in a letter to the registrar of voters that "very few of our members were able to vote privately/independently despite Santa Clara County's supposed 'accessible' touch screen machines." [7]

In response to the New York Times editorial discussed below, Barbara Silverstone, Chief Executive, Lighthouse International, wrote, "Lighthouse Internation . . . sees no contradiction between accessible voting and verifiable voting for all Americans. We support both concepts in the interest of fair elections." [915]

At its 2004 annual convention, the National Federation of the Blind (NFB) membership passed a resolution stating that nonvisual access was "presently achievable only through the use of DREs." [740] Yet, a December 2004 article in an NFB publication stated "The NFB does not oppose such paper trails in principle, but we insist that they must be just as accessible to the blind as they are to sighted voters. All reputable advocates of paper trails agree with our position, and have stated their agreement, although perhaps not as vociferously as we might have liked." [788] The article also spoke favorably of the Automark. A few months later Curtis Chong, President of the National Federation of the Blind in Computer Science, wrote a letter strongly recommending the Automark. [163] This machine is a ballot marking device, usable by voters with vision impairments and other disabilities, that prints voter selections on conventional optical scan ballots (see Chapter 5).

The neutral position taken by the NFB in the December 2004 article has been reinforced during the past several years, for example in testimony by NFB representatives in a public hearing held by the Colorado Secretary of State in February 2007. James Gashel, Director of Governmental Affairs for the NFB, also mentioned to Noel Runyan that NFB is officially neutral regarding electronic versus paper ballots. [862]

Prominent accessibility expert and Director of the TRACE Center at the University of Wisconsin, Gregg Vanderheiden, stated in May 2005, "Voter verifiability does not need to be inaccessible. Accessibility does not need to reduce vote verifiability. Ballot marking devices present a good solution." [977]

In July 2005 the American Council of the Blind issued a resolution on accessible VVPATs in which they authorized officers and staff "to take all necessary actions to ensure the accessibility of voting equipment and procedures including a VVPAT." [50]

Also in July 2005 Handicapped Adults of Volusia County (HAVOC) submitted an amicus curiae opposing the NFB lawsuit aimed at forcing Volusia County to purchase DREs for voters with disabilities. The amicus stated:

> Plaintiffs mistakenly seek to obtain advancement for the blind at the possible expense of the overall integrity of the vote. This is simply an unnecessary trade. The Diebold AccuVote machines championed by Plaintiffs produce no contemporaneous paper trail or other tangible record that would allow the County to accurately and reliably audit or reconstruct an election. ... Because it believes that their votes should be secure as well as accessible, HAVOC strongly supports the use of a voting system that produces a voter-verified paper ballot .... Nothing is accomplished by forcing insecure systems on all voters, disabled and not, as a method to help some subset of disabled voters vote better. [602]

In a January 2007 joint letter with the ACLU of Massachusetts, Stanley J. Eichner, Executive Director of the Disability Law Center, urged the Massachusetts Secretary of State to purchase ballot marking voting machines, specifically the Automark. "The AutoMARK device has consistently received the highest overall ratings from the disability community." [855] Two months later in a press release praising the purchase of Automarks, Eichner added, "We must debunk the myth that we have to choose between accessible voting and verifiable voting. Democracy requires that we have both." [12]

A Call for Accessible and Secure Voting Systems, a statement signed by over 40 disability advocates and released by Noel Runyan in May 2007, said in part:

> Electronic ballot systems such as the direct record electronic (DRE) machines (formerly called "touch screens") now in use have quickly proven to be neither fully accessible to all voters nor secure and accurate methods of recording, tallying, and reporting votes. While the goal of private voting has been achieved by some voters, this has often been without meaningful assurance that our votes have been counted as cast. Additionally, many other voters have been disappointed and frustrated because we have not been able to vote privately and independently as we had hoped and as voting-system vendors had promised.
>
> It is now clear that in order to guarantee reliability and security in our elections, it is necessary for the voter to be able to truly verify the accuracy of his or her ballot—the ballot that will actually be counted. The only voting systems that permit truly accessible verification of the paper ballot are ballot marking devices. These non-tabulating devices, either electronic or non-electronic, assist the voter in marking and verifying votes on paper ballots that can either be optically scanned or hand-counted. [866]

The statement calls for "an immediate ban on any voting system that fails to meet the twin requirements of full accessibility and election security."

9.4   Some Early Legislation and Litigation

According to a 2008 U.S. Census Bureau document, there are 41.3 million people 5 and older with some level of disability. In spite of Dickson's claim of 37 million disabled Americans waiting to get a secret ballot, only 1.8 million people 15 and older report being unable to see. There are 2.7 millions people 15 and older who use a wheelchair, and another 9.1 million who need ambulatory aid such as a cane, crutches, or walker. One million people 15 and older report being unable to hear. [972] The American Association of the Deaf-Blind estimates that there are between 40,000 and 70,000 deaf-blind people in the United States. [49] DRE voting systems do not support accessible voting for profoundly deaf-blind voters.

Polling place access can be difficult for voters in motorized wheelchairs or scooters, which tend to be bulkier than manual wheelchairs, require more space to maneuver, and may not fit under tables. Voting machine legs, doorways, and other impediments may prevent those voters from voting without assistance.

Numerous studies show that voters with disabilities vote at a low rate, although the voting rate has increased. [250] While a 1982 amendment to the *Voting Rights Act* (VRA) of 1965 contains a provision allowing voters with disabilities to bring someone to assist them at the polls, the VRA does not address accessibility issues directly. [200]

During the early 1970s, disability rights activists became more organized and politically involved. A key early victory was the inclusion of Section 504 in the *Rehabilitation Act of 1973*. [197] Section 504 prohibits the exclusion of people with disabilities from the benefits of any program receiving federal funding. Delays in the implementation of Section 504 led to groundbreaking national protests by people with disabilities in 1977.

Congress passed the *Voting Accessibility for the Elderly and Handicapped* in 1984. [201] The Act requires that polling places used for federal elections be accessible for people with disabilities. However, if the chief election officer of the state determines that no accessible polling place is available, the voter can be reassigned to an accessible polling place or provided with an alternative means for casting a ballot on Election Day.

The rights contained in the Rehabilitation Act were extended to the private sector in 1990, with the passage of the *Americans with*

Disabilities Act (ADA).[190] Title II of the ADA, which covers state and local programs, says that "no qualified individual with a disability shall, by reason of such disability, be excluded from participation in or be denied the benefits of services, programs, or activities of a public entity, or be subjected to discrimination by any such entity." The ADA does not rule out reassignment, absentee voting, or curbside voting as accessible options. [125]

The ADA has been the basis of a number of voting related lawsuits. An early lawsuit, *Lightbourn v. County of El Paso*, was filed in Texas in 1996. [120] With James Harrington as lead counsel, the class action lawsuit claimed that the state system of voting discriminated against people with disabilities. [425] The U.S. District Court for the Western District of Texas agreed, but the Court of Appeals reversed the judgment. Responsibility for the enforcement of the ADA eventually was assigned to local officials in El Paso. After the initiation of two more lawsuits and additional negotiations, Texas passed a law in 2000 mandating accessible voting systems. The law was repealed in 2006.

There also has been litigation in California and New York aimed at requiring that polling places be accessible. [609,933] Unfortunately, legislation mandating physical accessibility of polling sites is frequently ignored, sometimes because there is no adequate alternative. According to Ion Sancho, election supervisor in Leon County, Florida, churches traditionally have been chosen as polling places in Florida. However, church exemption from the ADA has resulted in a lack of physical access to some polling places, an understandable source of frustration for voters with mobility related disabilities. For some elderly voters, even the absence of a place to sit while waiting in line to vote can be an impediment.

Section 301(a)(3) of HAVA, passed in 2002, requires that "the voting system shall be made accessible for people with disabilities, including nonvisual accessibility for the blind and visually impaired." The accessibility requirement could be satisfied by having at least one DRE "or other voting system equipped for individuals with disabilities" at each polling place. Because providing all voters with the same equipment simplifies elections, Section 301 created a strong incentive to purchase DREs—an unfortunate consequence of specifying a particular technology.

Voters can have a wide range of disabilities, such as vision and hearing problems, severe arthritis, mobility impairments, loss of limbs, chronic fatigue syndrome, cognitive disabilities, paraplegia, quadriplegia, and developmental disabilities. Disabilities might require the use of a motorized vehicle, wheelchair, walker, cane, or crutches. There is no single voting system on which voters with all known disabilities could vote independently. Why, then, was a single system accessibility requirement written into HAVA? Why does HAVA reference only vision-related disabilities and favor a particular type of voting technology?

9.5 The AAPD

The American Association of People with Disabilities (AAPD) claims to be the largest national nonprofit cross-disability member organization in the United States. [46] By mid 2001 AAPD Vice President Jim Dickson was widely viewed as the lead spokesperson for both the blind and the cross-disability communities in national and state debates on voting machines. [257] Dickson is an effective, outspoken, and sympathetic supporter of paperless DREs, and an opponent of voter-verified paper ballots.

Dickson has traveled around the country, providing testimony in key states such as New York and California, attending statewide grassroots advocacy meetings, and appearing at numerous events, even some to which he had not been invited. [256,258,255] In California he threatened court action if Secretary of State Shelley were to decertify Diebold DREs: "I have in my hand a draft brief. If you decertify DREs, we will be in court the next day." [258] While Dickson followed through with his threat, he didn't have the success that he had hoped for (see American Association of People With Disabilities v. Shelley in Appendix A.1).

Following the passage of HAVA, Dickson was highly visible at events relating to voting machines. He was at a September 2003 AAAS workshop on electronic voting technology, the Claim Democracy Conference in November 2003, and the December 2003 NIST meeting on voting systems. In June 2005 Dickson appeared at a Volusia County, Florida Council meeting at which he lobbied for Diebold paperless DREs. A day later he spoke on an EAC panel in New York, where he attacked paper trails: "We have got this paper trail thing because there is this small segment of the computer world that's [sic] attitude is, you can't trust computers to do anything. I think of them as the cuneiform school of computer science. They cooked up an idea of a voter verified paper trail without testing it, without measuring it, without seeing if it will work." [260]

AAPD's Justice For All blog and state Disability Vote Projects (DVP) reach activists throughout the country. The DVPs, in turn, have close connections to the national network of independent living centers (CILs or ILCs) and their respective state organizations, the statewide independent living councils (SILCs). The CIL network and others, such as the network of agencies that serve people with developmental disabilities, provide AAPD access to the largest and most powerful group of disability activists in the nation.

Jim Dickson, James Gashel, Director of Governmental Affairs for the National Federation of the Blind (NFB), or a representative of the NFB testified at most national hearings on election reform in 2001. They were practically the only spokespeople for the disability rights community on the issue of voting and accessibility in pre-HAVA Congressional hearings.

9.5.1 Involving Other Organizations

Dickson has ties to most of the major disability rights organizations. Prior to moving to AAPD in 2001, Dickson had been employed by the National Organization on Disability (NOD). In addition, Dickson and AAPD are quite involved with the Leadership Conference on Civil Rights (LCCR), the country's largest and most influential civil rights coalition, representing more than 200 national organizations. A 2004 press release from HAVA co-sponsor Senator Christopher Dodd (D-CT), announcing Dickson's appointment to the Election Assistance Commission Board of Advisors,* referred to the influence Dickson has had on the LCCR, as well as his key role in the origins of HAVA. [277] Dickson's leadership role at the LCCR likely influenced not only the election reform position of the LCCR, which had strongly supported paperless DREs, but also many LCCR members, such as the League of Women Voters [584] (see Chapter 12).

Dickson and AAPD worked closely with key politicians and Congressional staffers, especially the HAVA co-authors. AAPD presented its *Justice for All Award* to Congressman Hoyer (D-MD) in 2002, Senator Dodd in 2003, and Congressmen Ney (R-OH) in 2004. [37] Dodd, together with Senator McConnell (R-KY), were the Senate sponsors of HAVA; Ney and Hoyer had the comparable role in the House. Hoyer was also given the *Spirit of ADA Award* in 2010. [45] Ney's 2004 award was "in recognition of his considerable work on the Help America Vote Act." [157]

Dickson made a habit of plugging his favorite "accessible" voting machines. In testimony at the National Conference of State Legislatures in May 2001, Dickson listed the following machines, together with contact information, as being accessible: Hart Intercivic E-Slate, QuadMedia Kiosk System, Election Systems & Software (ES&S), iVotronic, Global

---

*Dickson was Chair of the EAC Board of Advisors from 2009 to 2011.

Election (which became Diebold and ultimately Premier) Accuvote TS, and Sequoia AVC Advantage. [254]

While testifying at a June 2001 Senate hearing, prior to the passage of HAVA, Dickson included a list of six "Accessible Voting Machine Manufacturers." [252] He also provided a "list of manufacturers who produce accessible voting systems" in testimony before a House Committee in December 2001, adding:

> Mr. Chairman, I forgot to mention that two of the very accessible machines are here today. There are eight manufacturers who have machines that would allow people like myself to cast a secret ballot, and I would encourage the Members of the Committee and those in the audience to look at these exciting devices. [253]

In a press conference at the Ohio Statehouse on March 2002 Dickson arranged for five DRE vendors to demonstrate their wares to attendees of a meeting of the Ohio Developmental Disabilities Council. [255] AAPD subsequently acknowledged receiving financial contributions from three of those vendors—ES&S, Hart Intercivic, and Sequoia—in its May 2002 newsletter. [35] The same newsletter encouraged members to work closely with vendors to pass legislation.

> AAPD extends its appreciation to the voting machine manufacturers who were Silver Level sponsors of the February 27 Leadership Gala: Election Systems & Software, Inc., manufacturer of the iVotronic System; Hart Intercivic, manufacturer of the E-Slate System; and Sequoia Pacific Voting Machines, manufacturer of the AVC Advantage System.

> Because of the ongoing debate on Capitol Hill regarding voting accessibility (specifically the Equal Protection of Voting Rights Act of 2002), it is critical that AAPD and the voting equipment manufacturers work closely together to ensure equal voting accessibility and voting rights for all Americans. Additional thanks goes to the folks at Sequoia Pacific, who brought equipment to the Leadership Gala for demonstration purposes and were present to respond to questions.

In urging its members to organize accessible voting system expos, AAPD provided a list of vendors who would cover their own costs, namely Diebold, Hart Intercivic, Sequoia, ES&S, UniLect, and Microvote. [41] Following the list was the suggestion: "Feel free to tell the manufacturers that Jim Dickson of the American Association of People with Disabilities referred you to them." [42]

Dickson participated in a March 2004 media briefing sponsored by the Information Technology Association of America (ITAA), a trade association that at the time included voting machine vendors as members. [315] Joining Dickson were Maryland Administrator of Elections

Linda Lamone and Dan Tokaji, a law professor at Ohio State University, both strong supporters of paperless DREs, as well as the then ITAA President, Harris Miller.

9.5.2 AAPD Opposition to Voter Verified Paper Ballots

In the summer of 2003 AAPD issued their Policy Statement on Voter Verified Paper Ballots. [39] "The clique of VVPB supporters disputes the fact that touch screen voting machines are safe, secure, and reliable. They theorize that it is likely that computerized voting systems will accidentally miscount the ballots or that a rogue programmer will steal an election. Therefore, every touch screen must be attached to a printer and give the voter a paper ballot. . . . VVPB will violate the letter and spirit of HAVA by once again denying people with disabilities their right to a secret and independent vote." The statement also warned that the cost of elections would rise significantly.

As if to guarantee the correctness of its prediction, AAPD has consistently fought attempts to provide federal funding for voting systems that produce paper ballots, on the grounds that blind or vision impaired voters cannot verify paper ballots the same way that sighted voters can. Of course no voter can verify her ballot on a paperless DRE, and blind voters can still vote on DREs with VVPBs or ballot marking devices. For that reason, when the Department of Justice was asked if DREs with VVPBs discriminate against voters with vision impairments, it issued an October 2003 Memorandum finding that since DREs with or without VVPBs satisfy HAVA, there is no discrimination. [239]

The AAPD statement both suggested that the "clique" of VVPB advocates were insensitive toward people with disabilities and created apprehension within the disability rights community. One of the most incongruous claims, given that voting machines frequently spend days prior to an election in insecure locations such as poll workers' garages, was the reassurance that: "Election procedures provide multiple cross checks and access to the machines and software is guarded like Fort Knox." In support of their position, AAPD quoted CMU professor Michael Shamos, one of a tiny minority of computer scientists defending paperless DREs, as saying, "So-called voter-verifiable ballot systems are nothing of the kind. They simply replace electronic voting, which has a perfect security record, with a paper medium, which is easy to tamper with." In his critique, Shamos implies that the summary-screens of DRE machines are equivalent to the verifiability of paper, despite numerous studies documenting the differences, as we discuss in Chapter 5.

9.5.3 An Unnecessary Divide

By repeatedly warning that paper ballots would disenfranchise people with disabilities and that computer scientists were indifferent to their civil rights, Dickson and AAPD convinced many members of the disability rights community that computer scientists and election integrity activists were their enemies.

For example, a June 2004 article in the AAPD national Justice For All e-list alleged, "Barbara Simons wants the League [of Women Voters] to endorse a voter verified paper audit trail (VVPAT). Her arguments are that accessibility is not as important as security: that our rights should be sacrificed for the sake of a theory that has never been proven." [543] The personal attack was triggered by Simons' involvement with the member-led effort to end the League of Women Voter's support of paperless DREs. Simons, a strong civil rights advocate, never supported sacrificing the civil rights of voters with disabilities. Nonetheless, she was not contacted by AAPD beforehand, the allegation was never documented, and AAPD refused to publish a response or retraction. The LWV reversed its support of paperless DREs at its June 2004 convention (see Chapter 12).

9.6 Vendor Financial Contributions

9.6.1 The New York Times Editorial

On June 11, 2004 the New York Times published a dramatic editorial entitled "The Disability Lobby and Voting". [771] In discussing the National Federation of the Blind, which had been championing paperless voting machines, the Times observed that the NFB "has accepted a $1 million gift for a new training institute from Diebold, the machines' manufacturer, which put the testimonial on its Web site. The Federation stands by its 'complete confidence' in Diebold even though several recent studies have raised serious doubts about the company, and California has banned more than 14,000 Diebold machines from being used this November because of doubts about their reliability." The editorial continued:

> Disability-rights groups have had an outsized influence on the debate despite their general lack of background on security issues. The League of Women Voters has been a leading opponent of voter-verifiable paper trails, in part because it has accepted the disability groups' arguments.
>
> Last year, the American Association of People With Disabilities gave its Justice for All award to Senator Christopher Dodd, an author of the Help America Vote Act, a post-2000 election reform law. Mr. Dodd, who has actively opposed paper trails, then appointed Jim Dickson, an

association official, to the Board of Advisors of the Election Assistance Commission, where he will be in a good position to oppose paper trails at the federal level. In California, a group of disabled voters recently sued to undo the secretary of state's order decertifying the electronic voting machines that his office had found to be unreliable.

Some supporters of voter-verifiable paper trails question whether disability-rights groups have gotten too close to voting machine manufacturers. Besides the donation by Diebold to the National Federation of the Blind, there have been other gifts. According to Mr. Dickson, the American Association of People with Disabilities has received $26,000 from voting machine companies this year.

Some disability rights activists saw the Times' revelations as undermining national efforts. Shawn Casey O'Brien, a disability rights activist from California, wrote in his June 14, 2004 blog:

Sadly, this editorial serves only to confirm the conclusion that I and others have been compelled to reach. Namely, that the actions of AAPD and Jim Dickson have severely undermined the disability community's credibility on an issue affecting the voting rights of millions of disabled, senior and non English speaking voters. [791]

The next day O'Brien added:

For a rather pitiful sum AAPD has compromised its credibility on anything and everything having to do with Touch Screen Voting Machines—allegedly its number one political priority. Talk about a lack of strategic foresight! After all this, someone has to ask of AAPD and California Foundation: Who's in charge over there and what are they up to? How long are we going to let these "leaders" get away with this kind of behavior, because they have a disability—and everyone walks on eggshells because of it—no matter how craven and self serving these people become? [792]

O'Brien was not the only disability rights activist to react with dismay to the Times editorial. Mary Johnson, editor of Ragged Edge, a highly regarded on-line magazine for people with disabilities, wrote:

The problem is that AAPD also made a stupid, or naive, decision to accept money from the voting machine industry. Why the group did not realize that such funding had the potential to compromise their appearance of objectivity is anybody's guess. It can't be that they didn't care; it's more likely that it never occurred to them. Now it has come back to bite them, at a time when a national voice calling for accessible voting is more needed than ever. Whether justified or not, the group has lost credibility. [516]

9.6.2 Responding to the Editorial

Several days later Dickson issued a rebuttal to the Times editorial on the Justice For All e-list, suggesting that "the civil rights of people with disabilities" were at stake. [265] He also warned that in California "one million blind and disabled voters have had accessible voting machines removed for this fall's election because of the paper trail theory that has been championed by the New York Times and the California Secretary of State." Dickson acknowledged that AAPD had received money from vendors, but then immediately changed the subject to Diebold, even though the Times mentioned Diebold funding only in reference to the NFB:

> This year, voting manufacturers contributed $26,000 to support AAPD's leadership gala. AAPD has never received a contribution from Diebold, which is the controversial machine manufacturer mentioned by name in the New York Times editorial.

Since Dickson's response was written in 2004, he appears to have been saying that $26,000 was contributed to the AAPD by vendors in 2004, though he did not reveal which vendors made the contributions.

In the July 2004 Congressional Record, Ney chastised the Times for "more or less alleging that the representatives of these groups are selling out their own constituents as well as the American electorate in exchange for a pay-off." He also said that he had worked closely with both the NFB and AAPD as the legislation was being devloped. [774] Ney's indignation sounds hollow in retrospect, given his subsequent conviction for accepting expensive gifts from lobbyist Jack Abramoff. [242]

The same Congressional record contains a letter from Andrew Imparato, then President and CEO of AAPD, to the New York Times. In his letter Imparato stated, "The editorial correctly reported that the AAPD has received a total of $26,000 from voting machine companies this year."

Since charitable organizations are not required to reveal the names of their contributors, it is almost impossible to track contributions. However, AAPD informs its members of contributors to its Leadership Gala fundraiser. For the 2002 Gala, DRE vendors ES&S, Sequoia, and Hart Intercivic each contributed at least $5000. [36] For the 2003 Gala, Sequoia and Hart Intercivic also contributed at least $5000. [38] Thus, at least $25,000 was contributed to AAPD in 2002 and 2003. Dickson and Imparato stated that in 2004 AAPD received $26,000 from vendors, resulting in what appears to be a vendor contribution to AAPD of at least $51,000, as opposed to the $26,000 stated by the Times.

Another problem with determining the amounts contributed by vendors to AAPD is that comments by AAPD officials frequently conflicted. For example, in March 2006 Imparato acknowledged that AAPD accepted a contribution from ES&S, but added, "it was just $6000, not the $26,000 reported by the New York Times." [474] Since the New York Times referred to funding from all vendors, not just from ES&S, what Imparato was saying is unclear. Nor is it obvious how his 2006 comment relates to his letter to the New York Times that was published in the Congressional Record in 2004.

Dickson also made conflicting statements, as illustrated in an October 2004 Wired article by Kim Zetter:

> When asked in April, Jim Dickson, vice president of government affairs for the AAPD, told Wired News his organization had never received money from voting companies. But in June, he told The New York Times the organization had gotten money.
>
> Dickson didn't disclose the gifts at hearings in California this year, where he tried to convince officials not to decertify touch-screen voting machines made by Diebold and other companies. Nor did he disclose the information in Washington in May when he participated in hearings with the federal Election Assistance Commission.
>
> "He comes to states where he's not even registered to vote and he gives this very heartfelt testimony about how meaningful it is to vote independently," said Natalie Wormeli, an attorney in California who is blind. "But in his testimony he never says he's a professional spokesperson, he never says he's not a registered voter in the state, and he never discloses how he's getting paid." [1029]

At least one advocacy group for the disabled understood the implications of taking money from vendors and was able to just say no. Executive Director of the Catskill Center for Independence, Chris Zachmeyer, said that her organization, which had testified as to which voting machines should be purchased by Otsego County, N.Y., had been offered financial contributions by voting machine vendors. In an article in the Oneonta Daily Star, she refused to name any vendors. [400] But she was quoted as saying that if she had taken the money, "We would lose any credibility that we ever had, and no amount of money is worth it." She added that, "you have to realize there are hundreds of millions of dollars at stake just in New York state. ... I'm sure there have been a lot of back-door deals made or a lot of back-door deals offered ...."

9.6.3 The NFB

The NFB, which states that it is the largest and most influential membership organization of blind people in the United States, received one million dollars from Diebold to be paid out over five years as part of the October 31, 2000 legal settlement of an NFB lawsuit against Diebold inaccessible ATM machines. [742]

In July 2002, roughly four months before HAVA was signed into law, Walden O'Dell, then Diebold CEO, was on a panel at the NFB national convention together with Ney and Linda Lamone, Maryland's Administrator of Elections. [820] Lamone urged NFB members to lobby Congress "to pass federal legislation to help states pay for accessible systems," undoubtedly a reference to HAVA. O'Dell praised the partnership between Diebold and the NFB, and Ney thanked the NFB for their support in passing HAVA.

In the NFB's June 2004 newsletter, which came out shortly before the Times editorial, NFB President Marc Maurer mentioned that the NFB was partnering with Diebold on ATMs and voting machines. He also acknowledged that Diebold and the NFB had lobbied Congress together on HAVA.

> From this strange beginning [the legal settlement] a partnership has developed in which we have joined with Diebold to promote accessibility through ATMs, voting machines, and other devices to be built in the months to come ... Not long after our partnership came together, we approached members of Congress about the urgent need of the blind to be a part of the political process, with the result that the Help America Vote Act incorporates provisions requiring nonvisual access to polling places by 2006. [645]

Because the Diebold money was gifted to the NFB over a five-year period, it is likely that Diebold was making payments to the NFB while the NFB and Diebold were meeting with Congressional members before HAVA became law. [739] (The NFB-Diebold payment schedule does not seem to have been made public).

After the New York Times editorial appeared, Maurer defended the Diebold contribution in a July 2004 address at the NFB convention:

> The Times sought to imply that the good opinion of the National Federation of the Blind was available for sale and that Diebold was buying. The New York Times asserts that "a handful of influential advocates for the disabled" opposed electronic voting machines that produce paper receipts because the requirement that these machines be provided will slow the installation of accessible voting devices. ...

> We have worked with Diebold for several years, and we have examined their machines. We believe their machines are accessible. We have talked with officials who run boards of elections, and they tell us that the Diebold electronic voting machines are as accurate and safe as any on the market. [644]

We note that the NFB had no staff that was qualified to judge the security of voting systems.

The NFB and Ney

Ney's appearance at the 2002 NFB convention and his defense of the NFB against the Times editorial are just two instances of the close relationship the NFB had with Ney up to his resignation from office. For example, at the NFB-Ohio 2002 annual convention, held shortly after HAVA was signed into law, a resolution was passed praising Ney and Ohio Secretary of State Blackwell (R). The resolution said that Ney had "solicited the active support of the NFB" in passing HAVA. It also repeated the false claim that HAVA required that DREs be used for nonvisual accessibility. [743]

In the February 28, 2006 Congressional Record, Ney again referred to the assistance the NFB had provided in passing HAVA. [775]

One of Ney's last acts before leaving office was to introduce, co-sponsor, and marshal legislation for the minting of a new Braille coin commemorating the 200th anniversary of Louis Braille's birth. This time the NFB stood to receive a lot more than praise from Ney. The Braille coin legislation, signed into law on July 27, 2006, allocates up to $4 million in surcharges from the sale of the coins directly to the NFB. [741] Some members of the disability rights community questioned why only the NFB, and not any other organizations for the blind, received this windfall.

9.7 Lawsuits

9.7.1 Threats and Lawsuits by AAPD and the NFB

The most potent tools Dickson, AAPD, and a few other organizations have wielded have been lawsuits, threats of lawsuits, and intimidation of election officials and taxpayers. The threats were hardly idle, as the Appendix documents. AAPD's active solicitation of lawsuits is illustrated by the announcement that appeared in the October 2002 issue of AAPD's DVP (Disability Vote Project) News Notes:

> The Washington Lawyers Committee for Civil Rights, our attorneys for the DC and Florida lawsuits, are interested in filing suits in other jurisdictions. We are looking for counties or cities that have purchased inaccessible equipment within the passed [sic] 2 years and/or that have a significant number of inaccessible polling places.

One of Dickson's early threats was in testimony in New York City in July 2002:

> The disability community's patience, as we wait for polling places and

voting systems to be made accessible, is running thin, and there is a growing body of litigation. In fact, my organization has filed suits against the cities of Philadelphia, PA, Washington, DC and Jacksonville, FL. AAPD hopes that New York City will act quickly to offer a secret ballot to all of its voters, but we reserve our legal rights to litigate and take other actions. [256]

In February 2005 Dickson sent a warning letter to Ohio Secretary of State Kenneth Blackwell. [259] The letter encouraged Blackwell to reconsider his directive that included the Automark, a ballot marking system, on a state vendor list "in order to avoid major contentious action."

In August 2005 a similar letter was sent to several California election officials by John E. McDermott. While not mentioning any client, the letter warned: "Given that the AutoMARK is not accessible to physically disabled voters and unless reconsideration is agreed upon, a lawsuit challenging the recent [California] certification is imminent." [658] McDermott was the attorney from Howrey, Simon, Arnold & White for AAPD in two California lawsuits.

As mentioned earlier, Dickson lobbied for Diebold paperless DREs at a Volusia County, Florida Council meeting in June 2005. According to Susan Pynchon, who attended that meeting, "Dickson threatened a lawsuit, saying that the AAPD had plenty of money behind it, had already spent $2.2 million on lawsuits, and wouldn't hesitate for a second to bring a lawsuit against Volusia County." [829] Nonetheless, the County Council voted 4-3 to reject Diebold DREs.

Dickson's Volusia County visit was preceded by a May 2005 article in a Duval County, Florida paper about the $2.2 million in legal fees that had been demanded by AAPD's Howrey, Simon, Arnold & White, LLP attorneys from their Duval County lawsuit (American Association Of People With Disabilities v. Smith [Hood], see Appendix A.1). [903] The article quoted Ernest Muller, an attorney handling the case for Duval County: "They want $2.2 million in legal fees after they agreed to take the case pro bono. The machines are only going to cost us $1.1 million. The lawyer bill is bigger than the remedy." Duval County appealed a district court order to pay over $1.4 million in attorneys' fees and costs, and in May 2010 the 11th Circuit Court of Appeals sided with Duval County. [44,823]

While it is common for attorneys to file for legal fees after winning a case taken on a pro bono basis, the district court award was "one of the largest ever issued in a federal disabilities rights case against a local government," according to the lead Howrey attorney. [44] Whether intended or not, the large amount demanded by Howrey could have been viewed as a threat to counties throughout the country, as well as to Duval County's neighbor, Volusia County.

Volusia County did get hit with a lawsuit demanding that it purchase DREs—not by AAPD, but by the NFB. NFB President Marc Maurer's address at the July 2005 NFB annual convention included the following nation-wide warning:

> Last Wednesday, at the conclusion of a six-hour meeting, the Valusha [sic] County Board of Supervisors in Daytona Beach, Florida, voted not to have accessible voting technology installed. It isn't that they don't have the money. They have it. On Thursday, June 30th, I directed our attorneys to sue Valusha County. That suit has been filed today. Not only will we advocate for our rights in Congress, but we will also ensure that our rights are enforced in the courts when we must. Every political jurisdiction with responsibility for elections in America should take note. [646]

David Dixon, a Volusia County disability rights activist, expressed frustration with the out-of-town activists:

> Accessibility and auditability should not be conflicting values when it comes to voting equipment . . . . National advocates for the blind do the disabled community of Volusia County a disservice when they presume to speak on our behalf for flawed systems that we do not want. [213]

The threats had the desired effect of intimidating other election officials and discouraging counties and states from purchasing non-DREs. For example, at a meeting of the Wake County, North Carolina Board of Elections in September 2005, the Board was asked if they were considering the purchase of an Automark for each precinct. The reply was that Jim Dickson was threatening to sue any county that made such a purchase. [913]

9.7.2   Other Legal Action

The Department of Justice

The Department of Justice (DoJ) used HAVA to threaten or sue reluctant providers of new voting systems. The state of Massachusetts rented several systems for people with disabilities with the intent of testing them in November 2006 election. Because Massachusetts took a cautious route of testing first, the DoJ investigated the Massachusetts Secretary of State for failure to provide sufficient equipment for people with disabilities. [919] The DoJ subsequently accepted Massachusetts' decision to use the Automark. However, on March 15, 2007 Diebold filed a lawsuit against Massachusetts in an attempt to stop the Automark purchase. [931] Two weeks later the court rejected Diebold's request for an injunction to halt the purchase. Diebold subsequently withdrew the lawsuit.

The DoJ also sued New York State in early 2006 for not having a fully accessible voting system, though the DoJ later agreed to a plan that allowed New York to place one or more accessible ballot marking or vote-by-phone system in each county until 2007. [606,241] In August 2007 the DoJ notified the New York State Board of Elections that they had until the end of September 2007 to submit a plan for implementing fully accessible voting systems in 2008. In January 2008 a judge issued an order supporting the DoJ and demanding that New York provide accessible voting systems by September 2008 and replace lever voting machines by September 2009. [904]

Initially the New York State Board of Elections had been planning to allow DREs that produce a paper trail to be used as ballot markers only. [750] However, in January 2008 the Board rejected the use of DREs and instead voted to authorize only (non-DRE) ballot marking devices for use by voters with disabilities. [115] The decision was appealed by DRE vendor LibertyVote, and in early February 2008 Acting State Supreme Court Justice O'Connor overruled the decision of the Board of Elections. Perhaps out of concern that the ruling might be overturned yet again, only one county ordered Liberty DREs. [607] Because the DRE order was so small, Liberty cancelled the contract. As a result, New York State now uses only ballot marking devices for voters with disabilities.

By contrast with New York State, Pennsylvania, which was threatened by the DoJ in 2006, still deploys a large number of paperless DREs. [911]

A Different Kind of Lawsuit

James Harrington, founder of the Texas Civil Rights Project, litigated the groundbreaking Lightbourn v. El Paso case on behalf of blind voters. Ten years later he was the lead attorney on a lawsuit aimed at preventing the State of Texas from using "unreliable electronic voting machines" in the November elections. Harrington's position, in direct opposition to AAPD's narrow definition of ballot accessibility, is noteworthy, given his long history of championing voting rights for people with disabilities. [958] A June 2006 press release announcing the lawsuit quoted Harrington: "By using machines that provide no permanent record [a paper ballot], the state is failing in its constitutional duty to provide the people with an election in which they can trust the result." [959]

9.8 How Accessible are DREs?

While not directly related to accessibility, we note that deploying DREs for "access" for voters with disabilities when all other voters are using paper ballots is a segregated and second class system for accessible voting. Such a bifurcated system can even cause disenfranchisement, because of the unreliability of half-heartedly supported second class voting systems for voters with disabilities.

9.8.1 Problems with DREs

DREs can be difficult or impossible to use for voters confined to a wheelchair, especially if they have additional mobility problems. Figure 39 shows Merle Kuznik attempting to vote on an ES&S iVotronic touchscreen. Kuznik, who had a stroke in January 2006, had contractures of her legs and arm, along with paralysis on one side, and used a wheelchair because of her inability to walk. The photo also illustrates her lack of privacy. The screen, which would be shielded by a standing voter, is easily visible from some distance when the voter is in a wheelchair. In a letter written to Rep. Steny Hoyer in 2007, Kusnik discussed the problems she had with trying to vote on the ES&S DRE:

> I am unable to reach the "Vote" button at the top of the screen from my wheelchair, and last month during our most recent Primary election the screen itself would not respond to my touches, which I guess due to my stroke and age are not as strong as they need to be. I had to resort to becoming an "assisted voter" and ask my daughter to enter the booth with me to make my chosen selections on the screen and push the button to cast my ballot .... I can still use a pencil and would like to be able to vote on an optical scan system where I can mark my own paper ballot. I also want to be able to make sure that my vote is counted accurately. [577]

As we've seen from Noel Runyan's description of voting on a Sequoia DRE in the 2004 Presidential election, DREs can also be very difficult and frustrating to use for a voter who is blind. In fact, some of the systems are so inaccessible that some voters with disabilities have not been able to access them to vote privately and independently.

9.8.2 The California Top-to-Bottom Review

The California Top-to-Bottom Review included what is perhaps the most thorough analysis of accessibility in voting systems ever conducted. [864] The accessibility report concluded that, "Although each of the tested voting systems included some accessibility accommodations, none met the accessibility requirements of current law and none

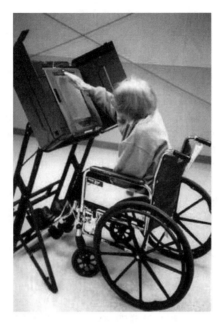

FIGURE 39 Merle Kuznik attempting to vote. Photo by Marybeth Kuznik.

performed satisfactorily in test voting by persons with a range of disabilities and alternate language needs." The report further stated that
the three tested systems, the Diebold Accuvote TSx, the Hart eSlate,
and the Sequoia Edge I and II, were "all substantially noncompliant
when assessed against the requirements of the HAVA and specified in
the 2005 VVSG guidelines."

Included in the report were photos and measurements illustrating
some of the problems. For example, the report found significant difficulties with positioning wheelchair users, interference with wheelchair
controls and armrests, problems with standing and seated use of voting
machines, and concerns with voting machine support stand stability.
The report also contained recommendations for mitigating some of the
usability defects, including better lighting for text on the VVPAT printout, privacy curtains that offer fully surrounding privacy, and chairs
and flat surfaces for voters. Recommendations more specific to voters
with disabilities included training poll workers to adjust the height and
angle of the touch screen for users with impaired dexterity, providing headphones with large easy to manipulate controls, and supplying
sip and puff controls with sanitary throw-away tube straws. However,

some of the voting systems' accessibility flaws, such as physical controls that are difficult to use for voters in wheelchairs or who have mobility problems, could not be repaired without fundamental modifications. Where possible, the report suggested design modifications that would significantly improve accessibility.

Given that some of the biggest selling points for the examined machines were their claims of accessibility, the documented inadequacies and failings illustrate yet again the need for skepticism about vendor claims, as well as the need for rigorous independent testing of the accessibility and usability of these machines.

9.9 What Lies Ahead?

In spite of serious security and accessibility problems of DREs uncovered during the past several years, Jim Dickson has continued to lobby against paper ballots. In November 2009 Dickson sent a letter to the Florida State Association of Supervisors of Elections. It incorrectly stated that no ballot marking device currently on the market or in serious development by manufacturers satisfies HAVA requirements. [263] In fact, the Automark machine, which was already on the market, satisfies HAVA better than any of the available DREs. [865]

On January 11, 2010, Dickson sent another letter, this one aimed at stopping Tennessee from purchasing Automark machines. Addressed to Mark Goins, Tennessee Coordinator of Elections, the letter urged Tennessee not to go ahead with a planned purchase of Automarks for people with disabilities. [264] Dickson wrongly claimed that the Automark is not accessible to people with mobility problems, even though the newer version of the Automark includes a feature (Autocast) that can deposit the ballot directly into a ballot box, so that the voter does not need to handle the ballot. [68] Dickson even exploited his role as Chair of the EAC Board of Advisors:

> As Chair of the Election Assistance Commission's Board of Advisors, I can confidently state that much more accessible and generally useable voting systems are just around the corner. It would be more than a shame if Tennessee spends millions of dollars to purchase equipment that is already obsolete. By delaying the purchase of new equipment, you will be able to purchase something that is accessible and secure and significantly reduce implementation costs.

It is likely that Dickson was aware of the Autocast option when he wrote the Florida and Tennessee letters, since a version of the Automark with Autocast had been certified at the federal level in August, 2009. It was also certified by the state of Florida two days after Dickson wrote to the Florida Supervisors of Elections. On January 12, the day after Dickson sent his Tennessee letter, the Tennessee Senate voted to delay for two years the implementation of legislation that had mandated paper ballots for 2010. [627]

Dickson continues to show little interest in working with computer scientists and election integrity advocates to ensure that the most accurate, secure, and accessible voting technology currently available is used for our elections. In an April 7, 2011 interview, he was quoted as saying:

> I think the computer folks who attack touch screens are doing it out of a narrow self-interest. It's their business. They get paid to say things don't work and they get paid to conduct research. What they basically say is, "I can't guarantee that this will be safe but if you pay me, you will be as safe as you can be." There's not been a single case where a computer in the polling place was able to being manipulated by a so-called computer expert. They are not connected to the Internet. In most polling places that use touch screens there will be three, five, seven different machines, they are not linked together so you cannot get into one machine and go to another. It's all just self-interested fear mongering. [362,374]

In fact, Dickson is wrong on several counts. As discussed in Chapter 5, several DRE voting systems do in fact use local networks within the polling place. Furthermore, as to the question of compensation, most of the computer scientists who uncovered security and accessibility problems in electronic voting systems received little or no compensation for their work, and that continues to be the norm. Many have also testified in court for minimal or no compensation. Scientists involved in the California Top-to-Bottom Review and the Ohio EVEREST Study were reasonably compensated for their time. By contrast, those willing to testify on behalf of electronic voting systems have been very well compensated. For example, Michael Shamos, who has frequently testified in favor of paperless DRE voting systems, including testimony on behalf of AAPD, has stated in court that he charges as much as $550 per hour for his expert witness work. [901]

Fortunately, Dickson's voice is no longer the only one being heard from within the disability rights community. Many national organizations and activists, having learned about the risks and inaccessibility of paperless DREs, have changed their views. While some of these changes were undoubtedly related to information that was not available during the years immediately following the passage of HAVA, we must also acknowledge the critical role being played by ballot marking devices now on the market that are far more accessible than DREs and offer accessible paper ballot marking and verification for voters with disabilities.

10

The Right to Vote: Voter Registration

Upon the honest and faithful maintenance of the registration books depends the purity of the ballot box. And upon the purity of the ballot box depends the success or failure of our democratic form of government.

Alden L. Powell and Emmett Asseff,
Registration of Voters in Louisiana, 1951 [824]

Dignity, justice, honor; at what point does the punished have the right to a simple chance to come back to society. ... Those whose lives we discuss today have served a sentence, as they should have; but what right have we here to add to that sentence. ... We should not confuse punishment with revenge.

Excerpts from Florida Governor Charlie Crist's (R)
Clemency Board Notes on the Restoration of Civil Rights, 2007 [215]

In April 2007, controversy erupted over a report commissioned by the Election Assistance Commission (EAC). Completed a few months earlier, *Voting Fraud and Voter Intimidation* was written by Job Serebrov and Tova Wang. [897] The EAC refused to publish the submitted report, and instead released its own version. [896] While saying that its report was based on the work of Serebrov and Wang, the EAC did not allow either researcher to address the ensuing controversy publicly, instead forcing them to adhere to confidentiality agreements they had signed.

After the original report was released, the New York Times observed:

> That report, which was released after intense pressure from Congress, found that voter identification laws designed to fight fraud can reduce turnout, particularly among members of minorities. In releasing that report, which was conducted by a different set of scholars, the commission declined to endorse its findings, citing methodological concerns.

241

A number of election law experts, based on their own research, have concluded that the accusations regarding widespread [voter] fraud are unjustified. And in this case, one of the two experts hired to do the report was Job Serebrov, a Republican elections lawyer from Arkansas defended his research in an email message. [973]

Part of Serebrov's email said, "Tova and I worked hard to produce a correct, accurate and truthful report. I could care less that the results are not what the more conservative members of my party wanted."

The version released by the EAC contained some modified claims. For example, the original report stated, "There is widespread but not unanimous agreement that there is little polling place fraud, or at least much less than is claimed, including voter impersonation, 'dead' voters, noncitizen voting and felon voters." By contrast, the EAC version said, "It also appeared . . . that there is no consensus on the pervasiveness of voting fraud and voter intimidation."

The original report discussed voter intimidation: "Abuse of challenger laws and abusive challengers seem to be the biggest intimidation/suppression concerns, and many of those interviewed assert that the new identification requirements are the modern version of voter intimidation and suppression." The EAC version stated: "It is also apparent from a review of . . . articles and books that there is no consensus on the pervasiveness of voting fraud and voter intimidation. . . . Voter intimidation is also a topic of some debate because there is so little agreement concerning what constitutes actionable voter intimidation."

Omitted from the EAC version were concerns raised in the original report about the Department of Justice (DoJ). The original report had argued that the DoJ was "bringing fewer voter intimidation and suppression cases now and is focusing on matters such as noncitizen voting, double voting and felon voting." Also omitted was the recommendation that violations under the Voting Rights Act have identical penalties. The penalty for voter fraud is $10,000, but only $5000 for acts depriving people of the right to vote.

The controversy reflects the tug of war between those anxious about voter disenfranchisement and those concerned about illegal voting by undocumented immigrants. It also reflects the difficulty of gathering accurate information on voter and election fraud, since election laws, oversight, complaint handling, and enforcement can vary considerably between states, and even localities.

There have been documented instances of election fraud, such as the 1997 mayoral primary election in Miami, FL., "a massive, well-conceived and well-orchestrated absentee ballot voter fraud scheme," in which large numbers of absentee ballots were fraudulently cast for one of the candidates.[712] But documenting widespread illegal voting by individuals, such as undocumented immigrants or disenfranchised felons, has proven to be a challenge. A significant initiative of the George W. Bush administration involving U.S. attorneys, FBI officials, and state and local election officials resulted in only 40 voters being indicted for the crime of illegal voting between 2002 and 2005. Only 26 of these indictments resulted in convictions.[712]

10.1 Some Background

One of the justifications for voter registration has been the corruption of big city bosses—politicians like Colonel Ed Butler, St. Louis Democratic Party boss at the beginning of the 20th century, who would brazenly shout across police lines on Election Day: "Are there any repeaters out here that want to vote again?"[415]

But while fraud prevention is one side of the story, voter disenfranchisement is another. At least as shocking as Butler's corrupt question was the comment of Carter Glass, a delegate to the Virginia Constitutional Convention in 1902: "[Virginia's felon disenfranchisement scheme] ... will eliminate the darkey as a political factor in this State in less than 5 years, so that in no single county will there be the least concern felt for the complete supremacy of the white race in the affairs of government."[454]

In many democracies, citizens are automatically registered to vote. The requirement in the United States that citizens take the initiative by registering is not only atypical, but also costly to administer. The absence of automatic voter registration can result in disenfranchisement, if mistakes are made or if citizens forget to re-register when they move. In November 2006 more than 65 million people, about 32% of eligible U.S. citizens, were not registered to vote.[1003]

In this chapter we examine both election fraud and voter disenfranchisement. We also discuss the new computerized statewide databases of registered voters, mandated by the Help America Vote Act (HAVA), and the likelihood that they will eliminate voter fraud and disenfranchisement.

10.1.1 Early History

Many of us believe that the right to vote in the United States has consistently expanded over the years, and is now at the point where we currently have total enfranchisement. However, there have been numerous times when the trend has been in the opposite direction.

In the early days of the Republic, voting restrictions meant that in most states only white male property owners, and in some cases white male taxpayers, were allowed to vote.* All white male adult residents, not just property owners, were allowed to vote in Virginia and Maryland until the middle of the seventeenth century. [431] Widows who owned property could vote in some Massachusetts towns and New York counties. New Jersey was more liberal, allowing property-owning women to vote from Revolutionary times until they were disenfranchised by the state in 1807. Women were not nationally enfranchised until 1920 with the passage of 19th Amendment. [555]

Non-citizens currently are not allowed to vote in most U.S. elections, but that was not always the case. For example, at the end of the 18th century in an effort to encourage settlement, the Federal government allowed aliens to vote in the Northwest Territories. [555]

While voter registration was first introduced by Massachusetts around 1800, it did not become widespread until near the end of the 19th century. [431] However, in response to large scale immigration during the middle third of that century, combined with rapid urbanization, some states developed policies that allowed voters to be challenged at the polls. A challenged voter was required to produce proof of citizenship, a precursor to voter registration. [420]

Between 1800 and 1830, most states removed religious and property restrictions for white male residents, a trend that was amplified during the Jacksonian era. [431] Jackson won the plurality of Electoral College votes in the 1824 presidential election, but then lost the presidency in the House of Representatives. So he set out to win the 1828 election by conducting the nation's first populist campaign. [415] The upshot was that the percentage of eligible voters who voted in 1828 was 58%, as compared to only 27% in 1824. The Jackson campaign also involved one of the first known instances of ballot fraud in a presidential election, when Jackson supporters from Tennessee cast ballots for dead people who had lived in neighboring states. [415] In part because of changes introduced by Jackson, voter turnout reached a high of 80% by 1840. [420]

After the Civil War, voter registration was introduced in a number of states, and by 1890 most states had some form of voter registration. In addition to preventing voter fraud, voter registration also was used to restrict voting by certain groups, especially recent immigrants and former slaves.

Sometimes, as happened in such diverse states as New Jersey and Louisiana, voter registration was required only of people living in the most populous cities. These requirements made voting more difficult for

---

*Vermont was a notable exception. The state constitution of 1777 eliminated all property and tax paying requirements for voting. Vermont continued to allow all adult men to vote after Vermont entered the Union in 1791.

urban residents—frequently new immigrants—than for rural ones.[420] For example, the Louisiana Constitution of 1852 required residents of New Orleans to register starting in 1854. Statewide registration requirements were established by the Louisiana Constitutions of 1864 and 1868. The Constitution of 1879 authorized the legislature to expand voter registration to the entire state, but it required only residents of New Orleans to register.[824]

As recently as 1951, several states still required voter registration only for residents of specific cities. In addition, some states required re-registration for each election.[824] For example, prior to 1952 registration in Louisiana took place every four years. In 1952, largely due to the efforts of the Louisiana League of Women Voters, permanent registration went into effect in Louisiana and is now part of the state constitution.

10.1.2 Ballot Fraud

Those arguing that voter registration would reduce voting fraud could point to numerous examples of fraud, including manipulation of elections by political machines. Tactics ranged from paying drunken bands of men to vote multiple times to arranging for the dead to vote.[415] Fraud and accusations of fraud were hardly limited to Jackson supporters and 19th century political machines. During the past several decades, both major political parties have charged the other party with election fraud. For example, in 1960 Republicans accused Democrats of stealing the Presidential election, a charge that was repeated by Democrats against Republicans in 2000. According to Republicans, the primary villain of the 1960 election was Mayor Richard Daley of Chicago (see Chapter 3.3). The hard to believe 89.3% Chicago turnout gave John F. Kennedy a margin of 456,000 votes in Chicago, thereby allowing Kennedy to carry Illinois by just 9400 votes.[415]

Republican presidential candidate Richard Nixon did not publicly contest the election, but others did. Cook County State's attorney Benjamin Adamowski, who had lost to a Democrat, requested a recount. While the Cook County recount resulted in additional votes for both Nixon and Adamowski, it failed to change the vote count sufficiently to overturn the outcome for either.[402] Since Kennedy's Electoral College win was 303 to 219, even if Nixon had received Illinois' 27 electoral votes, the outcome of the election would not have changed.

In 2000 the new villains, according to Democrats, were Jeb Bush, Governor of Florida and brother of Republican presidential candidate George W. Bush, and Katherine Harris, Florida Secretary of State and co-chair of George W. Bush's state election campaign. They were accused of using a variety of dirty tricks to steal the election, including a controversial felon purge list that disenfranchised large numbers of African Americans who were not felons.

10.1.3 Disenfranchisement

The felon purge list had been subcontracted by Florida to Database Technologies (DBT, which subsequently merged with ChoicePoint). According to DBT, the state asked them to include as many names as possible on the purge lists, claiming that it was up to county election supervisors to determine whether or not someone's name belonged on the list. [822] Because at that time Florida essentially disenfranchised convicted felons for life, and because the felon list used in the 2000 election contained the names of large numbers of non-felons, many Florida residents who were legally entitled to vote found their names removed from the lists of registered voters.* An estimated 50,000 names of African Americans were incorrectly deleted from the voting roles, leading to charges of election rigging and racism. [632,1025] The U.S. Commission on Civil Rights commented:

> DBT was not required to provide a list of exact name matches. Rather, the matching logic only required a 90 percent name match, which produced "false positives" or partial matches of the data. Moreover, the Division of Elections required that DBT Online perform "nickname matches" for first names and to "make it go both ways." Thus, the name Deborah Ann would also match the name Ann Deborah. [86]

In 2000 Al Gore lost Florida by 537 votes. He won the popular vote by 543,895 votes, and he would have won in the Electoral College as well, had he received Florida's electoral votes. [327]

Historical examples of disenfranchisement

The *Naturalization Act of 1790* limited naturalization to "free white persons." [880] That meant that no immigrant from Asia could become a citizen and hence vote. Anti-Chinese sentiment in California was reflected in the California constitution of 1879, which stated, "no native of China shall ever exercise the privilege of an elector in this State." The provision, intended to guard against a reversal of the anti-citizenship provision of the Naturalization Act and worded to thwart the 15th Amendment's prohibition of the use of race to restrict the vote, remained in effect until 1926. [555]

---

*Until 2007, felons who had served their sentences could have their voting rights restored only by the Board of Executive Clemency, which consists of the governor of Florida and the Cabinet. Since the Board met only four times a year and accepted only 50 appeals each time, almost all felons in Florida remained disenfranchised after completing their sentences.

The 14th Amendment, which granted citizenship to former slaves, also granted citizenship to U.S. born children of Asians. However, Japanese-Americans were disenfranchised during WWII, when they were forcibly sent to internment camps. They were not allowed to return to their homes to vote, and no provisions were made for them to cast absentee ballots. [805]

Incongruously, the 14th Amendment excluded Native Americans from citizenship; all Native Americans were finally made citizens with the passage of the *Indian Citizenship Act of 1924*. (Many had been granted citizenship during the 19th and early 20th centuries, but about a third had not been). Native Americans living in Arizona and New Mexico were not enfranchised until 1948. [943]

The first national post-Civil War disenfranchisement law, passed by Congress in 1867, mandated that all qualified male citizens living in former Confederacy states who were at least twenty-one years old take a loyalty oath in order to vote. Those taking the oath were required to swear that they had "not been disfranchised for participation in any rebellion or civil war against the United States"—in other words, that they had not fought for the Confederacy. [22]

Reconstruction, which lasted roughly a decade, was formally ended by the Compromise of 1877, resulting in the ascendancy to the presidency of Republican Rutherford B. Hayes. Hayes' victory was especially noteworthy, given that his Democratic opponent Samuel Tilden received about a quarter of a million more votes than Hayes. In exchange for the presidency, Republicans withdrew all remaining federal troops from the South, and Reconstruction was ended. [415]

The end of Reconstruction marked the beginning of disenfranchisement for the former slaves. In the South during the Jim Crow era that followed, African Americans were prevented from registering by a combination of poll taxes, literacy tests, felon disenfranchisement, and threatened or real violence. For example, there were 130,334 African American voters in Louisiana in 1896, but only 1,342 in 1904. [550] According to *Registration of Voters in Louisiana*,

> Six pages of [the Constitution of 1898] are devoted to suffrage and elections. The object of the convention was, of course, to establish white supremacy by reducing the number of Negroes voting to a minimum. The qualifications to vote as well as the entire system of registration were written in such a way that most Negroes could be disenfranchised. Other clauses were incorporated to permit the poor white to vote and yet not admit the Negro to the ballot. [824]

Disenfranchisement of former slaves was not unique to the South. Portions of the North disenfranchised black voters for a few years after the Civil War. [80]

Felon disenfranchisement

The United States is the only democracy in which lifetime disenfranchisement of former felons occurs, though laws vary considerably from state to state. [643] We are still living with the legacy of slavery and the Civil War.

The 15th Amendment, which prohibits states from using race, color, or previous condition of servitude to prevent citizens from voting, did not adequately protect the former slaves from felon disenfranchisement laws deployed in the post-Reconstruction South to significantly limit the number of African American voters, especially after 1890. The following is taken from a Mississippi Supreme Court decision upholding the state's disenfranchisement law:

> The [constitutional] convention swept the circle of expedients to obstruct the exercise of the franchise by the negro race. By reason of its previous condition of servitude and dependence, this race had acquired or accentuated certain peculiarities of habit, of temperament and of character, which clearly distinguished it, as a race, from that of the whites—a patient docile people, but careless, landless, and migratory within narrow limits, without aforethought, and its criminal members given rather to furtive offenses than to the robust crimes of the whites. Restrained by the federal constitution from discriminating against the negro race, the convention discriminated against its characteristics and the offenses to which its weaker members were prone.
> –Mississippi Supreme Court (Ratliff v. Beale) [80]

John B. Knox, chair of Alabama's 1901 constitutional convention, was explicit about one of the convention's major goals, which was: "to establish white supremacy in this State." [20] Consequently, the 1901 Alabama Constitution created laws that could be used to disenfranchise freed slaves, including crimes "involving moral turpitude," as well as being "convicted as a vagrant or tramp." Conviction for "assault and battery on the wife, bigamy, living in adultery, sodomy, incest, rape, miscegenation, [and] crime against nature" were also grounds for disenfranchisement. [21] "Moral turpitude," used to disenfranchise people convicted of misdemeanors, as well as felonies, was not eliminated as grounds for disenfranchisement until a 1985 U.S. Supreme Court decision. [949]

The negative impact of felon disenfranchisement on minorities and the poor is exacerbated in many states by requiring ex-felons to pay all court-imposed financial obligations before being eligible for restoration of voting rights. According to a 2009 ACLU study of disenfranchisement of Native Americans, "Those obligations can include docket and filing fees, court costs, restitution, and costs of incarceration. In Washington State, more than 90% of felony defendants are indigent at the time of their charge. Nationally, 31.2% of American Indians—compared with 11% of whites—live below the poverty line. It is not surprising, then, that many American Indians who accrue these legal financial obligations remain disenfranchised long after having concluded their prison terms." [660]

Felon disenfranchisement laws, especially those that continue to disenfranchise felons after they have served their sentences, remain controversial. In the 2000 presidential election, the number of Americans disenfranchised by felon disenfranchisement laws was estimated to be roughly 4.7 million, or 2.28% of the voting age population. [969] More than a third were ex-felons, as opposed to roughly a quarter who were currently in prison. Others were on probation (28%), on parole (10%), or serving felony sentences in jails (1%). [629]

Only Maine and Vermont, which allow felons to vote from prison, have no felon disenfranchisement laws. [891] Southern states are disproportionately represented among states with extensive felon disenfranchisement laws, as are states with large non-white prison populations. [80] African American males have been significantly impacted, with roughly one in six disenfranchised in the early 21st century because of felony convictions. [629]

Section 2 of the 14th Amendment forbids the disenfranchisement of male voters "except for participation in rebellion, or other crime." Ironically, the reference to "rebellion or other crime," initially directed at white supporters of the Confederacy, was the basis for *Richardson v. Ramirez*, a crucial 1974 U.S. Supreme Court decision upholding felon disenfranchisement laws.

On November 14, 2005, the U.S. Supreme Court declined to hear a challenge to Florida's felon disenfranchisement law. When the challenge was initiated in 2000, 14 states prohibited ex-felons from voting unless they went through an appeals process. By the time the Supreme Court rejected the appeal, only Florida, Virginia, and Kentucky disenfranchised all felons who had completed their sentences. [1018] However, in 2007 Florida Governor Charlie Crist (R) restored voting rights to all felons who had served their time, with the exception of those convicted of murder or other violent crimes. In 2011 the Crist reforms were rolled back by Governor Rick Scott (R). Even a nonviolent offender in Florida now has to wait five years after completing his sentence before being allowed to apply to have his voting rights restored.[991]

As of 2009, Virginia and Kentucky still had permanent felon disenfranchisement, except for government approval of individual rights restoration; eight states (AL, AZ, DE, FL, MS, NV, TN, WY) continued to disenfranchise some or all felons for life, depending on the type and/or number of convictions.[1017]

On January 5, 2010 the 9th Circuit Court of Appeals ruled 2-1 in favor of inmates who had challenged Washington State's felon disenfranchisement law, saying "Plaintiffs have demonstrated that the discriminatory impact of Washington's felon disenfranchisement is attributable to racial discrimination in Washington's criminal justice system."[954] On October 7, 2010 the full 9th Circuit Court reversed the ruling of its three judge panel, saying that the plaintiffs' claim that felon disenfranchisement violates the Voting Rights Act is not valid.[510]

Voter ID

As of this writing, proposals to require "voter ID", which typically is a non-expired state or federally issued photo ID, have been introduced in 32 states. Of the fewer than 50 people who were convicted or pled guilty to illegal voting at the federal or state level between 2002 and 2005, none would have been prevented by a photo ID requirement.[16] The paucity of examples is not surprising, since there are far better ways of stealing elections. Not only is illegal voting a felony, but the person committing the felony runs the risk of being unmasked at the polling place and arrested on the spot. In addition, tried and true methods such as ballot box stuffing, or more modern methods such as installing malicious code in voting machines, can be far more efficient.

Many voters with disabilities could be disenfranchised by voter ID laws. According to a letter co-signed by the American Association of People with Disabilities, 10% of all people with disabilities lack current state-issued identification.[48] In addition, a survey sponsored by the Brennan Center revealed that more than 21 million U.S. citizens do not have a government-issued photo ID. Citizens who currently lack government photo ID include:[116]

- 25% of African American voting age citizens—more than 5.5 million people,
- 15% of those earning less than $35,000 a year,
- 18% of those age 65 and above—more than 6 million voters,
- 20% of voters 18–29.

There can be significant costs of both time and money in obtaining documents necessary to satisfy voter ID requirements, even if the state provides the voter ID at no charge. Required documents may include a birth certificate or naturalization papers. A certified copy of a birth certificate could cost as much as $45, and naturalization papers could cost $200. An additional catch-22 is created in the 17 states that require a photo ID in order to obtain a birth certificate. In some cases birth certificate records have been misplaced or destroyed by fire or natural disasters, such as Hurricane Katrina. If the voter's name has been changed, he or she may be required to produce marriage or divorce records. [16]

States that do not charge for voter IDs can be confronted with major expenses at a time when most states are struggling to meet their financial obligations. For example, Indiana spent over $10 million to provide IDs to over 700,000 Indiana voters. In addition, states need to educate voters about new photo ID requirements. Missouri has estimated the education cost at $16.9 million over three years. [16]

Some opponents of voter IDs claim that the cost and time required to obtain the IDs amount to a new poll tax, which would be illegal. Others argue that voter IDs conflict with the constitutions of many states. In any case, voter ID laws are being challenged in the courts.

10.2   Issues Relating to Voter Registration

While the history of the suppression of the voting rights of African Americans in the South during the post-Reconstruction years is fairly well known, there is perhaps less understanding of the impact that variations in voter registration laws have had nationally. For example, in 1908 the only days on which New York City residents could register (registration was not required elsewhere in the state) were the Jewish Sabbath and the Jewish high holy day of Yom Kippur. [555] The obvious effect was to limit the registration of observant Jewish voters.

The 1998 election of Jesse Ventura as Governor of Minnesota illustrates what can happen when advanced registration requirements are eliminated. In Minnesota, one of a small number of states that allow Election Day registration, about 332,000 Minnesota residents registered and voted on Election Day in 1998. According to exit polls, the vast majority of these new voters voted for Ventura. [420] Since voters often start following elections during only the last few weeks of a campaign, a thirty day advanced registration requirement can prevent many potential voters, who belatedly become interested in an election, from voting. Consequently, states with Election Day registration are likely to have higher voter turnout than states requiring earlier voter registration.

Aside from Wyoming, which handles voter registration at the county level, and North Dakota, which does not require voter registration, all states have statewide voter registration requirements. (Wyoming lists "not a felon" and "not adjudicated mentally incompetent" as two statewide requirements).

10.2.1   What Information is Collected and How Is It Used?

Registration lists are public records that are typically provided to political parties, and sometimes sold to commercial entities. A California Voter Foundation 2004 report, *Voter Privacy in the Digital Age*, is the source for most of the following figures. [26] While there have been some changes since 2004, they have not been extensive. Twenty-one states and the District of Columbia allow commercial access to voter registration lists, while twenty-nine prohibit commercial use. Other groups, such as academics, journalists, political parties, and special interest groups, also utilize voter registration databases. Voter registration data are a source of names for juries in forty-three states. When state legislatures are engaged in redistricting, voter registration databases can be useful tools in drawing districts lines, especially if the goal is to keep certain districts safe for incumbents.

The issues of what information is collected, how it is stored, and who has access to that information have grown in importance with new HAVA regulations. With the exception of North Dakota, all states are required by HAVA to create centralized computerized databases of all registered voters. Because many people could have access to these centralized databases, their existence increases the risks of privacy invasion and identity theft. In addition, political parties and others who have access to computerized voter registration databases can combine them with commercially available databases containing additional information about voters, such as ethnicity, occupation, education, and income level. By merging databases, political parties and commercial entities can engage in profiling and targeted advertising. Slightly over half the states provide certain voters, such as judges and victims of domestic violence, with the option of having their registration records kept confidential. Privacy advocates are recommending that this option be made available to all voters.

There are reasons to require that a minimal part of the voter registration list be made public. In a democracy where the identity of those permitted to vote is not public, it becomes easy for the government to hide both disenfranchisement and padding of voter registration lists.

Proving that the government has systematically disenfranchised voters or padded the voter lists is very difficult if the voter lists are not available.

Every state with statewide voter registration requirements collects each voter's name, address, and signature; all states except for Alaska, where it is optional, obtain the voter's date of birth. Eleven states withhold part or all of the information about a voter's date of birth from secondary users; the rest provide that information. Forty-six states request the voter's telephone number, although twenty-eight states make that information optional. Only five states withhold telephone numbers from secondary users. Thirty-four states ask the voter's gender, with a small number making that information optional.

Most states do a poor job of telling voters which information is optional, and why. A number of states that request some or all of the voter's social security number fail to explain why this information is being requested, even though the Federal Privacy Act of 1974 mandates such an explanation. Only four states (NM, TN, TX, and IA) inform the registrant that voter registration information is a matter of public record. Finally, only Iowa makes reference to secondary use of voter registration data on its state form. California now requires that the forms state that "the use of voter registration information for commercial purposes is a misdemeanor." But California does not inform the voter of secondary uses that are permitted under California law.

10.2.2 Registration Legislation

The Voting Rights Act of 1965 (VRA). The VRA prohibits public officials from preventing any qualified person from voting, eliminates literacy tests, and prevents states from requiring people to register more than 30 days prior to a presidential election. Because of the VRA and the 1966 Supreme Court decision eliminating poll taxes, registration rates of African Americans rose throughout the South from 1964 to 1968. [420]

The National Voter Registration Act of 1993 (NVRA or "motor-voter law"). The goal of the NVRA is to facilitate voter registration. All states are compelled to use a uniform mail-in registration form, and state agencies—such as public schools, libraries, and offices that provide public assistance and unemployment compensation—are required to provide voter registration services. States also must provide residents who are obtaining or renewing driver's licenses the option of registering to vote. During the first few years after the law was enacted, voter registration increased: the number of voters registered in 1998 was the highest since reliable records of registration rates were first made available in 1960. [420]

Help America Vote Act (HAVA). HAVA required each state to create a statewide database of registered voters (Voter Registration Database or VRD) by January 1, 2006. As with voting machines, HAVA contains no federal standards or requirements that VRDs be accurate, secure, reliable, easily used, and protective of voters' privacy. (Although calling for a "minimum standard for accuracy" for VRDs, HAVA contains no accuracy standards or methods for measuring accuracy). Nor does HAVA mention any enforcement mechanism "to ensure that eligible voters are not removed in error from the official list of eligible voters."

By contrast, HAVA is far more demanding about verification of voter registration information, requiring either a current valid driver's license or the last four digits of the applicant's social security number. HAVA also stipulates that information in VRDs and departments of motor vehicles databases be shared, with the goal of verifying the accuracy of the information provided by the applicant. The Social Security Administration can be asked by the head of the state motor vehicle authority to verify information in the driver's license database.

The voter verification requirements have been used to disenfranchise voters by requiring exact matches between different databases, even though it is well known that the same name can be entered differently in different databases.

10.3   Studies and Proposed Reforms

Several studies on improving our electoral system have examined voter registration. One of the earliest was conducted by a state commission created by the Illinois legislature in 1931. The published report contained numerous recommendations, some of which, such as permanent voter registration, have been implemented. [431] More recently, the National Commission on Federal Election Reform assembled two blue ribbon panels that issued reports.

The Carter-Ford report. The initial report, published by the Commission in August 2001, was produced by a panel co-chaired by former Presidents Jimmy Carter and Gerald Ford. [354] The first policy recommendation from that study, given below, appears to have provided the basis for the statewide VRD requirement contained in HAVA.

In justifying the linking of the driver's license with voter registration, the report says that: 1) an estimated 92% of all registered voters also have driver's licenses; 2) more than 3/4 of all moves are intrastate, so voters will still be in the database; 3) members of low income groups are more likely to move than higher income groups, and therefore low income residents will benefit from not having to re-register whenever they move within a state; and 4) when an individual moves to another state, a driver is required to obtain a license from that state.

The 2001 report discussed the option of requiring all voters to produce official identification, such as a photo ID. Because a disproportionately large number of people who do not possess a driver's license are poor and urban, and because members of minority groups might fear that a photo ID requirement would be used to discriminate against them, the 2001 report took no position on voter IDs, aside from saying that states should be able to verify a voter's identity.

Another issue on which the 2001 report took no position was same day registration. While observing that Election Day registration might have a "modest effect (5-8%) in improving voter turnout," the commission argued that much of the evidence for improved voter turnout was gathered before the passage of the NVRA and hence might be no longer applicable. They appear to have discounted the impact that same-day registration had on the 1998 Minnesota governor's race.

The report addressed the issue of felon disenfranchisement by recommending that voting rights be restored to otherwise eligible citizens convicted of a felony "once they have fully served their sentence, including any term of probation or parole."

The recommendation for statewide VRDs from the Carter-Ford study (2001):

Every state should adopt a system of statewide voter registration.

1. *The statewide computerized voter file should be networked with and accessible to every election jurisdiction in the state so that any level can initiate registrations and updates with prompt notification to the others. It should include provisions for sharing data with other states.*

2. *When a citizen either applies for a driver's license or registers to vote, each state should obtain residential address and other information, such as a digitized signature, in a form that is equally usable for both the motor vehicle and voter databases. The address information can then be linked to a statewide street index.*

3. *Each state's driver's license and voter registration applications should require applicants to provide at least the last four digits of their Social Security number. States should also ask applicants if they are registered in another state, so that that state can be notified of the new registration.*

4. *Each state's voter registration applications should require a separate and specific affirmation that the applicant is a U.S. citizen.*

The Carter-Baker Report. The second report was issued by the Commission in September 2005, with James Baker replacing Gerald Ford as panel co-chair. [151] The Carter-Baker report strengthened some of the recommendations from the Carter-Ford report and took positions on some issues about which the first report had been noncommittal. The statewide VRD proposal was expanded by recommending that a) states, not local jurisdictions, be responsible for the accuracy and quality of voter lists and b) state VRDs be made interoperable, so that duplicate registrations could be removed, and a voter would have to register only once in his or her lifetime. To assist with interoperability, the report recommended a uniform template that included "a person's full legal name, date and place of birth, signature (captured as a digital image), and social security number."

The report acknowledged privacy concerns relating to the use of the social security number (SSN), and claimed that the concerns could be dealt with by limiting those allowed to access the SSNs to "authorized" (not defined in the text) election officials. It further suggested that the SSNs not be released to candidates, political parties, or anyone else. Nonetheless, given the widespread use of SSNs for identification, and the difficulty of securely restricting access, to say nothing of the problem of determining who should be authorized, the potential use of SSNs to identify voters increases the risks of identity theft.

Perhaps the most controversial recommendation from the Carter-Baker report was the use of a "uniform system of voter identification based on the 'REAL ID card' or an equivalent for people without drivers license [sic]." The REAL ID recommendation ignored the fact that most absentee voters are not required to present any ID, although some states require that a photocopy of a photo-ID be provided by the voter.

While the report urged states to provide photo IDs for free, Spencer Overton, a law professor at George Washington University, issued a strongly worded dissent in which he complained that the Real ID recommendation was "more extreme than any ID requirement adopted in any state to date" and "would prevent eligible voters from proving their identity with even a valid U.S. passport or a U.S. military photo ID card." Overton also objected to the absence of a serious cost-benefit analysis, saying that "the type of fraud addressed by photo ID requirements is extraordinarily small and that the number of eligible citizens who would be denied their right to vote as a result of the Commission's ID proposal is exceedingly large." He added, "The 2005 Carter-Baker Commission does not and cannot establish that its 'Real ID' requirement would exclude even one fraudulent vote for every 1000 eligible voters excluded."

Another dissent, authored by Tom Daschle and joined by Overton and Raul Yzaguirre, observed that obtaining the documents necessary for a REAL ID card could be difficult, even for those who have not suffered devastation such as that caused by Hurricane Katrina. The dissenters claimed that for some, the REAL ID proposal "constitutes nothing short of a modern day poll tax."

There were other criticisms of the REAL ID recommendation, such as a New York Times September 2005 editorial: "[I]f the solution [photo ID] risks disenfranchising hundreds of thousands, or even millions, of voters, it is a very bad reform. . . . The purpose of election reform should not be making it harder to vote. We all have a duty to make our election system as good as it can be—and not to disenfranchise people in the name of reform."

The Carter-Baker report repeated the suggestion from the Carter-Ford report that voting rights of ex-felons who have fully served their sentences be restored, with the exception of those "convicted of capital crimes or registered sex offenders." The recommendation that those two categories be excluded was absent from the earlier report. As with many previous reports, the Carter-Baker report recommended that "state election management bodies" be nonpartisan.

10.4   Voter Registration Databases (VRDs)

HAVA requires election officials to purchase VRDs, but most election officials, like most citizens, are not database experts. Yet, when election officials purchase an online system to authenticate registered voters, they are purchasing, among other things, a database system. There are good database systems and bad database systems; there are database systems that can provide a high level of security and those that cannot. Because there are no national requirements for these database systems and no federal certification, election officials have been on their own. Ideally, officials have had access to independent expert advice in making their purchasing decisions, assuming that they can find such experts, as opposed to accepting without question the claims made by vendors.

Even if one has purchased the "right" kind of database system (secure, reliable, accurate, privacy protecting, and easy to use), there is still the issue of the proper use of the system. The only people with the ability to insert or delete names in the database should be employees for whom this is part of their job. Furthermore, these employees should be given access to information about only those voters for whom they are responsible.

Any actions that modify the database should be tracked by a reliable audit trail, namely a record of who did what to the system and when was it done, so that if anything questionable happens, the officials in charge can determine who was responsible. At the very least, the system must be password protected, and employees who have access to the database must adhere to proper security policies, such as keeping their passwords secret. Of course an audit trail is of little use unless it is examined routinely for problems.

There is also the question of what can be viewed online or provided to political parties, candidates, the press, etc. While determining what information needs to be protected is a policy decision, properly implementing that policy in the database depends on a proper technical implementation. It should not be possible for an individual to access the online database and obtain sensitive voter information to which he or she is not entitled.

10.4.1 Problems with VRDs

An example of disenfranchisement by VRD matching. On November 2, 2005, California Secretary of State McPherson signed a Memorandum of Agreement with the Department of Justice. [244] A key portion of the agreement stated: "For each voter record presented, Cal-Validator will check the DMV (Department of Motor Vehicles) data to verify that the CDL (California driver's license) or CA ID (California Identification Card), if provided, matches the presented name and date of birth for the registrant." On December 12, McPherson adopted emergency regulations to implement the agreement by requiring that the voter registration information **exactly** match the information contained in either the DMV database or the Social Security Administration's database.

DMV databases are known to be unreliable. For example, women who marry and change their last names are sometimes lax about submitting updates. Furthermore, a name, especially a non-English one, may be entered in different ways in different databases. Because the regulations required an exact match, even a missing middle initial or an unhyphenated last name could have resulted in a rejection. [596,930]

On March 28, 2006 the California League of Women Voters wrote to McPherson expressing concerns that large numbers of registrations in Los Angeles County were being inappropriately rejected, and warned that, "**a failure to match the applicant or his/her data with another database must not result in the rejection of the applicant**" [511] [emphasis in the original]. The letter also stated that neither HAVA nor state law requires matching, and that there is a significant likelihood of errors in the database. Finally, the letter pointed out that "the absence of information does not suggest a problem. Only positive information of a disqualifying characteristic should result in the rejection of a voter in a database matching system."

The same day that the League sent its letter, then State Senator Debra Bowen wrote McPherson to warn that between January 1 and March 15, 2006, Los Angeles County had received 34,064 voter registration forms, of which 14,629, or nearly 43%, were rejected. [104] In response to the large number of rejections, McPherson weakened, but did not eliminate, the matching requirements. [143] We do not know how many people went to the polls thinking they were registered to vote, only to learn that their names were not on the VRDs.

An example of disenfranchisement by e-poll book failure. The critical importance of testing technologies that access VRDs under Election Day type conditions, and of having reliable backups in case of failure, was dramatically illustrated when Maryland began using Diebold electronic-poll books for the first time in the September 2006 primaries. Diebold e-poll books are small touchscreen computers, each of which contains the database of all voters registered in a particular county. [859] The e-poll books, which are connected by a network, can track who has already voted by sharing that information over the network. In other words, if a person votes at location A, all of the e-poll books in the entire county should be updated by the e-poll book at location A, thereby preventing that person from voting at another location.

Primary day did not start well in Maryland, with a number of polling places opening quite late. The cause, according to the President of the Baltimore Board of Elections, was that some poll workers arrived late, and many were not adequately trained in using the new e-poll books, though he claimed that problems were not unusual when dealing with new equipment. [440] Both voters and candidates expressed concern about voter disenfranchisement stemming from the delays. [440]

Problems were not limited to late polling place openings. Some of the Diebold e-poll books were excessively slow in synchronizing information about who had already voted. Computer scientist Aviel Rubin described problems he and his fellow election workers experienced with the e-poll books, starting a couple of hours into the election, when the poll workers realized that one of the poll books was not being synchronized with the other poll books. [859] If a voter were signed into the malfunctioning poll book, that voter would not be marked as having voted in the other two poll books for at least 20 minutes. Since a voter could in theory vote repeatedly by signing into the malfunctioning poll book multiple times, the poll workers stopped using the malfunctioning poll book. The resulting delays increased the wait time to almost an hour.

Rubin complained about inadequate support provided by Diebold, saying that the Diebold representative at his precinct had been hired just the previous day and had only six hours of training. As a result, Rubin explained some of the technical details to the Diebold representative, who, feeling that he was not doing anything useful, left early.

Diebold acknowledged that there was a software error after Maryland encountered significant problems with e-poll books. The workaround involved adding a computer mouse to each e-poll book. [439] Maryland Elections Administrator Linda Lamone then tested the system using more than 1000 mock voters—the kind of testing that she had not done prior to the primary. Diebold explained the synchronization problems by saying "software created exclusively for Maryland caused the machines' memories to fill up after about 40 people had checked in to vote." [222]

In addition to inadequate testing, the importance from a security and privacy perspective of limiting access to VRDs and of maintaining and overseeing audit trails was not understood by the State Board of Elections. A report issued by Maryland state auditors warned that the State Board of Elections was not exercising proper control over access to the VRD and changes made to the VRD.

10.4.2   VRD reports

There are a few studies that address policy issues relating to VRDs, including the previously discussed California Voter Foundation report on privacy issues.

Balancing Access and Integrity, a report issued by the Century Foundation, includes a number of recommendations, such as urging states to "take all appropriate measures to protect the privacy rights of voters when constructing and utilizing the statewide voter registration database." [992] The report recommends that "States also should make clear that information from the database may be used only for voter registration and election purposes." As we have seen, many states make voter registration information available for non-election and commercial purposes. In addition, the report advises states to make the re-enfranchisement of felons no more burdensome than voter registration.

In November 2005, Appleseed, the Brennan Center, and Latham & Watkins released a "best practices" booklet entitled *The Database Dilemma: Implementation of HAVA's Statewide Voter Registration Database Requirement.* [53] The booklet focuses on legal and policy issues related to creating the VRDs.

Making the List: Database Matching and Verification Processes for Voter Registration, published by the Brennan Center in March 2006, is an excellent source of information about different states' policies on database matching. [596] It discusses the kinds of problems that can arise when attempting to match names from different databases, both because of typing errors and because of variations in spelling. For example, Pierce might appear in one database, whereas Peirce, Pearce, Perce, or Pierrce might appear in another. Someone might be listed as Sam or Larry in one database, and Samuel or Lawrence in the other.

Electionline.org provides a 2008 listing of the state-by-state status of VRDs. [311]

10.4.3 A Technical Analysis of VRDs

The most extensive analysis of technological aspects of VRDs can be found in the ACM (the Association for Computing Machinery) report *Statewide Databases of Registered Voters* (one of us, Barbara Simons, co-chaired the study that produced the report). [447] Written for election officials and the general public, the report provides a check-off list of 99 recommendations. Had the relevant recommendations been followed in California and Maryland, many of the problems these states experienced would have been ameliorated, if not avoided altogether. The following recommendations are taken from the executive summary:

1. The policies and practices of entire voter registration systems, including those governing VRDs, should be transparent both internally and externally.
2. Accountability should be apparent throughout each VRD.
3. Audit trails should be employed throughout the VRD.
4. Privacy values should be a core element of the VRD, not an afterthought.
5. Registration systems should have strong notification policies.
6. Election officials should rigorously test the usability, security, and reliability of VRDs while they are being designed and while they are in use.
7. Election officials should develop strategies for coping with potential Election Day failures of electronic registration databases.
8. Election officials should develop special procedures and protections to handle large-scale merges with and purges of the VRD.

In addition to warning about the risks of large-scale merges and purges, the report urges that other databases (e.g. DMV databases) be used only for screening, and not to enroll or de-enroll voters automatically. Voters should be informed in a timely fashion if they are determined to be ineligible to vote, and they should be told the reason for that determination. It should be easy for voters to verify the accuracy of their records and to correct any mistakes. Voters also should be told why personal data is collected, informed about uses to which that data might be put, and supplied with a list of third parties who have been given or purchased access to the VRD.

To reduce security and privacy threats, the amount of information that is available to each election official who has access to the VRD should be minimized. In database security, this is called the "principle of least privilege." This means that users of the VRD should be allowed access only to that information that they need, and nothing more. Only well understood and well tested authentication techniques should be used, especially when providing access to individuals who have the capability of modifying the content of the VRD.

It is also critical that VRDs be protected as much as possible from attacks, both by outside "hackers" and by insiders. The report recommends securing all communication channels, implementing good firewalls, hardening mission-critical machines as much as possible, monitoring of possible intrusions, performing regular back-ups (including possibly off-site storage of backups), and having a plan for recovery from security failures. Attacks are a real threat, as was demonstrated by the 2011 breach of the Maine VRD. [709]

Finally, VRDs should be designed so that there is no single point of failure, and there should be fallback procedures in place to deal with failures when they do occur. Extensive and ongoing testing is crucial, including security audits and test runs of fallback procedures. VRDs also should be tested for usability by involving a wide range of users of different backgrounds, computer literacy, and experience. It is crucial that some of these tests simulate the kind of stressful conditions likely to prevail on Election Day.

10.5   The Future of VRDs

Voter registration legislation tends to assume that the underlying VRDs are relatively problem-free. Without national requirements or oversight of the VRDs themselves, such legislation might create unanticipated side effects. For example, in March 2009 legislation was introduced that would have allowed voters to register and to update their registration information over the Internet. [611] The bill did not appear to have adequate safeguards to prevent unauthorized access to the voter information or to deter wrongful modification or deletion of a voter's registration.

In 2009 the Brennan Center issued a report calling for Congress to establish a national mandate for universal voter registration within each state, provide federal funds, require that voters remain on the voting roles when they move, and mandate "fail-safe" procedures so that eligible voters can correct the voting rolls. [1003] Related legislation was considered, but not introduced.

While VRDs have not received the same scrutiny as voting machines, VRDs are nonetheless critical to the security of our elections. VRD mismanagement or failure can result in the disenfranchisement of voters or the padding of the voting roll. Exact matching, such as was used in California, can cause the names of large numbers of legitimate voters to be stripped from the voting rolls. As Maryland demonstrated, people also can be disenfranchised because of badly designed and inadequately tested VRDs, as well as the equipment used to access VRDs.

11

Internet Voting:
Voting Rights for Viruses?

The online system is incredibly secure: That was one of our biggest goals.

Lindsey Reynolds, Executive Director of Democrats Abroad [85]

Within 36 hours of the system going live, our team had found and exploited a vulnerability that gave us almost total control of the server software, including the ability to change votes and reveal voters' secret ballot.

University of Michigan Professor Alex Halderman, describing his team's break-in of the Washington, DC test Internet voting [419]

Coming up with "best practices for Internet voting" is like coming up with "best practices for drunk driving." You don't really want to go there ...

MIT Professor Ronald L. Rivest, in response to the EAC's request to NIST to come up with "best practices" for Internet voting [852]

11.1   The DC Pilot Test

In June 2010 the Open Source Digital Voting Foundation (OSDV) announced that they had been selected by the District of Columbia Board of Elections and Ethics (BOEE) to implement a "digital vote by mail" pilot project that would allow military and overseas voters to vote over the Internet, starting with the upcoming September primary. [804] The press release also stated that the BOEE anticipated having a "public review period" (test) during the summer in advance of the primary. Delays prevented the system from being used in the primary.

11.1.1 The Blank Ballot Bug

Because of further delays, the test was scheduled to run from September 28 until October 6, with voting in the real midterm election scheduled to begin October 11 or 12. On September 30 computer scientist David Jefferson discovered that the selections he had made on his test ballot had all been lost, so that he ended up casting a blank ballot.

Jefferson determined that his system's PDF "save as" command, which voters were instructed to use, saved only a blank ballot. Clearly, the type of system he used (an Apple Macintosh computer with the Safari browser) had never been tested. There are so many different versions of computers, browsers, and operating systems that it would have been impractical for all possible combinations to have been tested, though the combination used by Jefferson is fairly common. Jefferson's discovery illustrates one of the problems with Internet voting: you can never be certain that a voting system will work with any possible software running on some computer, since you can never test all possible combinations.

More significant for the pilot test, Jefferson's discovery meant that some segment of real voters would have been disenfranchised by the system, since they would not have been warned that they were about to cast blank ballots.

11.1.2 The Break-In

By October 1 people testing the system were surprised to hear the Michigan Fight Song played 15 seconds after they submitted their ballots. [276] A Michigan team, which had taken over the system within 36 hours of the start of the tests, had exploited a vulnerability in the software, giving them almost total control. The attackers remained in control for two business days, until the BOEE halted the test the afternoon of October 1, possibly after learning of the fight song.

Of course an attacker wanting to subvert an election would never leave an obvious "calling card." The delay between the break-in and the shutting down of the system illustrates the difficulty in determining that a break-in has occurred, even when the "culprits" announce themselves with music."

In an October 5 blog, Michigan Prof. Alex Halderman revealed that, in addition to installing the fight song, his team had changed ballots already cast, they could modify future ballots, and they could violate voters' secret ballot rights. [419] On the same day the BOEE restarted the test, with the song removed. Testers were told to print out and mail in their ballots, i.e. no Internet return of voted ballots. Figure 40 shows the hacked ballot with write-in candidates selected by the Michigan team.

Official Ballot
District of Columbia Mock Election
PRECINCT 22
September 17, 2010

INSTRUCTIONS TO VOTER

1. TO VOTE YOU MUST DARKEN THE OVAL TO THE LEFT OF YOUR CHOICE COMPLETELY. An oval darkened to the left of the name of any candidate indicates a vote for that candidate.
2. Use only a pencil or blue or black medium ball point pen.
3. If you make a mistake DO NOT ERASE. Ask for a new ballot.
4. For a Write-in candidate, write the name of the person on the line and darken the oval.

DELEGATE TO THE U.S. HOUSE OF REPRESENTATIVES	AT-LARGE MEMBER OF THE COUNCIL	UNITED STATES REPRESENTATIVE
Vote for not more than (1)	Vote for not more than (1)	Vote for not more than (1)
[ ] **Alice Example** Democratic	[ ] **Joan Example** Statehood Green	[ ] **Latoya Example** Republican
[ ] **Bob Example** Republican	[ ] **Kimberley Example** Democratic	[ ] **Marcus Example** Statehood Green
[ ] **Carol Example** Statehood Green	[ ] **Liam Example** Republican	[ ] **Newton Example** Democratic
(●) or write-in	(●) or write-in	(●) or write-in
Skynet	Johnny 5	Colossus

MAYOR OF THE DISTRICT OF COLUMBIA	MEMBER OF THE COUNCIL WARD ONE	MEMBER OF ADVISORY NEIGHBORHOOD COMMISSION 1B DISTRICT FOUR
Vote for not more than (1)	Vote for not more than (1)	Vote for not more than (1)
[ ] **Duane Example** Republican	[ ] **Mary Example** Republican	[ ] **Orlando Example** Democratic
[ ] **Edward Example** Democratic	[ ] **Nitan Example** Democratic	[ ] **Phyllis Example** Statehood Green
[ ] **Frances Example** Statehood Green	[ ] **Odell Example** Statehood Green	[ ] **Quincy Example** Republican
(●) or write-in	(●) or write-in	(●) or write-in
Master Control Pro	GLaDOS	Deep Thought

CHAIRMAN OF THE COUNCIL	MEMBER OF STATE BOARD OF EDUCATION WARD ONE	Thank you for voting. Please turn in your ballot
Vote for not more than (1)	Vote for not more than (1)	
[ ] **Gregory Example** Statehood Green	[ ] **Abigail Example** Republican	
[ ] **Helen Example** Republican	[ ] **Yvonne Example** Democratic	
[ ] **Inez Example** Democratic	[ ] **Zachary Example** Statehood Green	
(●) or write-in	(●) or write-in	
HAL 9000	Bender	

FIGURE 40 The Rigged Ballot, courtesy of Alex Halderman.

Halderman was the star of an October 8 oversight hearing, where he dropped additional bombshells. Since the beginning of the test his team had control over the routers and switches of the pilot network, because the default master password (four characters long), which the team obtained from the owner's manual, had not been changed. This capability allowed them to "monitor, change and redirect data flowing through network," thereby providing an alternative route for stealing votes in a real election. Control of the network permitted the Michigan team to watch network operators configure and test the equipment. In addition, the team detected that a pair of security cameras in the data center that were connected to the pilot system did not have passwords. So they could see what operators were doing and capture images directly from the cameras. Halderman brought some of these security camera photos to the hearing.

Halderman even discovered a file used to test the system that consisted of copies of 937 letters sent to real voters. Each letter included the voter's name, id, and 16 character PIN for use in the real Internet election. The file would have allowed the team to cast ballots for actual voters in the real election. Finally, Halderman revealed that attempts to break into the system were coming from Iran and China. Since the attempts involved trying to guess the network password, the team modified the password to defend the network. The Chinese and Iranian attempts illustrate how dangerous the Internet is, with powerful adversaries from around the world constantly attempting to break into systems.

11.1.3 Implications of the Attack

As the DC attack demonstrated, Internet voting can be attacked from anywhere. Almost any complex software system has an abundance of vulnerabilities, and attackers need exploit only one. Once the team changed all the votes, it was impossible for DC officials to reconstruct the original ballots. The team could determine the outcome of the election, while not being detected and leaving no traces. Consequently, the wrong people could have been elected without anyone noticing. It took over a day for DC officials to realize that they had been successfully attacked, even though the attackers thoughtfully played the Michigan fight song after each ballot was cast. By the time officials discovered the attack, it was too late to recover from it.

While the BOEE did not allow the system to be used for the return of voted ballots, they had been prepared to accept voted ballots over the Internet. If there had been no pilot test, or if the Michigan team had been unable to participate, members of the military and civilians living abroad who vote in Washington DC would have been casting their ballots over a very vulnerable system. The BOEE did the right thing by setting up a test and then canceling the ballot return portion when vulnerabilities were uncovered. Unfortunately, other states have not been so responsible. In the 2010 midterms, 33 states allowed some kind of Internet voting—including web based Internet pilots and the return of voted ballots over the Internet via email attachment or fax— without first encouraging independent experts to test the system. [982]

One of us (Jones) has consulted with several election offices, including the BOEE. He observed that the election office in the District of Columbia is above average in terms of physical and human resources. Many big city election offices have less technical expertise, and the average county election office outside of urban areas has far less. Jones' observations suggest that the mistakes found by the Michigan team were not the result of isolated incompetence, but rather were typical of the best we can expect under current circumstances.

The bottom line is that security is hard. Even major corporations with considerable security expertise have been compromised. We know that elections offices are under-resourced and have a lot of other problems to worry about. They also lack security expertise. Therefore, it is completely unrealistic to expect extraordinary security competence from elections office.

11.2   Internet Risks

As we've seen from the DC pilot, a risk of Internet voting is that the computer receiving the voted ballots (*server*) could be attacked over the Internet by individual hackers, political operatives, foreign governments, terrorists, or even Univ. of Michigan graduate students. Nonetheless, the DC attack exploited only a subset of Internet voting vulnerabilities.

11.2.1   The Server

Internet voting, whether web-based or via email, involves having a computer (*client*), typically that of the voter, communicate via the Internet with a server. Since national races in the U.S. cost vast amounts of money, a very small fraction of which would be an exceedingly large bribe, there could be considerable financial, as well as ideological, incentives for individuals to perpetrate attacks.

Corporate and Government Vulnerabilities

A survey of roughly 1000 large organizations stated that in 2008 the average loss per company due to intellectual property cybertheft was about \$4.6 million.[535] A December 2009 report from the Computer Security Institute surveying 443 companies and government agencies found that 64% had experienced malware infections in the preceding year.[612]

A major China-based Internet attack on Google and dozens of other companies illustrates that even major corporate sites are vulnerable. The attack targeted Google intellectual property, including systems used by software developers to build code, as well as Gmail accounts of Chinese human rights activists.[673] As many as 34 companies—such as Yahoo, Adobe, Juniper Networks, defense contractor Northrop-Grumman, and Symantec, a major supplier of anti-virus and anti-spyware software—were targeted.[978] The attacked companies employ large numbers of computer security experts and have vastly more security expertise and resources than relatively small Internet voting vendors.

The attacks looked as if they came from trusted sources, so that victims would be tricked into clicking on a link or file. Then, using a vulnerability in Microsoft's Internet Explorer, the attacker downloaded and installed malicious software, thereby gaining complete control over the compromised system.[576] George Kurtz, Executive Vice President and Worldwide Chief Technology Officer of McAfee (an Internet security company), expressed dismay at the implications:

> In addition to worrying about Eastern European cybercriminals trying to siphon off credit card databases, you have to focus on protecting all of your core intellectual property, private nonfinancial customer information and anything else of intangible value.[576]

Government sites are also vulnerable. In a March 2010 talk, FBI Director Robert Mueller said that the FBI's computer network had been penetrated and that the attackers had "corrupted data."[673] General Michael Hayden, former Director of the CIA and the National Security Agency, has stated: "The modern-day bank robber isn't speeding up to a suburban bank with weapons drawn and notes passed to the teller. He's on the Web taking things of value from you and me."[448]

In spite of devoting large sums of money and resources to cybersecurity, computers at major corporations and government agencies have been successfully attacked. What chance would underfunded local election officials, with little or no security expertise, have in defending themselves against attacks?

11.2.2 Insider attacks

Although this didn't happen in Washington, a risk of any computerized voting, including Internet voting, is that one or more insiders (e.g. programmers) could rig an election by manipulating election software. While many security discussions tend to focus on outsider attacks, insider attacks may be even more dangerous. Even if the system is extensively tested, vote rigging software may not be uncovered if it is well hidden. If it were easy to detect incorrect or malicious software, software vendors would not have to produce frequent security patches, since they would detect all possible problems initially.

A trusted insider, such as former CIA agent Aldrich Ames, who turned out to be a spy, can do tremendous damage before he is caught—if he is ever caught.

11.2.3 The Voting Terminal

Cybertheft tools used to steal personal information or money have become increasingly sophisticated. Many of these tools could be modified to steal Internet elections. While some cybertheft tools are designed for specific systems, the sheer number of attacks and the difficulty of preventing any one of them is a big part of the problem.

Viruses and *worms* are types of malicious software (malware). Just as a human virus spreads from human to human, a computer virus spreads from computer to computer by attaching itself to an email or an input device such as a CD. A virus or worm can infect public or privately owned machines linked to the Internet without the owner's knowledge or permission. If a virus or worm replicates quickly, or if it is widely distributed via popular web pages or candidate websites, attached to spam, etc., it might infect a large number of machines prior to detection. Once a computer is infected, the attacker might be able to modify or destroy the voter's ballot, steal information, delete files, and read email. An election-rigging virus or worm that erases itself after the person votes could be impossible to detect. The damage, however, will have been done.

Many viruses or worms allow their creators to seize control of infected machines. Infected computers remotely controlled by the malware distributor are called *zombies*; a network of infected computers is called a *botnet* (short for robot net). Some botnets have consisted of millions of infected computers. According to the FBI, the Mariposa Botnet may have infected 8,000,000 to 12,000,000 computers internationally.[324] The virus used to create the Mariposa Botnet can steal credit card data and online banking passwords, as well as prevent people from accessing a particular website (a Denial of Service or DoS Attack). The creator of the virus also sold customized versions with augmented features. By 2007, it was estimated that 20% to 40% of all home computers had been "recruited" into botnets, most of which are used to send spam.

The biggest threat posed by malware is to the voter's computer. The existence of large botnets demonstrate that it is not even necessary to send out special election-rigging malware. Many voters' computers (yours, dear reader?) are already infected.

Anti-virus software works by checking for known viruses and worms. Therefore, whenever a new virus appears, the anti-virus software must be updated. There can be many days or even weeks between the time when the virus begins to spread and when it is recognized and analyzed. After that, the virus fix needs to be distributed, and victims need to disinfect their machines. Because anti-virus software has limited capabilities for recognizing unknown malware, a new virus or worm may well escape detection for a while, especially if it remains dormant until, say, Election Day. Even if the virus or worm is detected, removal can be quite difficult, as most PC owners who have had to deal with adware and spyware are well aware.

One study showed that anti-virus software has become less effective over time, with recognition of malware by most anti-virus software falling from 40%–50% at the beginning of 2007 to 20%–30% at the end of that year.[418] Another set of experiments conducted at the University of Michigan demonstrated that the number of malware samples detected decreased significantly as the malware became more recent; when the malware was only one week old, the detection rate was very low.[789] Given that an election-stealing virus or worm would likely be spread silently with no symptoms in order to infect the maximum number of machines, it could be impossible to determine if votes were modified, or even which computers had been infected.

Hackers, criminals, or countries could manipulate Internet-based elections by inserting election-rigging malware into voters' computers. The Conficker worm, discovered in November 2008, illustrates the risk. Conficker rapidly infected between 9 and 15 million machines and had the capability of "calling home" for more instructions.[1006] In other words, the unknown creator of Conficker could instruct an infected machine to install additional malware remotely without the computer owner's knowledge.[953] For example, the new instructions could be targeted at specific candidates and elections, and fine tuned for each election.

While many viruses and worms are planted without the knowledge of the computer owner, people are sometimes willing to download software of highly questionable provenance. In August 2009 a spam message circulate that said, "If You dont [sic] like Obama come here, you can help to ddos his site with your installs." ("ddos" stands for Distributed Denial of Service, a Denial of Service attack involving large numbers of computers). According to CNET News, people who clicked on the email link were offered money in exchange for downloading the software. They were even told to return to the website for updated versions if their virus detection software deleted the original download. [711]

The source of the software is not known. The goal could have been to disrupt websites associated with Obama, to engage in identity theft, or even to infect machines of Obama opponents, something that could be especially useful if Internet voting were to become an option in the United States.

On-Line Banking Attacks

Computer security expert Harri Hursti, who has been involved with selling on-line banking software, made the following observation: [478] "Our sales point was always, 'Yes, we will introduce more fraud. However, we will introduce cost savings which will greatly offset the increased amount of fraud.'" He added that commercially available malicious software has introduced new targets and made it easier to attack small regional banks. Hursti concluded, "So, I think the good lesson is on-line banking was never meant to put fraud down. It was just to save more than the increased cost of the fraud."

Banks might tolerate fraud, because they still end up saving money. But they can make a rational business decision only if they can quantify the cost of fraud. Unfortunately, the fraud v. cost trade-off to which Hursti referred appears to be getting worse, as viruses such as Zeus become increasingly sophisticated. In elections, unlike banking, a "small amount of fraud" is unacceptable, since that fraud might change the election outcome.

A Threat Example: The Zeus Virus

The following example illustrates how a virus can manipulate what a voter sees and change the voter's selection. While Zeus has been used mainly to steal money, it would not be difficult to reprogram Zeus to steal votes instead.

In April 2009 we learned that malicious software, which redirected visitors to an IP address in Amsterdam, had been inserted into Paul McCartney's website. The Amsterdam site contained software that exploited vulnerabilities on the victims' machines to install the very dangerous Zeus virus on those machines. [500] The infection, planted shortly before McCartney's New York reunion concert, was timed to catch as many victims as possible before discovery.

The German edition of Wikipedia was also a source of infection. [449] A bogus article about another dangerous piece of malware contained a link to software that supposedly would fix the problem. However, anyone who downloaded the "fix" was actually downloading a copy of Zeus. In 2009 it was estimated that Zeus had infected about 3.6 million PCs in the U.S. alone. [703]

Zeus' was built to steal money from on-line financial accounts. When the victim logs onto her bank's website, Zeus copies her credentials and sends them to a remote location. It then uses those credentials to remove money from her account. Zeus can even simulate the victim's financial statements. [967] When the victim checks her on-line statement, everything looks as it should. The victim typically learns of the theft only when checks start to bounce or financial transactions cannot be finalized because of insufficient funds. At that point it's too late to retrieve the money, which has been sent off-shore.

The Zeus virus has also mimicked (spoofed) verification systems used by Visa and MasterCard when enrolling new users (Figure 41). [289] Zeus thereby obtained sensitive information such as social security number, card number, and PIN from the unknowing victim, who would think he was providing that information to the bank. This information, sent to the attacker's computers, was used to defraud the victim.

Yet another attack was reported in August 2010 by M86 Security. The report stated that about 3000 bank customers in the U.K. were victimized by a form of the Zeus virus. [622] The announcement accompanying the report's release, which did not provide the bank's name, described the attack:

> Unprotected customers were infected by a Trojan—which managed to avoid detection by traditional Anti-Virus software while browsing the Internet. The Trojan, a Zeus v3, steals the customer's online banking ID and hijacks their online banking sessions. It then checks the account balance and, if the account balance is bigger than £800 value, it issues a money transfer transaction.

> From July 5, the cyber criminals have successfully stolen £675,000 (c. $1,077,000) and the attack is still progressing. [623]

On September 29, 2010 UK police announced the arrest of 19 individuals accused of using the Zeus crimeware toolkit to steal £6,000,000 from thousands of victims over a three month period. [598] Nonetheless, new Zeus attacks continue to be discovered. For example, in October 2010 Computerworld revealed that Zeus was attacking Charles Schwab investment accounts. [548] Victims' machines were infected by links to malicious sites hidden in bogus LinkedIn reminders.

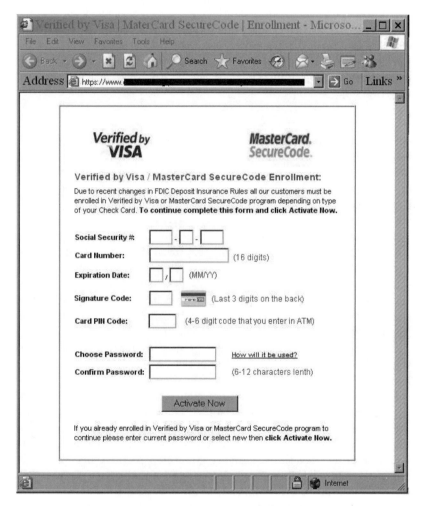

FIGURE 41 The Bogus Enrollment Screen Displayed by Zeus.
Screen capture by Amit Klein, CTO of Trusteer.

In light of the many successful attacks being conducted against governments, major banks, and the world's technology leaders, it should be relatively easy to entrap large numbers of voters who are not technologists. Once a voter's computer is infected by a malicious virus, all bets are off. The virus can make the computer screen show the voter a ballot image that correctly represents the voter's intent. But the virus can then send something entirely different over the Internet. In other words, *it is the virus that votes, not the voter.* The voter will never know, because it is impossible for the voter to see what is actually sent.

11.2.4 Counterfeit Websites

Another Internet risk involves counterfeit websites, or *spoofing.* Because fake websites can be made to look very much like legitimate ones, spoofing is used to entrap victims into revealing sensitive information such as credit card and social security numbers. In the case of Internet voting, spoofing could trick a voter into thinking that he or she has actually voted, when in fact the vote will never arrive at the legitimate website.

For example, suppose I want to defeat a candidate, let's call him Thomas Jefferson, in the upcoming Senatorial election. I create a website called JeffersonForSenate.com that looks like an official Jefferson.com website and has a link that says, "Click here to vote for Thomas Jefferson." The link would be to a fake website that looks exactly like the real one used for voting. Because the website is not legitimate, none of the "votes" on that website would be counted.

JeffersonForSenate.com could also be used to download malware on the voter's computer. I could post a notice on the website saying, "For more information, click here." Next, I send fake newsletters to the people who respond. These newsletters include an attached video of Jefferson, accompanied by software for viewing the video. Unfortunately for the unwary voter, the software also contains a virus that emulates the official voting website. When voters who download the video attempt to vote, they think they are connected to the official website, but in fact they are communicating only with malicious software that has been installed on their machines. If the voter selects Jefferson, the software can change the vote and send the modified vote to the official website. The voter will never know what happened.

A variation on spoofing is called *phishing.* Phishing involves email appearing to be from a legitimate organization, for example a credit card company. The phony email contains an authentic-looking link that appears to go to the legitimate organization's website, but actually goes to the criminal website. Because the emails and websites tend to be well designed, the victim who goes to the fake website frequently ends up providing sensitive information, such as a credit card number.[553] While phishing usually steals personal information, the same techniques could be used to trick the voter into voting from a fake website.

Yet another use of a fake voting website is to create a *man in the middle* attack. By eavesdropping on communications between the voter and the real voting website, the attacker can use intercepted information, such as a password, to impersonate the voter and cast the voter's vote for Jefferson's opponent. A man in the middle attack could also be used to monitor the voter's selections, thereby violating the voter's right to a secret ballot. Such monitoring could be useful for vote buying schemes or in situations involving coercion of the voter.

A good way to avoid counterfeit websites is to rely on a trusted entity (certificate authority or CA) to authenticate that a website is legitimate. This job typically is done by the user's browser, which checks that the website has a valid "certificate" issued by a trusted entity known to the browser. The certificate digitally identifies the organization or individual with whom it is associated. If the browser does not recognize (trust) the issuer of the certificate, it will ask the computer user if she still wants to access the questionable website. If a user does not understand the significance of what the browser is asking, she may naively instruct the browser to access the possibly counterfeit website.

But even if the voter is very careful and links only to what she believes are legitimate websites, she could still be victimized. First, it is possible to trick many browsers into going to the attacker's, rather than the legitimate, website.[1035] Second, some CAs have not been validating the identities of sites they vouch for.[807] Finally, the voter could be vulnerable to an attack on the routing infrastructure of the Internet.[636] Such an attack could take her to a fake voting website without her knowledge. This attack is a bit like stealing mail (in this case the voted ballot) out of the voter's mailbox.

11.2.5 Denial of Service Attacks

A *Denial of Service (DoS)* attack occurs when so many corrupted computers attempt to access a website that legitimate users are unable to do so. A *Distributed Denial of Service (DDoS)* attack involves large numbers of computers (botnet) that typically are controlled by some widely distributed malware. There are many documented instances of DDoS attacks, such as the massive 2007 DDoS attack on Estonia, discussed in Section 11.7.6. It appears that both the Estonian attack and an attack on the Republic of Georgia, which occurred around the time of the Georgian invasion of South Ossetia, originated in Russia. Other victims of DDoS attacks have included Twitter, Facebook, Google, Yahoo, eBay, and Amazon.

A DDoS attack could prevent certain groups from voting or could even disrupt an entire election, as may have occurred in a leadership vote by the New Democratic Party (NDP) in Canada. Internet voting for the NDP election lasted from January 2 through convention day of January 25, 2003. On January 25, the same day that the Slammer worm was attacking large numbers of (unpatched) Windows 2000 servers on the Internet, the NDP voting site reportedly was down or effectively unusable for several hours. [155]

Because of the secrecy surrounding the technical aspects of the NDP election, we do not know if the NDP voting site was brought down by a denial of service attack or if it was a victim of the Slammer worm. The vendor, election.com, claimed to have patched the servers against the Slammer worm and maintained that they experienced a denial of service attack. However, election.com provided neither logs nor other proof that the servers were patched; nor did they permit expert examination of the records. There was no transparency and hence no way for an independent outsider to determine what had happened.

11.2.6   No Post-Election Audit or Recount

Accountability is a critical aspect of any election. In order to address security concerns, we need to be able to verify after the election that the technology has operated correctly and that the right person has been declared the winner. Just as businesses routinely conduct audits, so too should elections be routinely audited, or, if necessary, recounted, as happened in the 2008 Minnesota Senatorial race. In order to conduct a post-election audit or recount, election officials must possess accurate copies of all legally cast ballots, something that is impossible with current Internet voting technology. Allowing the voter to print a copy of her ballot for her own use is meaningless because there is no way to verify that the paper copy matches the electronic version that reached the election official.

Some systems, such as Helios [452] and Remotegrity, [843] provide cryptographic tools to allow the voter to verify that an accurate version of her ballot has been received and counted. Encryption does not protect against Denial of Service attacks, spoofing, coercion, design flaws, and many kinds of ordinary software bugs. [318] If a serious problem is uncovered in an election, there is no way to conduct a recount. While these systems have been used for some small elections, the general consensus is that they are not ready for use in a major election. As Ben Adida, the creator of Helios, put it:

We now have documented evidence ... that viruses like Stuxnet that corrupt nuclear power plants by spreading from one Windows machine to the other have been built. And so if you run a very large scale election for a president of a G8 country, why wouldn't we see a similar scenario? Certainly, it's worth just as much money; it's worth just as much strategically. ... All the verifiability doesn't change the fact that a client side corruption in my browser can flip my vote even before it's encrypted, and if we ... must have a lot of voters verify their process, I think we're going to lose, because most voters don't quite do that yet. [14]

11.2.7 False Flag Attacks

Yet another risk of Internet voting is a *false-flag attack* in which attackers penetrate a system to plant bogus evidence of an attack coming from somewhere else in order to provoke retaliation. With Internet voting, a false flag attack that made it appear that an attack had come from a particular country, say Iran, could trigger a retaliatory attack against a falsely implicated enemy state. Needless to say, such a occurrence could be highly destabilizing and dangerous.

11.2.8 Loss of the Secret Ballot

States that allow the return of voted ballots via fax or email attachments have been asking voters to sign a statement relinquishing the right to a secret ballot. The same may also happen with web-based Internet voting that does not use special encryption techniques to protect the voter's privacy once the ballot has been received by the local election official. The threat to eliminate the secret ballot for a class of voters is disturbing for several reasons. First, it makes such voters second class citizens, deprived of a right that other citizens take for granted. Second, there is no need to eliminate the secret ballot for overseas voters, as we discuss in Section 11.6.7. Third, and perhaps most important, ballot secrecy protection is not just an individual right but also a systemic requirement, essential for fair, honest elections that reflect the voting public's choices. Without ballot secrecy, voters, especially those in hierarchical organizations such as the military, can be subjected to coercion. An election in which a subset of voters could be pressured to vote a particular way by their superiors or others is not a free and fair election.

11.3 Early Reports

Many of the risks we have discussed were recognized in early reports. In 2000 and 2001 three reports on Internet voting, as well as a more general report issued by a commission co-chaired by former Presidents Carter and Ford, were released. In addition, a U.S. General Accounting

Office (GAO) report on elections included a chapter on Internet voting that focused on "formidable technical and social challenges." [369] All of the reports expressed significant reservations about voting in federal elections over the Internet. The security risks described in these reports remain as relevant today as they were when the reports were issued, as has been demonstrated by the serious problems caused by post-2001 viruses and worms such as Blaster, Slammer, MyDoom, Conficker, and Zeus.

The California Internet Voting Task Force Report was the first major report to address security issues of Internet voting. [137] The report, commissioned by the California Secretary of State and released in January 2000, warned of "the possibility of 'Virus' and 'Trojan Horse' software attacks on home and office computers used for voting." While the report optimistically stated that such attacks are preventable, it realistically observed that attacks "could result in a number of problems ranging from a denial of service to the submission of electronically altered ballots." In light of many security problems, the report recommended against deploying a system that allows voting from home, office, or any Internet connected computer "until a satisfactory solution to the malicious code and remote control software problems is offered."

The Report of the National Workshop on Internet Voting (NWIV): Issues and Research Agenda was published in 2001 in response to a 1999 request to examine the possibility of Internet voting made by President Clinton to the National Science Foundation. (One of us, Barbara Simons, was a member of the study group that produced the report). Below is a quote from the Executive Summary:

> *Remote Internet voting systems pose significant risk to the integrity of the voting process, and should not be fielded for use in public elections until substantial technical and social science issues are addressed.* [Italics in original] The security risks associated with these systems are both numerous and pervasive, and, in many cases, cannot be resolved using even today's most sophisticated technology. [505]

The Caltech/MIT Voting Technology Report: What Is, What Could Be, published in July 2001, stated: "Remote Internet voting poses serious security risks. It is much too easy for one individual to disrupt an entire election and commit large-scale fraud." [144]

The National Commission on Federal Election Reform, co-chaired by former Presidents Carter and Ford, strongly recommended against Internet voting in its August 2001 report:

> Our concerns about early and remote voting plans are even stronger as we contemplate the possibility of Internet voting. In addition to the

more general objections, the Commission has heard persuasive testimony that Internet voting brings a fresh set of technical and security dangers all its own. This is an idea whose time most certainly has not yet come. [354]

Finally, the GAO's October 2001 report *Elections: Perspectives on Activities and Challenges Across the Nation* warned: "For remote Internet voting, the problem of malicious software (such as computer viruses, worms, or 'Trojan horses') is acute—that is, such software could be introduced into computers without voters being aware of its presence. Hackers could thus alter ballots, spy on citizens' votes, or disrupt Web sites, preventing voters from voting." [369]

11.4 Misconceptions

Despite all the warnings from independent studies and commissions, as well as sensational news stories about hacking and viruses, some widely held misconceptions about Internet voting persist: (1) because we can bank or make purchases over the Internet (e-commerce), we can safely vote over the Internet; (2) Internet voting will increase voter participation, especially among young people; and (3) Internet voting will save money. We have already discussed the risks of Internet banking; we now address each of the other issues.

11.4.1 Comparing Internet Voting to E-Commerce

Internet voting has many complications that do not arise with e-commerce:

- A secret ballot protects against vote buying and coercion, but it also prevents election officials from checking with me that they received an accurate copy of my vote. By contrast, when I make an Internet purchase, the seller can document who I am and what I am buying.

- I know if amazon.com has received a correct order from me. But with most commercial Internet voting schemes, I cannot know whether or not a correct copy of my vote was received. I could print a copy of my voted ballot, but so long as that paper ballot stays with me and is not in the possession of election officials, it cannot be a check on my electronic ballot, nor can it be used to audit or recount the election. An email confirming my vote is unreliable, since the email could be forged or my infected computer could lie to me. While amazon.com could attempt to cheat me by overcharging, I would detect the cheating on my credit card statement. Because my ballot is secret, no such checking is available for my ballot.

- If a commercial website fails, transactions conducted prior to the failure are not impacted. But, failure of a voting website on Election Day could mean that some people get to vote and others do not.

- In the event of an e-commerce failure, there is a good chance that the situation will be rectified, or that I can stop my credit card payment. But, if my vote is not successfully cast on Election Day, I probably won't know, and I almost certainly will be unable to revote.

- Since Internet voting is done remotely, it is difficult to verify a person's identity. It might be legal for my spouse to make a purchase using my credit card. But in most countries it is illegal for my spouse to vote on my behalf, unless for some reason I am unable to do so myself, e.g. I have a disability that prevents me from voting independently.

- amazon.com might try to sell me products, or my browser might display an ad in a pop-up window. Such actions may be annoying, but they are not illegal. However, with online voting political ads could be displayed while I'm voting, something that may not be currently illegal, but probably should be—just as posting political posters in voting booths is illegal.

- Unlike commercial activities, vote buying and selling is illegal. In the 2000 U.S. Presidential election, an online system designed to broker Nader and Gore votes was created, but it was forced to shut down by the California Attorney General. There is no evidence that any votes were actually traded. Internet voting could eliminate the need for an honor system by allowing voters to sell their voting credentials on a website. The website might even automatically cast the actual ballot.*

11.4.2 Voter Participation

As early as 1964 V. K. Zworykin, who had been Vice-President of RCA Laboratories, was calling for instant direct democracy using remote electronic voting. [1039] Since there was no Internet at the time, he suggested using modified telephones. A third of a century later, similar ideas were reappearing. In 2000 the Knight-Ridder News Service claimed: "Californians could be voting over the Internet in five years with a computerized system that could revolutionize the state's voting process and boost sagging voter turnout." [158] However, Internet voting does not necessarily increase voter turnout. For example, a May 2009

---

*There are many legitimate situations, such as family members voting on their home computer and people voting from the same work location, in which multiple voters have the same Internet location (IP address). Therefore, while it would be possible to detect multiple votes coming from the same IP address, it would be problematic to prohibit such votes.

local election in Honolulu that allowed people to vote only over the Internet or via phone saw an 83% drop in voter participation, compared to the similar election in 2007.[561] The vendor, Everyone Counts, also ran the 2007 Swindon, UK Internet election and the 2008 Democrats Abroad primary, both discussed below. The Electoral Commission, established by the UK Parliament, determined that the Internet voting in Swindon had a negligible effect on voter turnout.

We know of no rigorous study of overall voter participation in Internet elections. Conducting such a study would be difficult, since voter turnout can vary enormously from election to election. But even if Internet voting were to increase overall participation, the increase would be a Pyrrhic victory if the entire election were jeopardized by insecure Internet voting.

11.4.3 Cost

Internet voting costs, especially upfront charges, can be quite steep. For example, 2009 cost estimates from Everyone Counts were so large that Washington State legislation that would have allowed Internet voting for UOCAVA (military and overseas) voters, was killed in committee.[100] The estimated costs, obtained by John Gideon via an open records request, included:[234]

- 6 weeks consulting to understand state requirements: $40,000–$60,000;
- 10 weeks consulting to develop processes specific to state requirements: $100,000–$200,000;
- 12 weeks consulting to conduct initial pilot + 8 weeks engineering/consulting to evaluate the pilot and recommend changes: $300,000–$700,000;
- 12 weeks consulting to conduct training for new counties, conduct pilots, evaluate the processes, and recommend for next pilot: $500,000–$900,000;
- 20 weeks consulting to conduct training, build ballots, test ballots, conduct the general election, evaluate the processes, and make recommendations for the next election: $1,500,000–$2,500,000;
- 4 weeks consulting to provide the final report, etc.: $60,000–$80,000;
- Primary and general election ongoing annual license fee per county: $20,000–$120,000 per year + $2–$7 per registered UOCAVA voter.

In other words, upfront cost would have ranged from $2,500,000 to $4,440,000. After that, each county would have been hit with an annual fee, combined with additional per-voter charges.

11.5 Ignoring the Obvious

While this section focuses on Democratic Party primaries, the Democratic Party is hardly unique in holding insecure elections over the Internet. The 2000 ICANN election, the 2000 Arizona Democratic primary, the 2008 Arizona Libertarian Party primary, and Internet elections in a few countries are all discussed on our website. The following examples are illustrative of an all too common lack of understanding of security issues, denial of the possibility of any problems, and failure to consult independent security experts.

11.5.1 The Michigan Democratic Party 2004 Caucuses

In 2003 the Democratic National Committee (DNC) passed a resolution stating:

> [T]he DNC goes on record demanding that all electronic voting equipment used in public elections must incorporate an accessible voter-verified paper audit trail as soon as practical, but in no case any later than the November 2004 general election. [235]

Nonetheless, for their 2004 caucuses the Michigan Democratic Party (MDP), on the basis of unchallenged assurances from the vendor, chose to provide voters with the option of voting via absentee mail ballots or over the Internet, as well as at conventional polling locations. In spite of the DNC resolution, the Internet voting scheme did not incorporate an accessible voter-verified paper audit trail.

The company managing the Internet voting was Election Services Corp. (ESC), an offshoot of election.com. In a heavily redacted email from ESC to the Compliance Director of the MDP, ESC stated, "We have been audited ... by the Carter Institute for our ICANN election. The US Department of Defense has reviewed our security procedures in anticipation of an international Internet election pilot ...." [312] ESC did not mention, at least in the unredacted portion, that there were major problems with the ICANN election, or that a security review of the Department of Defense project, one that would ultimately call for its cancellation, was ongoing.

In the belief that Internet voting would increase participation by young people, MDP Chair Mark Brewer declared, "Polls show that this [Internet voting] is very popular with young people, and they have one of the worst rates of participation." [887]

The MDP argued that those who raised issues about the Michigan scheme "can offer only *speculation*—they offer *no evidence* of any *actual incidents* of Internet voting security problems" [emphasis in the original]. [118] In spite of a spate of highly publicized Internet viruses and worms, the MDP asserted, "Internet voting is secure" and "The voting infrastructure also is secure." However, instead of providing evidence to support their claims, the MDP declared that it was the responsibility of the challengers to prove that "the system is *not* secure by 'clear and convincing' evidence" [emphasis in the original]. In addition, the MDP maintained that "extensive and reliable security features provided by an experienced vendor will protect the integrity of the Internet voting option." However, all of the security system features listed in MDP documents related to security at the vendor's site; none addressed security threats to the users' computers or to the Internet infrastructure.

In claiming that there have been "numerous successful public, private and political party elections in the United States and throughout the world using Internet voting without security problems," the MDP ignored both the secrecy that has made rigorous analysis of previous Internet elections impossible and the fact that, because there is nothing that can be audited, it is almost impossible to determine whether or not security related incidents have occurred.

The MDP contended that ESC would not have been chosen by the Department of Defense for its upcoming Internet voting project "unless its security were adequate." As discussed below, that project was terminated because of security concerns. The cancellation became public on February 5, just before the close of Internet voting in Michigan.

The MDP had been planning to allow Internet voting for their 2008 caucuses, even though they had not provided any analysis of the 2004 process and, so far as we know, had not obtained any assessment of software and security risks from independent computer security experts. However, since the Michigan legislature established a state-administered presidential primary for 2008, the MDP did not hold its party-run caucus, and Internet voting was not deployed.

11.5.2   The Democrats Abroad 2008 Primary

Democrats Abroad (DA), the overseas branch of the Democratic Party, allowed members to vote over the Internet in a real primary in 2008. Again, officials unquestioningly accepted vendor claims, ignored recent news about Internet vulnerabilities, and did not consult with independent outside security experts.

According to Robert Checkoway, International Secretary of DA, "There is no requirement that DA voters be registered to vote in their home state. There is also no requirement that they be registered Democrats. There is no way we could verify either of those things." [161] The Internet portion of the primary was run by Everyone Counts, the same company that had been commissioned to run the Internet portion of the 2008 MDP primary. Software used for the DA primary was not inspected by outside experts or by any state or federal entities.

DA did not coordinate with state Democratic Parties before allowing someone to vote in their primary. Therefore, in spite of the NO DOUBLE VOTING! warning, people could vote both in their state primaries and in the DA primary. Typifying the lack of security, voters were sent their ballot numbers and Personal Identification Numbers (PINs) in unencrypted emails. In other words, anyone intercepting the email could easily impersonate the voter. DA even encouraged people to print a copy of their ballot, something euphemistically referred to as a paper trail, in an attempt to reassure the voter, as acknowledged by Everyone Counts CEO Lori Steele. She was quoted as saying, "Some customers demand paper as a comfort for their voters, and that's what we provided." [398]

There was no way for the voter to know whether or not the printed copy corresponded to the vote record that was transmitted.* DA paid Everyone Counts $40,000; 11,162 people voted over the Internet. [411,236]

Emails obtained via an open records request by Washington State resident John Gideon reveal that in early January 2009, Meredith Gowan Le Goff, then Chair of the Europe/Middle East/Africa regions for Democrats Abroad, was introduced to Washington State policy makers by Everyone Counts CEO Lori Steele. According to one state official, "She [Gowan Le Goff] had wonderful things to say about your company, and on countering the anti-Internet skeptics." [942] In addition to assisting Everyone Counts, DA officials claimed in statements to the press, such as the one at the beginning of this chapter, that the system was secure.

11.6   Military Voting

Frequent moves on short notice, deployment to distant bases, and rough field conditions can make conventional postal absentee voting difficult for overseas military personnel. Expatriates living abroad, especially in countries with unreliable mail service, can also have problems. Members of uniformed services, their families, and non-military citizens living overseas are called UOCAVA voters. (UOCAVA comes from the Uniformed and Overseas Citizens Absentee Voting Act of 1986.) UOCAVA voters have complained that absentee ballots were never delivered or that their returned voted ballots arrived too late to be counted.

---

*Since the primary votes were not private, in theory voters could have contacted the DA leadership to check that their votes had been properly recorded. However, this option was not provided.

Consequently, and in spite of multiple warnings, repeated efforts have been made to allow UOCAVA voters to vote in national elections via fax or over the Internet, even though such transmissions use telecommunications infrastructures of other countries, some of which may be hostile to the U.S. (Even friendly countries may have an interest in manipulating U.S. elections).

11.6.1 The 2000 Election

The Federal Voting Assistance Program (FVAP), housed in the Department of Defense (DoD), is charged with facilitating voting for all UOCAVA voters, including civilians. In 2000, FVAP conducted a small-scale Internet voting project called VOI (Voting over the Internet). At a cost of $6.2 million, the 84 real votes from four states (Florida, South Carolina, Texas, and Utah) cost roughly $73,800 each. The assumption was that there was little incentive to attack or subvert such a small-scale "experiment". Given that the Florida race, which provided the winning Electoral College votes in the 2000 Presidential election, was decided by only 537 votes, such an assumption can be dangerous.

A 2001 FVAP-sponsored report on VOI warned that:

> [Remote Internet voting] is subject to the same security concerns as the current VOI System. For this reason, we cannot recommend [it] as an immediate follow-on development to the VOI Pilot .... Therefore, we recommend that research continue on these security issues so that this alternative could be implemented in the future when adequate security measures are available to counteract the malicious software (e.g., virus and Trojan Horse) threat and denial of service attempts. [123]

11.6.2 SERVE

Despite the warning in the report it commissioned, FVAP allocated $22 million to build the Secure Electronic Registration and Voting Experiment (SERVE) system so that UOCAVA voters could register and vote over the Internet in the 2004 primaries and general election. Participation by states and counties within those states was voluntary.

Voters could use their own computers, so long as they ran Windows, or they could use public computers in any country, such as those found in libraries and cybercafes. Voters were responsible for the security of whatever computers they used. The vendor for SERVE was Accenture.

In 2003, FVAP assembled a group of experts called the Security Peer Review Group to evaluate SERVE. Following two 3-day meetings with FVAP officials and lead technical staff of SERVE, the four computer scientists who attended both meetings, including one of us, Barbara Simons, released *A Security Analysis of the Secure Electronic Registra-*

tion and Voting Experiment (SERVE), on January 20, 2004.[515] The conclusion of that report stated:

> Because the danger of successful, large-scale attacks is so great, we reluctantly recommend shutting down the development of SERVE immediately and not attempting anything like it in the future until both the Internet and the world's home computer infrastructure have been fundamentally redesigned, or some other unforeseen security breakthroughs appear.

At the time the report was issued, 50 counties in seven states (AR, FL, HI, NC, SC, UT, WA) were planning to participate in SERVE. FVAP had estimated that the maximum overall vote total would be approximately 100,000, including both primaries and the general election. On January 30, DoD Secretary Paul Wolfowitz issued a memo stating that the Pentagon "will not be using the SERVE Internet voting project in view of the inability to assure legitimacy of votes that would be cast using the system, which thereby brings into doubt the integrity of election results." [1004] On February 5, news that SERVE would not be used in the 2004 election became public. [331] SERVE was subsequently terminated.

FVAP has referred to the report authors as "a minority of members of a peer review group for SERVE"; however, there was neither another peer review group nor a "majority" report. [333]

It is fortunate for our democracy that SERVE was halted. If SERVE had been deemed successful in 2004, it is likely that a similar program would have been made available first to UOCAVA voters and then to the entire country—despite the impossibility of proving the absence of either serious software bugs or successful election rigging attacks. Even if we could have known with certainty that SERVE had not been attacked in 2004, there is no guarantee that a similar system would not be attacked in a future election, since an attacker could have far more impact if many more people were voting over the Internet. Nonetheless, Internet voting for the military is an idea that refuses to die.

11.6.3 Fax Voting

A program that allows voted ballots to be returned via fax, called the Electronic Transmission Service (ETS), was started by the DoD in 1990 for military involved in Operation Desert Shield. ETS capabilities were expanded in 2003 to include fax to email conversion. [333]

Not only does fax voting requires the voter to give up her right to a secret ballot, but it also raises security issues, especially if the voter is living or stationed abroad. It is not possible for the DoD to guarantee the security of telecommunications outside the U.S. Faxes sent from computers are subject to the same security threats as computer-based Internet voting. It is relatively easy to forge both the contents and originating telephone number of a fax.

11.6.4 IVAS 2004

In September 2004, well after the cancellation of SERVE, the DoD's Interim Voting Assistance System (IVAS) was implemented.[333] IVAS allowed DoD overseas personnel and their families to request and download blank ballots over the Internet. The voted ballot was then sent by regular mail to the voter's local election official. Of the 108 counties in nine states that participated in the 2004 IVAS, only 28 counties received and processed ballot requests. Voters downloaded only seventeen ballots.

Email voting in Missouri, North Dakota, and Utah

While the official IVAS 2004 documents we have read speak only of providing blank ballots to military voters, IVAS also deployed an email-voting scheme for the 2004 Presidential election. The email-voting proposal was first announced in August 2004 by Missouri Secretary of State Matt Blunt (R), who was a candidate for governor.[96] While Blunt's announcement applied to Missouri, subsequently North Dakota and Utah stated that they also would be allowing the military to vote via email.

The plan was described in an email from the Chief Counsel of the Senate Committee on Rules and Administration dated September 24, 2004:

> [IVAS] uses a 3rd party contractor, Omega Technologies, Alexandria, VA, as a middleman in transmitting completed ballots by FAX to local election authorities. Although this program has been operational since 2000 through the Electronic Transmission Service (when 334 completed ballots were transmitted by FAX and another 62 in 2002), last week an extension of this program—IVAS—went live.

> IVAS transmits blank ballots electronically through email. This same system has been expanded to allow military in Iraq and Afghanistan to scan completed ballots into a computer and then email the pdf file back to Omega, who then prints the ballot and transmits it to the local election authority by FAX. So far, only Missouri, North Dakota and Utah are accepting completed ballots returned to Omega by email.

> At a recent briefing, DOD officials indicated that that *this technology had not been subjected to a security review.*[375] [emphasis added]

Email voters were required to sign a statement acknowledging that they were relinquishing their right to a secret ballot. Because voters' names were transmitted with their ballots, DoD and contractor employees could know how the voter voted, as could local election officials. In some states such as Pennsylvania, where voters have a constitutional right to a secret ballot, requiring voters to give up this right would be illegal. The scheme also appears to have been illegal in Missouri. According to a New York Times editorial from November 3, 2004, "the Missouri Supreme Court held as early as 1895 that its State Constitution requires that voting be by secret ballot." [770] This raises an interesting question: Is it ever—or should it be—legal for voters to waive their rights to a secret ballot? If those rights can be waived, then voters may be forced to vote according to the wishes of a vote buyer or of someone in a position of authority.

The security risks of the email-fax-voting proposal were breathtaking. There were no independent outside observers or representatives of political parties or candidates watching the "trained professionals" who downloaded the email. There was no impartial inspection, qualification, or certification of the system used by Missouri, North Dakota, and Utah. There was no formal review of the code; independent computer security experts were not brought in to examine the system or the code for security vulnerabilities. The software used is not publicly known, nor is it publicly known if it was commercial or custom software. The names of the Omega employees working in the DoD were not made public.

Emails can get caught in spam filters or lost in other ways. The "From" field on emails can be forged, as can unencrypted contents. Because emails travel over the Internet, they are incredibly insecure. The combination of excessive secrecy and an insecure voting process means that we cannot know if all of the votes were received, if votes for the "wrong" candidates were "lost," if selections were added to partially voted ballots by the people processing the emails, if voters felt pressured to vote a certain way because their commanding officers might know how they voted, if votes were forged, or if people processing the ballots attached the signature portion to a different ballot.

By contrast, for the 2004 presidential election the city of Chicago used email and faxes to deliver blank ballots, but required that the completed ballot be returned via regular mail—a far more secure option. [332]

11.6.5 The Integrated Voting Alternative Site (IVAS)

In September 2006, FVAP publicly announced that it had created a new Internet voting system for the November 7, 2006 midterm elections, also called IVAS. [514] The name was subsequently changed to the Integrated Voting Alternative Site, but the IVAS acronym was retained. [164] IVAS was designed and built in only 79 days, a very short period of time for such a complex and critical system. [278] We have not seen any final assessment of the system, including the cost and number of users. A September 2006 document put the cost at $1,300,940.74. [504]

Unlike SERVE, no external review of IVAS was conducted. However, an internal DoD review expressed concern about the security of the system.

> The transmission of voting materials by unsecured email is a concern from both a privacy and security concern. Email traffic ... is easily monitored, blocked and subject to tampering. In addition, the publication of e-mail addresses of voting officials subject those offices to attack, effectively blocking voters. E-mails can be easily and reliably signed and encrypted to reduce the risk of tampering ... However, at the time of this report, there is no plan to digitally sign or encrypt e-mail communications .... [T]he risk that tampering could occur is significant and may reflect negatively on FVAP or DoD. [503]

Despite the security risks described in the DoD review, states were encouraged to participate in IVAS, as illustrated by a letter signed by Dr. David Chu and others in the DoD:

> Consider a faxing/email option for return of voted ballots. If your state does not allow voting materials to be transmitted via email, but does allow faxing, FVAP has enhanced its Electronic Transmission Service to receive faxed voting materials and forward them as email attachments. This option will provide a viable alternative to Uniformed Service members stationed in combat zones and other overseas areas. Due to the security measures taken by the military, the capability for unclassified fax transmission is not available to most of our service members in these regions, but email transmissions are an option for many. After receiving an email from Uniformed Service members and other overseas voters, FVAP can forward the transmission to the states as a fax document to comply with state law. [504]

As discussed earlier, voting by fax or email not only entails serious security risks, but also requires voters to relinquish their right to a secret ballot.

11.6.6 Operation BRAVO

Operation BRAVO (Op BRAVO) is illustrative of the tendency to claim that pilot projects have been successful, regardless of the results. It also demonstrates the risk common to all voting systems that security warnings will be ignored because of the need to let people vote.

In November 2007 the tax exempt Operation BRAVO (Bring Remote Access to Voters Overseas) Foundation announced the Okaloosa Distance Balloting Project (ODBP). The goal of ODBP was to provide UOCAVA voters from Okaloosa County, Florida with the option of voting over the Internet in the 2008 presidential election. Scytl Secure Electronic Voting, a privately owned company headquartered in Barcelona, Spain, developed the voting system; the effort was financed by the Op BRAVO Foundation.

Two key people in Op BRAVO were Carol Paquette and Pat Hollarn. Hollarn was both Supervisor of Elections of Okaloosa County and President of the Op BRAVO Foundation Board during the election, though she subsequently retired as Supervisor of Elections in December, 2008. Paquette, former program manager for VOI and SERVE, was the Foundation Secretary.[111]

The ODBP created one voting location in each of England, Germany, and Japan. Okaloosa County residents could vote from any of these locations using a commercial laptop computer located in a secure voting kiosk. Once the voter finalized the ballot, it was first encrypted and digitally signed and then sent over a secure connection (OpenVPN) to a voting server in the data center. In addition, the voter was asked to review a paper Voter Choice Record and, if it accurately reflected the voter's choices, to deposit the Voter Choice Record in a receptacle at the kiosk. Finally, each voter was given a "counted as cast" receipt that allowed the voter to verify that his ballot had been received, but not whether or not it had been accurately counted.[110]

While not federally certified, the Okaloosa system was provisionally certified under Florida state standards. Also, the Scytl voting software was reviewed by a team of outside experts, commissioned by the State of Florida as part of the state certification process. The team included computer security expert Alec Yasinsac, who worked with Op BRAVO in the design of the system.[171]

The code review team found that the system was defended against outsider threats, such as Internet hackers, "as well as can reasonably be expected, given current technology." Their comment about the insider threat was more pointed:

> The system is vulnerable to attack by trusted insiders (such as elec-

tion officials behaving maliciously). Defending against such attacks can be challenging in any voting system. In Scytl's system, Voter Choice Records are pivotal to this defense. *Manual counts of the Voter Choice Records, as well as procedural controls on insider access to the system before and during an election, are the only way we have identified to secure the system against insider threats.* [emphasis added]

The Voter Choice Records were delivered to the Okaloosa Elections Office on November 4, where they were manually counted by Op BRAVO officials, though there were no outside witnesses. Op BRAVO announced that the paper and electronic records produced the same results, but their press release made no mention of discrepancies later uncovered by University of Miami Law Professor Martha Mahoney: Voter Certificates attesting to eligibility were signed by 95 people, but only 93 ballots were cast, and only 92 Voter Choice Records were included in the audit. [625] Part of the explanation, as mentioned on the Op BRAVO website, is that a voter may have interrupted the voting process, and not tried a second time. However, as Mahoney observed:

> Seven voters from precinct 46 signed in at the kiosks, including two voters in Japan, but only six ballots from that precinct were counted, only one from Japan. A handwritten note from the project manager stated that a kiosk worker from Japan "will prepare incident report" on two voters: an unnamed voter who had an incident involving a Voter Choice Record, and a named voter who was one of those from precinct 46. However, there is no incident report on that voter and no explanation of why a second ballot was not counted from that precinct.

In addition to the audit discrepancies, critical compromises were made in security that was promised, but not delivered. Because no follow up analysis by the Op BRAVO team has been made public, the security compromises, discussed below, have come to light only because of Mahoney's investigation.

In a pre-election response to the code review team's report, Scytl stated that the voting software could not run unless a key security condition was satisfied (the digital signature was verified by the voting computer). [886] Nonetheless, it appears that Scytl knowingly circumvented that security condition by instructing poll workers to ignore the security warning (accept an expired certificate) and continue. [626]*

---

*The Bouncy Castle certificate used to verify the digital signature had a warning saying that it had expired. There was also a warning that the application would be run "without the security restrictions normally provided by Java," because the system could not verify the digital signature (generated by an untrusted certificate) on the Java voting application.

Another security violation occurred in Japan, where the computer was unable to verify the operating system (using a cryptographic hash) which was uploaded into volatile memory daily from a CD, even though it had succeeded in doing so twice before. Because volatile memory loses its contents whenever the computer is turned off, the code review team had warned about the difficulty of verifying that executed software matched the certified software, adding that "there may be no way to check whether malicious code was introduced." Nonetheless, poll workers followed instructions and ignored the unsuccessful verification. There were phone and email incident reports, but no follow-up investigation, even though all the ballots from the Japanese kiosk, and that kiosk alone, had the same choice for president.

It appears that Florida did not approve the security circumventions, despite the state requirement that a new certificate be obtained for any system configuration change.

Scytl spent about $500,000, and Okaloosa County made two $50,000 payments to Scytl, resulting in a total cost of $600,000. [625] In addition, material obtained from an open records request of the Florida Voters Coalition estimated that over $46,000 of services will have been provided pro bono. [876] The resulting per-voter cost was over $6000.

What are the implications of the Okaloosa pilot project?

Instructing poll workers to ignore security warnings desensitizes poll workers to the importance of treating security warnings as serious risks. This is not the kind of lesson a pilot should be conveying.

Furthermore, the Okaloosa project violated fundamental principles of a meaningful pilot. Because significant discrepancies were ignored and no meaningful post-election analysis released, the level of transparency and accountability was unprofessionally low, and claims of success were unsubstantiated. Nonetheless, Op BRAVO has been lauded by the Election Assistance Commission and others. [626] The widespread perception that the pilot was successful could be exploited to justify a significant expansion of Internet voting. In fact, the Op BRAVO Foundation proposed a project, not implemented, to extend the Okaloosa kiosk model to combat zones in the 2010 election.

The Okaloosa County experiment dealt with only a single county. Expanding kiosk-based Internet voting to cover all service people would be very difficult, since the system would need to deal with a multitude of state and county laws, such as straight party voting, full face ballots, etc. These sometimes conflicting requirements would significantly increase cost and complexity.

The Op BRAVO Foundation has claimed in sales material that its system will provide voter-verified paper records, but there has been no explanation as to how paper records or ballots from all over the county would be dealt with. It would be necessary to sort the paper ballots by voting districts and send the sorted ballots to the corresponding local election officials. For the paper records to have any value, they would need to arrive in time to be audited or recounted. These constraints in turn raise issues about the chain of custody of ballots, expense, which almost certainly would be considerable, and privacy—especially when there is only a small number of voters from a particular precinct.

Furthermore, the only real protection against the insider threat, which could come from Scytl employees, as well as from malicious election officials or other insiders, is the manual count of the Voter Choice Records. In other words, the paper ballots or records must be manually audited or counted *before* an election is certified. This requirement, which creates additional time constraints for returning the paper records or ballots to local election officials, suggests that the Okaloosa model would face major, if not insurmountable, problems dealing with voters from multiple counties in multiple states.

Instead, why not simply allow remote voters to download a blank ballot from the Internet and return the voted ballots by mail? If the blank ballot is posted early, most voted ballots should arrive in time. Such a system may not have the pizazz of Internet voting, but it would have far fewer security issues and would almost certainly be less expensive. That is the idea behind the MOVE Act.

11.6.7 The MOVE Act

In October 2009, the Military and Overseas Voter Empowerment (MOVE) Act (incorporated into the National Defense Authorization Act) was passed. Designed to address the problems of UOCAVA voters, MOVE requires states to make blank ballots available electronically at least 45 days prior to any Federal election. UOCAVA voters may request and receive voter registration and absentee ballot applications electronically. MOVE also provides free expedited mail service for voted ballots of overseas uniformed service voters. By eliminating postal mail requirements for voter registration requests and absentee ballot deliveries, together with other reforms, MOVE dramatically reduces the amount of time required by UOCAVA voters to register and vote.

The Military Postal Service Agency (MSRA) conducted an analysis of its effectiveness in handling absentee ballots during the 2010 General

Election. [707] There were problems with getting postal ballots to members of the military. However, the time required to return the paper ballots, many of which had been electronically downloaded, filled out by the servicemember, and then returned via postal mail, was impressive. According to the report:

> The overall transit average was 5.2 days which is under the 7 day deadline directed by the MOVE Act. 92% of absentee ballots reached election offices within 7 days of acceptance at overseas MPOs [Military Post Offices].

Only 118 out of 23,900 voted ballots took at least 20 days to be returned from an MPO, and most or all of these ballots likely originated in Afghanistan and Iraq. The time required to get a voted ballot from a service member to an MPO ranged from 2–20 days. [147] Therefore, if election officials provide downloadable blank ballots at least 45 days before the election, essentially all members of the military could return their voted paper ballots in time. As stated by the MSRA: "Election officials must adhere to the MOVE Act requirement for dispatching absentee ballots to voters no later than 45 days prior to the election date. This provides adequate time for ballots to reach absentee voters in the most remote locations to vote and mail back their ballot for the election."

Not satisfied with the significant speed-up provided by MOVE and the MSRA statement that the MOVE Act provides adequate time for voters to return their voted ballots by postal mail, Internet voting enthusiasts are advocating that *voted* ballots be returned over the Internet—either by casting a vote on a website or by attaching a voted ballot to an email. Providing an insecure system that can be attacked from anywhere is not a solution, and it does a major disservice to the people it is intended to help.

11.7 Some Other Countries

11.7.1 Switzerland

Because a large number of its citizens live outside Switzerland, the Canton of Geneva initiated its eVoting project in 2001 as a third option in addition to polling station and postal voting. The goal was to develop an Internet voting system that would be as secure as postal voting, which is to say only somewhat secure. Even though Geneva's system does not protect against denial of service attacks or election-rigging malware on the voters' computers, in February 2009 Geneva voters ratified a constitutional amendment guaranteeing Internet voting in Geneva. [371]

11.7.2 The Netherlands

In the 2006 Dutch parliamentary elections, the option of Internet voting was provided as an alternative to postal voting for Dutch citizens living or working abroad. [842] The system, Rijnland Internet Election System (RIES), had a relatively modest goal, namely that the "capacity, reliability, security and transparency of the Internet voting system must be on at least the same level as the system of postal voting." In spite of the cost and questions about the security of the system, the official evaluation of the system recommended that Internet voting be made a permanent option for Dutch citizens living or working abroad. [841] However, primarily as a result of efforts by a group called "We Don't Trust Voting Computers," the Netherlands banned DREs in September 2007. A subsequent analysis of software and structural security issues in RIES was published by the same group. [397] The portion of the government that administered RIES responded by saying in essence that they would fix the software bugs, but the response did not address the serious structural issues. [999] In June 2008, the DRE ban was followed by an Internet voting ban.

More details about the Geneva and Dutch systems are on our website.

11.7.3 Finland

Scytl software was used for pilots in three municipal elections in Finland on October 26, 2008. Unlike Op BRAVO, there were no Voter Choice Records. Voters could vote with paper ballots or via an electronic terminal connected to the Internet by Scytl's secure connection (a virtual private network or VPN). Out of 12,234 cast ballots, 232 were lost. In the municipality of Vihti, the 122 lost votes could have changed the result of a council election in which a candidate won by only 77 votes. In early April 2009, the Supreme Administrative Court ordered new municipal elections for the three municipalities in which the Internet pilots had been held, overruling an earlier court decision. The Minister of Justice estimated the cost of the new elections to be 130,000 euros. [453]

Usability issues, i.e. voters who didn't complete the voting process on the machines, were blamed for the lost votes. There has been no independent review. [848]

11.7.4 The UK—Swindon

The UK conducted its first Internet voting pilot in 2002, when the town of Swindon gave voters the option of voting over the Internet in a local election. [79] Swindon also offered Internet voting for local elections in

2003 and in May 2007. Four other localities (Councils) provided an Internet voting option in the 2007 election, but given its history, we shall focus on the Swindon election.

The 2007 Swindon pilot election allowed people to vote by paper ballot at an assigned polling place, via telephone, or over the Internet. Internet voting could be from any of five locations prior to polling day, or from any of 64 electronic polling stations that provided a "vote any-where" environment on polling day. Everyone Counts, the same company that ran the Democrats Abroad primary, provided the Internet voting software.

The entire Swindon pilot election was analyzed by the Electoral Commission, an independent body established by the UK Parliament.[121] The Commission concluded that while the pilot scheme facilitated and encouraged voting, it had a negligible effect on voter turnout. The Commission also determined that "The pilot scheme led to an overall increase in expenditure by the Council ... The average cost of the 2007 pilot scheme per elector was £8.33, compared with £2.30 for a conventional election, while the cost per electronic vote cast was £102.50." In other words, each Internet vote was over 44 times more costly than a conventional vote.

The Commission found serious usability problems, including non-intuitive screen layouts that could cause the elector to "very easily miss additional unseen candidates at the bottom of the ballot paper," a user interface that "did not include high-contrast, clearly labelled buttons" (thereby increasing the chance for error), and a voter interface that "seemed to contain several more steps than the equivalent manual voting process." As a result of the additional steps, electronic voting "took an average of three minutes compared with 30 seconds for manual voting."

A second report was issued by the non-profit Open Rights Group (ORG), which organized teams of volunteers to oversee several of the pilot projects, including Swindon. Their *May 2007 Election Report* expressed serious concerns about the pilots.[798] Among these concerns were the lack of an independent or governmental analysis of any of the software, inadequate audit trails, and the absence of a manual audit of electronically counted ballots—though they observed that an audit could not be conducted of the votes cast over the Internet. They complained that "accredited observers encountered difficulties with the observation process and at times had to deal with arbitrary decisions and limited access." They also noted that "the supplier concerned confirmed that only 'about 100 people [in Swindon] had used the service' to check their receipts." [798]

ORG observed that security of the laptops used for voting in Swindon seemed lax at best. Prior to the election, residing officers were allowed to take home laptops used for voting. There were also a number of unsecured laptops at the voting locations. Observers were told that those laptops would not be used to tabulate votes, but they were not told how the laptops would be used. In addition, a majority of the polling stations experienced problems with the laptops that were used for e-voting.

An ORG volunteer visited a polling station after having received conflicting reports about what appeared to be malfunctioning (Internet-linked) voting equipment. There she met Lori Steele, CEO of Everyone Counts. When asked if the laptops were experiencing problems, such as had been observed elsewhere in Swindon, Steele responded that the machines were "up and running." However, after Steele left, the observer asked the same question of the Presiding Officer, who responded that there were "technical glitches." When pressed about Steele's comment, the Presiding Officer said that she was being "diplomatic." [798]

11.7.5 Norway

Norway is planning to allow voters in eleven municipalities to vote over the Internet in municipal and council elections in 2011. [786] Scytl was selected as the vendor; the source code will be publicly available. The complexity of Norway's elections led them to offer only a partial proof to voters, sent to their cell phones, that their vote was correctly recorded. They also count the votes behind closed doors, although they do allow an inside auditor. It is still possible for malware on the voter's computer to change the voter's selection, so long as the change is consistent with the partial proof, or if the voter does not check that partial proof. As of this writing, the election has not yet taken place.

11.7.6 Estonia

In 2007 Estonia became the first country to hold national parliamentary elections that provided the option of voting over the Internet to all citizens. During the most recent election, which occurred in March 2011, Internet voting was an option from February 24 to March 2; polling-place voting occurring on March 6. [802] Unlike the more modest goal of the Dutch Internet voting system, the stated goal of the Estonian system is to make Internet voting "at least as secure as regular voting." [320] To minimize coercion of Internet voters, early paper balloting and repeat Internet voting were allowed, with the early paper ballot or, if there was none, the Internet vote with the latest time stamp being the official vote. [321]

Unlike most countries, including the U.S., Estonia has national ID cards and computers with smart card readers. The Estonian system rests on a public key infrastructure or PKI provided by their national ID cards. A PKI allows its users to attach cryptographically secure digital signatures to electronic documents. During the election, voters used their ID cards both for authentication and to digitally sign their ballots. Over 140,846 people, about a quarter of all voters, voted online in 2011.[802]

After connecting to the election server, the voter authenticates herself by using her ID card. The server then provides the voter with the candidate list on the website. After making her selections and finalizing her ballot, the voter's computer generates a random number r, which is concatenated to the ballot. The purpose of the random number is to prevent an adversary from using exhaustive search to determine the contents of encrypted ballots (by encrypting all possible choices using the voting system's public key). Her computer next encrypts and digitally signs the concatenated ballot, which is sent to the election server. The election server verifies the voter and stores the encrypted ballot. Before the ballots are counted, the voter's signature is stripped from the ballot. The system was developed by Cybernetica, an Estonian company.[220]

The election was observed by a team from the OSCE/ODIHR (Organization for Security and Cooperation in Europe/Office for Democratic Institutions and Human Rights). They found a number of serious problems, including that the project manager could update the software without any formal procedure. This is a significant security vulnerability, since the project manager could intentionally or inadvertently insert election rigging code into the software, or even trigger malware that had already been installed. There is no way to check or analyze any last minute code insertions.

The OSCE/ODIHR team was told that one programmer had "verified" the software, but the results were secret. Paavo Pihelgas, an Estonian graduate student who had submitted a complaint about the Internet election, subsequently learned that the programmer had become ill, and there was no written report. The OSCE/ODIHR team also observed that, while the National Election Commission can invalidate the Internet voting results, there are no specifications stating the basis for and circumstances under which the results could be invalidated. There is also no plan describing how to inform voters that they would need to recast paper ballots on election day.

Denial of service attacks are a risk. Indeed, a massive denial of service attack against Estonian web sites began on April 27, 2007 and continued through part of May. [559] Because Estonia had become heavily dependent on Internet communications, the attack created problems for governmental and private institutions. There was speculation that the attack, which originated in Russia, was triggered by Russian anger over Estonia's decision to move a Soviet war memorial. [340] While voters would have had the option of polling place voting in the event that a successful denial of service attack had occurred during the election, voters who had planned to vote over the Internet could have been disenfranchised.

As we have stated repeatedly, the election server is vulnerable to an attack from anywhere, and the voters' computers are vulnerable to election-rigging malware. Pihelgas had pointed out the malware risk in his complaint, which was rejected. Estonian cryptographer Helger Lipmaa summed up the threat:

> Voter computers are an obvious problem: most of the people are computer illiterate, and are not able to check if their computers are not infected. Even if they have the newest antivirus (which we can't be sure of), that antivirus itself might not be able to detect a piece of new malware that has been written specifically for *that* election and is unleashed just before it. (Note: in Estonia e-voting lasts for 3 days.) That malware could do a lot of damage, like hijack the connection between you and the ID card (basically letting the ID card to sign wrong votes), between the GUI and what actually happens inside the computer, etc. I would *not* be surprised if such a piece of software was written by a high-school kid. [608]

Estonia requires anyone wishing to view the election software to sign a non-disclosure agreement. Prominent independent computer security experts are willing to inspect the system, but they refuse to do so unless they are allowed to inform the public of any risks they uncover. Aside from the DC pilot, we know of no Internet voting scheme where outside computer security experts have been allowed to attempt to break into the system.

11.8 The Future of Internet Voting

Proposals to conduct voting pilots using real elections continue to reappear both in the U.S. and elsewhere, seemingly independent of warnings from computer security experts. While the appeal of Internet voting is obvious, the risks, unfortunately, are not, at least to many decision makers.

As we have seen, people running pilots are likely to declare success, in spite of any problems that might crop up. However, it is dangerous to draw conclusions from what appears to be a successful Internet voting pilot. If the election is insignificant, there is little to no motivation to sabotage the election. Even if the election is significant, a malicious player might hold off from attacking the first election in the hope that the election will be declared a success, thereby resulting in future Internet elections. Having claimed success, independent of any verifiable proof of the accuracy of the election, Internet voting enthusiasts could push to extend Internet voting to a broader group of voters, thereby seriously undermining the security of our electoral system.

An attacker is not going to publicize an attack—just as the credit card thieves don't advertise that they are stealing credit card numbers. When election officials or policy makers ask for proof that voting systems have been attacked, it is important to keep in mind that well devised attacks by their very nature can be difficult or impossible to detect. Furthermore, most Internet voting systems do not include a proactive search to see if the system was compromised, thereby making the attacker's job all the easier.

A serious failure of Internet voting in a major election would have significant societal repercussions. Since the U.S. legal system is not designed to rerun compromised elections, an Internet voting attack detected during the election would create chaos. If there were no back-up voting scheme, the country could be thrown into disarray. If voters depended on the compromised system to vote, then even if the election were to be rerun, we would be confronted with holding another election on a system already shown to be insecure. It is not clear what would happen if the failure were detected after the winners had been declared.

Perhaps some day a paperless encryption-based Internet voting system will be sufficiently secure, accurate, and transparent for it to be used safely in major elections. However, as stated by the National Commission on Federal Election Reform, Internet voting "is an idea whose time most certainly has not yet come."

12

Missed Opportunities:
How to Kill a Bill

On Election Day 2004, How Will You Know If Your Vote Is Properly Counted? Answer: You Won't.

Press Release issued by the office of Rep. Rush Holt [466]

DREs [direct-recording electronic voting machines] are extremely sophisticated machines and most DREs store information in multiple formats and in multiple places within its program. To tamper with a DRE someone would need to know each and every format and storage capacity and be able to manipulate it undetected ... And why would we assume that, if the total from a paper count and the total from a machine count are different, the paper count is accurate? Is it not just as easy to tamper with an election by "losing" a couple of paper ballots or miscounting them during a recount?

The League of Women Voters, June 11, 2003 [585]

On October 23, 2006, the first Election Assistance Commission (EAC) Chair, the Rev. Dr. DeForest B. Soaries, Jr. (R), and former EAC Vice-Chair, Ray Martinez (D), appeared on the Lou Dobbs TV Show. At that point both had already resigned from their EAC positions. [928]

Dobbs: [O]ne third of voters this November will be using new voting equipment. Thirty-eight percent will be using electronic voting equipment. Deforest, what do you think is going to happen?

Soaries: Well, I think we're going to have frustration at the polls. Many poll workers will be inadequately prepared for the use of this equipment. And if there's a close race, there will be tremendous frustration because there will be difficulty confirming what the real results were, given the lack of any paper to verify what happened at the polls.

Dobbs: And Ray, looking at another statistic that everybody might as well start getting comfortable with, the 2000 voting machines, they malfunctioned in 25 states. I mean, are we going to see ... something that widespread ... in this election, or will it be even worse?

Martinez: Well, I certainly hope it's not anything of that magnitude, Lou. And I think the American public ought to demand that election officials around the country do their due diligence to ensure that we don't see problems like that. You know, election administration is comprised of three essential parts, Lou, the technology we use, the processes that we have in place and the people that run our elections. And we've seen a lot of problems when it comes to the technology, but we've also seen equal amounts of problems when it comes to the people aspect of election administration. We have to emphasize that as well.

Dobbs: Lots of wonderful people volunteer, Deforest, around this country to work in polling booths and work for the election offices all across this country. As part of the Help America Vote [Act], billions of dollars put into play here, jurisdictions all over the country buying these machines. Are we better off, in your judgment today, than we were in 2000?

Soaries: Well, I think we're worse off because in 2000, at least we knew what we didn't know. And the hanging chad became center stage in 2000. Today six years later after spending $2.5 billion, we don't know what we don't know. We don't know about security, we don't know enough because the EAC never got enough money for research. The Congress passed a law that authorized $30 billion for research [sic: $20 million was authorized]. EAC to this date has received zero of those dollars. The Republican party ...

Dobbs: Zero.

Soaries: The Republican-led Congress and the Republican White House have failed. And what Ray and I were invited to do was really a charade. And I think the public, as Ray said, should be outraged and demand results from the local to the federal level.

Dobbs: Ray?

Martinez: Well, I think that's right, Lou. I mean, I certainly agree with my friend and former colleague Buster Soaries, who was an outstanding leader for the EAC.

Look, I think that it's time for us to make our elections work in this country, Lou. I mean, that's the bottom line. And obviously we have a great deal of work to do to make that happen. It's time for us to bring together the best and brightest from the high-tech industry, Lou, the business industry, election officials, et cetera, for us to make things work. You know, Friday, this coming Friday, we'll celebrate—or actually mark, I suppose some people might scorn the passage—it's the four-year anniversary of the passage of the Help America Vote Act this coming Friday, of Congress passing that historic law.

It's time, four years later, Lou, six years removed from Florida in 2000, it's time for us to achieve a consensus on exactly what we have to do to really improve the process of election administration.

Although Soaries and Martinez were keenly aware of HAVA's failings (see Section 12.2), repeated efforts to reform those failings have been unsuccessful. [191] As a result, in many parts of the country we are still voting on insecure or unaudited voting systems. This chapter is the story of Congress' failure to legislate.

12.1 The Role of Public Interest Groups

The failure of legislative attempts to require secure voting technology and audited elections is in part a reflection of an unhealthy national divide between the science/technical community and the liberal arts community that impacts both policy makers and the leadership of public interest groups. People who lacked a science or technology background were put in the position of having to judge the validity of arguments made by salespeople and advocates of particular technologies. Fortunately, sometimes policy makers have access to technically knowledgeable staff or research organizations.

Regrettably, the leadership of many well-known public interest groups, for whom voting is a key issue, had inadequate or no technical expertise. They tended not to consult independent computer security experts, even though many qualified experts would have been happy to assist in evaluating proposed voting technologies. Instead, the leaders listened almost exclusively to the small handful of computer scientists who mirrored their views about paperless voting machines. When prominent computer security experts pointed out the risks of paperless voting systems, they were often dismissed as being uninformed, biased, or even Luddites.

Organizations that should have been concerned about voting integrity and security issues were instead making almost identical incorrect arguments about the benefits of paperless voting, while denigrating more secure alternatives. These groups included the American

Civil Liberties Union (ACLU), the League of Women Voters (LWV), the American Association of People with Disabilities (AAPD), and the Leadership Conference on Civil Rights (LCCR—an umbrella organization of public interest groups). Since several leaders of the organizations were friends and colleagues, they reinforced each other's hostility towards paper. For example, Jim Dickson, vice-president of the AAPD, co-chaired the LCCR's Help America Vote Act Task Force. The President of the LWV, as well as the Executive Directors of the ACLU and the AAPD, have been members of the Executive Committee of the LCCR.

12.1.1 Reactions to Florida 2000

To understand why certain public interest groups advocated for paperless DREs, we begin with Florida 2000. Difficulties with tabulating and recounting punch card ballots led some people to conclude that paper ballots of any type could not be counted accurately, even though businesses, banks, lotteries, and many other entities in our society rely on paper to ensure accuracy. After the 2000 election, paperless DREs were touted as a solution to "the Florida problem." Replacing hanging chads with paperless electronic technology, proponents claimed, would result in accurate election counts and an end to ambiguity about voter intent.

The DRE bandwagon gained momentum because of support from many election officials who believed these machines would be modern, inexpensive, easy to use, and more reliable than the old voting systems. Paper ballots can be expensive to print, and machines that tabulate paper ballots may be prone to jamming. Eliminating time consuming and labor intensive manual recounts of paper ballots was appealing, especially after the spectacle of the Florida recount. As we discuss in Chapter 9, prominent disability rights advocates also promoted paperless DREs as the way to allow voters with disabilities to vote independently and in private.

Less than a month after the issuance of the LWV statement quoted at the beginning of this chapter, the LCCR released a policy analysis opposing HAVA-reform legislation. The analysis stated that " 'Voter-Verified Paper Trails' are not needed to keep elections from being stolen." [584] The LCCR analysis also mirrored the LWV arguments: "DREs are highly sophisticated, with most of them storing ballot records in multiple formats and in multiple locations.... In order to rig a DRE, an individual would need to be intimately familiar with its software, gain access to it long enough to change its code, conceal the changes during pre- and post election testing, and do this on enough machines to actually alter the outcome of an election. While such rigging is possible in theory, in practice it is highly improbable —in fact, in practice, it would be far easier to simply 'lose' paper ballots." An April 6, 2004 AAPD letter reiterated the arguments made by the LWV and the LCCR, again almost verbatim. [43]

The LCCR now states that the 2003 analysis no longer represents their position. [541]

12.1.2 The League of Women Voters

There are several problems with the LWV statement that begins this chapter. First, as any experienced computer user knows, storing information in multiple formats and locations provides little defense against software bugs or election rigging. Multiple copies may protect against loss or alteration, but they do not guarantee that the voter's selection, as seen on the screen, is identical to what is stored in the computer's internal memory. The LWV statement also ignores the fact that historically most election fraud has involved insiders. [415] Finally, it would be vastly easier to replace or steal a credit card size memory card than to walk off with a box of paper ballots.

Given the LWV's reputation for thoughtful analysis, many computer experts and League members were surprised by the League's support of paperless DREs. While the LWV prides itself on reaching positions via a consensus process, the membership was not consulted about DREs. An April 30, 2003 posting on an LWV listserv stated that the LWV had no position on a "paper trail" at that time. [955] But by late May 2003, Kay Maxwell, then President of the LWV, had sent a letter to the editor of the New York Times downplaying concerns about paperless DREs expressed in a Times article. [648] The Maxwell letter began, "The concerns raised about electronic voting machines in 'To Register Doubts, Press Here' (May 15) are worrisome because they unnecessarily scare voters and ignore the larger problem: reforming election systems."

As the League became increasingly outspoken in support of paperless DREs, members started challenging the League's position. Maxwell attempted to silence opposition by distributing a statement entitled *Applying League Positions* that said, "once the League's stance on [an] issue has been determined, the organization speaks with one voice. Individual League members are, of course, free to express differing personal views, so long as they do not speak in the name of the League." The statement added, "The [League] does not believe that an individual paper confirmation for each ballot is required to achieve those goals; in fact this is unnecessary and can be counterproductive." [647]

In November 2003 the LWVUS issued a set of questions and answers on DREs, presumably, as suggested by the first question, in response to "controversy over Direct Recording Electronic (DRE) voting systems." The document assured the voter that there was nothing to worry about. Instead, it argued that the debate was triggered by people who were:

> uncomfortable with or distrustful of new technologies, even though we rely on such technologies to fly our airplanes and operate our banking systems so long as there are appropriate management systems to provide safeguards. Finally, computer specialists with limited experience with election systems have focused narrowly on the DRE machines themselves without taking into account the management systems and safeguards that can protect against tampering and without acknowledging the problems associated with other voting systems such as punchcard machines. [587]

With controversy within the League increasing, Maxwell became more explicit in her opposition to a voter-verified paper trail (VVPT). In a December 2003 letter to the New York Times she wrote:

> In our view, a system requiring a voter-verified paper trail will fail to add significantly to security while adding costs and complications to the voting process and undermining disability and language access (editorial, Dec. 8). [649]

In January 2004 the LWV Board sent a memo to state and local League Presidents. That memo reiterated the League's anti-VVPT position, repeated the flawed argument that VVPTs discriminate against people with disabilities and language minorities, and listed the experts with whom the LWV consulted.

> The League does not support a voter-verified paper trail (VVPT) system ...A VVPT system limits access for persons with disabilities or limited English proficiency, does not meet federal certification standards, and creates additional problems for election administration. ...Throughout the debate over DREs, the League has consulted with many recognized experts in the fields of technology and elections, including Dr. Michael Shamos, Dr. Britt [sic] Williams, Dr. Ted Selker, the American Civil Liberties Union (ACLU), and the Leadership Council [sic] on Civil Rights (LCCR) .... Other expert opinion that was reviewed includes that of Dr. David Dill, Dr. Barbara Simons, Georgia Secretary of State Cathy Cox and the Congressional Research Service (CRS). [621]

While the LWV statement mentions Dill and Simons, neither was consulted. Instead, the LWV turned to Shamos, Williams, and Selker, the most vocal of the small group of computer scientists opposing

VVPTs. [586] Indeed, when Simons sent the LWVUS Board a rebuttal to the DRE questions and answers document mentioned above, she received no response. [917]

The League's positive reputation, combined with its public support of paperless DREs, could be used by election officials to justify DRE purchases, something that upset many League members who did not agree with the leadership's endorsement of paperless DREs. In 2003 some members posted an open letter to President Maxwell stating their opposition to the LWVUS anti-paper position. By the time of the 2004 League national convention, the letter organizers, led by Genevieve Katz, had gathered 924 signatures from 35 states. [590]

DREs were among the main topics of discussion among attendees at the 2004 convention. Even the Associated Press followed the issue. [570] Delegates challenging the League's position on paperless voting were dismayed by a plenary session on HAVA, moderated by Maxwell, in which all of the speakers (Michael Shamos, Conny McCormack, and Angela Maria Arboleda of the National Council of La Raza) attacked the use of paper ballots. Nonetheless, by the end of the convention, League members had voted to support only voting systems that are "Secure, Accurate, Recountable, and Accessible (SARA)." [589] Following the convention, the League leadership claimed that "recountable is not a code word for paper." [588] The anti-paper claim galvanized members disappointed by the leadership's response, and at the next convention in 2006, a far stronger resolution was adopted calling for "a voter-verifiable paper ballot or other paper record, said paper being the official record of the voter's intent." [591] SARA was expanded even further to include "transparent" (SARAT) at the 2010 convention. [592] The 2006 resolution, combined with SARAT, now comprise the official LWV position.

12.1.3 The ACLU

In April 2003 the Los Angeles Voter Empowerment Circle, which included the ACLU of Southern California, the Los Angeles LWV, People For the American Way, the Green Party, the Asian Pacific American Legal Center, and other organizations, wrote a draft working paper that strongly supported paperless DREs, and by implication opposed HAVA reform legislation. [615] The draft justified the recommendation against a "contemporaneous" paper trail by saying:

> The State of California should not at this time require that DRE systems have a contemporaneously generated paper trail. While such a paper trail may have some benefits in terms of security and confidence, it goes beyond the requirements of state and federal law. They may

also result in mechanical problems, complicating the voting process and resulting in longer lines at the polls. Mandating a contemporaneously generated paper trail for all DRE's could deter counties from moving to this technology, and that [sic] they might instead choose optical scan systems which are less desirable.

In addition to attacking paper trails and optical scan systems, the Empowerment Circle draft claimed that DREs are better for voters with disabilities, linguistic minorities, and people of color; it gave no documentation for these claims.

On December 5, 2003 the national ACLU issued a *Statement of Principles* on DREs.[29] The ACLU argued that:

1. Election officials would resort to a "verified paper trail" only in the case of a recount or contest, which a hacker can prevent or deter.

2. The voter-verified paper trail could be used by a sophisticated fraud to give voters a false sense of security that their vote was correctly tallied.

In its eagerness to support paperless voting machines, the ACLU undermined its own arguments by implicitly acknowledging that hacking of voting machines could occur. The ACLU statement also demonstrated a lack of rigor by ignoring optical scan systems, even though the paper ballots of optical scan systems are a "verified paper trail." Combined with mandatory manual post-election audits, optical scan systems are resistant to the very fraud of concern to the ACLU.

The ACLU statement was posted on the LWV website for several months, in apparent violation of an accompanying cover letter saying that the statement should not be redistributed. Although several LWV members objected to the posting, the statement was removed from the LWVUS website only because of opposition from some ACLU members and ACLU affiliates to the ACLU's anti-paper statement.

In October 2004 the national ACLU Board of Directors approved an official policy, *Electronic Voting Systems*, that recognized some of the problems with DREs, but that also consigned ballot marking systems to footnotes.[30] In stressing that DREs are needed "to ensure independent voting access for persons with disabilities and language minorities," the ACLU policy ignored the fact that ballot marking devices tend to be significantly more accessible than DREs (see Chapter 9). The policy correctly stated, "There is presently no field-tested means of conducting a true independent recount when elections are conducted with paperless electronic devices (DREs)." Unfortunately, that observation was deleted from the ACLU's revised policy, issued in November 2007. Other references to limitations of paperless DREs were also deleted.[31] The 2007 revised policy is currently the official national ACLU position.[659]

Some state ACLUs, such as Massachusetts, New York, and Florida, split with the national ACLU on the issue of paperless DREs.*

12.1.4 Organizations supporting Reform

The Brennan Center for Justice, especially through the efforts of Larry Norden, became a core supporter of meaningful reform. Their reports on post-election audits and voting machine security drew on input from a number of technology experts and election officials.[785,784] Initially lukewarm about legislation introduced by Rep. Rush Holt to require voter-verified paper audit trails in 2004, People For the American Way (PFAW) ultimately became a strong supporter of the 2007 iteration of the Holt bill[812] (see Section 12.3). With the appointment of Chellie Pingree as President of Common Cause in 2003, that organization also became a staunch supporter of reform, issuing a statement in 2004: "We believe it is critical at this point to *provide a voter-verifiable paper audit trail as one of the essential requirements of voting systems*" [emphasis in the original].[183]

Organizations such as Verified Voting, TrueMajority, VoteTrustUSA, and numerous state and local election integrity groups consistently supported Holt's legislation calling for voter-verified paper ballots or records. Growing concerns among computer scientists led ACM (the Association for Computing Machinery), a 96,000 member educational and scientific society of computing educators, researchers, and professionals, to issue a statement on electronic voting, calling for a "physical record" that the voter can use to verify his or her vote.[412]

12.2 The Help America Vote Act (HAVA)

HAVA created the Federal Election Assistance Commission (EAC) to oversee both the disbursement of federal funds and the development of new voting machine standards. However, the first EAC Commissioners were not appointed until December 2003. The EAC had insufficient funds to properly oversee the disbursement of $1.495 billion allocated in fiscal year 2003 to buy voting systems, a matter of great concern to EAC Chair, DeForest Soaries.[177] The Technical Guidelines Development Committee, charged by HAVA with writing new voluntary voting system standards, was not even empaneled until June

---

*For example, in 2007 the Florida ACLU issued a press release praising the Florida legislature for passing a law requiring paper ballot voting technology.[33]

2004.[293] Meanwhile, states were supposed to have replaced their voting systems by the November 2004 elections, or January 2006 at the latest.

12.2.1 Problems with HAVA

Instead of the promised major reform, HAVA engendered new kinds of election problems. Although DREs had been in use since the 1980s, an unrealistically short deadline, together with a lack of reasonable standards, triggered a massive deployment of faulty, flawed, and expensive equipment. This deployment has led to security and integrity crises for which there are no clear-cut legal remedies.

We've already discussed the problems that arose from the use of paperless DREs in Sarasota County, FL. in the 2006 election. An earlier example involved the paperless UniLect Patriot DRE, used in Carteret County, North Carolina for early voting in the 2004 election. Because the machine had a storage capacity of only 3005 ballots and the number of early voters far exceeded the machine's capacity, 4438 ballots were lost. Only 2287 votes separated the Republican and Democratic candidates for state Agricultural Commissioner, and a rerun of the Agricultural Commissioner election seemed an obvious solution. The State Board of Elections' decision to hold a revote in Carteret County only was struck down by the court.* The Board of Elections then called for a statewide revote. That, too, was struck down, and the bitterly divided Board was ordered to resolve the election some other way.

Eventually, 1352 affidavits were collected by the leading candidate from voters claiming to have voted for him.[772] Since there were enough affidavits to guarantee the election of the leading candidate, and since the judge appeared ready to accept the affidavits, the other candidate conceded. This may be the first time that an election in the United States was decided by affidavits.

Post-HAVA problems should not have come as a surprise. As early as 1975, Roy Saltman warned about problems with using computers in elections.[868] Well before the passage of HAVA, computer scientists Rebecca Mercuri and Peter Neumann issued similar warnings.[696,748] In 1985 David Burnham wrote about the dangers of computerized voting in the New York Times.[126] Mae Churchill, who helped found the Urban Policy Research Institute in California, cautioned in 1990 that, "The proprietary interests of voting system vendors have been allowed to drive the standards drafting procedure ... The privatizing of elections is taking place without the consent or knowledge of the governed."[416]

---

*It might have been possible to allow only those voters whose votes had been lost to recast their ballots, but that approach was not considered.

Many of the problems that have since come to light involve usability or human factors. A central promise of DRE technology was that it would offer an easy, accessible user interface that would reduce the rate of voter errors and enfranchise more voters. Instead, several studies have demonstrated that DRE voting systems have not lowered error rates, nor have they proven to be particularly accessible, as we discuss in Chapters 5 and 9. [456,145,864]

12.3   Efforts to Reform HAVA

After the passage of HAVA, awareness within the computer science community about the move to purchase unauditable voting machines increased significantly as a result of Stanford professor David Dill's petition, circulated in early 2003 (see Chapter 8). As press reports about voting machine failures began appearing, large numbers of other citizens also became concerned.

Because of the lack of adequate guidelines, the absence of regulations mandating significant security measures, and the impossibility of conducting a meaningful post-election audit or recount of paperless voting machines, many citizens felt that HAVA needed revision. In an effort to reform HAVA before a lot of money was spent on insecure and inadequate machines, less than seven months after HAVA's passage, Congressman Rush Holt (D-NJ) introduced the Voter Confidence and Increased Accessibility Act of 2003 (H.R. 2239). H.R. 2239 was never voted on, and Holt introduced increasingly strong versions of the bill over the next several years.

As of this writing, the only piece of HAVA reform legislation voted on by either chamber of Congress was H.R. 5036, a 2008 Holt bill that would have allowed states to opt-in to receive emergency reimbursements for converting to a paper ballot voting system, offering emergency paper ballots, and/or conducting hand counted audits. [470] Since H.R. 5036 was reported out of committee without opposition, it was put to a vote under "suspension of the rules," a procedure used for non-controversial bills that requires a 2/3 supermajority. The bill received a majority of "yes" votes, but not the required 2/3 support. A majority of Republicans, including some who had not opposed the bill in committee, voted no—most likely as a result of a statement opposing the bill that was issued by the Bush Administration and circulated to Members on the day of the vote. [793]

Given the large number of questions and problems with paperless DREs, why has Congress failed to pass reform legislation?

12.3.1 The Holt Legislation

Changes in successive HAVA-reform bills introduced by Holt reflect a deepening understanding of how to deal with the risks of computerized voting machines.

While drafting H.R. 2239 Holt, a Ph.D. physicist, consulted with several computer scientists, including the authors, about the accuracy, integrity and security of electronic voting machines. Holt also showed a draft of the bill to Jim Dickson. According to Holt, one of Dickson's primary concerns was that HAVA delayed the requirement of accessible voting systems for the disabled until 2007, while other voting system standards had a 2006 deadline. To accommodate Dickson and preserve accessibility, H.R. 2239 moved HAVA's 2007 disability access deadline forward to 2006. [469]

Introduced on May 22, 2003, H.R. 2239 called for a) a voter-verified paper record suitable for a manual audit, b) no undisclosed software, and c) manual mandatory random audits of the voter-verified paper records for federal elections in 0.5% of each state's jurisdictions. Had the bill passed, paper records and audits would have been required for the November 2004 election, and verifiable voting systems would have been made available for voters with disabilities by January 1, 2006, earlier than mandated by HAVA. [466]

In early February 2005 Holt introduced a second version of his bill. H.R. 550 would have taken effect in time for the next Federal election, which would have been the November 2006 mid-term elections. The legislation also required a voter-verified paper record and random manual audits—this time in 2% of all jurisdictions. It again prohibited the use of undisclosed software, wireless communications devices in voting systems, and voting machine components connected to the Internet. The most substantial differences between H.R. 2239 and H.R. 550 were in the audit section, which grew from one paragraph to more than six pages. The new audit material was in direct response to the manner in which the 2004 Ohio recount was conducted. [467]

Holt introduced a third version of his bill, H.R. 811, in February 2007. [468] A companion bill, S. 559, was introduced in the Senate by Sen. Bill Nelson (D-FL). [747] Like its predecessors, H.R. 811 called for random manual audits, as well as the public disclosure of voting system software and a ban on Internet connections for voting machine components. Also like its predecessors, the bill was vetted with computer security experts and voting integrity and disability activist groups, as well as election officials.

H.R. 811 mandated voter-verified paper ballots, instead of records.

Responding to the problems in Cuyahoga County, Ohio in May 2006, where 10% of the paper printout-outs from new DRE machines were lost, damaged or otherwise compromised, the bill required paper ballots to be "durable," i.e. capable of withstanding multiple recounts by hand. Because of concerns that ballot marking devices might create problems for voters with mobility impairment, the bill called for the entire process of ballot verification and vote casting to be equipped for individuals with disabilities. Based on recommendations from the Brennan Center, the strengthened auditing provisions included a "tiered" system to reflect the closeness of announced election results.[784]* The bill also required audits to be publicly observable. H.R. 811 was marked up by the committee of jurisdiction, but was not voted on by the House. ("Mark-up" refers to the process by which a legislative committee debates proposed legislation and agrees to changes in language or to a compromise version).

H.R. 2894, introduced by Holt in June, 2009, was based on the mark-up version of H.R. 811. H.R. 2894 required voter-marked or ballot-marking-device paper ballots for the November 2010 elections, made the paper ballot the vote of record (as had all earlier versions), mandated the same tiered audits as H.R. 811, and banned wireless devices, Internet connections, and uncertified and undisclosed software in voting and tabulating machines.[471] The ballot marking requirements would have banned DREs. Sen. Nelson again introduced a Senate companion bill, S. 1431. Although supported by the broadest range of organizations of any version of the bill (including the American Council of the Blind, the Advancement Project, the Brennan Center, Common Cause, the Electronic Frontier Foundation, Voter Action, and Verified Voting), and endorsed in a New York Times editorial, the bill received no committee action and no floor vote.[471,773]

12.3.2 Support for the Holt Legislation

Many good government groups either initially supported Holt's legislation or moved to a position of support by the time that H.R. 811 was introduced. For example, Barbara R. Arnwine, Executive Director of the Lawyers' Committee for Civil Rights Under Law, released a statement in support of H.R. 811:

> Responsive and effective elections are the right of every eligible Ameri-

---

*If the margin of victory between the two leading candidates was: a) less than 1%, then at least 10% of all precincts would be audited; b) between 1% and 2%, then at least 5% of all precincts would be audited; and c) greater than 2%, then at least 3% of all precincts would be audited. If the winning candidate had no opposition or received at least 80% of the total votes, then no audit would be required.

can. To ensure that right, there must be comprehensive and meaningful reform of how our elections are administered. ... This bill addresses a key element to that reform by demanding needed improvements to voting machines; allowing voters to verify their ballots in a way that protects accessibility for people with disabilities and language minority voters. The Bill makes the voters interests—and not the profits of the machine company—the focus of the election machine business by requiring manufacturers to balance their intellectual property interests with the interests of election officials to know the security pitfalls that are possible in their voting systems. Finally, the bill requires mandatory audits of election results, which we think moves us towards restoring public faith in the veracity of election outcomes.

In a letter supporting H.R. 811, the Brennan Center stated, "There is a consensus among experts who have studied electronic voting machines in the United States that they are insecure and unreliable. As a nation, we cannot afford another divisive federal election marred by voting machine glitches." People for the American Way also supported the legislation, saying "[W]ith millions of voters disenfranchised in each election cycle, our citizens have lost confidence that their votes are counted accurately—or even counted at all. The recent debacle in Sarasota County, where inexplicably some 18,000 votes were not recorded on the paperless voting machines, is only the tip of the iceberg."

Most election integrity advocates had supported all of Holt's bills, but some, who had supported early versions, opposed H.R. 811, because it did not explicitly ban DREs. (The earlier bills hadn't either). Still, H.R. 811 was ultimately co-sponsored by 216 members of Congress from both parties.

Related legislation

One of the most outspoken opponents of paperless voting machines has been Senator John Ensign (R-NV). In February 2005 Sen. Ensign, who had introduced HAVA reform legislation in 2004, reintroduced his Voting Integrity and Verification Act. The 2005 bill, S. 330, eventually collected 13 co-sponsors from both parties. Ensign's concern about paperless voting machines stems from his personal experience:

> I understand better than most the importance of the integrity of the ballot box. I was at the mercy of a paperless-machine election in my 1998 race for the U.S. Senate. When the votes were tallied with a difference of only a few hundred, I asked for a recount in Clark County, the only county at the time using electronic voting machines. The result of the recount was identical to the first count. That is because there was nothing to recount. After rerunning a computer program, the computer predictably produced the same exact tally. I conceded

that race and was elected to Nevada's other Senate seat in 2000. But that experience made me realize the importance of ensuring Americans that their votes will count—it is absolutely fundamental to our democracy. [317]

The first bill that would have eliminated DREs altogether, in this case by 2012, was introduced on November 1, 2007 by Senators Bill Nelson and Sheldon Whitehouse (D-RI). [947] Modeled on the version of H.R. 811 that came out of committee in May, S. 2295 added a ban on DREs, consistent with a decision made by Governor Charlie Crist (R) of Florida in 2007. [746]

During the past few years, legislation to reform HAVA also has been introduced by a number of members of Congress, including Senators Hillary Clinton (D-NY), Barbara Boxer (D-CA), and Diane Feinstein (D-CA). None of those bills received much attention.

Examples from Congressional hearings

When the Senate held its first hearing on Voter Verification in June 2005, Sen. Ensign and computer scientist David Dill testified in support of voter verified paper audit trails. [230] Dill remarked, "Computer systems are so complex that no one really knows what goes on inside of them." [271] He also observed that, "Paper has specific properties . . . that we don't know how to replicate in electronic media. For example, most voters can verify the contents of a paper ballot without computer mediation; paper can be written indelibly; and the procedures for handling critical paper documents are easily understood by ordinary poll workers and voters."

In a July 2006 House hearing on Voting System Standards, the subject of verification and audits came up repeatedly. [475] David Wagner, a computer science professor at U.C. Berkeley, was blunt. [988] After stating that "The federal qualification process is not working," Wagner observed "[federally]-approved machines have been found to contain numerous security defects that threaten the integrity of our elections." Wagner listed many examples and concluded by warning that "the 2005 [federal] standards contain significant shortcomings regarding the security, reliability, and auditability of electronic voting."

At the same hearing Minnesota Secretary of State Mary Kiffmeyer (R) supported Wagner. [557] "[T]he 2005 [federal standards] are not sufficiently comprehensive to ensure security in our election systems. The use of technology for voting increases the risk that security of the voting system will be breached, if proper safeguards are not taken."

More directly related to Holt's legislation was a September 2006 House hearing at which Princeton professor Ed Felten demonstrated how a computer virus could be inserted easily into a Diebold DRE. He elaborated:

> From a security standpoint, what distinguishes computerized voting systems from traditional systems is not that computers are easier to compromise, but that the consequences of compromise can be so much more severe. Breaking into an old-fashioned ballot box can affect a few hundred ballots at most; injecting a virus into a single computerized voting machine can affect an entire election. [337]

Congressional support

Congressional support for the Holt bills had grown steadily. H.R. 2239, which had no co-sponsors when it was introduced, eventually had 157 bi-partisan cosponsors. H.R. 550 had 50 co-sponsors when it was introduced, and over 100 co-sponsors within two weeks. By the end of the Congressional session the number of co-sponsors for H.R. 550 was 222, a majority of House members, of whom 23 were Republicans. One of those Republicans was Rep. Tom Petri (R-WI), who in a statement of support said:

> It is typical for computer vendors to insist that their systems are reliable and, when properly handled, secure from malicious invasion. Common experience with home and business computers, however, shows that computers can crash due to software or hardware failure, suffer power surges and outages, and be hacked by programmers intent on altering the information inside. Accordingly, for me it's a "no-brainer" that electronic voting machines should produce paper trails so that ballots can be counted by hand if necessary. Due to the importance of elections, we simply cannot be expected to take on faith any vote total that an election system displays on a computer screen. [813]

A relentless series of voting system problems throughout the 2006 primaries and mid-term elections culminated in the contested Sarasota Florida Congressional election. [986] That race caused such concern that Sen. Diane Feinstein asked the Government Accountability Office to investigate. [334] Consequently, when H.R. 811 was introduced, most observers thought that it would easily pass, especially since Democrats, newly in control of Congress, had expressed strong support. A spokesman for House Speaker Nancy Pelosi (D-CA) had stated that "Democrats are committed to election-reform legislation that requires all voting machines produce a paper trail." [395] The incoming chair of the Senate Rules and Administration Committee, Sen. Feinstein, had announced her intention to introduce legislation calling for some of the provisions in H.R. 550. [724]

12.3.3 Opposition to Reform Legislation

H.R. 811 is a story of dashed hopes and expectations. It also provides a case study of how legislation is modified, weakened, and ultimately killed. Why did Congress not pass any of the Holt bills?

Opposition from HAVA co-authors

In March 2004 the HAVA co-authors, Sen. Mitch McConnell (R-Ky.), Sen. Chris Dodd (D-Conn.), Rep. Robert Ney (R-Ohio), and Rep. Steny Hoyer (D-Md.), circulated an anti-H.R. 2239 letter that ignored the availability of ballot marking devices and complained that:

> The proposals mandating a voter-verified paper record would essentially take the most advanced generations of election technologies and systems available and reduce them to little more than ballot printers. ...Most importantly, the proposals requiring a voter-verified paper record would force voters with disabilities to go back to using ballots that provide neither privacy nor independence, thereby subverting a hallmark of the HAVA legislation. [777]

Pushback from good government and disability rights groups

Support of paperless DREs by the LCCR, the LWV, and the ACLU initially led to opposition to the Holt legislation, starting with H.R. 2239. [584]

Even though the H.R. 2239 deadline for accessible voting systems had been moved earlier to 2006 to accommodate Jim Dickson, AAPD charged in an April 2004 letter, signed by several disability rights organizations, that: "H.R. 2239 erodes the rights of voters with disabilities under HAVA by creating a waiver for HAVA's requirement that each polling place have one accessible voting machine by 2006, and removing the requirement under HAVA that all voting systems purchased beginning in 2007 be accessible to voters with disabilities." [47]

Not only did the letter misrepresent the H.R. 2239 deadline for accessible voting systems, but it also misrepresented HAVA itself. HAVA says nothing about requiring accessibility for *all* voting systems. Rather, HAVA stipulates "at least one direct recording electronic voting system or other voting system equipped for individuals with disabilities at each polling place."*

---

*The deadline included in HAVA's disability access provision is 2007. While the deadline language is ambiguous, it cannot be construed to mean that all voting systems must be accessible by then. Indeed, between 2006 and 2008, jurisdictions serving 10 million voters replaced their DRE voting systems with optical scan machines as the primary voting system, and since 2006 (HAVA's overall deadline for voting system standards) every county that changed voting systems purchased optical scan machines as the primary voting system. [109]

Dickson indirectly attacked the second Holt bill, H.R. 550, in June 2005 Senate testimony in which he denigrated supporters of voter verified paper audit trails (VVPATs), as well as the VVPAT principle:

> Supporters of a VVPAT claim to support access for voters with disabilities. In state after state, county after county, they have prevented jurisdictions from purchasing equipment that meets HAVA's January 1, 2006 deadline. From the hysterical supporters of VVPAT, we continuously get lip service about supporting accessible, secret and independent voting and organized efforts which prevent it. [261]

The reality is that supporters of voter verifiable systems have long advocated for voting systems that are both accessible and verifiable. For example, in 2006 Verified Voting, an organization working on making voting systems and elections verifiable, conducted a survey on the accessibility of polling places and the accessible features available or absent from voting systems being deployed. [980] The survey was part of an Election Transparency project that was aimed at involving citizens in gathering information about the quality and problems of voting machines. [981] The survey also helped inform election reform advocates of accessibility issues that existed—and continue to exist.

Dickson also attacked H.R. 550 in testimony in the 2006 House committee hearing (the one at which Felten demonstrated his virus attack), where he claimed that a paper ballot is not accessible, even though paper ballot marking computerized voting machines and paper tactile ballots are accessible. [262] And he denounced H.R. 811 in a disability rights publication, stating: "I think the Holt bill is the worst piece of election legislation that I have seen in 25 years of working on election law. It's not just bad for us, it's bad for the country." [130]

Opposition from election officials

Large numbers of local and state election officials, as well as organizations representing them, have opposed the Holt bills. In Chapter 8 we discuss why a number of election officials are protective of computerized voting systems and opposed to HAVA reform. Furthermore, Holt's repeated attempts to enact reform as of the next national election, which reflected his concerns about the insecurity of our elections, created some tension. While many experts felt there was sufficient time to make the necessary changes if any of the bills had passed quickly, the more time that elapsed without each bill passing, the more difficult it became to make the changes. Of course organizations representing election officials could have proposed a later deadline, if they agreed with the principles of the legislation but were concerned about the timing. That did not happen.

There has also been resistance by election officials to mandated manual post-election audits. Organizing and running elections require a vast amount of work, and Election Day is exhausting for everyone involved. It is understandable that election officials who have never conducted audits would be concerned about having to audit elections manually. This may explain the reluctance of many election officials to acknowledge that voting system software could be buggy or contain election rigging code, in spite of demonstrations by computer scientists such as Ed Felten and Harri Hursti showing how to rig an election.

Fortunately, a number of enlightened election officials support post-election audits. For example, in September 2006 Connecticut Secretary of State Susan Bysiewicz was quoted in a press release as saying, "These random audits will ensure that we are using funds wisely to purchase equipment that is reliable and accurate. These audits are also a means for assuring Connecticut voters that each of their votes will be counted properly and that we will continue our tradition in the state of fair, secure elections." [129]

By contrast, 2005 Senate testimony of Los Angeles County Registrar Conny McCormack exemplifies the Panglossian attitude of some election officials:

> It goes without saying that all of the members of Congress seek the same overriding goal for election administration—the accurate casting, tabulation and reporting of all votes in accordance with the voters' intentions. *The fact is that existing DRE systems without VVPAT have the proven track record of doing the best job of all available voting systems in achieving that goal.* [Underlined in original] ... The suppositions and theories espoused by critics contending that DRE systems are more susceptible to tampering are completely unfounded. There is not one scintilla of evidence to support such claims. By contrast, there is ample, documented evidence that fraud has been perpetrated with paper-based voting systems. DRE tabulation software must be installed in each individual touch screen unit which entails thousands of standalone units in large electoral jurisdictions. Such decentralization down to each unit makes DRE systems less vulnerable to tampering than paper-based ballot systems. [655]

The notion that installing software in individual touch screen units makes them less vulnerable to tampering has no technical or scientific grounding. Even if the software differed somewhat between machines with different ballots, each machine would have identical underlying software used to run and tabulate the elections. The shared software could be a vehicle for wholesale fraud.

The National Association of Counties (NACo) opposed H.R. 811 because it would have had the practical effect of banning DREs in all paperless jurisdictions without funding their replacements in what NACo felt was enough time. [983] NACo was explicit, warning that the bill would "require all votes in the 2008 federal election to be cast on 'durable' paper ballots (i.e. all DREs will have to be junked in favor of optical scan)." [733]

Opposition from activists

Despite initially supporting DREs with VVPATs, most voting integrity activists later concluded that they were so poorly engineered and unreliable that they should all be banned. Because H.R. 811 did not explicitly ban DREs (even though NACo interpreted it as doing so as a practical matter, as noted above) or because H.R. 811 did not require only hand counted paper ballots, a number of individuals and groups who had supported earlier Holt bills opposed H.R. 811. Given that the vast majority of jurisdictions in the U.S. had been using computer based voting systems for several years, the demand for hand counted paper ballots was politically unrealistic and helped undermine H.R. 811. There was further concern that the Election Assistance Commission, which many election integrity activists did not trust, was being reauthorized or given extra power to oversee elections, a provision that was removed in the committee mark-up.

Other activists blamed Holt for changes negotiated during the mark-up. For example, author Mark Crispin Miller accused Holt of doing the bidding of Microsoft and voting system vendors: "In other words, companies like Microsoft, Diebold and ES&S had problems with the early version of Holt's bill; and Holt himself not only listened to them, but obliged them, so that his 'election reform' bill would now make our system even more undemocratic than it is already."

Miller did not acknowledge, or perhaps did not even know, that all of Holt's bills had called for all software relating to voting systems to be made publicly available. Holt's legislation was modified by the legislative committee of jurisdiction—not by Holt—because of pressure from Microsoft, when it appeared that the bill might actually pass. At that point, Microsoft intervened to oppose the voting machine software disclosure provision.* Microsoft lobbyists persuaded some committee members that the bill as written would have a negative impact on the software industry. Consequently, the originally scheduled mark-up

---

*One of us, Barbara Simons, was among the computer scientists consulted during the negotiations.

was delayed, while staff negotiated a compromise that would satisfy committee members' concerns.

In early May an amendment to the original bill reflecting the compromise negotiated with Microsoft was adopted. The introduced bill would have made "source code, object code, executable representation, and ballot programming files available for inspection promptly upon request to any person." By contrast, the negotiated version limited disclosure by defining a notion of "election-dedicated voting system technology" that excluded commercially available software and hardware. Voting system technology was to be held in escrow by an accredited laboratory and disclosed only to a "qualified" person who signed a non-disclosure agreement (NDA) or to someone who was legally allowed to inspect the technology under state law. While Microsoft was able to eliminate the requirement that all voting system software be available for inspection by anyone, the revised legislative text included some meaningful restrictions on the scope of any required NDA. The signatory could not be prohibited from analyzing and executing the software, and disclosure of evidence of a crime, vulnerabilities to tampering, risks, failures, and other problems was allowed.

Opposition from computer scientists

The small number of computer scientists who have consistently opposed Holt's legislation have received a disproportionately large amount of government and media attention. Foremost among this group is Carnegie Mellow University professor Michael Shamos. Shamos consistently minimizes the seriousness of DRE security and accuracy problems uncovered by computer security experts. In testimony at the September 2006 hearing in the House of Representatives mentioned earlier in the chapter, Shamos attempted to play down the gravity of security vulnerabilities uncovered by Felten and Hursti by arguing that those vulnerabilities could be "easily remedied." [900] Even if Shamos were right, his comments ignored the widespread use of insecure legacy voting machines in previous critical elections, as well as the inevitable lag time in repairing those machines, if they are ever repaired.

Shamos discounted the significance of voting machine problems in a January 2008 New York Times article. [960] While acknowledging that about 10% of DREs fail in each election, he added, "In general, those failures result in the loss of zero or one vote." Shamos gave no reference for his claim, and it is highly unlikely that he could ever prove such an assertion. Finally, Shamos has consistently stated, such as in expert witness testimony in September 2008, that "not a single case is known in which a single vote has been lost or stolen from [a DRE] by malicious intrusion." [902] While literally correct, Shamos' argument ignores the very serious security problems uncovered by the Top-to-Bottom Review and the EVEREST Study, both of which had been release in 2007. He also ignores the fact that the lack of a paper trail combined with little to no post-election audits of DREs means that it is almost impossible to be able to prove that malware on a DRE has impacted any election.

Opposition from vendors

Not surprisingly, vendors have tried to minimize the seriousness of problems with their systems. For example, in written testimony before a Congressional committee, John S. Groh, speaking on behalf of the vendors, claimed that, "Many, if not most, of the problems ... are not directly technological, but involve humans and their interactions with technology." He went on to warn that the " 'perfect should not be the enemy of good.' ... What may be perfect for an aspect of security may be a limiting factor on usability." [409]

12.3.4   How to Kill a Bill: the Death of H.R. 811

In spite of pockets of opposition, initially things looked positive for H.R. 811, in large part because of strong support from House Speaker Pelosi. [948] Rep. Zoe Lofgren (D-CA), who chaired the Subcommittee on Elections, held a series of hearings involving a wide range of stakeholders in March 2007. There was also a full committee hearing immediately prior to the April recess.

Unlike its predecessors, H.R. 811 was marked up and eventually reported out of committee in May 2007 on a party line vote, with six Democrats supporting the bill and three Republicans voting against it. What follows is a description of some of the machinations that prevented this strongly supported legislation from being voted on by the House.

The bill reported out of committee included a compromise to accommodate concerns of election officials who had just deployed touch screen voting machines equipped with VVPAT printers: the mark-up delayed the original deadline for all voting systems to have durable, accessible, and privacy-protecting paper ballots from 2008 to 2010 in jurisdictions that already had DREs with VVPATs, while retaining the requirement for those jurisdictions that had no VVPATs. [170] The bifurcated deadlines were subsequently used as justification to further weaken the bill.

With H.R. 811 reported favorably out of committee and enjoying the co-sponsorship of almost half the House members, supporters anticipated a floor vote in May or June of 2007. But, instead of a floor vote, some disability rights activists intervened to delay and weaken the bill. Despite Rep. Holt's extensive prior negotiations with a broad range of disability rights advocates, Majority Leader Hoyer asked the bill's supporters to negotiate further changes with specific representatives of the disability advocacy communities. [283]

During the negotiations, the disability rights advocates raised mobility issues relating to ballot marking devices.* As a result, H.R. 811 supporters contacted a leading vendor to ask if it was possible to address the needs of voters with severe mobility problems. The response was yes, the vendor's system could be modified so that the voter would not have to touch the ballot, which instead would eject into a privacy sleeve or separate envelope. When this information was shared with one of the advocates, she responded that such a solution would be acceptable.

Nonetheless, expressing apprehension about appropriating funds for equipment that did not completely meet the needs of voters with severe mobility problems, some advocates argued for more implementation time. [393] They also protested the "lack of parity" of allowing the retention of DREs with VVPATs that did not provide accessible verification for blind voters until 2010, a change inserted in the mark-up at the request of election officials. [170]

The resulting compromise, which may have created as many problems as it solved, delayed the requirements for both durable paper ballots and accessible verification to 2012. [192] After objecting to the retention of DREs with VVPATs until 2010, the only compromise some disability advocates would accept was one that allowed yet more usage of DREs with VVPATs for a longer period of time than H.R. 811, as marked up, allowed. As a practical matter, the introduced version and committee mark-up would have required election officials to replace paperless DREs with optical scan systems combined with ballot marking devices by 2008. The negotiated language, by contrast, would have allowed jurisdictions to replace paperless DREs with DREs with VVPATs. Although blind voters can verify their paper ballots on ballot marking devices, but not on DREs with VVPATs, the compromise could have resulted in increasing the number of DREs with VVPATs on which blind voters would be voting from 2008 through 2012. This was precisely the lack of parity the disability rights advocates complained about.

In addition, a new provision was inserted that mandated "mechanisms that do not require a voter to manually handle the paper ballot,

---

*One of us, Barbara Simons, was aware of the negotiations.

which may include mechanisms that provide voters with the option of automatically placing the ballot into a secure container for subsequent counting." [192] While such a requirement would probably have caused the vendors to replace or retrofit the old systems, the timing of the bill also would have allowed vendors to develop new voting systems which would eliminate the need to manually handle the paper ballot.

Funding mechanisms also were changed. The committee mark-up would have provided one billion dollars for states to meet requirements for durable auditable paper ballots. The negotiated version provided one billion dollars for 2008 and "such sums as may be necessary" for 2009 to fund any additional upgrades not covered by the amounts provided in FY 2008. [192] In other words, the 2008 money could have been used to purchase either DREs with VVPATs or optical scanners and ballot marking devices. Inaccessible DREs would no longer have been legal in 2012, while ballot marking devices might have needed modifications by 2012 to automatically deposit the ballot into a secure container. The 2009 money could have been used to replace newly purchased DREs or to pay for a ballot marking device upgrade. Depending on how it was spent, the increased funding could have resulted in a huge waste of taxpayer money, while being highly profitable for DRE vendors.

Finally, the negotiations resulted in the insertion into the bill of a statutory requirement guaranteeing a private entity, namely the Association of Assistive Technology Act Programs, a voice in determining which voting systems would be considered accessible. [192] This provision circumvented public bidding requirements. It also appeared to reflect a conflict of interest for then ATAP Board member Diane Golden, who was directly involved with the negotiations that named her organization in the bill.

The result of the negotiation, known as the "Manager's Amendment," ran into additional opposition, even though the Manager's Amendment was far weaker than the version of H.R. 811 reported out of committee. The National Association of Counties (NACo) redoubled its opposition, as did the AAPD, whose letter in opposition to the Manager's Amendment, signed by Jim Dickson and AAPD President Andrew J. Imparato, was circulated by Rep. Vern Ehlers (R-MI). [495,672] According to an AP article, R. Doug Lewis, Executive Director of the Election Center, said of the Manager's Amendment "the bill was so objectionable that, if passed, he would recommend that state and local election officials refuse to run federal elections." [6]

There was also considerable resistance from Blue Dog Democrats, even some who were co-sponsors. In addition, a small contingent of

Democrats, including Dennis Kucinich (D-OH), objected to the Manager's Amendment because it didn't ban DREs. But perhaps most damaging were initial public criticisms of the bill by Alcee Hastings (D-FL) and the New York Congressional delegation, including Rules Committee Chair Louise Slaughter (D-NY). According to *Roll Call*, "Slaughter said her concerns have been appeased because leadership agreed to allow New York to continue using lever voting machines until the 2010 elections." [238] Ironically, New York State eliminated all lever machines prior to the 2010 midterms. [162]

Despite the weakening of the Holt bill, many election integrity advocates and organizations supported the Manager's Amendment. For example, although VerifiedVoting.org criticized some of the provisions introduced in the negotiations, they observed that "the good in the bill outweighs the changes" and urged Congress to implement VerifiedVoting.org's suggestions and to pass the bill. [979]

At the end of July, the New York Times published a report confirming that negotiations between Rep. Holt and Majority Leader Steny Hoyer concerning remaining disability access issues had been resolved. [284] Nonetheless, unfortunately, there was never a vote on H.R. 811 by the full House.

12.4   The 2008, 2010, 2012 Elections and Beyond

In spite of a promising beginning, none of the HAVA reform legislation was passed by either the House or Senate. Consequentially, for the 2008 presidential election and the 2010 mid-term elections, there was no mandatory national random audit of voting systems, and many millions of voters used unreliable voting machines with known security vulnerabilities. Insecure and unaudited voting is likely to continue in many parts of the county through the 2012 presidential election and—until there is an acknowledged disaster or citizens start demanding serious reform—for many years to come.

13

Voting, Counting, and Auditing: Building Confidence in Elections

The annual federal budget amounts to over $2 trillion. Why bother auditing government spending down to dollars and cents, when you can't audit the process of choosing those who spend the money?

Richard Kennedy (R), New Hampshire House [549]

The initial count in the 2010 race for Senate District 7(SD 7) in New York showed Republican Jack Martins beating Democratic incumbent Craig Johnson by 42,942 to 42,491, a margin of only 451 votes. New York State has a law requiring that 3% of the optical scan machines be audited. Irreconcilable differences between the hand and machine counts could lead to escalations of 5%, 12%, or a total recount. [937] The drama was increased with SD 7, because if Martins were declared the winner, Republicans would control the State Senate by 32–30, whereas a win for Johnson would result in a tied Senate.

Since SD 7 had 249 machines, the 3% rule meant that 7 machines were randomly selected and audited. The initial audit size was far too small to draw any conclusions for such a close race, even if no errors were found. In fact, four errors were found on 3 of the 7 machines, one favoring Johnson and 3 favoring Martins. [940] While correcting the errors gave Johnson two votes, Martins' supporters claimed that since all the errors could be "explained" (e.g. a ballot was not counted initially), those errors didn't count towards the audit law's escalation requirement.

The judge apparently agreed and ruled against escalation. His decision was upheld by the Appellate Court and the Court of Appeals, New York's highest court. The judge may have thought that the error rate found in the audit could be extrapolated to all the machines, much as one slice of cake is similar to another. So, 4 errors on 7 machines would suggest 142 errors on 249 machines, about 1/3 of the number of votes needed to change the election outcome. But, there is no reason to assume that other machines had the same error rates. Instead of comparing voting machines to cake slices, it would be better to compare them to chocolate chip cookies. One cookie might have very few chips, while another might have many.

In such a close election, it would not have taken much error to change the outcome: the audit needed to examine many more machines to give strong evidence that the right person had been elected, even if it found no additional errors. This was never done.

13.1 Manually Counting Ballots

Several countries, such as Canada and Israel, manually count all ballots in national elections. The ballots used in these countries tend to be simple, typically with only one race per ballot, so counting is very fast. Nationwide results are usually available within one day, or even hours after the close of the election.

There are a number of jurisdictions throughout the U.S., including 122 in New Hampshire, where ballots are counted by hand. According to Anthony Stevens, Assistant Secretary of State for New Hampshire, the cost of the hand counts ranges from 3 to 7 cents per choice on a ballot, depending on how efficiently the counts are conducted and assuming a labor cost of $10/hour. Since the number of choices on a ballot may range from 12 to 17 in hand count towns, the total cost for manually counting every contest on the ballot can range from $0.36 cents to $1.19 per ballot. (Many towns make effective use of volunteer counters, thereby reducing costs well below the above range.) In these contests, management time is not devoted to challenges from candidates; rather, questioned ballots are acted on by the moderator and the team of election officials.

Stevens observed that an accurate and efficient method of counting for contests in which instructions are "vote for not more than 1" is "the sort and stack method," in which two-person teams sort all ballots into separate piles for each candidate and then count each candidate stack twice. This is the same method we discussed in Chapter 2 used to count partisan paper ballots in the 19th century. An alternative counting method, one used particularly for multi-seat contests, involves one team member calling out each vote, and another team member writing it down. This method is less intuitive than the sort and stack method, so it is advisable to have an extra team member to check the person reading the ballot and another to check the person marking the tally sheet. [945]

Ideal conditions for hand counting are polling places with fewer than 1300 registered voters, proactive election management and poll worker recruitment practices, healthy levels of civic engagement, and reliance on sound counting techniques, including ballot accounting that catches errors every 50 ballots or so. Otherwise, hand counting can be error prone.[392] While some activists want all elections to be hand-counted,[156] the best path forward is to rely on judiciously chosen technology backed by hand counts for audits and recounts.

13.1.1 Checking DRE Voting Machines

Because it is impossible to conduct a meaningful recount or audit of paperless DRE voting machines, *parallel testing* has occasionally been recommended for those systems, as discussed in Chapter 5. In such a test, machines are randomly selected before the election and separated from the remaining machines. While the polls are open, test ballots are cast on the selected machines. After the election, the tabulated test DRE results are compared with the pre-determined test ballot results. If they match, the assumption is that all the voting machines worked correctly. If they do not, careful investigation is required.

Our experience with voting machine testing shows that errors in following the test script are extremely common and determining the cause of an incorrect result is extremely difficult without a video recording of the entire test session. Even with a video recording, the investigation is very labor intensive. As a result, few jurisdictions have the resources needed to test more than a very small fraction of their machines in this fashion.

While parallel testing may be the best available check for paperless DREs, it is inadequate. First, the assumption that if the test machines work correctly then all the machines work correctly may be unfounded, because malicious voting machine software could easily recognize a typical voting machine test script and behave correctly. Second, if a serious election day discrepancy is uncovered, there is no recourse, aside from rerunning the election. The inability to conduct an audit or recount on paperless DRE machines makes their use unacceptable.

DRE machines that produce a voter verified paper audit trail (VVPAT) are an improvement over paperless machines. However, the paper used in most of these machine is continuous roll thermal printer paper, similar to a gas station receipt. As we discuss in Chapter 5, many voters don't check the VVPATs, and manually counting ballots on thermal printer tape is even harder than manually counting conventional paper ballots.

13.1.2   Recounts

Most large jurisdictions use computer based voting systems, thereby exposing themselves to risks of programming errors, software bugs, and hidden election-rigging software. Problems such as flawed scanner calibration or use of the wrong kind of pen can also impact an election outcome. To catch and correct possible election-changing errors, as well as intentional manipulation, we need a check on the computers and related voting equipment. Currently, the only known check is to examine paper ballots that accurately represent citizens' votes. One way to verify the results is to conduct a manual election recount. As Richard "Stretch" Kennedy, Republican member of the New Hampshire House wrote in 2004, states that routinely conduct such recounts experience multiple benefits:

> Easy recounts bear major benefits over time, and have led to early adoption of good practices in elections. In 1974, the recount resulting from the closest U.S. Senate election in American history obliged New Hampshire to tighten up its election laws. By 1986, multiple recounts of punch card ballots revealed the hanging chad problems and caused the state to eliminate punch cards. In 1988, the State Republican Convention enacted a resolution calling for a recountable paper ballot. In 1994, after a recount involving voting machines without a paper trail, Manchester Representative Leo Pepino got the Legislature to enact the nation's first law requiring that voting machines use paper ballots. [549]

In addition to the benefits discussed by Kennedy, recounts confirm the outcome of an election. As a matter of law in most jurisdictions, the hand count result is the correct result. The issue is whether the machine count finds the same winner that a hand count would find.

The cost of conducting a recount can be kept under control by proper planning, as well as by sensible election laws. For example, an October 2010 study by Pew Charitable Trusts compared the 2008 Minnesota recount for the U.S. Senate with the 2004 Washington gubernatorial recount. [656] The report found that Washington spent over 39 cents per choice on a ballot. By contrast, Minnesota spent less than half as much, roughly 16 cents per choice on a ballot. One of the reasons, according to the report, is that Minnesota conducted only one manual recount, whereas Washington was required first to conduct a re-tabulation of the machines and then a manual recount—in essence two recounts. The cost for just the manual recount in Washington was estimated at 31 cents per choice on a ballot, still roughly double the cost in Minnesota. Another difference is that in Minnesota challenged ballots were sent to a centralized state board, while in Washington the counties had to deal with the time-consuming activity of resolving ballot disputes.

In addition, Washington had to process provisional ballots, whereas Minnesota, which allows election day registration, is not required to provide provisional ballots.

In 2008 and 2010, recounts in New Hampshire contests cost an average of about 24 cents per choice on a ballot, after costs of travel to bring ballots to the state capital, storage space, security, utilities, counting team and management time are considered. Some recounts involve opening many partially filled boxes of ballots from many distant towns, whereas other recounts involve opening relatively few full boxes from one or two large jurisdictions that are close by. In New Hampshire, unlike many other states, recounts are conducted at the state capital. This entails additional costs of bringing ballots to a central location and storing them securely. The advantages are that candidates are able to coordinate their efforts more easily and that decisions on contested ballots may be more consistent. Since any and all ballots may be challenged by candidates, candidates effectively determine how much staff and management time is used in the recount. [945]

13.2 Post-Election Audits and Recounts

A report on Minnesota's 2008 post-election audit and recount was released by Citizens for Election Integrity Minnesota (CEIMN), a non-partisan, non-profit citizens' organization, in partnership with the League of Women Voters Minnesota and Common Cause Minnesota. [421] Like Stevens, the report recommends a two-person manual counting protocol. It also suggests that counting locations post the audit or recount tallies at the end of each day, so that they can be reviewed by the public. Because of chain of custody concerns, the report calls for the unsealing and sealing of ballots, as well as their transportation to and from a secure location, to be publicly observable. Two elected officials should always be present whenever ballots are retrieved from or returned to locked storage.

In addition to auditing voted ballots, it is also important to examine all of the secondary records produced by the voting equipment. There is no point in recording event logs if those logs are not subject to regular scrutiny. Such reviews can provide assurance that the polls were opened and closed in a timely manner, as well as a variety of useful management information. Audits performed primarily for management purposes can be performed after the election results have been certified. These are sometimes referred to as *cold audits* to distinguish them from the *hot audits* performed before final certification of the election results.

13.2.1 Ballot Auditing Issues

Computer-declared election results cannot be checked by having the
same voting system recompute those results. At the very least, the
checking must be done with a completely independent system. If that
system itself involves a machine, it may be subject to the same questions
that were asked about the original computer.

Ultimately, the only check we can be certain of is one performed
by people in plain public view. Audits and recounts should be publicly observable; at a minimum, independent observers and candidate representatives should be allowed to observe the process. In
the modern era, it is reasonable to ask that the audit process be
shown on the local government cable channel or streamed on the Internet.

Most post-election ballot auditing involves manual counting a set of
ballots for comparison with the original machine count results for the
same ballots. Although close elections may require a total recount, in
most cases a well designed post-election manual audit will give strong
evidence that the declared outcome is correct after counting a small
fraction of the ballots.

Sometimes determining a voter's selection on a hand-marked paper
ballot can be a challenge, as discussed in Chapter 4. Solid rules governing what constitutes a legal vote can reduce contention over whether
to credit a particular vote to a specific candidate, but it is difficult to
eliminate grey areas. In addition, ballot scanners can make mistakes
that a human would not, confusing smudges or printing defects for
votes, or missing clearly made marks because the voter used the wrong
kind of pen. Properly conducted recounts and audits can identify the
prevalence of such problems.

Precinct-based audits

Early thinking about election auditing focused on how many precincts
to audit. For example, the oldest audit law, passed by California in
1965, requires selecting precincts from each county at random for audit
until the total number of precincts selected is at least one percent of the
number participating in the election. [134] Like California, a number of
states require fixed percentage audits of precincts. A fixed percentage
audit is better than no audit at all, but fixed percentage audits may
examine too few ballots in a close election and far too many in a land-
slide election. That is why U.S. Rep. Rush Holt of New Jersey, in an
effort to make audits more reflective of election results without being
overly complicated, introduced the notion of a "tiered" audit system,
as discussed in Chapter 12.

A defect in the audit laws of California and some other states is that there is no requirement for escalating the audit. Those drafting the laws probably assumed that there would be a demand for an escalation if an audit uncovered problems. But, they may not have realized that without strong statistical evidence that the outcome is correct, something that might not be obvious to the non-statistician, the audit should be escalated. Only a few states currently require escalation when an audit fails to provide adequate evidence to support the machine-declared results. [783]

Randomness

Selecting the audit units at random is a critical component of audits. For example, if an audit is precinct-based and the precincts subject to audit are known at advance, crooks can confine their manipulations to those precincts that will not be audited. If randomness is not required or well defined, auditors may simplify their life by cherry-picking audit units that are known to be defect free. This actually happened in Cuyahoga County, Ohio in 2004, as discussed in Chapter 7. Merely relying on a machine such as a bingo cage or a computer to give a random number is not secure, since machines may be rigged.

It is notoriously difficult to generate random numbers on a computer; the best that can be done is to use a "pseudo-random number generator," and many of these are flawed and challenging to use properly. [809] Hardware accessories that use physical random processes such as radioactive decay are available, but they are rare. Whether pseudo-random or physically random processes are used, it is extremely difficult to convince a suspicious observer that any particular machine is actually producing random numbers, as opposed to pre-selected numbers that are under the complete control of the machine's owner.

A simple way to create publicly verifiable random numbers is to have all the participants in the process contribute a random number, chosen in whatever way the participant wishes. If there is at least one honest participant who produces a genuinely random value and if the numbers are combined the correct way, the result will be random. For example, each participant can roll dice to contribute one decimal digit of the value. [208] The Brennan Center report on post-election audits describes several alternatives. [783]

Other audit units

There are alternatives to precinct-based audits. The "audit unit" does not have to be a precinct. In vote-by-mail jurisdictions an audit unit can be a "batch," where ballots are divided into batches as they arrive at the election office. Better yet, if it is possible to connect the interpretation of the image of each ballot back to the original paper document without compromising ballot privacy, the audit unit can be the individual ballot.

Ballot-level auditing is a very recent idea. Calandrino et al. published a proposal in 2007 for a specialized recount machine that would scan and count ballots after the initial tabulation had been completed. The recount machine's results would then be checked using a smaller manual ballot-level audit. [132]

How do you determine the number of ballots that need to be counted in order to be fairly certain that any errors that are uncovered are not enough to change the election outcome? Statisticians have concluded that the answer depends on a number of factors, including the margin of victory in the election, and they have developed schemes called *risk limiting audits*. When combined with ballot-level auditing, risk limiting audits minimize the number of ballots that must be recounted to obtain any particular level of confidence in the election outcome.

13.2.2 Risk-Limiting Post-Election Audits

The *risk-limiting* audit is the gold standard of audits. Risk-limiting means that if the machine-reported count is incorrect, "there is a large, pre-specified chance that the audit will reveal the correct outcome." [34] Risk-limiting post-election audits are designed to minimize the size of the audit when the outcome is correct, while with very high probability correcting the outcome, if it is incorrect, by counting all the ballots. The audit continues until there is sufficiently strong statistical evidence that the apparent outcome is right, or until all the ballots have been manually counted.

There are several factors that determine the size of the audit. Two are the closeness of the race being audited and the total number of ballots cast in that race. To understand why, imagine an election with 100,000 votes where the machine results show candidate A beating candidate B by 100 votes. A relatively small number of votes for B that either were incorrectly counted for A or not counted at all could change the result and determine that B was the actual winner. Since a few potentially election-changing discrepancies might not be uncovered by a small audit, a large audit is needed. If, however, the machine results show A beating B by a wide margin of 20,000 votes, but B actually beat A, there would have to be a large number of B votes given to A or not counted at all to change the outcome. Therefore, if only a relatively small number of audit units is examined, it would be highly likely that a large number of wrongly recorded votes would be uncovered.

A third factor is the size of the batches for which auditable totals are available. The smaller the batches, the fewer ballots will have to be examined, with individual ballot audits being the most efficient. The following food example from Philip Stark is instructive.[938] Suppose there are 100 bags of 100 jelly beans each, with some bags having a mixture of flavors and others consisting of a single flavor only. Suppose also that each bag is covered with aluminum foil, so that nobody can tell which is which by looking at the bags. I love coconut jelly beans and I want to estimate the number of coconut beans in all 100 bags. One option would be to choose a bag at random, open it, and count all the beans. I could then estimate the total number of coconut beans by multiplying the number in that bag by 100. If I chose a bag that contained only coconut beans, I would estimate that all 10,000 beans were coconut; if the bag consisted of entirely a different flavor, I would estimate that none of the 10,000 beans was coconut; and if I picked a mixed bag, I would assume the ratio of all 10,000 beans was the same as that in the bag I had picked.

Suppose instead the jelly bean bags are all opened by someone else, dumped into a large pot, and stirred well. Suppose I then choose 100 beans at random from the large pot and count the number of coconut beans in that group. The estimate I get in this case will be far more reliable than the estimate I would get by looking at the contents of a single bag, even though in both cases I'm examining 100 jelly beans. To get a similarly reliable estimate on the number of coconut jelly beans in all the bags by drawing individual bags at random, I would have to examine far more bags and count many more jelly beans.

The basic structure of a risk-limiting audit follows the following framework: Hand count ballots until the evidence is strong that the outcome is correct. The number of ballots counted will depend on the errors you observe and the particular method being used. If you see no errors or predominantly errors that, if corrected, help the apparent winner, you need to look at fewer ballots than if you see errors that, if corrected, predominantly help the apparent loser. In sum, the number of ballots that need to be examined depends on the data.[940] There are also time-saving techniques for doing a risk-limiting audit of all of the ballot races simultaneously,[939] although hand-counting multiple races at once may be significantly harder than counting just one race by the sort and stack method.

In 2009 Colorado modified its election law to require risk-limiting audits by 2014.[180] The following year the American Statistical Association issued a statement endorsing risk-limiting post-election audits.[34] In the same year AB 2023 became law in California. AB 2023 authorizes "the Secretary of State to establish a postcanvass risk-limiting audit pilot program in five or more voluntarily participating counties for the purpose of verifying the accuracy of election results." [135]

In 2011, California and Colorado were two of several states and counties that received EAC grants to conduct pilot post-election audits. Prior to AB 2023, risk-limiting audits were conducted in Marin County (2 elections, 2 contests total), Santa Cruz County (1 contest), and Yolo County (2 elections, 3 contests total). As of this writing, twenty California counties have committed to conducting risk-limiting audits under AB 2023 and the EAC California grant, and audits have been conducted in Alameda (4 contests), Humboldt (3 contests), Orange (one contest), Merced (2 contests), Monterey (1 contest), San Luis Obispo (2 contests), Stanislaus (one contest), and Ventura (one contest). Risk-limiting audits have also been conducted in Boulder, Colorado and Cuyahoga, Ohio.

13.3 Examining Other Aspects of Elections

While verifying that the declared winners were the actual winners is of critical importance, there are many other aspects of elections that also should be audited. Historically, elections have been conducted without the accountability and transparency expected of legitimate businesses. Some states and precincts rarely conduct any kind of post-election analysis or audit, even though such audits could help identify problems in a current election and prevent similar problems in future elections.

13.3.1 Chain of Custody Issues

In 2002 plastic ballot box lids were found floating in San Francisco Bay. [657] Many people assumed that someone had dumped full ballot boxes into the Bay, but it appears that the lids, which had been used as containers for pens and other office supplies, were blown off a pier where they had been left after being hosed down by city workers. [867] While that explanation seems correct, the incident highlights the need for cautious handling of all materials related to elections.

Elections cannot be secure unless all the components of elections, including ballots, hardware, software, and audit logs, are handled, transported, and stored securely. If jurisdictions do not have sound chain of custody procedures for these items, there is the risk of election error, manipulation, or theft. Chain of custody procedures, together with explanations for why each is needed, should be made available for public review well in advance of an election and should be subjected to frequent audits. In 2007 the Brennan Center issued a report containing recommendations for the secure storage of voting system components: [783]

- Before and after elections, voting systems should be locked in a county warehouse that is frequently checked by security guards and has perimeter alarms, secure locks, and video surveillance.

- Sensitive areas of the machines, such as vote data media compartments, communication ports, and the seams of the voting system case, should be protected by tamper-evident seals.

- To increase accountability, access to the warehouse should be limited to regular staff who are required to sign in with some automatic logging device, such as a card key.

The report also addresses steps to be taken after an election, starting with placing all audit information in packets or boxes protected by numbered tamper-evident seals. (We note that tamper-evident seals are not secure. There are techniques for bypassing, removing, and replacing the seals without detection, and duplicate seals often can be obtained).[52] The audit information, including event logs, voter verifiable paper records, paper ballots, and machine printouts of vote totals, should be delivered to the local election center by two officials from opposing parties. Once at the election center, the containers should be logged and the numbers on the seals checked to ensure that the seals have not been replaced. Given how easily seals can be defeated, good protocols, combined with well-designed training, are needed for checking the seals and reporting evidence of tampering. The containers should then be stored in a location with the same or greater security and access control as the voting systems warehouse. The audit material should be protected by security guards and local police officers.

13.3.2 Comprehensive Election Auditing

There are many ways in which overall audits of elections, such as checking that that the ballot layout is not confusing and that the ballot is correct (e.g. all candidates and issues listed), can help improve the overall conduct and accuracy of elections. For that reason, the League of Women Voters commissioned a task force to examine all aspects of election-related audits. (One of us, Barbara Simons, was a member of the LWV task force.) Released in January 2009, the *Report on Election Auditing*, recommends that election audits examine:[286]

1. Activities typically undertaken before or between elections, such as evaluation of the following: the voter registration process, the voting machines to be used, the electronic poll books, and all procedures for running the election;

2. Procedural aspects of the election, such as wait times, polling place worker performance and whether there were appropriate

controls on the chain of custody for all election equipment, materials, and ballots; and

3. Procedures to determine the accuracy of the reported election results themselves. Properly performed audits will guard against both deliberate manipulation of the election and software, hardware or programming problems, since any of these factors could alter the election outcome.

The report also contains three sets of useful guidelines, including both goals and performance measures. The first set relates to auditing of election procedures and processes, namely transparency, testing, physical protection of voting systems, education and training, and polling place procedures during voting. The second deals with post-election audits, including preparatory steps to be taken in advance of an election, risk limiting audits, and escalation procedures. The final set applies after an election, including polling place checking of totals, problem ballots, and provisional ballots; accounting for all provisional and absentee ballots; verifying that provisional ballots are approved or disapproved for statutorily acceptable reasons; protecting ballot secrecy; properly dealing with all forms of paper records; and preserving records as required by law.

Every aspect of an election should be subject to examination, including proprietary software and hardware. All ballots, including mail-in, early-voting, provisional, and emergency ballots should be inspected. Spoiled or cancelled VVPATs should be analyzed to see if the voters had problems because of DRE voting machine errors or malicious code; ballots with overvotes or undervotes should be checked, since they might be symptomatic of faulty scanner calibration or poorly written instructions. Significant problems or discrepancies should be investigated to determine the cause, even if the discrepancies almost certainly did not change the election outcome. Otherwise, the same problems might reoccur in future elections. Much of the auditing activity recommended by the League report is best classified as cold auditing, since it can be done after the election results are certified.

13.4   Other Voting Models

Up to this point our discussion has largely ignored the question of how the winner in an election is determined, although the tacit assumption has been that the votes for each candidate are simply added to get a grand total and then the winner or winners are determined, depending on who gets the highest total. This is sometimes called the *first-past-the-post* system. There are alternatives to this model:

13.4.1 Ranked Choice Ballots

Ranked-choice ballots allow the voter to express preferences among candidates, as opposed to voting for only a single candidate. On a typical ranked-choice ballot, voters are asked not only who their first choice is, but also their second, third, and later choices. There are a number of ways to conduct ranked choice elections, but the one that is gaining the most traction in the U.S. is called *Instant Runoff Voting (IRV)*

In a single seat IRV election, the ballot counting process begins by counting all of the first choice votes. If no one wins a majority, the candidate with the fewest first choice votes is eliminated and that candidate's ballots are re-distributed, each going to the highest ranked candidate on the ballot who has not yet been eliminated. Elimination rounds continue until some candidate gets a majority or only one candidate remains.

One of us, Douglas Jones, worked with the student government leadership at the University of Iowa to implement their first IRV election. In the process, he became convinced that many of the leaders who had pushed for IRV did not understand significant details. Ties between the winners of an election are unlikely, but what the students did not realize is that in an IRV system, ties between the losers must be broken. The outcome of an IRV election can change significantly, depending on how such ties are broken, particularly if the two losing candidates are at the opposite extremes of the political spectrum.

Confusion over IRV is not limited to University of Iowa students. San Francisco has held IRV elections for several years. Yet, of the San Francisco voters who participated in a 2011 survey by the San Francisco Chamber of Commerce, 55% expressed some confusion as to how the system works. [87] An earlier study had shown that, while a significant majority of voters (87%) said they understood the system "fairly" or "perfectly" well, those with the lowest understanding tended to be minority and lower income voters. [745]

Auditing IRV Ballots

As with first-past-the-post elections, the most efficient way to conduct a post-election audit of any election using ranked-choice ballots is to do so at the ballot-level, with a link between each paper ballot and its electronic representation. If the voting technology does not allow for such a link, then a link can be created by marking the paper ballots with unique identifying numbers after the election and then rescanning them. Software is needed that will interpret the ballot image and link that interpretation back to the paper ballot. Unfortunately, rescanning is not always an option.

An interesting example is the 2011 San Francisco mayoral race, in which there were 16 candidates. Since the Sequoia voting system used in San Francisco did not allow a linkage between the paper and electronic versions of the ballot, in order to conduct a ballot-level audit or recount, it would have been necessary to rescan all of the paper ballots, roughly 480,000 pieces of paper. To do that in a few days would have required ballot interpretation software, along with a team of about 25 people and six $16,000 scanners. The city had neither the room nor the necessary staff to do this.[941]

California law requires a post-election manual ballot count of 1% of precincts, randomly selected. Because ballot-level auditing is not currently an option, San Francisco instead conducts audits that ignore the fundamentals of IRV voting. For the selected precincts, the city manually counts the 1st, 2nd, and 3rd choices for each voting machine, as if they were separate elections. (San Francisco uses a modified version of IRV in which the voter chooses only his or her top three choices.)

To complete its strange audit process, San Francisco runs a mini-IRV election for the selected precincts, even though the outcome determined by the mini-IRV election could easily differ from the outcome of the full election when all ballots are tabulated.

The problems of conducting an audit in San Francisco illustrate the important difference between "built-in" and "bolt-on" audits. In small jurisdictions, an audit can be "bolted-on" to existing systems fairly easily. But to audit efficiently in a jurisdiction as large as San Francisco requires a voting system that facilitates or automatically associates electronic images of voted ballots with the individual paper ballots. The limitations of the voting system used by San Francisco, combined with the use of IRV, has resulted in an audit procedure that does not provide a useful check on the accuracy of the machine tabulation.

A manual recount of the 2011 mayor's race would have been a nightmare. For a first-past-the-post election, each ballot contains only a single vote for mayor, and therefore needs to be examined only once. With IRV, each time a candidate is eliminated, that candidate's ballots are manually redistributed. The process would be very time consuming and prone to error.

Other Rank Choice Methods

A simpler method of counting ranked-choice ballots is known as the *Borda count*. In a Borda Count race where voters are allowed to vote for their top three choices, as in San Francisco, the voter's first choice gets 3 votes, the second choice 2 votes, and the third choice one vote. Determining the winner is a simple matter of adding up the votes.

The candidate with the most votes wins. Audits with this scheme can be done locally, and the precinct results can be published locally. The Borda count system has many of the advantages of IRV, but it is far simpler to count and audit.

Another approach, *range* voting, allows voters to express differing preferences for candidates, without requiring a complete ordering. This avoids forcing voters to make choices between candidates they like or dislike equally. With range voting the voter assigns a number to each candidate that reflects the voter's enthusiasm for the candidate. In a 3-way race, the ballot might allow voters to rank each candidate on a scale of 0 to 5. The counting and auditing for range voting is the same as for Borda count, making it another simple alternative to IRV. *Approval voting* is a special case of range voting in which the scale is 0 or 1. In other words, the voter can give a 1 to all the candidates the voter likes, and a 0 to all the others.

We understand the appeal of a ranked-choice ballot, but we do not understand why a large portion of the election reform community has advocated for IRV, since among all schemes for counting ranked-choice ballots, it is the hardest to explain, the hardest to audit, and the hardest to recount. If we are going to modify the way in which ballots are voted and counted, we should avoid complicated systems that don't address the underlying problems and that make tabulations, audits, and recounts unnecessarily difficult.

13.4.2 National Popular Vote

A proposal that has already been enacted into law in several states is the *National Popular Vote (NPV)*. NPV bypasses the Electoral College without the need for a constitutional amendment by requiring an NPV state to provide all of its electoral votes to the presidential candidate receiving the most votes nationally, independent of the state-wide winner. Consequently, in order to validate the national vote count, there would need to be a national post-election audit that included all the states.

Whether or not NPV is a good idea at this time, the lack of uniformity and fairness in how different states run their elections would impact an NPV election. For example, some states allow convicted felons to vote, with varying restrictions, while others make it almost impossible for convicted felons ever to vote. Some states have ballot rotation, whereas others give the top slot on the ticket to the party controlling the governorship. Some states conduct audits and recounts, whereas others do not. Some states facilitate post-election recounts, while others make recounts almost impossible. Obviously, these disparities impact

Electoral College elections as well, but at least the damage done by a poorly or corruptly run state election is limited to that state's Electoral College votes. Furthermore, a state-wide post-election recount, where possible, is less daunting than a national recount.

We conjecture that if NPV laws end up reversing election results from what would have been determined by the Electoral College, we will see yet another major battle at the Supreme Court. The risk of the kind of divisiveness triggered by Bush v. Gore is not a reason to oppose NPV, but it is a concern. Perhaps a greater concern is that NPV might be used by some states to argue against instituting the kinds of reforms needed to make our elections accurate and secure—possibly on the grounds that instituting too many reforms at the same time is a bad idea, or, paradoxically that state-level results are no longer so important, since only the national count matters.

While even a handful of states continue to hold insecure, non-transparent, and potentially inaccurate elections, we are at risk of having national elections wrongly decided or even stolen. We can debate if the risk of incorrect or fraudulent elections is greater with NPV or with the current Electoral College system. What is certain is that we desperately need major reforms that are independent of NPV.

13.5   Why Audits Matter

Elections are complicated processes that involve voters, election officials, voting systems, and volunteers. Because there is much that can go wrong with elections, ranging from careless errors to vote rigging, and because some elections are for very high stakes, it is critical that we have policies and procedures in place that will justifiably create voter confidence in the declared results. As Richard Kennedy said:

> This debate is not about who wins or loses. It's about whether we can trust the system. For the election to be a success, the loser must be convinced the outcome is legitimate. The issue is whether voters in states with recountable ballots can trust the results of states without a credible recount process. [549]

14

Conclusion: Where Do We Go From Here?

In many ways, I think voters and counties are the victims of a federal certification process that hasn't done an adequate job of ensuring that the systems made available to them are secure, accurate, reliable and accessible.

California Secretary of State Debra Bowen (D) [105]

By 2008 most California counties were using only optical scan voting systems, except for a minimum number of direct-recording electronic voting systems to meet the needs of voters with disabilities. In Humboldt County, California, a group of citizens, called the Humboldt Election Transparency Project (ETP), worked with Humboldt County Registrar of Voters Carolyn Crnich to post all the voted ballots on a website, so that anyone could verify the election results. Their tools were a high speed scanner that made images of all the ballots, combined with open source software written by volunteer Mitch Trachtenberg. The software, which allowed the ballots to be sorted by precinct or contest, also counted the ballots for about 98% of the scans.

After the scanning was completed, the ETP volunteers realized that they had scanned more ballots than the number reported by the Premier (formerly Diebold) GEMS version 1.18.19 software. Working together with officials from the election office, they made the surprising discovery that the officially certified election results from Humboldt County were incorrect: 197 ballots had not been tabulated by GEMS. After multiple phone calls with Premier, Crnich learned that if a deck of ballots was deleted from the count, something that election workers might do to correct a mistake in entering the ballots, GEMS might also delete the first deck that had been fed into the machine (Deck Zero).

In the 2008 election, Deck Zero contained the vote-by-mail ballots from Precinct 1E-45.[407]

It turned out that Premier already knew about the "Deck Zero" software bug:

> Chris Riggall, a spokesman for Premier Elections Solutions, said in a previous interview with the Times-Standard that the company had known of the programming error since 2004. Saying the certification process is too lengthy and time-consuming to have had the software re-certified, Riggall said Premier instead simply issued "work-around" orders to its customers instructing them how to take steps to avoid the problem.[406]

An earlier email from Premier documenting the work-around did not explain why it was necessary, and the Humboldt County Elections Manager who received the email neglected to share it with Crnich.[107] Neither the EAC nor the State of California knew of the defect, which had not been uncovered by California's Top-to-Bottom Review. It is disquieting to realize that the GEMS product defect could have been used to "lose" certain ballots by putting those ballots in Deck Zero, and then arranging for all Deck Zero ballots to disappear from the final tally. We have no evidence to suggest that this was ever done, but given the lack of checks on the computer-declared results, we cannot prove that it was not done.

While praising Crnich for her openness, (then) EAC Commissioner Rosemary Rodriguez added:

> There's this very confidential relationship between counties and vendors, and I think issues have been resolved as they've arisen with these kinds of work-arounds, but who knew. The voters certainly didn't know, and elections officials aren't going to necessarily want their voters to know there are problems. So, it's resulted in this kind of unhealthy situation.[406]

Rodriguez also said that the EAC would inform election officials throughout the country of the Deck Zero software bug, and that the new EAC certification process would require vendors to tell the EAC of known problems. But in 2008 the EAC already required vendors to report "any known malfunction of a voting system holding an EAC Certification ... which causes the system to cease operation during a Federal election or otherwise results in data loss." The requirement, which allows potentially election-changing defects to be reported as much as two months after an election, does not apply to voting systems, such as GEMS 1.18.19, that were certified before the introduction of EAC certification. It also does not apply to problems uncovered outside of an election, for example in pre-election testing. As of this writing, there is no federal requirement for vendors to report known product defects in legacy voting systems still in use. [301]

The fact that Premier did not make public information about a known defect that could change the outcome of an election was not the only surprise. It turned out that the voting system event logs, which were supposed to track operator actions, did not track either intentional deletions or unintended erasures. [1034] Consequently, the logs were practically useless. Worse yet, a report later issued by Bowen found "three 'deficiencies' in the system's audit logs that placed incorrect data-entry time stamps in the logs, allowed operators to delete decks of ballots without a paper trail, and even allowed system operators to, intentionally or inadvertently, erase the system's audit logs." [408] The last revelation was especially disturbing, since log deletions could make it impossible to conduct a post-election forensic examination to determine operator actions.

At the end of March 2009, Bowen withdrew approval of GEMS version 1.18.19 because of its "serious software flaws." [108] Bowen also sponsored SB 1404, a bill that was signed by Gov. Schwarzenenegger at the end of September, 2010. [138]

SB 1404 forbids unauthorized changes to voting systems and requires voting system vendors to notify the state in writing "of any defect, fault, or failure of the hardware, software, or firmware of the voting system or a part of the voting system within 30 calendar days after the vendor learns of the defect, fault, or failure." Businesses that produce blank ballots are required to "notify the Secretary of State and the affected local elections officials in writing within two business days after it discovers any flaw or defect in its ballot card manufacturing or finishing process or manufactured or finished ballot cards that could adversely affect the future casting or tallying of votes."

14.1   Recommendations

In the course of writing this book, we have pointed out numerous problems with the current state of election administration in the United States. We would be remiss if we did not make recommendations to address these problems. In many cases, we have already stated our recommendations in the body of the text, but we are presenting them here in consolidated form. Many of our recommendations will require federal or state legislation. We are well aware of the difficulty of getting reform legislation passed, and we realize that we are aiming high. We also realize that some of our recommended reforms may require additional funding; however, careful planning should minimize those costs.

We believe that voting is an area in which we should not be making compromises. Having secure and honest elections is a cornerstone of our democracy and a national security issue.

Technology-related recommendations

1. Vendors should be required to report all known product defects for all election-related technologies, especially defects that could alter the outcome of an election. (Chapter 14)

   • Vendors should be required to repair major defects in election-related technologies at no charge. (Chapters 7, 8, and 14)

2. Voting system standards and practices that will increase the uniformity, accuracy, security, accessibility, usability, and transparency of elections should be mandated. We have presented ample evidence, notably in Chapter 4 and 6, that the current weak system of "voluntary guidelines" is not adequate.

   • The standards should be reviewed periodically, not just in response to crisis situations, and all phases of the process should be open to public input and scrutiny.

   • The standards must govern not only the machinery, but also the procedures that surround the use of the machinery. Attempting to write technical standards without making assumptions about the procedures, as is the case with today's federal guidelines, does not work.

   • States should develop uniform legislation. Federal standards will never cover all aspects of election administration, and the current lack of uniformity drives up costs and serves as a serious deterrent to potential new vendors.

3. All of the above requirements should apply to Voter Registration Databases, as well as to technologies that record and tabulate votes. Electronic pollbooks and similar new technologies are making it difficult to separate registration from other aspects of election management. (Chapter 10)

   • Standards are needed that govern privacy protection, accuracy, reliability, security, and usability, as well as testing of Voter Registration Databases.

4. Use of the Internet to return voted ballots should be forbidden. As we discuss in Chapter 11, Internet security is both poor and getting worse. We emphasize that ballot return by email is transmission over the Internet, and that fax technology is no better than Internet tech-

nology, even when faxes are sent entirely over the dialed telephone network. Phone voting is equally dangerous.

5. Be cautious about introducing new technology. The history of voting technology we have presented in Chapters 2 through 5 shows that technological change has frequently introduced serious problems, and as we have made clear in Chapter 11, we believe that the new technical options available today are no different. We do not oppose change, as such, but we urge a conservative approach, avoiding change unless:

   - There is a demonstrated problem to solve,
   - The solution has been shown to work, and
   - The apparent risks have been independently assessed and shown to be outweighed by the advantages of the technology.

Recommendations to facilitate audits and recounts

1. Only voting systems that facilitate easy audits and recounts should be permitted. As we discuss in Chapter 13, auditing can be an extraordinarily powerful tool for answering questions about the integrity of an election.

   - All voting systems should facilitate ballot level audits by allowing easy matching of individual paper ballots with their electronic images without violating the right to a secret ballot.
   - All voting systems should maintain accurate audit logs that cannot be deleted by poll workers or election officials, so that they are available for post-election forensic analysis.

2. Legislation mandating risk-limiting post-election audits, preferably at the ballot level, should be passed. As we note in Chapter 13, auditing a fixed percentage of the ballots can be expensive and, when done at the precinct level, can fail to assure a useful level of integrity.

3. All voting systems should be strongly software-independent, that is, it should be possible to detect and correct any error caused by software. This is a prerequisite for meaningful audits, as we discuss in Chapter 6.

4. The time between the end of an election and the date by which the final election outcome is certified must allow for meaningful audits and any needed recounts, as we observe in Chapter 13. In many states, current laws do not provide nearly enough time. We recognize that some auditing activities are best done after election certification, but:

   - Audits that might overturn an election should be done before the results are final.

- If an audit or recount determines that the computer-declared result was incorrect, then the correct winner should be declared the legal winner.
- If it is impossible to determine who actually won the election, then the election should be rerun.

General recommendations

1. Election officials need sufficient funding to run elections. These costs cannot be reduced by outsourcing, nor can they be reduced by equipment rental. Costs that must be covered include:
   - The purchase or rental price of voting equipment.*
   - The cost to store and maintain voting equipment between elections.
   - The cost of recounts and routine audits.

2. The right to a secret ballot needs clarification and protection. As we mention in Chapter 2, there are multiple interpretations of this right. When states have moved to permit fax or Internet voting, voters have been asked to waive their right to a secret ballot. (Chapter 11) We believe that this is a mistake and that:
   - The secret ballot was instituted to protect against voter intimidation; as such, each voter has a right to the assurance that other voters have not been intimidated into disclosing their ballots or into voting a particular way.
   - While there may be special cases in which it might be possible to construct a link between a voter and that voter's ballot, we must not jeopardize the secret ballot by providing tools such as ballot ID numbers or serial numbers that can be used to create such links.
   - Relying on the honesty of election officials is dangerous; where officials have access to information that could be abused to link voters to ballots, this information should be stored so that no single release of information is sufficient to reveal such a linkage.
   - We recognize that auditing may release sufficient information to link an occasional voter to their ballot. The probability of such a

---

*While rental of voting equipment can sometimes be desirable, routine rental is usually a bad idea for two reasons: First, rental is accompanied by loss of control and transparency. When the owner of the equipment is responsible to stockholders and not the general public, the rights of the public are at risk. Second, renting is generally more expensive than ownership. Over the life of the equipment, renters pay not only the full purchase price, but they also cover the rental agency's profit margin. Furthermore, rental agencies will adjust their rental charges up to account for the risk that the renter will terminate the lease early, for example because the machines have been shown to be unreliable.

release must be very small, and it should be impossible for anyone to know in advance which ballots may have their secrecy compromised.

3. The penalties for depriving citizens of the right to vote should be at least as great as the penalty for other forms of election fraud. As we discuss in Chapters 3 and 10, control of who is allowed to vote can be just as potent a tool for election manipulation as buying votes or rigging voting machines.

4. Felon disenfranchisement laws should be reformed. Like literacy tests and other discriminatory measures, many felon disenfranchisement laws were passed in order to disenfranchise voters. (Chapter 10). It strikes us as obvious that, at a minimum, voting rights ought to be automatically restored for felons who have served their sentences.

5. In order to reduce costs and increase election transparency, ballots should be simplified. As we have shown in Chapter 3, the complexity of U.S. elections has been a driving factor behind the use of voting machines. This complexity is also a barrier to effective auditing. (Chapter 13).

   • There may be justification for some variation from state to state, but the current situation does nothing but drive up costs and confuse voters. Voting system vendors must research and support the diverse requirements of 50 states and 4 territories, and when voters move across state lines, they must learn new rules that serve no real purpose.

   • The structure of districts and sub-districts creates a proliferation of ballot styles. In some jurisdictions, the number of ballot styles has proliferated to the point that a small number of voters may be the only ones casting votes on the ballot styles assigned to them. This destroys the right to a secret ballot while running up the cost of ballot preparation and printing.

   • Printing the entire text of referenda on paper ballots or displaying that text on computerized ballot displays disrupts voter concentration and increases the cost of the entire voting system. States should explore ways to reduce the amount of text printed on the ballot.

   • The number of offices and issues on most ballots should be significantly reduced. When voters are faced with choices between candidates they have not heard of or issues they do not understand, democracy becomes meaningless.

Our election rules lack uniformity and simplicity

We are not political theorists, so we cannot say if uniformity should be achieved by a federal mandate or by cooperative action among the states. The federal government could enforce a uniform code of election law, or the states could enact a Uniform Election Code following the long-established model of the Uniform Commercial Code. Here are some examples of the needless complexity that is created by widely varying state laws:

- Some states list candidates in order of the popularity of their political parties in the previous election, thereby tending to favor the dominant party, since there is a statistical advantage to being listed first. Other states rotate the order in which candidate names appear, but different states, for example California and Iowa, have different rotation rules.

- Some states provide straight party voting, while others do not. Among those that allow straight party voting, the rules again differ. For example, in North Carolina, straight-party voting does not apply to the race for president. This variation serves only to raise the price of voting equipment and confuse voters.

- Different states have different rules for ballot typography. These rules gratuitously raise the price of ballot preparation and display software, while few of the differences actually lead to better readability.

- Different states have different residency requirements for being able to vote. Some of these needlessly increase the cost of elections.

- Felon disenfranchisement rules vary widely, ranging from allowing felons to vote from prison (Maine and Vermont) to permanent felon disenfranchisement (Virginia and Kentucky). We see no justification for this extreme range of variation.

- Voter ID rules differ, with some states having no voter ID requirements (e.g. California) while others require a photo ID at the polls (e.g. Kansas).

- State laws for registration of new voters differ. Local election officials can reject a new voter registration application under Florida's "no match, no vote" law if there is not a match between the name on the application and the name in other state databases. By contrast, Minnesota, Iowa and several other states allow voters to register to vote on election day.

14.2　Looking Ahead

This book is an effort to communicate the history and concerns about the technological side of elections. Despite our emphasis on technology, we hope that all stakeholders will work together to improve elections in ways that do not trade one benefit for another, that do not look at improving our elections as an either-or proposition. There are bottom line attributes, such as auditability, accessibility, accuracy, security, reliability, and usability, that our voting systems must meet collectively. These are not mutually exclusive goals, but rather goals that complement each other.

The easiest and most obvious way for a concerned citizen to get involved with our elections is as a volunteer during the election, during pre-election testing, or during post-election audits. Honest elections require a broad range of volunteers:

- Election office and polling place staff. While every election office has a few professionals permanently on the payroll, the vast majority of election workers are temporary employees, paid for just one or a very few days of work. We estimate that a well-run election in the United States requires close to one percent of the electorate to run the election.

- Candidate and party volunteers. Candidates and parties need active help. The primary job of party volunteers working at the polls on election day is to track who has voted to support get-out-the-vote drives. The same volunteers also play a fundamental role as election observers on behalf of their party or candidate. They are frequently the first to report irregularities at the polls. It is almost always representatives of the losing party who ask the really difficult questions and uncover the most serious problems.

- Independent observers. Independent observers are—or should be—welcome at many points in the election cycle from pre-election testing to post-election canvassing. The rules vary from state to state, but there are numerous election protection organizations, both nationally and local, that can use volunteers.

All voters are important, not only for the votes they cast, but also as witnesses of whatever parts of the election process they happen to observe. Voters can and must ask questions if they are confused by any aspect of an election. If local pollworkers cannot provide adequate answers, then the election office should be held accountable. All aspects of our elections, including ballot design, vulnerabilities of voting systems, testing of those systems, counting the voted ballots, and pre- and post-election testing and audits must be made transparent and open to inspection.

Transparency is a key attribute of an honest and trustworthy election system. Whenever election work is conducted behind closed doors and out of sight, there is the potential for fraud. Voters should demand change where states exclude members of the public from being observers. There are, of course, cases where the number of observers must be limited to avoid disruption, but in the modern era, video cameras and Internet connections can allow unlimited observation of key activities in the election office.

Almost every state can improve the way it holds elections, though some states have farther to go than others. In states that still use paperless direct-recording electronic voting machines, we recommend that election officials read Ohio's EVEREST Study and California's Top-to-Bottom Review. [322,141] Regardless of what voting machines are used, it is worthwhile for voters to inspect the maintenance contract for the voting machines. In most cases, these contracts are with the vendor who sold the equipment, and in many cases, these maintenance contracts have become cash cows.

In large jurisdictions, we are convinced that it is almost always less expensive for the jurisdiction to pay for training for their own staff, rather than to rely on vendor technicians for routine maintenance. As we pointed out in Chapter 8, as things are currently run, vendors have an effective monopoly on servicing their equipment, thereby forcing jurisdictions into far too close a relationship with their vendors.

The good news is that average citizens and some truly dedicated election officials have already had a considerable positive impact on how elections are conducted. The Humboldt County Ballot Transparency Project with which we began this chapter is but one example. We have seen similar local successes in Miami-Dade County and elsewhere. In many states a handful of committed individuals have been able to get good legislation passed. But even in those states, the struggle is not over; some states there have been attempts to overturn positive regulations or legislation via legal challenges and judicial efforts.

We believe that the trend is in the right direction. Elections today are more honest than they were a century ago. Nonetheless, the battle is far from over, and we would be presumptuous to claim that we will ever achieve a perfect democracy. This is an area in which, time after time, individual citizens have made a difference. We hope that our readers feel inspired to join in this work.

Appendix

Disability Rights Groups' Lawsuits

A.1 Lawsuits involving Jim Dickson or the AAPD

National Organization on Disability v. Tartaglione, filed 4/19/2001.[806] Dickson was at NOD when the lawsuit was filed. The lawsuit was settled in 2003 when the city of Philadelphia agreed to provide at least one electronic voting machine for each polling place. [885] A supporting Amicus brief was submitted by AAPD.

American Association Of People With Disabilities v. The District of Columbia, filed 9/05/2001. Dickson was one of the plaintiffs. [832] The District of Columbia settled by agreeing to purchase enough DREs to have at least one at every polling place. [844]

American Association Of People With Disabilities v. Smith [Hood], filed 11/08/2001. The firm of Howrey, Simon, Arnold & White, LLP filed the case for AAPD, initially pro-bono. In a Declaratory Judgment John Stafford, the Supervisor of Elections in Duval County, FL, was ordered to have at least one DRE in each voting place. The order specifically mentioned Diebold, saying, "If the Diebold touch screen machines with audio ballot capabilities are not certified on or before May 14, 2004, and/or the Diebold touch screen machines do not permit a manually impaired voter to vote alone via mouth stick, Defendant Stafford is directed to select and procure another vendor's acceptable touch screen machines with audio ballot capabilities in time for use during the August 2004 primaries." [28] A 2010 ruling by a panel of the 11thCircuit Court of Appeals dismissed the case and ruled that that the plaintiffs' attorneys were not entitled to attorney fees or costs. [823]

American Association Of People With Disabilities v. Shelley, filed 3/08/04 by John McDermott of Howrey, Simon, Arnold & White, LLP. [40] The original goal was to require four California counties to install paperless DREs prior to the November 2004 election. The suit was subsequently expanded to attempt to enjoin Shelley's April 30, 2004 Directive decertifying the Diebold TSx for violating California election law. When the judge refused to issue a preliminary injunction, the case was withdrawn.

PVA [Paralyzed Veterans of America] v. McPherson, filed 8/1/06. AAPD was one of the plaintiffs.[808] The California case, for which John McDermott of Howrey, LLP again was the attorney for the plaintiffs, challenged the use of the Automark, as well as DREs with VVPATs. The plaintiffs based their claim on both HAVA and the 14th Amendment. The HAVA claim was dismissed in 2006, but 14th Amendment rights were not resolved.[738] After a September 2008 ruling threw out the Automark complaints, as well as most of the remaining claims, the case was settled on October 31, 2008.

A.2   Lawsuits involving the NFB

Poole v. Lamone, et al., filed 11/05/02. The Maryland ACLU brought the suit, and the NFB were intervenor-plaintiffs. The case was settled when the Board of Elections agreed to install Diebold AccuVote DREs in time for the (Maryland) March 2004 primary.[661]

National Federation of the Blind et al. v. Blackwell et al., filed 4/20/04. The goal was to obtain an injunction forcing Ohio counties to purchase DREs. There also was a request for payment of attorneys' fees and costs. The NFB withdrew their lawsuit the day the New York Times editorial on disability lobbying appeared.[821]

Linda Schade et al. v. Maryland State Board of Elections and Linda Lamone, filed 4/21/04. The NFB was an intervenor. Schade had sued to require Maryland to decertify Diebold DREs, charging that the Diebold system violated state recount law that required "an original record of voter intent." The NFB supported the state and opposed the decertification effort. The case is ongoing.[817]

National Federation of the Blind et al. v. Volusia County et al., filed 7/05/05.[314] The NFB wanted Volusia County, Florida, to purchase DREs (at one point the attorney said that Volusia County should be purchasing Diebold DREs, though Diebold's name was subsequently stricken from the record), and also requested that the county cover their legal costs.[828] After a preliminary injunction request was denied, AAPD submitted an amicus brief to the appeals court in which they argued that the decision from the AAPD v. Hood case should apply. The appeal also was denied. In June 21, 2006 the NFB and Volusia County issued a joint status report in which they notified the court that they had reached a tentative agreement.

References

Material cited on the web is subject to change. Generally, the original can be found using the Internet Wayback machine at http://www.archive.org/ and specifying the date given in the reference.

[1] Abbott, Robert P., Mark Davis, Joseph Edmonds, Luke Florer, Elliot Proebstel, Brian Porter, Sujeet Shenoi, and Jacob Stauffer. 2007. Red team report on the Diebold Election Systems, Inc. voting system (Diebold GEMS 1.18.24/AccuVote). Technical report, California Sec. of State. Jul. 2007.

[2] ABC7 News. 2005. Complaint against SF Housing Authority commissioner unsealed, Julie Lee faces eight felony counts. Apr. 8, 2005.

[3] Abissi, Carl F. 1960. U.S. Pat. 2,949,292: Perforating apparatus. Aug. 16, 1960.

[4] Abrahams, Rebecca. 2006. Exclusive: Leaked 2003 report on Maryland's Diebold voting systems reveals serious security concerns were withheld from election board, governor, public. *Brad Blog* Nov. 2, 2006. URL http://www.bradblog.com/?p=3719#more-3719.

[5] Abrahams, Rebecca. 2006. The two faces of Diebold. *Huffington Post* Nov. 2, 2006.

[6] Abrams, Jim. 2007. Congress looks to paper again to guarantee election counts. *Boston Globe* Sept. 9, 2007.

[7] Ackerman, Elise. 2004. Blind voters rip e-machines. *San Jose Mercury News* May 15, 2004.

[8] Ackerman, Elise. 2004. E-voting regulators often join other side when leaving office. *San Jose Mercury News* Jun. 15, 2004.

[9] Ackerman, Elise. 2004. Election officials rely on private firms. *San Jose Mercury News* May 30, 2004.

[10] Ackerman, S. J. 1998. The vote that failed. *Smithsonian* Nov. 1998.

[11] ACLU. 2001. ACLU files CA voting rights lawsuit, saying punch cards belong in junkyard, not voting booth. press release. Apr. 16, 2001. URL http://www.aclu.org//votingrights/er/13049prs20010416.html.

[12] ACLU Massachusetts and Disability Law Center. 2007. ACLU and Disability Law Center applaud Secretary Galvin's decision on new voting technology. press release. Mar. 15, 2007.

[13] Adams, Arlin M., James Hunter III, and A. Leon Higgenbotham Jr. 1979. Opinion of the court: United States of America v. Ransom F. Shoup II. U.S. Court of Appeals, 3rd Circuit. Oct. 26, 1979.

[14] Adida, Ben. 2011. Panelist remarks – Internet voting panel. EVT/WOTE'11, the Electronic Voting Tech. Workshop / Workshop on Trustworthy Elections. Aug. 9, 2011. URL http://www.usenix. org/events/evtwote11/stream/benaloh_panel/index.html.

[15] Adrine, Ronald B., Thomas J. Hayes, and Candice Hoke. 2006. Cuyahoga election review panel final report. *Cuyahoga Co., Ohio* Jul. 20, 2006. URL http://www.docstoc.com/docs/88696218/CERP_Final_Report_20060720.

[16] The Advancement Project. 2011. What's wrong with this picture? new photo id proposals part of a national push to turn back the clock on voting rights. Apr. 13 2011. URL http://www.advancementproject.org/sites/default/files/publications/Picture%20ID6%20low.pdf.

[17] Aguayo, Terry and Christine J. Sexton. 2007. Florida acts to eliminate touch-screen voting system. *N.Y. Times* May 4, 2007.

[18] Ahmann, John E. 1981. U.S. Pat. 4,258,249: Stylus for tabulating device. Mar. 24, 1981.

[19] Ahmann, John E. 1987. U.S. Pat. 4,642,450: Punching stylus for handicapped users. Feb. 10, 1987.

[20] Alabama, State of. 1901. 2nd day, May 22. In *Proc. Constitutional Convention*, page 12. Montgomery: Brown.

[21] Alabama, State of. 1901. 82nd day, May 22. In *Proc. Constitutional Convention, 82nd Day*, page 1709. Montgomery. Brown.

[22] Alabama legislature. 1867. Reconstruction Acts of 1867. March 1867. URL http://www.legislature.state.al.us/misc/history/constitutions/1868/1868enablinginst.html.

[23] Alexander, Kim. 2005. More on the Diebold TSx rejection. *California Voter Foundation* Jul. 29, 2005. URL http://calvoter.org/news/blog/2005_07_01_blogarchive.html.

[24] Alexander, Kim. 2005. Secretary of State announces security measures – good, but not good enough. *California Voter Foundation* Oct. 6, 2005. URL http://calvoter.org/news/blog/2005_10_01_blogarchive.html#112861509455193694.

[25] Alexander, Kim. 2006. Public verification of software vote counts and California's manual count law. *California Voter Foundation* Feb. 22, 2006. URL http://www.calvoter.org/issues/votingtech/manualcount.html#text.

[26] Alexander, Kim and Keith Mills. 2004. Voter privacy in the digital age. California Voter Foundation. May 2004. URL http://www.calvoter.org/issues/votprivacy/index.html.

[27] Allen, David. 2003. Secret meeting of the Black Box Yakuza. http://blackboxvoting.com/s9/index.php?/archives/2003/08/22.html. Aug. 22, 2003.

[28] Alley, Wayne. 2004. Court order: American Association of People with Disabilities et. al. v. Glenda E. Hood, et. al. U.S. Dist. Court, Middle Dist. of Florida, Jacksonville Div. No. 3:01CV1275J. Mar. 26 2004.

[29] American Civil Liberties Union. 2003. ACLU statement of principles on touch screen (DRE) voting systems. Dec. 5, 2003. URL http://www.lwv.org/join/elections/hava_aclu_votingmachines.html.

[30] American Civil Liberties Union. 2004. Electronic Voting Systems, Policy #322b. ACLU Board of Directors. Oct. 16-17, 2004.

[31] American Civil Liberties Union. 2007. Electronic Voting Systems, Policy #322b [Proposed Revision]. ACLU Board of Directors. Oct. 2007.

[32] American Civil Liberties Union of Florida. 2002. Analysis of September 10th voting fiasco in Miami Dade demonstrates disproportionate impact on racial minorities, ACLU says. press release. Oct. 21, 2002.

[33] American Civil Liberties Union of Florida. 2007. ACLU applauds Florida legislature on scrapping flawed voting machines. press release. May 3, 2007. URL http://www.aclufl.org/news_events/?action=viewRelease&emailAlertID=2685.

[34] American Statistical Association. 2010. Statement on risk-limiting post-election audits. Apr. 17, 2010. URL http://www.amstat.org/outreach/pdfs/Risk-Limiting_Endorsement.pdf.

[35] Amer. Assoc. of People with Disabilities. 2002. 2002 AAPD leadership gala sponsors. *AAPD News* 4(2). May 2002.

[36] Amer. Assoc. of People with Disabilities. 2002. AAPD leadership gala sponsors. AAPD website. Feb. 27, 2002. URL http://www.aapd-dc.org/gala/gala02/galasponsors.html.

[37] Amer. Assoc. of People with Disabilities. 2003. 2003 Justice for All award recipients. *AAPD News* 5(3). Aug. 2003.

[38] Amer. Assoc. of People with Disabilities. 2003. AAPD Leadership Gala Information Sheet. AAPD website. Mar. 4, 2003. URL http://www.aapd-dc.org/gala/gala03/galainfo03.html.

[39] Amer. Assoc. of People with Disabilities. 2003. AAPD policy statement on voter verified paper ballots. AAPD website. URL http://www.aapd.com/dvpmain/elreform/aapdballots.html.

[40] Amer. Assoc. of People with Disabilities. 2004. AAPD wins in Florida, files suit in California. AAPD News 6(2). Spring 2004. URL http://www.aapd.com/AAPDnews/newsletter.html.

[41] Amer. Assoc. of People with Disabilities. 2004. Organize an Accessible Voting System Expo in Your Area. AAPD website. URL http://www.aapd.com/dvpmain/votemachines/votingexpo.html.

[42] Amer. Assoc. of People with Disabilities. 2004. Six Voting Machines are Certified for Use in Federal Elections. AAPD website. URL http://www.aapd.com/dvpmain/votemachines/machinemanufact.html.

[43] Amer. Assoc. of People with Disabilities. 2004. Voter Confidence and Increased Accessibility Act of 2003. AAPD website, letter to members of Congress. Apr. 6, 2004. URL http://www.aapd-dc.org/policies/vciaact.html.

[44] Amer. Assoc. of People with Disabilities. 2008. Duval County Supervisor of Elections continues to litigate after being ordered to pay $1.4 million to advocates for disabled voters. press release. URL http://www.washlaw.org/pdf/090508_pressrelease.pdf.

[45] Amer. Assoc. of People with Disabilities. 2010. 2010 Leadership Gala fact sheet. URL http://www.aapd.com/site/c.pvI1IkNWJqE/b.5607121/k.CF71/2010_Leadership_Gala_Fact_Sheet.htm.

[46] Amer. Assoc. of People with Disabilities. 2010. About us. Apr. 21, 2010. URL http://www.aapd.com/staff.html.

[47] Amer. Assoc. of People with Disabilities et al. 2004. Letter opposing the Voter Confidence and Increased Accessibility Act of 2003. AAPD website. Apr. 6, 2004. URL http://www.aapd-dc.org/policies/vciaact.html.

[48] Amer. Assoc. of People with Disabilities et al. 2011. Election Protection Partners urge Montana State Senate to oppose voter ID bill. Mar. 4, 2011. URL http://www.866ourvote.org/newsroom/publications-testimony?id=0030.

[49] Amer. Assoc. of the Deaf-Blind. 2006. Definition of deaf-blindness. Mar. 10, 2006.

[50] Amer. Council of the Blind. 2005. Resolution 2005-16 submitted by ACB of Maryland – accessible voter verifiable paper audit trail. ACB General Session Record, 44th Annual Convention. Jul. 8, 2005. URL http://www.acb.org/board-minutes/convention-2005.html.

[51] Anno, Julien, Russel F. Lewis, and Dale A. Cone. 1993. U.S. Pat. 5,189,288: Method and system for automated voting. Feb. 23, 1993.

[52] Appel, Andrew. 2011. Security seals on voting machines: A case study. *ACM Trans. on Information and System Security* 14(2). Sep. 2011.

[53] Appleseed and Latham and Watkins LLP. 2005. The database dilemma: Implementation of HAVA's statewide voter registration database requirement. Nov. 2005. URL http://www.appleseednetwork.org/LinkClick.aspx?fileticket=Z7d-P9sxvc0%3D&tabid=609.

[54] Arizona Sec. of State. 2003. Certified vote tabulating equipment pursuant to A.R.S. 16-442. Oct. 22, 2003.

[55] Arizona Sec. of State. 2004. Official canvass: 2004 primary election. Sep. 20, 2004.

[56] Arizona Sec. of State. 2004. Official canvass: 2004 primary recount. Sep. 24, 2004.

[57] Arnold, Edward G. 1999. *History of Voting Systems in California.* California Sec. of State.

[58] Arnold, Edward G. 1999. *History of Voting Systems in California,* pages 25–27, 56–62. California Sec. of State.

[59] Arnold, Edward G. 1999. *History of Voting Systems in California,* chapter Appendix 1: Voting Systems Used in each County, pages 46–54. California Sec. of State.

[60] Arnold, Edward G. 1999. *History of Voting Systems in California,* pages 62–68. California Sec. of State.

[61] Ash, Arlene and John Lamperti. 2008. Florida 2006: Can statistics tell us who won congressional district-13. *Chance* 21(2): 18–24.

[62] Associated Press. 2003. Receipts reflect fears over electronic votes. *N.Y. Times* Feb. 26, 2003.

[63] Associated Press. 2004. Solano County pays $415,000 to get out of e-voting contract. *Monterey Herald* Sept. 1, 2004.

[64] Associated Press. 2005. CEO quits embattled Diebold. Dec. 13, 2005.

[65] Associated Press. 2005. Maryland to spend more than $10 million for voting machines. *WJLA News (ABC)* Aug. 31, 2005.

[66] Associated Press. 2005. Report shows problems with Montgomery voting machines. *WTOP* Mar. 31, 2005.

[67] Associated Press. 2007. Cuyahoga Co. elections director resigns. *Newsnet5* Feb. 6, 2007.

[68] AutoMark. 2010. Products and Services; ES&S AutoMARK. URL http://www.essvote.com/HTML/products/automark.html.

[69] Automatic Voting Machine Corp. 1957. Behind the freedom curtain. URL http://www.archive.org/details/Behindthe1957/. Promotional film depicts deliberate ballot mutilation by a teller.

[70] Avante Intl. Tech. Inc. 2002. First voter-verifiable touch-screen voting system debuted in Sacramento county, California. press release. Nov. 18, 2002. URL http://www.avantetech.com/uploads/pdf/Sacramento.pdf.

[71] AVM Corporation. 1954. The history and development of voting machines. Technical report, Sequoia Voting Systems. Reprinted 2003, 2008.

[72] Axtman, Chris. 2000. A vote for change. *Schenectady Gazette* page H6. Dec. 31, 2000. (Christian Science Monitor).

[73] Bacon, Steuben. 1878. U.S. Pat. 203,525: Improvement in ballot-boxes. May 14, 1878.

[74] Bailey, Gilbert L. 1860. U.S. Pat. 28,339: Ballot-box. May 22, 1860.

[75] Bailey, Gilbert L. 1883. U.S. Pat. 272,011: Apparatus for registering votes. Feb. 6, 1883.

[76] Baquet, Dean. 1990. Machine politics: Slow search for a better booth. *N.Y. Times* Jun. 5, 1990.

[77] Baquet, Dean. 1990. New York picks a voting machine supplier. *N.Y. Times* Oct. 3, 1990.

[78] Barr, Cameron W. 2006. Voting machines had defective part. *Washington Post* Oct. 26, 2006.

[79] BBC News. 2007. Swindon's enthusiasm for e-voting. *BBC News* May 2, 2007. URL http://news.bbc.co.uk/2/hi/uk_news/england/wiltshire/6608809.stm.

[80] Behrens, Angela, Christopher Uggen, and Jeff Manza. 2003. Ballot manipulation and the 'menace of negro domination': Racial threat and felon disenfranchisement in the United States, 1850–2002. *American J. of Sociology* 109(3): 559–605. Nov. 2003.

[81] Bemiss, R.D. 1915. Testimony. In *Chicago Voting Machine Investigation: Report of the legislative committee appointed under House joint resolution no. 23 of the forty-eighth Illinois General Assembly*, pages 578–581. Illinois General Assembly. Testified Apr. 21, 1914.

[82] Bennett, Linda. 2006. Memo to Florida users. Leon Co. Supervisor of Elections public records. Aug. 15, 2006. Bennett was the ES&S Regional Account Manager.

[83] Berger, H. Stephen. 2003. Profile. TEM Consulting, LP. Apr. 28, 2003. URL http://www.temconsulting.com/support%20pages/Resume%20-%20Stephen%20Berger.htm.

[84] Berger, Stephen. 2004. Written testimony. Election Assistance Comm. May 5, 2004.

[85] Bernstein-Wax, Jessica. 2008. Americans abroad can now vote online. *The Associated Press* Jan. 21, 2008. URL http://www.bluemassgroup.com/showDiary.do?diaryId=10146.

[86] Berry, Mary Frances (Commission Chair). 2001. Voting irregularities in Florida during the 2000 Presidential Election. Technical report, U.S. Commission on Civil Rights. Jun. 2001. URL http://www.usccr.gov/pubs/vote2000/report/main.htm.

[87] Binder, David. 2011. 2011 CityBeat poll results. San Francisco Chamber of Commerce. Feb. 2011. URL http://www.sfchamber.com/2011CityBeatPoll/2011pollresults.pdf.

[88] Binette, Chad. 2002. Election systems face a big test. *Sarasota Herald-Tribune* page 1B. Sep. 9, 2002.

[89] Binette, Chad. 2002. Rate of undervotes drops only slightly. *Sarasota Herald-Tribune* page 2B. Mar. 21, 2002.

[90] Bishop, Matt. 2007. Overview of Red Team reports. California Sec. of State. Jul. 27, 2007. URL http://www.sos.ca.gov/voting-systems/oversight/ttbr/red-overview.pdf.

[91] Bishop, Matt, Loretta Guarino, David Jefferson, David Wagner, and Michael Orkin. 2005. Analysis of volume testing of the AccuVote TSx/AccuView. California Sec. of State. Oct. 11, 2005. URL http://www.ss.ca.gov/elections/voting_systems/vstaab_volume_test_report.pdf.

[92] Blake, Peter. 1992. Svelte vote machine carries heavy price. *Rocky Mountain News* Jan. 29, 1992.

[93] Blaze, Matt. 2007. California voting systems code review now released. *Exhaustive Search (blog)* Aug. 2, 2007. URL http://www.crypto.com/blog/ca_voting_report.

[94] Bleck, James H. and Stephen A. Wagner. 1990. U.S. Pat. d312,251: Memory cartridge for electronic voting system. Nov. 20, 1990.

[95] Bleck, James H., Scott H. Wakefield, and Stephen A. Wagner. 1991. U.S. Pat. d319,459: Voting machine. Aug. 27, 1991.

[96] Blunt, Matt. 2004. Blunt announces new voting option for Missouri military personnel. press release. Aug. 25, 2004. URL http://www.sos.mo.gov/news.asp?id=375.

[97] Bolton, Steve. 2006. Email to Douglas Jones. Jul. 20, 2006.

[98] Bolton, Steve, Tim Cordes, and Herb Deutsch. 2005. U.S. Pat. 6,854,644: Method of analyzing marks made on a response sheet. Feb. 15, 2005.

[99] Bolton, Steve, Robert Hogzett, and Michael Dammann. 2008. U.S. Pat. 7,387,244: Electronic voting system and method with voter verifiable real-time audit log. Jun. 17, 2008.

[100] Bonifaz, John. 2009. Washington State Internet voting bill defeated. Feb. 18, 2009. URL http://www.voteraction.org/print/807.

[101] Boram, Robert J. 1987. U.S. Pat. 4,641,240: Electronic voting machine and system. Feb. 3, 1987.

[102] Boram, Robert J. 1987. U.S. Pat. 4,641,241: Memory cartridge for electronic voting system. Feb. 3, 1987.

[103] Boulton, Clint. 2004. Diebold to settle with California. *internetnews.com* Dec. 17, 2004. URL http://www.internetnews.com/bus-news/article.php/3449691.

[104] Bowen, Debra. 2006. Letter to the Honorable Bruce McPherson, Secretary of State. California Progress Report. Mar. 28, 2006. URL http://www.californiaprogressreport.com/2006/03/problem_with_st.html.

[105] Bowen, Debra. 2007. California Secretary of State Debra Bowen decertifies Diebold, Hart InterCivic and Sequoia Voting Systems – late submitted ES&S system "InkaVotePlus" used in Los Angeles to be reviewed. *California Progress Report* Aug. 4, 2007. URL http://www.californiaprogressreport.com/2007/08/california_secr_1.html.

[106] Bowen, Debra. 2007. Post-Election Manual Tally Requirements. California Sec. of State. Oct. 25, 2007. URL http://www.sos.ca.gov/voting-systems/oversight/ttbr/post-election-req.pdf.

[107] Bowen, Debra. 2009. California Secretary of State Debra Bowen's report to the Election Assistance Commission concerning errors and deficiencies in Diebold/Premier GEMS Version 1.18.19. Mar. 2, 2009. URL http://www.sos.ca.gov/voting-systems/vendors/premier/sos-humboldt-report-to-eac-03-02-09.pdf.

[108] Bowen, Debra. 2009. Secretary of State Debra Bowen withdraws state approval of Premier voting system; legislation to require disclosure of product flaws clears first hurdle. press release. Mar. 31, 2009. URL http://www.sos.ca.gov/elections/elections_vs_premier.htm.

[109] Brace, Kimball W. 2008. Nation sees drop in use of electronic voting equipment for 2008 election—a first. Technical report, Election Data Services. Oct. 17, 2008.

[110] BRAVO Foundation, Operation. 2007. Bring remote access to voters overseas, executive summary. Sep. 2007. URL http://www.votetrustusa.org/pdfs/OVF/OpBRAVO_ExecSumm_FINAL_ver101907.pdf.

[111] BRAVO Foundation, Operation. 2009. About us. URL http://www.operationbravo.org/about_us.html.

[112] BRC Holdings Inc. 1995. SEC Form 10K. Dec. 31, 1995. Item 1. Business Historical Background.

[113] BRC Holdings Inc. 1997. SEC Form 8K. Nov. 20, 1997. Exhibit 99.1: BRC Announces Restructuring.

[114] Breed, Allen G. 2002. Senior poll workers in eye of voting storm. *Sarasota Herald-Tribune* page 3B. Sep. 17, 2002.

[115] Brennan Center. 2008. Brennan Center applauds decision of NYS Board of Elections to reject full-face DREs. press release. Jan. 24, 2008.

[116] Brennan Center for Justice. 2006. Citizens without proof. Voting Rights & Elections Series. Nov. 2006. URL http://www.brennancenter.org/dynamic/subpages/download_file_39242.pdf.

[117] Brent, Peter. 2005. The Australian ballot: not an Australian first. In *Australasian Poli. Studies Assoc. Conf.*

[118] Brewer, Mark. 2003. Brief of Michigan Democratic Party in support of hearing officer's dismissal of challenge. Oct. 10, 2003.

[119] Bridgman, Raymond L. 1888. *Ten Years of Massachusetts.* D.C. Heath.

[120] Briones, David. 1995. Lightbourn v. county of El Paso, Texas. U.S. Dist. Court, W.D. Texas, El Paso Div. Nov. 22, 1995.

[121] British Electoral Commission. 2007. Electoral pilot scheme evaluation Swindon borough council. Aug. 2007.

[122] Brody, Alan. 2007. Lamone: Don't give up on voting machines. *Maryland Gazette.net* Jan. 19, 2007.

[123] Brunelli, Polli. 2001. Voting over the Internet pilot project assessment report. Jun. 2001. URL http://www.fvap.gov/services/voireport.pdf.

[124] Brunner, Jennifer. 2007. Study: Voting systems vulnerable. Ohio Sec. of State press release. Dec. 2007.

[125] Bundy, Hollister. 2003. Election reform, polling place accessibility, and the voting rights of the disabled. *Election Law J.* 2(2). Jun. 2003.

[126] Burnham, David. 1985. Computerized systems for voting seen as vulnerable to tampering. *N.Y. Times* Jul. 29, 1985.

[127] Butts, Lucas I., Robert S. Jones, J.H. Jayne, R.J. Barr, F.A. Landee, John M. Chamberlin, and Edward J. King. 1915. Conclusion. In *Chicago Voting Machine Investigation: Report of the legislative committee appointed under House joint resolution no. 23 of the forty-eighth Illinois General Assembly*, pages 43–47. Illinois General Assembly.

[128] Byrd, David. 2006. Diebold Election Systems response to the Princeton University AccuVote-TS analysis. press release. Sep. 13, 2006.

[129] Bysiewicz, Susan. 2006. Secretary Bysiewicz announces random audits to be performed following elections to ensure reliability of new voting machines. Connecticut Sec. of State press release. Sep. 21, 2006. URL http://www.ct.gov/sots/LIB/sots/RELEASES/2006/9_21_06ElectionsAudits.pdf.

[130] Byzek, Josie. 2007. Voting: Talking with the advocate. New Mobility blog. URL http://www.newmobility.com/browse_thread.cfm?blogid=10&id=56.

[131] Calandrino, Joseph A., Ariel J. Feldman, J. Alex Halderman, David Wagner, Harlan Yu, and William P. Zeller. 2007. Source code review of the Diebold voting systems. Technical report, California Sec. of State. Jul. 20, 2007.

[132] Calandrino, Joseph A., J. Alex Halderman, and Edward W. Felten. 2007. Machine-assisted election auditing. In *Proc. EVT'07, the USENIX/ACCURATE Electronic Voting Tech. Workshop*.

[133] California, State of. 1898. *Report of the Commission on Examining, Testing and Investigating Voting Machines to the Senate and Assembly of the State of California*. Enquirer.

[134] California, State of. 1965. § 336.5: One percent manual tally. Cal. Elections Code, Div. 0.5, Chapt. 4.

[135] California, State of. 2010. § 15560: Postcanvass risk-limiting audit pilot program. Cal. Elections Code, Div. 15, Chapt. 8.5. Jul. 19, 2010. Originated as Assembly Bill 2023.

[136] California Association of Clerks and Election Officials. 2003. press release. Nov. 21, 2003. URL http://www.electionline.org/site/docs/pdf/CACEO+11-21-03.pdf.

[137] California Internet Voting Task Force. 2000. A report on the feasibility of Internet voting. Jan. 20, 2000. URL http://www.sos.ca.gov/elections/ivote/final_report.pdf.

[138] California legislature. 2010. SB 1404 an act to amend ... the elections code. Sep. 2010. URL http://e-lobbyist.com/gaits/text/60828.

[139] California Sec. of State. 2004. Meeting transcript, State of California, Secretary of State, Voting Systems and Procedures Panel. Apr. 22, 2004.

[140] California Sec. of State. 2007. Public Hearing Transcript. Jul. 30, 2007.

[141] California Sec. of State. 2007. Top-to-bottom review web page. URL http://www.sos.ca.gov/voting-systems/oversight/top-to-bottom-review.htm.

[142] California Voter Foundation. 2005. Governor signs landmark bill to require public audits of software vote counts. press release. Oct. 11, 2005. URL http://www.calvoter.org/news/releases/101105release.html.

[143] *California Chronicle.* 2006. Secretary of State submits request to change voter database regulations. Chronicle California political desk. Apr. 19, 2006.

[144] Caltech-MIT Voting Technology Project. 2001. Voting: What is, what could be. Technical report, Caltech/MIT. Jul. 2001. URL http://vote.caltech.edu/drupal/node/10.

[145] Campbell, Brian A. and Michael D. Bryne. 2009. Now do voters notice review screen anomalies? In *Proc. EVT/WOTE'09, the Electronic Voting Tech. Workshop / Workshop on Trustworthy Elections.*

[146] Campbell, Tracy. 2005. *Deliver the Vote: A History of Election Fraud – 1742-2004*, chapter 4: The Holiest Institution of the American People, section: Approaching the Gates of The Penitentiary, pages 94–96. Carroll & Graf.

[147] Carey, Bob, Dir. FVAP. 2011. Email to Barbara Simons. Aug. 22, 2011.

[148] Carroll, Fred M. 1940. U.S. Pat. 2,195,848: Voting machine. Apr. 2, 1940.

[149] Carson, William H. 1987. U.S. Pat. 4,649,264: Electronic voting machine. Mar. 10, 1987.

[150] Carson Manufacturing Company. 2011. Microvote election system. http://www.carson-mfg.com/manufacturing-microvote.asp. Mar. 2011.

[151] Carter, Jimmy, James A. Baker, III, et al. 2005. Building Confidence in U.S. Elections. National Commission on Federal Election Reform. Sep. 2005. http://www.american.edu/ia/cfer/report/full_report.pdf, Spencer Overton's dissent can be found at http://www.carterbakerdissent.com.

[152] Cassels, Edwin H. 1912. Lessons of the election. *City Club Bulletin* V(21): 351–355. Nov. 27, 1912.

[153] Castro, Daniel. 2007. Stop the presses: How paper trails fail to secure e-voting. Technical report, Information Technology & Innovation Foundation. Sep. 2007. URL http://www.itif.org/files/evoting.pdf.

[154] Catt, Carrie Chapman. 1904. Speech favoring education tests for suffrage. *Woman's Jour.* Feb. 20, 1904.

[155] CBC News. 2003. Computer vandal delays leadership vote. Jan. 25, 2003. URL http://www.cbc.ca/news/story/2003/01/25/ndp_delay030125.html.

[156] Center for Hand Counted Paper Ballots. 2011. Website. URL http://www.handcountedpaperballots.org/.

[157] Cervenka, Stacy. 2004. AAPD presents six Justice for All awards. *AAPD* 6(3). Summer 2004. URL http://www.aapd.com/AAPDnews/downloads/AAPD%20Summer04.pdf.

[158] Chaney, Tyson. 2000. Using the Internet to improve voter turnout (netocracy). *Spark Online* May 2000. URL http://www.spark-online.com/may00/esociety/tyson_chaney.html.

[159] Charlton, Paul K. 2006. Letter to Linda Weedon, Re: Federal Investigation into District 20 Recount. Maricopa Co. public records. Nov. 30, 2006.

[160] Chaum, David. 2004. About us. http://votemeter.com/aboutus.html. Apr. 17, 2004.

[161] Checkoway, Robert. 2008. International secretary, Democrats Abroad. email. Mar. 11, 2008.

[162] Chen, David W. 2010. City finally poised to give up lever voting machines. *N.Y. Times* Jan. 4, 2010.

[163] Chong, Curtis. 2005. Letter to Mr. Robert Resuali, Automark Technical Systems. Mar. 12, 2005. URL http://www.verifiedvoting.org/downloads/LetterNFBComputerScience.pdf.

[164] Chu, David S. C. 2006. Statement of the Under Secretary of Defense for Personnel and Readiness. Senate Armed Services Comm. hearing on the Fed. Voting Assistance Prog. Sep. 28, 2006. URL http://armed-services.senate.gov/statemnt/2006/Sep./Chu09-28-06.pdf.

[165] Chung, Kevin Kwong-Tai and Victor Jun Dong. 2005. U.S. Pat. 6,892,944: Electronic voting apparatus and method for optically scanned ballot. May 17, 2005.

[166] Chung, Kevin Kwong-Tai, Victor Jun Dong, and Xiaoming Shi. 2006. U.S. Pat. 7,077,313: Electronic voting method for optically scanned ballot. Jul. 18, 2006.

[167] Chung, Luke. 2004. Microsoft Access or Microsoft SQL Server: What's right in your organization. Technical report, Microsoft Corp.

[168] CIBER Huntsville and CIBER's Global Security Practice. 2006. Diebold Election Systems, Inc. Source Code Review and Functional Testing. Technical report, CIBER, Inc. Feb. 23, 2006. URL http://www.sos.state.tx.us/elections/forms/diebold_code_review.pdf.

[169] Clark, Eric. 2001. Report of the Secretary of State's select task force on election procedures and technology. Technical report, Mississippi Sec. of State. Nov. 2001.

[170] Clark, Eric. 2007. Testimony. House Admin. Comm. Elections Subcomm., 110th Congress, Hearing on Election Reform: Machines and Software. Mar. 15, 2007.

[171] Clarkson, Michael, Brian Hay, Meador Inge, Abhi Shelat, David Wagner, and Alec Yasinsac. 2008. Software review and security analysis of Scytl remote voting software. Sep. 19, 2008. URL http://election.dos.state.fl.us/voting-systems/pdf/FinalReportSept19.pdf.

[172] Cobb, Sue M. 2006. Letter to the honorable Ion V. Sancho. Leon Co. Public Records. Mar. 3, 2006. URL http://www.leoncountyfl.gov/elect/includes/General%20Information/PDFs/SOS%20March%203%202006.pdf.

[173] Cohen, Adam. 2004. The results are in and the winner is ... or maybe not. *N.Y. Times* Feb. 29, 2004.

[174] Cohen, Robert C., Russell Michaels, and Simon Ardizzone. 2006. Hacking democracy (film). Home Box Office. Nov. 2, 2006.

[175] Cohn, Cindy. 2003. letter to Daniel J. Senese, Don Wright, Gerald H. Peterson and Malcom Thaden. Electronic Frontier Foundation. Jul. 28, 2003.

[176] Cohn, Cindy. 2003. letter to Stephen Berger, Brit Williams, Lowell Johnson and Vern Williams. Electronic Frontier Foundation. Sep. 18, 2003.

[177] Coleman, Kevin J. and Eric A. Fischer. 2011. The Help America Vote Act and elections reform: Overview and issues. Technical Report RS20898, Congressional Research Service. Jan. 11, 2011.

[178] Collaborative Audit Committee. 2007. Collaborative public audit of the November 2006 general election. *Cuyahoga Co. Board of Elections* Apr. 18, 2007. URL http://urban.csuohio.edu/cei/public_monitor/cuyahoga_2006_audit_rpt.pdf.

[179] Collin, Charles A. (ed.). 1892. *Revised Statutes of the State of New York*, volume V, chapter 127, page 3520. Banks & Brothers.

[180] Colorado, State of. 2009. § 1-7-515: Risk limiting audits – pilot program. Col. Revised Statutes, Title 1, Article 7, Part 5. Originated as House Bill 09-1335, Section 12.

[181] Comisar, Gerald G. and Fred L. Carter. 1975. U.S. Pat. 3,944,788: Vote-recording apparatus. Mar. 16, 1975.

[182] Common Cause. 2004. The Help America Vote Act: Will it help or hinder NY voters? *Connect the Dots* Nov. 2004.

[183] Common Cause. 2004. Statement on voting machines. position paper. Mar. 3, 2004.

[184] Compuware Corp. 2003. Direct recording electronic (DRE) technical security assessment report. Technical report, Ohio Sec. of State. Nov. 21, 2003.

[185] Conaughton, Gig. 2007. County officials fear new voting standards will be hard to meet. *San Diego North County Times* Aug. 5, 2007.

[186] Conaughton, Gig. 2007. San Diego County hires Vu as assistant registrar. *San Diego North County Times* Apr. 12 2007.

[187] Conaughton, Gig. 2007. San Diego faces registrar search again. *San Diego North County Times* Apr. 2, 2007.

[188] Conference on Security and Cooperation in Europe. 1990. Charter of Paris for a new Europe. Nov. 21, 1990.

[189] Conference on Security and Cooperation in Europe. 1990. Document of the Copenhagen meeting of the conference on the human dimensions of the CSCE. Jun. 29, 1990.

[190] Congress, 101st. 1990,. Public law 101-336: Americans With Disabilities Act. 42 U.S.C. 12101. Jul. 26, 1990,.

[191] Congress, 107th. 2002. Public law 107-252: The Help America Vote Act of 2002.

[192] Congress, 110th. 2007. Draft [floor] manager's amendment to H.R. 811, as reported [from committee]. Jul. 27 2007. URL http://www.votetrustusa.org/pdfs/Bills/MANAGAMEND7-27-4-48%20%282%29.pdf.

[193] Congress, 112th. 2011. H.R. 235: The Cut Unsustainable and Top-heavy Spending Act of 2011.

[194] Congress, 112th. 2011. H.R. 672: To Terminate the Election Assistance Commission, and for Other Purposes. Feb. 11, 2011.

[195] Congress, 86th. 1960. Public law 86-449: The Civil Rights Act of 1960.

[196] Congress, 92nd. 1972. Public law 92-225: The Federal Election Campaign Act of 1971.

[197] Congress, 93rd. 1973. Public law 93-112: Rehabilitation Act of 1973. 29 U.S.C. 701 et. seq. Sep. 26, 1973.

[198] Congress, 93rd. 1974. Public law 93-443: Federal Election Campaign Act Amendments of 1974.

[199] Congress, 96th. 1980. Public law 96-187: Federal Election Campaign Act Amendments of 1979.

[200] Congress, 97th. 1982. Public law 97-205: To Amend the Voting Rights Act of 1965. 42 U.S.C. 1973 et. seq. Jun. 29, 1982.

[201] Congress, 98th. 1984. Public law 98-432: Voting Accessibility for the Elderly and Handicapped Act. 42 U.S.C. 1973ee-1(b). Sep. 28, 1984.

[202] Cookson, Brian. 2000. Election mess casts vote of confidence for Olathe company. *Kansas City Business Journal* Nov. 19, 2000.

[203] Cooper, Florence-Marie. 2004. Order denying plaintiff's application for temporary restraining order, or, in the alternative, preliminary injunction. U.S. Dist. Court, Central Dist. of California, Case No. CV 04-01526 FMC (PJWx). Jul. 6, 2004.

[204] Cooper, Henry C. H. 1898. U.S. Pat. 614,419: Voting-machine. Nov. 15, 1898.

[205] Corcoran, Katherine. 2003. Santa Clara County faces key decision on electronic ballots. *San Jose Mercury News* Feb. 24, 2003.

[206] Corcoran, Katherine. 2003. Security of e-voting machines targeted. *San Jose Mercury News* Feb. 8, 2003.

[207] Cordero, Arel and David Wagner. 2008. Replayable voting machine audit logs. In *Proc. EVT'08, the USENIX/ACCURATE Electronic Voting Tech. Workshop.*

[208] Cordero, Arel, David Wagner, and David Dill. 2006. The role of dice in election audits – extended abstract. In *IAVoSS Workshop On Trustworthy Elections (WOTE 2006).*

[209] Coronado, Michael. 2004. Registrar of voters defends Florida trip. *Riverside Press-Enterprise* Apr. 1, 2004.

[210] Coronado, Michael. 2004. Voting system under scrutiny. *Riverside Press-Enterprise* Apr. 19, 2004.

[211] Council of Europe Committee of Ministers. 2004. Legal, operational and technical standards for e-voting, rec(2004)11. Sep. 30, 2004.

[212] Cowett, Patricia Y. 2008. San Diego Co. Superior Court. Jan. 22, 2008. Ruling denying declaratory judgment: County of San Diego v. Bowen.

[213] Coyne, Brendan. 2005. Electronic voting law splits Florida disabled advocates. *New Standard* Jul. 20, 2005.

[214] Craig, Tim and Mary Otto. 2004. Voters fight discard of paper ballots. *Washington Post* May 27, 2004.

[215] Crist, Charlie. 2007. Governor Charlie Crist's clemency board notes on the restoration of felon civil rights, 2007 (Florida Governor 2007: Crist, Series S 2068). Florida State Library & Archives. Apr. 5, 2007. URL http://www.floridamemory.com/FloridaHighlights/crist/.

[216] Cross II, E. Vincent, Gregory Rogers, Jerome McClendon, et al. 2007. Prime III: One machine, one vote for everyone. In *Proc. University Voting Systems Competition,.*

[217] Cudahay, Richard D., John L. Coffey, and Frank H. Easterbrook. 1992. Business Records Corp. v. Carl D. Lueth, 981 F.2d 957. U.S. Court of Appeals, 7th Circuit. Dec. 14, 1992.

[218] Cummings, Alan. 1858. U.S. Pat. 20,256: Ballot box. May 18, 1858.

[219] Cummings, Eugene M. 2003. U.S. Pat. 7,080,779: Ballot marking system and apparatus. Dec. 11, 2003.

[220] Cybernetica AS. 2008. Corporate web page. URL http://www.cyber.ee/cms-en.

[221] Danaher Industrial Controls. 2005. Danaher: A history of innovation. URL http://http://www.dancon.com/content.aspx?id=15.

[222] Davenport, Christiani and Ann E. Marimow. 2006. Ehrlich wants paper ballots for Nov. vote; state election chief staff toiling to fix electronic glitches. *Washington Post* Sep. 21, 2006.

[223] Davey, Monica. 2006. New fears of security risks in electronic voting systems. *N.Y. Times* May 12, 2006.

[224] Davis, George D. 1874. U.S. Pat. 149,202: Ballot-boxes. Jan. 30, 1874.

[225] Davis, Kelly. 2007. "And that's it": County dismisses critics of election-office hires. *San Diego CityBeat* May 30, 2007.

[226] Davis, Sylvanus E. 1894. U.S. Pat. 526,668: Voting machine. Sep. 25, 1894.

[227] Davis, Sylvanus E. 1895. U.S. Pat. 549,631: Voting machine. Nov. 12, 1895.

[228] Davis, Sylvanus E. 1895. U.S. Pat. 549,901: Voting machine. Nov. 19, 1895.

[229] Davis III, John M. and Shelby Thomas. 1996. U.S. Pat. 5,583,329: Direct recording electronic voting machine and voting process. Dec. 10, 1996.

[230] DC Pol Sci (pseudonym). 2005. Breaking: Verified voting Senate hearing, unpublicized, untelevised, convenes. Daily KOS blog. Jun. 21, 2005. URL http://www.dailykos.com/story/2005/6/21/10245/1805.

[231] DeAngelis, Mary and Carol Leonnig. 1998. Culp enjoyed carte blanche with office, critics say. *Charlotte Observer* Jul. 12, 1998.

[232] DeArmond, Michelle. 2004. Update: County votes to sue state over voting machines. *Riverside Press-Enterprise* May 4, 2004.

[233] DeArmond, Michelle. 2006. Vote count appeal fails. *Riverside Press-Enterprise* Feb. 8, 2006.

[234] DeGregorio, Paul. 2009. UOCAVA voting scoping strategy. Washington Sec. of State Public Records. Jan. 18, 2009. URL http://www.votersunite.org/info/WA-PRR-ScopingStrategy.pdf.

[235] Democratic Nat. Comm. 2003. Resolution Supporting Election Reform. Oct. 4, 2003. URL http://www.verifiedvoting.org/downloads/DNC_Resolution.pdf.

[236] Democrats Abroad. 2008. Democrats Abroad global presidential primary, results report, revised. Feb. 21, 2008. URL http://www.democratsabroad.org/sites/default/files/DA%20Global%20Primary%20Results%20FINAL%20REVISED.pdf.

[237] Dennis, Steven T. 2003. Voting security debated. *Maryland Gazette.Net* Nov. 14, 2003.

[238] Dennis, Steven T. 2007. Democrats try to salvage election reform bill. *Roll Call* Sept. 6, 2007.

[239] Dept. of Justice. 2003. Whether certain direct recording electronic voting systems comply with the Help America Vote Act and the Americans with Disabilities Act. Oct. 10, 2003. URL http://www.justice. gov/olc/drevotingsystems.htm.

[240] Dept. of Justice. 2006. Justice Department sues New York state over voting rights. press release. Mar. 1, 2006. URL http://www.justice. gov/opa/pr/2006/March/06_crt_108.html.

[241] Dept. of Justice. 2006. Lawsuit seeks to vindicate rights of disabled voters, Federal election reform efforts. press release. Mar. 1, 2006. URL http://www.verifiedvotingfoundation.org/article. php?id=6342.

[242] Dept. of Justice. 2007. Former congressman Robert W. Ney sentenced to 30 months in prison for corruption crimes. press release. Jan. 19, 2007. URL http://www.justice.gov/opa/pr/2007/Jan. /07_crm_027.html.

[243] Dept. of Justice. 2010. Divestiture will restore competition in voting equipment systems, nine state attorneys general join in department's resolution. press release. Mar. 8, 2010. URL http://www.justice. gov/opa/pr/2010/March/10-at-235.html.

[244] Dept. of Justice and California Sec. of State. 2005. Memorandum of agreement. Nov. 2, 2005. URL http://www.usdoj.gov/crt/voting/ hava/ca_moa.htm.

[245] *Desert Weekly.* 1892. Voting by machinery. *Desert Weekly* XLIV(21). May 14, 1892.

[246] Deutsch, Herb. 2006. Email to Douglas Jones. Mar. 3, 2006.

[247] Deutsch, Herb. 2006. Email to Douglas Jones. Feb. 21, 2006.

[248] Deutsch, Herb. 2006. Email to Douglas Jones. Oct. 23, 2006.

[249] Devereaux, Michael D. 1998. Revised addendum to the response of AIS to RFP no. 97-295 of Dallas County Texas, Exhibit A. Attached to and cited in County of Dallas Commissioners Court Order 98,552. Aug. 11, 1998.

[250] Diament, Michelle. 2009. People with disabilities voting in record numbers. *Disability Scoop* Jul. 2, 2009. URL http://www. disabilityscoop.com/2009/06/29/disabilities-vote/3893/.

[251] Diaz, Madeline B. 2002. Miami-Dade outlines election problems. *Fort Lauderdale Sun Sentinel* Sep. 18, 2002.

[252] Dickson, James C. 2001. Prepared statement. Senate Comm. on Rules and Admin., Hearing on Election Reform. Jun. 27 2001. URL http:// www.access.gpo.gov/congress/senate/pdf/107hrg/82483v1.pdf.

[253] Dickson, James C. 2001. Testimony. Hearing before Comm. on the Judiciary, House of Representatives, 107th Congress, on H.R. 3295 (The Help America Vote Act of 2001). Dec. 5, 2001.

[254] Dickson, James C. 2001. Written testimony. Nat. Conf. of State Legislators Election Reform Task Force. May 31, 2001. URL http://www.ncsl.org/LegislaturesElections/ElectionsCampaigns/VotingSystemsfortheDisabled/tabid/16515/Default.aspx.

[255] Dickson, James C. 2002. Quoted in: Accessible voting machines are right of all Americans. *DD Quarterly, Ohio Developmental Disabilities Council* pages 3–5. Spring 2002. URL http://www.ddc.ohio.gov/Pub/DDSpring02.pdf.

[256] Dickson, James C. 2002. Testimony before the New York City Council committees on Mental Health, Mental Retardation, Alcoholism, Drug Abuse and Disability Services, and Governmental Operations. Disabilities Network of New York City. Jul. 22, 2002. URL http://www.dnnyc.net/Issues/testimony/aapd.html.

[257] Dickson, James C. 2003. James C. Dickson. Amer. Assoc. of People with Disabilities website. May 1, 2003. URL http://www.aapd-dc.org/dvpmain/JimDicksonbio.html.

[258] Dickson, James C. 2004. Oral testimony. Public Hearing, California Sec. of State Voting Systems and Procedures Panel. Apr. 22, 2004.

[259] Dickson, James C. 2005. AAPD Automark letter to OH SOS Blackwell. Amer. Assoc. of People with Disabilities website. Feb. 5, 2005. URL http://web.archive.org/web/20050309042309/http://www.aapd-dc.org/dvpmain/votemachines/blackwell.html.

[260] Dickson, James C. 2005. Oral testimony. Public Hearing, U.S. Election Assistance Comm. Jun. 30, 2005.

[261] Dickson, James C. 2005. Testimony. Senate Comm. on Rules and Admin. Hearing on Voter Verification in the Federal Election Process. Jun. 21, 2005.

[262] Dickson, James C. 2006. Testimony. Hearing before Comm. on House Administration on Electronic Voting Machines: Verification, Security, and Paper Trails,. Sep. 28, 2006.

[263] Dickson, James C. 2009. AAPD letter to Florida supervisors of elections. Nov. 9, 2009.

[264] Dickson, James C. 2010. Letter to Mark Goins. Tennessee Division of Elections public records. Jan. 11, 2010.

[265] Dickson, James C. and Dan Tokaji. 2004. Response to NYT article on voting. *Justice For All email list* Jun. 15 2004. URL http://www.jfanow.org/jfanow/index.php?mode=A&id=1986.

[266] Diebold Election Systems. 2003. About Us. Feb. 16, 2003. URL http://www.diebold.com/aboutus/history/default.htm.

[267] Diebold Election Systems. 2003. Checks and balances in elections equipment and procedures prevent alleged fraud scenarios. Jul. 30, 2003. URL http://www2.diebold.com/checksandbalances.pdf.

[268] Diebold Election Systems. 2003. Diebold Election Systems announces restructuring of compliance and certification process. PR Newswire. Dec. 18, 2003.

[269] Diebold Election Systems. 2007. Statement of Diebold Election Systems on California Secretary of State's top-to-bottom review of voting systems. press release. Aug. 4, 2007.

[270] Diebold Election Systems. 2009. Diebold sells U.S. elections systems business to ES&S. press release. Sep. 3, 2009. URL http://phx.corporate-ir.net/phoenix.zhtml?c=106584&p=irol-newsArticle&ID=1327351.

[271] Dill, David. 2005. Written testimony. Senate Comm. on Rules and Admin., Hearing on Voter Verification in the Federal Election Process. Jun. 21, 2005. URL http://www.verifiedvoting.org/article.php?id=5789.

[272] Dill, David L. 2003. California task force recommends a voter verifiable audit trail be required on all voting equipment. *Voter Verification Newsletter* 1(6). Jul. 3, 2003. URL http://www.verifiedvoting.org/article.php?id=66.

[273] Dill, David L. 2003. Computerized voting systems pose unacceptable risks unless they provide a voter-verifiable audit trail, technologists warn. press release. Jan. 31, 2003. URL http://verify.stanford.edu/EVOTE/01312003release.html.

[274] Dill, David L. 2003. Resolution on electronic voting. URL http://verify.stanford.edu/dill/EVOTE/statement.html.

[275] Dill, David L. and Dan S. Wallach. 2007. Stones unturned: Gaps in the investigation of Sarasota's disputed congressional election. http://www.cs.rice.edu/~dwallach/pub/sarasota07.pdf. Apr. 13, 2007.

[276] District of Columbia and J. Alex Halderman. 2010. Thank you! (hacked version with Michigan fight song). URL http://www.cse.umich.edu/~jhalderm/pub/dc/thanks/.

[277] Dodd, Christopher. 2004. Dodd appoints Carnahan, Dickson to Election Assistance Commission Board of Advisors. Senatorial press release. Apr. 30, 2004.

[278] Dominguez, Michael L. 2006. Response from the Under Secretary of Defense to question 6 by Rep. Carolyn Maloney. Sep. 20, 2006. URL http://accurate-voting.org/wp-content/uploads/2006/10/IVAS-UnderSecDef.pdf.

[279] Dominion Voting Systems. 2010. Dominion Voting Systems Corporation acquires assets of Sequoia Voting Systems. press release. Jun. 4, 2010.

[280] Dougan, Kennedy. 1890. U.S. Pat. 440,545: Ballot holder. Nov. 11, 1890.

[281] Dougan, Kennedy. 1890. U.S. Pat. 440,547: Mechanical ballot and ballot holder. Nov. 11, 1890.

[282] Dougherty, John. 2006. GOP honchos keep hiding the truth about election foul-ups, as it's learned that local ballots may have been stored illegally. *Phoenix New Times* Jan. 19, 2006.

[283] Drew, Christopher. 2007. Overhaul plan for vote system will be delayed. *N.Y. Times* Jul. 20, 2007.

[284] Drew, Christopher. 2007. Scientists' tests hack into electronic voting machines in California and elsewhere. *N.Y. Times* Jul. 28, 2007.

[285] Driehaus, Bob. 2007. Audit finds many faults in Cleveland's '06 voting. *N.Y. Times* Apr. 20, 2007.

[286] Duffy, Judy, Norman Turrill, et al. 2009. Report on election auditing. League of Women Voters of the U.S. Jan. 2009. URL http://www.lwv.org/files/Report_ElectionAudits.pdf.

[287] Dugger, Ronnie. 1988. Annals of democracy: Counting votes. *New Yorker* Nov. 7, 1988.

[288] Duke, Lloyd L. 1915. The Duke statement. In *Chicago Voting Machine Investigation: Report of the legislative committee appointed under House joint resolution no. 23 of the forty-eighth Illinois General Assembly*, pages 35–37. Illinois General Assembly.

[289] Dunn, John E. 2010. Trojan attacks credit cards of 15 U.S. banks. *Techworld* Jul. 14, 2010.

[290] Edison, Thomas A. 1869. U.S. Pat. 90,646: Improvement in electrographic vote-recorder. Jun. 1, 1869.

[291] Ehrlich, Jr., Robert L. 2006. Letter to Gilles Burger, chair, State Board of Elections. Maryland Governor's Office. Feb. 15, 2006. URL http://www.bradblog.com/Docs/EhrlichLetter_021506.pdf.

[292] Election Assistance Comm. 2004. Annual report: Fiscal year 2003. Apr. 2004.

[293] Election Assistance Comm. 2004. U.S. EAC forms technical committee to create new voting standards. press release. Jun. 17, 2004. URL http://www.eac.gov/news_061704_2.asp.

[294] Election Assistance Comm. 2005. 2004 Election Day Survey, Table 9b. URL http://www.eac.gov/clearinghouse/2004-election-day-survey/.

[295] Election Assistance Comm. 2005. EAC adopts 2005 Voluntary Voting System Guidelines. press release. Dec. 13, 2005.

[296] Election Assistance Comm. 2005. Fiscal year 2004 annual report. Feb. 17, 2005.

[297] Election Assistance Comm. 2005. *Voluntary Voting System Guidelines: Volume I – Voting System Performance Guidelines*. United States Election Assistance Commission.

[298] Election Assistance Comm. 2005. *Voluntary Voting System Guidelines: Volume II – National Certification Testing Guidelines*. United States Election Assistance Commission.

[299] Election Assistance Comm. 2006. Fiscal year 2005 annual report. Jan. 31, 2006.

[300] Election Assistance Comm. 2007. Commission votes to terminate CIBER interim accreditation. press release. Jun. 13, 2007.

[301] Election Assistance Comm. 2007. Testing and certification program manual. Jan. 1, 2007.

[302] Election Assistance Comm. 2009. Annual report: Fiscal year 2008. Jan. 2009.

[303] Election Assistance Comm. 2010. Annual report: Fiscal year 2009. May. 2010.

[304] Election Center. 2006. About the election center. URL http://www.electioncenter.org/about.html.

[305] Election Data Services Inc. 2002. Voting Equipment Report – Year 1980. Nov. 10, 2002. URL http://www.electiondataservices.com/images/File/VotingEquipStudies%20/ve1980_report.pdf.

[306] Election Data Services Inc. 2006. Voting Equipment Report – Year 1992. Nov. 11, 2006. URL http://www.electiondataservices.com/images/File/VotingEquipStudies%20/ve1992_report.pdf.

[307] Election Data Services, Inc. 2006. Voting equipment summary by type as of: 11/07/2007. Feb. 1, 2006. URL http://www.electiondataservices.com/VE+Summary+by+Type+20061107_counties.pdf.

[308] Election Systems & Software. 2002. California Deputy Secretary of State joins Election Systems & Software. press release. Oct. 15, 2002.

[309] Election Systems & Software. 2006. Executive summary, enhancing the City of New York election process: Proposal for an automated voting system. N.Y. City Board of Elections public records. Dec. 6, 2006.

[310] Election Systems & Software. 2007. Model 650 best practices manual. Mar. 1, 2007.

[311] electionline.org. 2008. Statewide voter registration database status. Jan. 23, 2008. URL http://www.pewcenteronthestates.org/uploadedFiles/voter%20reg%20db%20status.pdf.

[312] Election Services Corporation (ESC). 2003. Email to Jody Maye Weissler, compliance dir., Michigan Democratic State Central Comm. Jul. 25, 2003.

[313] Electronic Frontier Foundation. 2003. Diebold backs down, won't sue on publication of electronic voting machine flaws. press release. Dec. 1, 2003. URL http://w2.eff.org/effector/16/34.php#II.

[314] Electronic Frontier Foundation. 2005. National Federation of the Blind v. Volusia County. EFF website. URL http://www.eff.org/cases/national-federation-blind-v-volusia-county.

[315] Emery, Gail Repsher. 2004. Budgets, mandates slow adoption of e-voting. *Washington Technology* Mar. 31, 2004.

[316] Engelhardt, Joel and Scott McCabe. 2001. Poll workers ignored flaws in pre-vote machine tests. *Palm Beach Post* Dec. 31, 2001.

[317] Ensign, John. 2005. Remarks on the introduction of S. 330, a bill to amend the Help America vote Act. *Congressional Record – Senate* 151(2): 1854. Feb. 9, 2005.

[318] Estehghari, Saghar and Yvo Desmedt. 2010. Exploiting the client vulnerabilities in Internet E-voting systems: Hacking Helios 2.0 as an example. USENIX EVT/WOTE 2010. Aug. 9, 2010.

[319] Estep, Bill. 2010. Jury convicts all 8 defendants in Clay vote-buying case. *Lexington Herald-Leader* Mar. 26, 2010.

[320] Estonian Nat. Electoral Comm. 2005. E-voting system overview. URL http://www.vvk.ee/elektr/docs/Yldkirjeldus-eng.pdf.

[321] Estonian Nat. Electoral Comm. 2009. Elections and e-voting. May 2009. URL http://www.valimised.ee/teema_eng.html.

[322] EVEREST Project. 2007. EVEREST testing reports. Technical report, Ohio Sec. of State. Dec. 14, 2007. URL http://www.sos.state.oh.us/Text.aspx?page=4519.

[323] Everett, Sarah P. 2007. *The Usability of Electronic Voting Machines and How Votes Can Be Changed Without Detection.* Ph.D. thesis, Rice University.

[324] FBI. 2010. FBI, Slovenian and Spanish police arrest Mariposa botnet creator, operators. press release. Jul. 28, 2010. URL http://www.fbi.gov/pressrel/pressrel10/mariposa072810.htm.

[325] Fechter, James L. and Everett E. Stallard. 1960. U.S. Pat. 2,940,663: Automatic vote tallying machine. Jun. 14, 1960.

[326] Federal Election Comm. 1990. *Performance and Test Standards for Punchcard, Marksense, and Direct Recording Electronic Voting Systems.* Federal Election Commission.

[327] Federal Election Comm. 2001. 2000 Presidential popular vote summary for all candidates listed on at least one state ballot. Oct. 12, 2001. URL http://www.fec.gov/pubrec/fe2000/prespop.htm.

[328] Federal Election Comm. 2002. *Voting System Performance and Test Standards: An Overview.* Federal Election Commission.

[329] Federal Election Comm. 2002. *Voting System Performance and Test Standards: Volume I – Performance Standards.* Federal Election Commission.

[330] Federal Election Comm. 2002. *Voting System Performance and Test Standards: Volume II – Voting System Qualification Testing Standards.* Federal Election Commission.

[331] Fed. Voting Assistance Prog. 2004. *e-Voting Initiatives.* URL http://fvap.gov/services/evoting.html.

[332] Fed. Voting Assistance Prog. 2004. Notice on City of Chicago and suburban Cook County uniformed services voting project. FVAP Voting News Release 11. Aug. 17, 2004. URL http://www.fvap.gov/pubs/releases/2004/11-2004.html.

[333] Fed. Voting Assistance Prog. 2006. Report on IVAS 2006 as required by Section 596 of the Nat. Defense Auth. Act for F.Y. 2007. Dec. 2006. URL http://accurate-voting.org/wp-content/uploads/2006/12/ivas.pdf.

[334] Feinstein, Diane. 2007. Senator Feinstein asks Government Accountability Office to investigate Sarasota County electronic voting systems. press release. Feb. 14, 2007. URL http://feinstein.senate.gov/07releases/r-e-voting-fl.htm.

[335] Feldman, Ariel J., J. Alex Halderman, and Edward W. Felten. 2007. Security analysis of the Diebold AccuVote-TS voting machine. In *Proc. EVT'07, USENIX/ACCURATE Electronic Voting Tech. Workshop*. Boston, MA.

[336] Felten, Ed. 2006. Refuting Diebold's Response. *Freedom to Tinker (blog)* Sep. 20, 2006. URL http://www.freedom-to-tinker.com/?p=1065.

[337] Felten, Edward W. 2006. Testimony. House Admin. Comm., 109th Congress, Hearing on Verification, Security and Paper Records. Sept. 28, 2006.

[338] Fidlar & Chambers. 2000. Contract between Fidlar & Chambers Co., and the Surry County Board of Commissioners. Surry Co. North Carolina public records. Jan. 26, 2000.

[339] Fielder, James C. 1973. U.S. Pat. 3,708,656: Tabulating type ballot. Jan. 2, 1973.

[340] Finn, Peter. 2007. Cyber assaults on Estonia typify a new battle tactic. *Washington Post* May 19, 2007.

[341] Fischer, Eric A. 2003. Election reform and electronic voting systems (dres): Analysis of security issues. Technical report, Congressional Research Service Report RL32139. Nov. 4, 2003.

[342] Fischer, Eric A. and Kevin J. Coleman. 2008. Election reform and local election officials: Results of two national surveys. Technical Report RL34363, Congressional Research Service. Feb. 7, 2008.

[343] Fisher, Lawrence M. 1998. Reynold Johnson, 92, pioneer in computer hard disk drives. *N.Y. Times* Sep. 18 1998.

[344] Fletcher, Ed. 2002. Ex-state analyst defends his ethics. *Sacramento Bee* Oct. 31, 2002.

[345] Florida, State of. 2002. 1S-2.027 Clear indication of voter's choice on a ballot. Florida Administrative Code. Jun. 6, 2002.

[346] Florida, State of. 2008. 1S-2.027 Standards for determining voter's choice on a ballot. Florida Administrative Code. Oct. 6, 2008.

[347] Florida, State of. 2010. Title IX, 102.166 Manual recounts of overvotes and undervotes. Florida Statutes.

[348] Florida Dep. of State. recurring. Election results. Div. of Elections.

[349] Florida Legislature. 2001. SB 1118: Florida Election Reform Act of 2001. Jun. 2001.

[350] Florida Legislature. 2007. HB 537: An act relating to elections. May 2007.

[351] Florida Senate. 2001. *Ethics and Elections: CS/SB 1118 – Florida Election Reform Act of 2001*, pages 143–147. Florida Senate.

[352] Fogel, Jeremy. 2004. Court order: Online Policy Group v. Diebold. U.S. Dist. Court, N.D. California, San Jose Div. Sep. 30, 2004. URL http://www.eff.org/files/filenode/OPG_v_Diebold/OPG%20v.%20Diebold%20ruling.pdf.

[353] Fogg, M. Charles, Charles F. Krieger, and John R. Veale. 1984. U.S. Pat. 4,479,194: System and method for reading marks on a document. Oct. 23, 1984.

[354] Ford, Gerald R., Jimmy Carter, Robert H. Michel, Lloyd N. Cutler, et al. 2001. To assure pride and confidence in the electoral process. National Commission on Federal Election Reform. Aug. 2001. URL http://www.reformelections.org/ncfer.asp#finalreport.

[355] Fowler, Jerry M., L. J. Hymel, Richard Crane, Brian A. Jackson, and James S. Lemelle. 2000. Factual basis and plea agreement: United States of America v. Jerry M. Fowler. U.S. Dist. Court, Middle Dist. of Louisiana. Nov. 27, 2000.

[356] Framboise, Guy R. and Merle P. Prater. 1961. U.S. Pat. 3,007,620: Card punching device. Nov. 7, 1961.

[357] Republic of France. 1795 [1904]. Constitution of the year III, 5 Fructidor, year III [Aug. 22, 1795]. In Frank M. Anderson (ed.), *The Constitutions and other Select Documents Illustrative of the history of France, 1789-1901*. Minneapolis: The H. W. Wilson Company.

[358] Fredrickson, Tom. 1997. Company focus: High-tech voting machines lighter, faster. *Newport News Daily Press* Oct. 12, 1997.

[359] Freeman, David N. 1994. Electronic voting machines and LANs. In *5th Ann. West Chester Univ. Connectivity and Tech. Symp.*, pages 99–104.

[360] Freeman, Steven. 2005. Certification test for the Diebold Election Systems, Inc. (DESI) GEMS 1.18.24, AV-OS 1.96.6, AV-TSX 4.6.4 with AccuView printer module, and voter access card utilities. California Sec. of State. Nov. 11, 2005.

[361] Frutchey, Fred P. 1938. Chapter V: Developments in test scoring and analysis. *Rev. of Educational Research* 8(5): 537–541. Sep. 1938.

[362] Gagliardi, Andrea, Cynthia Medina, Weida Li, and Zita De Pooter. 2011. Interview transcript – part 3: Manipulation of the machine. Georgetown U. Communication Culture & Technology project blog. May 2, 2011. URL http://506technology.wordpress.com/2011/05/02/interview-transcript/.

[363] Garavan, Thomas N., Barra O. Cinneide, Mary Garavan, and Anna Cunningham. 1996. *Cases in Irish Business Strategy and Policy*, chapter 22: Jefferson Smurfit Group, page 443. Oak Tree Press, Dublin.

[364] Garber, Marie. 2005. Telephone interview with Douglas Jones, subsequent email. Sep. 1–2, 2005.

[365] Gardner, Ryan, Alex Yasinsac, Matt Bishop, Tadayoshi Kohno, Zachary Hartley, John Kerski, David Gainey, Ryan Walega, Evan Hollander, and Michael Gerke. 2007. Software review and security analysis of the Diebold voting machine software. Technical report, Security and Assurance in Info. Tech. Lab., Florida State U. Jul. 27, 2007. Prepared for the Florida Dept. of State.

[366] Garland, Greg and Andrew A. Green. 2004. Elections board places Lamone on paid leave. *Baltimore Sun* Sep. 3, 2004.

[367] Geissinger, Steve. 2003. Election flap spurs state audit. *Oakland Trib.* Nov. 13, 2003.

[368] Geminus. 1964. It seems to me. *New Scientist* (387): 165. Apr. 16, 1964.

[369] General Accounting Office. 2001. Elections: Perspectives on Activities and Challenges Across the Nation. Oct. 15, 2001. URL http://www.gao.gov/new.items/d023.pdf.

[370] General Accounting Office. 2001. Elections: Status and use of federal voting equipment standards. October 2001.

[371] Geneva, Canton of. 2009. E-voting – Internet voting in Geneva, frequently asked questions (faq). URL http://www.geneve.ch/evoting/english/faq-internet-voting.asp.

[372] Ghose, Carrie Spencer, Thomas J. Sherran, and Mike Baker. 2006. Ohio struggles to fix voting problems. *Associated Press* May 4, 2006.

[373] Gibson, Gerald A. 2001. Iacreot election reform commission. *The Bell* 2(1): 11–12. Jan., 2001.

[374] Gigliardi, Andrea. 2011. Email to Barbara Simons. Gigliardi is one of the students who interviewed Dickson.

[375] Gill, Kennis. 2004. Email. Sep. 24, 2004.

[376] Gillespie, Alfred J. 1883. U.S. Pat. 275,818: Stringing pianos. Apr. 17, 1883.

[377] Gillespie, Alfred J. 1887. U.S. Pat. 365,593: Stringing pianos. Jun. 28, 1887.

[378] Gillespie, Alfred J. 1888. U.S. Pat. 375,871: Cord-fastener and label-holder for mailbags. Jan. 3, 1888.

[379] Gillespie, Alfred J. 1895. U.S. Pat. 533,191: Pneumatic dispatch apparatus. Jan. 29, 1895.

[380] Gillespie, Alfred J. 1897. U.S. Pat. 576,570: Voting machine. Feb. 9, 1897.

[381] Gillespie, Alfred J. 1899. U.S. Pat. 628,792: Voting machine. Jul. 11, 1899.

[382] Gillespie, Alfred J. 1899. U.S. Pat. 628,905: Voting machine. Jul. 11, 1899.

[383] Gillespie, Alfred J. 1904. U.S. Pat. 773,140: Interlocking device for voting machines. Oct. 25, 1904.

[384] Gillespie, Alfred J. 1905. U.S. Pat. 799,556: Register or counter. Sep. 12, 1905.

[385] Gillespie, Alfred J. 1907. U.S. Pat. 857,800: Voting-machine. Jun. 25, 1907.

[386] Gillespie, Alfred J. 1914. U.S. Pat. 1,088,816: Voting machine. Mar. 3, 1914.

[387] Glasner, Joanna. 2003. Silicon Valley to vote on tech. *Wired* Feb. 1, 2003.

[388] Glen, William Cunningham. 1873. *The Ballot Act, 1872, With Copious Notes and Index.* Shaw & Sons.

[389] Global Election Systems. 2000. Global Election appoints new president. Marketwire. Jul. 31, 2000.

[390] Global Election Systems. 2000. Global Election Systems' touch screen voting system to be used on election day in Mahoning County. Business Wire. Nov. 7, 2000.

[391] Global Election Systems Inc. 2001. SEC Form 10-KSB. Oct. 12, 2001.

[392] Goggin, Stephen N., Michael D. Bryne, Juan E. Gilbert, Gregory Rogers, and Jerome McClendon. 2008. Comparing the auditability of optical scan, voter verified paper audit trail (VVPAT) and video (VVVAT) ballot systems. In *Proc. EVT'08, the USENIX/ACCURATE Electronic Voting Tech. Workshop.*

[393] Golden, Diane. 2007. Testimony. House Admin. Comm. Elections Subcomm., 110th Congress, Hearing on Election Reform: Machines and Software. Mar. 15, 2007.

[394] Goldfarb, Zachary. 2006. As elections near, officials challenge balloting security. *Washington Post* Jan. 22, 2006.

[395] Goldfarb, Zachary A. 2007. Campaign strengthens for a voting paper trail. *Washington Post* Feb. 19, 2007.

[396] Goldsmith, Sir James. 1975. Statement before the Subcommittee on Monopolies and Commercial Law of the Committee on the Judiciary. House of Representatives, Washington, D.C. Oct. 7, 1975.

[397] Gonggrijp, Rop, Willem-Jan Hengeveld, Eelco Hotting, Sebastian Schmidt, and Frederik Weidemann. 2008. RIES – Rijnland Internet Election System: very quick scan of published source code and documentation. Jul. 2008. URL http://wijvertrouwenstemcomputersniet.nl/images/7/7f/RIES.pdf.

[398] Goodin, Dan. 2008. US expat casts ballot from Vienna, wonders if anyone got it. *The Register* Feb. 6, 2008.

[399] Gorman, Judith. 2002. letter to House-Senate conference committee members. unpublished. May 24, 2002.

[400] Grace, Tom. 2006. Advocate for disabled says group didn't take voting-machine money. *Oneota Daily Star* Aug. 2, 2006.

[401] Gray, Joseph A. 1899. U.S. Pat. 620,767: Voting machine. Mar. 7, 1899.

[402] Greenberg, David. 2000. Was Nixon robbed? *Slate* Oct. 16, 2000. URL http://www.slate.com/id/91350/.

[403] Greene, Kristen K. 2010. *Effects of Multiple Races and Header Highlighting on Undervotes in the 2006 Sarasota General Election: A Usability Study and Cognitive Modeling Assessment.* Ph.D. thesis, Rice U.

[404] Greenhalgh, Gary L. 1987. Letter to James H. Douglas. Mar. 12, 1987.

[405] Greenhalgh, Gary L. 2011. LinkedIn profile. http://www.linkedin.com/in/tkback2.

[406] Greenson, Thadeus. 2008. Federal Election Commission eyes Humboldt. *Eureka Times-Standard* Dec. 29, 2008.

[407] Greenson, Thadeus. 2008. Software glitch yields inaccurate election results. *Eureka Times-Standard* Dec. 5, 2008.

[408] Greenson, Thadeus. 2010. SOS report: Numerous 'deficiencies' in elections software. *Eureka Times-Standard* Feb. 13, 2010.

[409] Groh, John S. 2006. Testimony. House Admin. Comm., 109th Congress, Hearing on Voting System Standards. Jul. 19, 2006. URL http://web.archive.org/web/20070425220530/http://cha.house.gov/images/stories/Documents/groh_testimony.pdf.

[410] Gross, Grant. 2005. Diebold to market paper-trail e-voting system. *Computerworld* Jan. 27, 2005.

[411] Grossman (Treas., Democrats Abroad), Stanley. 2008. Some questions about the Internet primary. Email to DemsAbroad@yahoogroups.com. Mar. 10, 2008.

[412] Grove, Jeff. 2004. ACM statement on voting systems. *Comm. ACM* 47(10). Oct. 2004.

[413] Guadagno, Vic. undated, late 1990s. Corporate sales video for worldwide election systems. http://www.bordertownonline.com/FullCircle/html/elect.html.

[414] Gumbel, Andrew. 2004. Down for the count. *L.A. City Beat* Jun. 24, 2004. URL http://lacitybeat.com/article.php?id=1013&IssueNum=55.

[415] Gumbel, Andrew. 2005. *Steal This Vote: Dirty Elections and the Rotten History of Democracy in America*, chapter 9: Levers, Punch Cards, and the Fallacy of the Technological Fix, pages 173–175,184–185. Nation Books.

[416] Gumbel, Andrew. 2006. E-voting in the United States: a cautionary tale. In *Proceedings of the Workshop on Electronic Voting and e-Government in the UK*. Edinburgh.

[417] Gustafson, Craig. 2007. Review shows S.D. voting machines can be breached. *San Diego Union Tribune* Jul. 28, 2007.

[418] H Security. 2007. Antivirus protection worse than a year ago. Dec. 20, 2007. URL http://www.h-online.com/security/news/item/Antivirus-protection-worse-than-a-year-ago-735697.html.

[419] Halderman, J. Alex. 2010. Hacking the D.C. Internet voting pilot. *Freedom to Tinker (blog)* Oct. 5, 2010. URL http://www.freedom-to-tinker.com/blog/jhalderm/hacking-dc-internet-voting-pilot.

[420] Halperin, Jason P. W. 1999. A winner at the polls: a proposal for mandatory voter registration. *New York U. J. of Legislation and Public Policy* 3(1): 69–123. Winter 1999. URL http://www.law.nyu.edu/journals/legislation/issues/volume3number1/ECM_PRO_060619.

[421] Halvorson, Mark and Sarah Martyn Crowell. 2009. Eyes on the vote count: Non-partisan observer reports of Minnesota's 2008 post-election audit and recount. Technical report, Citizens for Election Integrity, MN. May 26, 2009. URL http://ceimn.org/files/ceimn.report_color.pdf.

[422] Hamilton, Arthur S. 1901. Voting machines. *Appletons' Annual Cyclopedia and register of important events of the year 1900* V: 761–762.

[423] Hanley, John. 1892. U.S. Pat. 475,013: Folding election booth. May 17, 1892.

[424] Harmon, Steven. 2007. Are strange bedfellows sharing a voting booth? critics again questioning county election officials' cozy relationship with voting machine manufacturers. *The Contra Costa Times* Aug. 20, 2007.

[425] Harrington, James C. 1999. Pencils within reach and a Walkman or two: Making the secret ballot available to voters who are blind or have other physical disabilities. *Texas J. on Civil Liberties & Civil Rights* 4(2).

[426] Harris, Bev. 2003. Embezzler programmed voting system. *Scoop (blog)* Dec. 23, 2003. URL http://www.scoop.co.nz/stories/HL0312/S00191.htm.

[427] Harris, Bev. 2003. Exclusive Breaking News: Voting System Integrity Flaw. *Scoop (blog)* Feb. 5, 2003. URL http://www.scoop.co.nz/stories/HL0302/S00036.htm.

[428] Harris, Bev. 2003. Interview with Georgia Diebold election machine installer. *Interesting People (blog)* Aug. 8, 2003. URL http://www.interesting-people.org/archives/interesting-people/200308/msg00029.html.

[429] Harris, Bev. 2004. *Black Box Voting: Ballot Tampering in the 21st Century*, chapter 8: Company Information. Talion.

[430] Harris, Bev. 2004. *Black Box Voting: Ballot Tampering in the 21st Century*, chapter 9: The first public look – ever. Talion.

[431] Harris, Joseph P. 1934. *Election Administration in the United States*. Washington, DC: Brookings Institution.

[432] Harris, Joseph P. 1934. *Election Administration in the United States*, chapter VII Voting Machines, pages 247–264. Washington, DC: Brookings Institution.

[433] Harris, Joseph P. 1934. *Election Administration in the United States*, chapter IX Election Frauds, pages 354–376. Washington, DC: Brookings Institution.

[434] Harris, Joseph P. 1934. *Election Administration in the United States*, chapter II A Model Election Administration System, pages 40, 61–62. Washington, DC: Brookings Institution.

[435] Harris, Joseph P. 1934. *Election Administration in the United States*, chapter VI The Conduct of Elections, pages 236–237. Washington, DC: Brookings Institution.

[436] Harris, Joseph P. 1934. U.S. Pat. 1,947,157: Voting and counting machine. Feb. 13, 1934.

[437] Harris, Joseph P. 1965. U.S. Pat. 3,201,038: Data registering device. Aug. 17, 1965.

[438] Harris, Joseph P. 1966. U.S. Pat. 3,240,409: Data registering device. Mar. 17, 1966.

[439] Harris, Melissa. 2006. Lamone delays decision on election equipment; she is awaiting test results for modified e-poll books. *Baltimore Sun* Oct. 4, 2006.

[440] Harris, Melissa. 2006. Long delays reported as primary gets underway. *Baltimore Sun* Sep. 12, 2006.

[441] Hart Intercivic. 2003. Kathryn Ferguson, former California and Texas election official, joins Hart InterCivic to head company's voter registration group. Business Wire. Oct. 27, 2003. URL http://www.highbeam.com/doc/1G1-109283176.html.

[442] Hart Intercivic. 2007. Initial Hart InterCivic response to California Secretary of State Bowen's decision on the use of electronic voting systems. press release. Aug. 4, 2007. URL http://www.hartintercivic.com/pr_view.php?prid=66.

[443] Hart Intercivic. 2009. Amended complaint: Hart Intercivic, Inc. v. Diebold, Inc. and Election Systems & Software, Inc. U.S. Dist. Court, Delaware. Sep. 14, 2009. URL http://www.wired.com/images_blogs/threatlevel/2009/09/hart-v-diebold-and-ess.pdf.

[444] Hart Intercivic. 2010. Product catalog.

[445] Hart Intercivic. 2011. About Hart: Company history. http://www.hartintercivic.com/pages/194.

[446] Hastings, Deborah. 2010. Angry New Yorkers hate new voting machines. *N.Y. Times* Sep. 15, 2010.

[447] Hawthorn, Paula, Barbara Simons, et al. 2006. Statewide databases of registered voters. ACM U.S. Public Policy Comm. Feb. 2006. URL http://usacm.acm.org/images/documents/vrd_report2.pdf.

[448] Hayden, Michael. 2010. Hackers force Internet users to learn self-defense. *PBS Newshour* Aug. 11, 2010. URL http://www.pbs.org/newshour/bb/science/Jul.-dec10/cyber_08-11.html.

[449] Head, Will. 2006. Hackers use Wikipedia to spread malware. *IT News for Australian Business* Nov. 6, 2006. URL http://www.itnews.com.au/News/67796,hackers-use-wikipedia-to-spread-malware.aspx.

[450] Hearst, William Randolph. 1912. Challenge from Mr. Hearst: To those who inspired the Chicago voting machine charges. *N.Y. Times* Apr. 11, 1912.

[451] Hedges, Lori. 1990. Trimble fiscal court agrees to buy new voting machines. *Madison (Kentucky) Courier* page 3. Mar. 30, 1990. URL http://news.google.com/newspapers?id=479JAAAAIBAJ&sjid=pxANAAAAIBAJ&pg=5073%2C7466780.

[452] Helios. 2011. Helios Website. URL http://heliosvoting.org/.

[453] Helsingin Sanomat, International Edition. 2009. Supreme Administrative Court orders new municipal elections for Vihti, Karkkila, and Kauniainen. Apr. 2009.

[454] Hench, Virginia E. 1998. The death of voting rights: The legal disenfranchisement of minority voters. *Case Western Reserve Law Rev.* 48: 727–798. Summer 1998.

[455] Henderson, Albert N. 1850. U.S. Pat. 7,521: Aye and nay apparatus. Jul. 22, 1850.

[456] Herrnson, Paul S., Richard G. Niemi, Michael J. Hanmer, Benjamin B. Bederson, Frederick G. Conrad, and Michael Traugott. 2006. The not so simple act of voting: an examination of voter errors with electronic voting. Presented to the Midwest Political Science Association. Apr. 20-23, 2006.

[457] Hinkley, Aaron and John Welch. 1892. U.S. Pat. 480,925: Voter's compartment and shelf. Aug. 16, 1892.

[458] Hintz, Jeff. 2002. Re: AccuVote-TS quality production stop – reboot issues. Diebold internal email. Mar. 12, 2002.

[459] Hoffman, Allison and Tim Reiterman. 2003. Secretary of State orders audit of all counties' voting systems. *L.A. Times* Nov. 13, 2003.

[460] Hoffman, Ian. 2004. Diebold knew of legal risks. *Oakland Trib.* Apr. 20, 2004.

[461] Hoffman, Ian. 2004. E-voting not living up to campaign promises. *Oakland Trib.* Mar. 7, 2004.

[462] Hoffman, Ian. 2004. State approves limited e-voting – 11 counties throughout California are allowed to use touchscreens. *Oakland Trib.* Aug. 12, 2004.

[463] Hoffman, Ian. 2005. Paper trail may clog e-voting advances. *Oakland Trib.* Aug. 17, 2005.

[464] Hoffman, Ian. 2007. "Minor hiccups" mark balloting across state. *Oakland Trib.* Jun. 7, 2007.

[465] Holovka, Jr., Charles. 1960. U.S. Pat. 2,923,452: Perforating mechanism for record cards. Feb. 2, 1960.

[466] Holt, Rush. 2003. On election day 2004, how will you know if your vote is properly counted? Answer: You won't. Congressional press release. May 22, 2003. URL http://holt.house.gov/issues2.cfm?id=5996.

[467] Holt, Rush. 2005. H.R. 550: The Voter Confidence and Increased Accessibility Act of 2005. Introduced, 109th Congress. Feb. 2, 2005.

[468] Holt, Rush. 2007. H.R. 811: The Voter Confidence and Increased Accessibility Act of 2007. Introduced, 110th Congress. Feb. 5, 2007.

[469] Holt, Rush. 2007. telephone interview with Barbara Simons. Sept. 29, 2007.

[470] Holt, Rush. 2008. Holt introduces emergency bill to help ensure accuracy, integrity of 2008 election. Congressional press release. Jan 17, 2008. URL http://www.house.gov/apps/list/press/nj12_holt/011708.html.

[471] Holt, Rush. 2009. H.R. 2894: The Voter Confidence and Increased Accessibility Act of 2009. Introduced, 111th Congress. Jun. 16, 2009. URL http://www.gpo.gov/fdsys/pkg/BILLS-111hr2894ih/pdf/BILLS-111hr2894ih.pdf.

[472] Holzer, Gerold, Norman Walker, and Harry Wilcock. 1965. U.S. Pat. 3,218,439: Vote tallying machine. Nov. 16, 1965.

[473] Homewood, John P., Thomas E. Keeling, Paul D. Terwilliger, and Marc R. Latour. 2006. U.S. Pat. 7,111,782: System and method for providing security in a voting machine. Sep. 26, 2006.

[474] Hopkins, Jared S. 2006. Paper trail voting machines split disabled advocacy groups. *Capital News Service* Mar. 8, 2006.

[475] House Administration. 2006. Hearing on voting system standards. House Admin. Comm., 109th Congress. Jul. 19, 2006.

[476] Hursti, Harri. 2005. Critical security issues with Diebold optical scan design. Technical report, Black Box Voting. Jul. 4, 2005. URL http://www.blackboxvoting.org/BBVreport.pdf.

[477] Hursti, Harri. 2006. Diebold TSx evaluation: Security alert. Technical report, Black Box Voting. May 11, 2006. URL http://www.blackboxvoting.org/BBVreportIIunredacted.pdf. Unredacted version released Jul. 2, 2006.

[478] Hursti, Harri. 2010. Remarks in internet voting: The great debate. Overseas Vote Foundation. Mar. 22, 2010. URL http://www.youtube.com/user/OverseasVote#p/u/5/WBKYVuwxmHw.

[479] IBM Archives. 2010. IBM special products (vol. 1). URL http://www.ibm.com/ibm/history/exhibits/specialprod1/specialprod1_1.html.

[480] IBM Archives. 2010. Supplies Division history. URL http://www.ibm.com/ibm/history/exhibits/supplies_history.html.

[481] Idaho, State of. 2010. Title 34, 34-2305 manner of recounting. Idaho Statutes.

[482] Idaho Sec. of State. 2007. Idaho certified voting systems as of may 1, 2007. Includes history of Idaho certification from 1990.

[483] Idaho Sec. of State. 2008. Ballot inspection process: What is to be counted as a vote? Sep. 4, 2008.

[484] IEEE Project 1583. 2001. IEEE P1583 operating procedures, version 1.2. Nov. 9, 2001.

[485] IEEE Project 1583. 2001. P1583 voting standards meeting synopsis. Nov. 2, 2001.

[486] IEEE Project 1583. 2001. P1583 working group meeting. Sep. 11, 2001.

[487] IEEE Project 1583. 2001. Working group P1583 meeting minutes. Aug. 7, 2001.

[488] IEEE Project 1583. 2001. Working group P1583 meeting minutes. Nov. 15-16, 2001.

[489] IEEE Project 1583. 2002. IEEE voting equipment standards project 1583. http://grouper.ieee.org/groups/scc38/1583/. Feb. 20, 2002.

[490] IEEE Project 1583. 2003. IEEE P1583 membership list. Jul. 17, 2003.

[491] IEEE Project 1583. 2003. IEEE voting equipment standards project 1583. http://grouper.ieee.org/groups/scc38/1583/. Oct. 1, 2003.

[492] IEEE Project 1583. 2003. Minutes: P1583 teleconference. Sep. 16, 2003.

[493] Iles, Urban G. 1893. U.S. Pat. 500,001: Ballot registering device. Jun. 20, 1893.

[494] Illinois, State of. 1913. *Laws of the State of Illinois Enacted by the Forty-Eights General Assembly*, chapter Investigations: Voting Machines in Chicago, House Joint Resolution No. 23, pages 627–639. Illinois State Jour.

[495] Imparato, Andrew J. and Jim Dickson. 2007. Dear colleague letter. Circulated to House members by Rep. Vern Ehlers. Sept. 4, 2007.

[496] Indiana Election Commission. 2001. Minutes. Aug. 7, 2001.

[497] Indiana Election Commission. 2001. Minutes. Nov. 15, 2001.

[498] Indiana Election Commission. 2002. Minutes. Feb. 28, 2002.

[499] Indiana Sec. of State. 2010. Voter information: Optical scan ballot card and direct recording voting systems used by indiana counties. Election Div. Jan. 8, 2010.

[500] Info Security (magazine). 2009. *McCartney site serves up Zeus malware*. Apr. 8, 2009. URL http://www.infosecurity-us.com/view/1178/mccartney-site-serves-up-zeus-malware/.

[501] Infosentry Services, Inc. 2003. Volume 1 computerized voting systems security assessment: Summary of findings and recommendations. Technical report, Ohio Sec. of State. Nov. 21, 2003.

[502] Ingram. 1996. Political watch: Getting in touch with voters. *Decatur Herald & Review* page B1. Dec. 22, 1996.

[503] Interim Voting Assistance System. 2006. Independent review final report for the Interim Voting Assistance System (IVAS). Aug. 2006. Prepared for the Princip. Deputy Under Sec. of Defense for Personnel and Readiness.

[504] Interim Voting Assistance System. 2006. Report on the status of the Interim Voting Assistance System (IVAS) ballot request program. Sep. 2006. URL `http://accurate-voting.org/wp-content/uploads/2006/10/ivas.pdf`.

[505] Internet Voting, National Workshop on. 2001. Report of the National Workshop on Internet Voting: Issues and research agenda. Technical report, Internet Policy Inst. Mar. 2001. URL `http://news.findlaw.com/cnn/docs/voting/nsfe-voterprt.pdf`.

[506] Iowa, State of. 1998. Minutes of examination and test. Iowa Board of Examiners for Voting Machines and Electronic Voting Systems. Dec. 16, 1998.

[507] Iowa, State of. 1998. Minutes of examination and test. Iowa Board of Examiners for Voting Machines and Electronic Voting Systems. Jan. 9, 1998.

[508] Iowa, State of. 2000. Minutes of examination and test. Iowa Board of Examiners for Voting Machines and Electronic Voting Systems. Oct. 17, 2000.

[509] Iowa, State of. 2009. Section 52.4: Examiners – term – removal. Iowa Code of 2009.

[510] Jackson, Brian. 2010. Ninth Circuit upholds Washington ban on felon voting. *Jurist Legal news & Research* Oct. 8, 2010. Univ. of Pittsburgh School of Law.

[511] Jacobberger, Jacqueline. 2006. Letter to the Honorable Bruce McPherson, Secretary of State. League of Women Voters of California. Mar. 28, 2006. URL `http://ca.lwv.org/lwvc/action/letters/mcpherson_2006mar.html`.

[512] Japsen, Bruse. 1990. Four bids received for voting machines. *Dubuque Telegraph Herald* page 3A. Feb. 5, 1990.

[513] Jazbutis, Anatolijus. 1964. U.S. Pat. 3,162,362: Voting machine and system. Dec. 22, 1964.

[514] Jefferson, David, Aviel Rubin, Barbara Simons, and David Wagner. 2006. Internet voting revisited: Security and identity theft risks of the DoD's interim voting assistance system. Oct. 25, 2006. URL `http://www.servesecurityreport.org/ivas.pdf`.

[515] Jefferson, David, Aviel D. Rubin, Barbara Simons, and David Wagner. 2004. A security analysis of the Secure Electronic Registration and Voting Experiment (SERVE). Jan. 20, 2004. URL http://servesecurityreport.org/.

[516] Johnson, Mary. 2004. Waiting—Again—for The Vote. *Ragged Edge online* Jun. 17 2004.

[517] Johnson, Reynold B. 1938. U.S. Pat. 2,113,620: Examination paper grading device (electrical). Apr. 12, 1938.

[518] Jollie, Samuel C. 1858. U.S. Pat. 21,684: Ballot box. Oct. 5, 1858.

[519] Jones, Douglas W. 2000. E-voting: Prospects and problems. Apr. 13, 2000. URL http://www.cs.uiowa.edu/~jones/voting/taubate.html. Talk presented at the Paul D. Scholz Symposium.

[520] Jones, Douglas W. 2001. Some comments on the Help America Vote Act of 2001. Submitted to the House Science Comm. Nov. 26, 2001. URL http://www.cs.uiowa.edu/~jones/voting/hr3295.html.

[521] Jones, Douglas W. 2001. Testimony: Problems with voting systems and the applicable standards. House Science Comm. Hearing, Improving Voting Technologies: The Role of Standards. May 22, 2001.

[522] Jones, Douglas W. 2002. Human factors in voting technology. Talk presented to the Council on Government Ethics Laws, Ottawa. Sep. 29, 2002.

[523] Jones, Douglas W. 2003. The case of the Diebold FTP site. U. of Iowa web site. Oct. 2003. URL http://www.cs.uiowa.edu/~jones/voting/dieboldftp.html.

[524] Jones, Douglas W. 2004. Confusion of myth and fact in Maryland. U. of Iowa web site. Jul. 19, 2004. URL http://www.cs.uiowa.edu/~jones/voting/myth-fact-md.html.

[525] Jones, Douglas W. 2004. The European 2004 draft e-voting standard: Some critical comments. Oct. 11, 2004. URL http://www.cs.uiowa.edu/~jones/voting/coe2004.shtml.

[526] Jones, Douglas W. 2004. Observations and recommendations on pre-election testing in Miami-Dade County. Report to the County Dep. of Elections. Sep. 9, 2004.

[527] Jones, Douglas W. 2004. Recommendations for the conduct of elections in Miami-Dade County using the ES&S iVotronic system (revised). Report to the County Dep. of Elections. Jun. 7, 2004.

[528] Jones, Douglas W. 2006. Affidavit regarding the revised draft voting systems standards proposed by the New York State Board of Elections in Feb. 2006. N.Y. Board of Elections public comment. Feb., 24, 2006.

[529] Jones, Douglas W. 2006. Affidavit regarding the voting systems standards proposed by the New York State Board of Elections in Dec. 2005. N.Y. Board of Elections public comment. Jan, 23, 2006.

[530] Jones, Douglas W. 2006. Expert report: Conroy et al v. Dennis. Sep. 5, 2006. URL http://www.cs.uiowa.edu/~jones/voting/conroy_v_dennis_jones.pdf. Redacted and approved for public release.

[531] Jones, Douglas W. 2006. Regarding the optical mark-sense vote tabulators in Maricopa County. Statement delivered to Arizona Senator Jack Harper. Jan. 12, 2006.

[532] Jones, Douglas W. 2010. Kazakhstan: The Sailau e-voting system. In Michael Yard (ed.), *Direct Democracy: Prospects and Pitfalls of Election Technology*, pages 57–70. IFES.

[533] Jones, Jackson. 1892. U.S. Pat. 481,571: Election booth. Aug. 30, 1892.

[534] Kallina, Jr., Edmund F. 1988. *Courthouse over White House: Chicago and the Presidential Election of 1960*, pages 87–88, 163–164, 254. Univ. Press of Florida.

[535] Kanan, Karthik, Jackie Rees, and Eugene Spafford. 2009. *Unsecured Economies: Protecting Vital Information*. McAfee, Inc. Feb. 2009. URL http://resources.mcafee.com/content/NAUnsecuredEconomiesReport.

[536] Kane, Gary. 2001. Caveat lector: Tests find how much pressure voter must apply to remove chad. *Palm Beach Post* Jan. 13, 2001.

[537] Kane, Greg. 2005. Paper ballots for voters. *Stockton Record* Jul. 30, 2005.

[538] Kansas Sec. of State. 1997. What is a voting system? *Canvassing Kansas* page 5. Sept., 1997.

[539] Kansas Sec. of State. 1998. Voting equipment certification process evolves. *Canvassing Kansas* pages 6–7. Sept., 1998.

[540] Kansas Sec. of State. 2006. Certified voting systems in Kansas. Dec. 4, 2006.

[541] Kao, Maggie. 2010. Email to Barbara Simons, re: the LCCR position on electronic voting. Apr. 27, 2010.

[542] Kataoka, Mike, Bettye Wells Miller, and Bradley Weaver. 2004. Riverside County elections chief to retire. *Riverside Press-Enterprise* Jun. 21, 2004.

[543] Katsakis, Angela. 2004. Voting accessibility under attack! Justice For All email list. Jun. 7, 2004. URL http://www.jfanow.org/jfanow/archive.php?mode=A&id=1979.

[544] KCBS Radio. 2007. Napa county registrar blasts decertification of voting machines. Aug. 6, 2007. URL http://www.kcbs.com/pages/766720.php?contentType=4&contentId=760951.

[545] Keane, Kevin. 2006. Telephone interview with Barbara Simons. Apr. 5, 2006. Managing Ed., Oakland Tribune.

[546] Keiper, Frank. 1911. Voting machines. *Encyclopædia Britannica* 28: 217–218.

[547] Keisler, Peter, H.S. Garcia, et al. 2005. Supplemental brief for appellee – Gregorio Igartúa-de la Rosa v. United States of America in the Court of Appeals for the 1st Circuit. U.S. Dept. of Justice. Apr. 13, 2005.

[548] Keizer, Gregg. 2010. Zeus botnet gang targets Charles Schwab accounts. *Computerworld* Oct. 16, 2010.

[549] Kennedy, Richard. 2004. Vote recounts are good for America. *Keene Sentinel* Nov. 21, 2004.

[550] Kennedy, Stetson. 1959. *Jim Crow Guide: The Way it Was*. Florida Atlantic U. URL http://www.stetsonkennedy.com/jim_crow_guide/index.html.

[551] Kennesaw State University. 2001. *Graduate Catalog 2001–2002*, chapter Graduate Faculty. Kennesaw State University.

[552] Kentucky Board of Elections. 2011. Certified voting systems. Mar. 3, 2011.

[553] Kerstein, Paul L. 2005. How can we stop phishing and pharming scams. *CSO Magazine* Jul. 19, 2005.

[554] KeyBanc Capital Markets. 2007. Diebold downgraded to "hold" update. Aug. 13, 2007. URL http://www.newratings.com/analyst_news/article_1591766.html.

[555] Keyssar, Alexander. 2000. *The Right to Vote*. New York, NY: Basic Books.

[556] Kiayias, A., L. Michel, A. Russell, and A. A. Shvertsman. 2007. Integrity vulnerabilities in the Diebold TSx voting terminal. Technical report, U. of Connecticut Voting Tech. Research Center. Jul. 17, 2007.

[557] Kiffmeyer, Mary. 2006. Written testimony. House Admin. Comm., 109th Congress, Hearing on Voting System Standards. Jul. 19, 2006.

[558] Changing Times – Kiplinger Magazine. 1967. What good are voting machines. *Kiplinger Magazine* pages 39–41. Jun. 1967.

[559] Kirk, Jeremy. 2007. Estonia recovers from massive denial-of-service attack. *InfoWorld* May 17, 2007.

[560] Kitkin, David. 2004. Election board won't count paper ballots. *Baltimore Sun* Jul. 2, 2004.

[561] KITV news. 2009. Voting drops 83 percent in all-digital election. May 26, 2009. URL http://www.kitv.com/politics/19573770/detail.html.

[562] Klein, Stanley A. 2003. Email quoted by Vern Williams re: Plan for Going Forward. Nov. 10, 2003. URL http://grouper.ieee.org/groups/scc38/1583/emailtg1/msg00146.html.

[563] Klein, Stanley A. 2007. Email to Barbara Simons re: The start date of P1583. unpublished. Aug. 3, 2007.

[564] Knight, Will. 2003. E-voting system flaws 'risk election fraud'. *New Scientist* Jul. 25, 2003.

[565] Kohno, Kadayoshi, Adam Stubblefield, Aviel D. Rubin, and Dan S. Wallach. 2004. Analysis of an electronic voting system. *Symp. on Security and Privacy* May 2004.

[566] Komp, Catherine. 2006. Cold shoulder for e-voting whistleblowers. *The NewStandard* May 17, 2006.

[567] Konrad, Rachel. 2003. Critics: Convicted felons worked for electronic voting companies. *San Jose Mercury News* Dec. 17, 2003.

[568] Konrad, Rachel. 2003. Electronic vote security uncertain. *Associated Press* Sep. 11, 2003. URL http://www.cbsnews.com/stories/2003/09/11/tech/main572704.shtml.

[569] Konrad, Rachel. 2004. California election raises e-voting concerns. *Associated Press* Aug. 28, 2004.

[570] Konrad, Rachel. 2004. E-voting issue splits League of Women Voters. *Associated Press* Jun. 10, 2004.

[571] Konrad, Rachel. 2004. Judge sides with Riverside County in dispute over electronic voting records. *San Jose Mercury News* Sept. 27, 2004.

[572] Kotob, Moutaz, Ralph J. Anderson, Jay C. Bennett, Jr., Paul T. VanCamp, and David J. Steil. 2004. U.S. Pat. 6,799,723: Automated voting system. Oct. 5, 2004.

[573] Kucinich, Dennis J. 2003. Diebold internal memos reveal knowledge of software flaws. Congressman's web site. URL http://kucinich.house.gov/issues/issue/?issueid=1572#Privatized%20Voting,%20Private%20Interests.

[574] Kumler, Preston and S. Bowles King. 1912. Annual report of the Committee on Political Nominations and Elections. *City Club Bulletin* V(16): 267–269. Sep. 28, 1912.

[575] Kunerth, Keff and Jim Leusner. 2001. Some had 1 from 'column A,' 1 from 'column B'. *Orlando Sentinel* Jan. 28, 2001.

[576] Kurtz, George. 2010. *Operation "Aurora" Hit Google, Others.* McAfee Security Insights Blog. Jan. 10, 2010. URL http://siblog.mcafee.com/cto/operation-%E2%80%9Caurora%E2%80%9D-hit-google-others/.

[577] Kuznik, Merle Smith. 2007. Letter to the honorable Steny Hoyer. Jun. 20, 2007. URL http://www.votepa.us/newsletters/9-4-07.html.

[578] Kyle, Mark, Marc Carrel, Kim Alexander, David Dill, David Jefferson, Robert Naegele, Shawn C. O'Brien, Mischelle Townsend, Charlie Wallis, and Jim Wisley. 2003. Ad hoc touch screen task force report. California Sec. of State. Jul. 1, 2003.

[579] Laffont, Jean-Jacques and Jean Tirole. 1991. The politics of government decision-making: A theory of regulatory capture. *Quarterly J. of Economics* 106(4): 1089–127. Nov. 1991.

[580] Lamone, Linda. 2007. Letter to Mark Radke, director of marketing for Diebold. *Maryland Board of Elections* Jun. 28, 2007.

[581] Lampson, Butler W. 2004. *Software Components: Only the Giants Survive*, pages 137–146. Springer.

[582] Langenberg, Linda and Sue Wold. 2007. History of voting equipment in Linn County. Linn Co. Iowa Auditor. Apr. 2007.

[583] Lawrence Tech News Center. 2006. Splash! new landmark fountain at Lawrence Tech to symbolize watershed improvements. press release. Feb. 6, 2006.

[584] Leadership Council on Civil Rights. 2003. Policy analysis of DRE voting machines: 'voter-verified paper trails' are not needed to keep elections from being stolen. LCCR website. Jul. 9, 2003.

[585] League of Women Voters. 2003. Direct recording electronic (DRE) voting machines and HAVA implementation. LWV website. Jun. 2003. URL http://www.lwv.org/where/promoting/votingrights_hava_drevm.html.

[586] League of Women Voters. 2003. Help America Vote Act: HAVA implementation resources. Oct. 2003. URL http://www.lwv.org/join/elections/hava_resources.html.

[587] League of Women Voters. 2003. Questions and answers on direct recording electronic (DRE) voting systems. Nov. 24, 2003. URL http://www.lwv.org/join/elections/HAVA_QAonDRE.pdf.

[588] League of Women Voters. 2004. Convention 2004: Engaging members. *National Voter* 54(1). Oct. 2004.

[589] League of Women Voters. 2004. Convention 2004 summary. Jul. 1, 2004. LWV members only at http://www.lwv.org/.

[590] League of Women Voters. 2004. An open letter to President Kay Maxwell. League Issues website. URL http://www.leagueissues.org/openletter.shtml.

[591] League of Women Voters. 2006. Report of convention action. Jun. 11, 2006. LWV members only at http://www.lwv.org/.

[592] League of Women Voters. 2010. Report of convention action. Jun. 14, 2010. Publicly available at http://www.lwv.org/.

[593] Leonard, Lloyd J. 2001. Testimony. Hearing before Comm. on the Judiciary, House of Representatives, 107th Congress, on H.R. 3295 (The Help America Vote Act of 2001). Dec. 5, 2001.

[594] Frank Leslie's Illustrated Newspaper. 1856. Stuffer's ballot box. *Frank Leslie's Illustrated Newspaper* Jul. 19, 1856.

[595] Leutwiler, A. O. 1915. Testimony. In *Chicago Voting Machine Investigation: Report of the legislative committee appointed under House joint resolution no. 23 of the forty-eighth Illinois General Assembly*, pages 378–394. Illinois General Assembly.

[596] Levitt, Justin, Wendy R. Weiser, and Ana Muñoz. 2006. Making the list: Database matching and verification processes for voter registration. Brennan Center for Justice. Mar. 24, 2006. URL http//\www.brennancenter.org/dynamic/subpages/download_file_35559.pdf.

[597] Lewis, R. Doug. 2001. Testimony. Senate Government Affairs Comm. May 9, 2001.

[598] Leyden, John. 2010. UK cybercops cuff 19 Zeus banking Trojan suspects. *The Register* Sep. 29, 2010.

[599] Liberty Election Systems, LLC. 2003. Liberty election systems home page. Apr. 19, 2003. URL http://www.libertyelectionsystems.com/.

[600] Liberty Election Systems, LLC. 2005. DRE voting machines—system description. Jul. 29, 2005.

[601] Liebling, Abbot J. 1970. *The Earl of Louisiana*, pages 136–137. LSU Press.

[602] Liggo, Jeffrey M., Cindy A. Cohn, and Matthew J. Zimmerman. 2005. Amicus curiae brief: National Federation of the Blind et al. v. Volusia County et al. U.S. Dist. Court, Middle Dist. of Florida, Orlando Div. No. 6:05-cv-997-Orl-28DAB. Jul. 14, 2005.

[603] Lindquist, Everet F. 1939. U.S. Pat. 3,050,248: Method and apparatus for processing data. Aug. 21, 1939.

[604] Lindsey, Nedra. 2004. McComish's District 20 2nd-place finish confirmed. *Arizona Republic* Sep. 24, 2004.

[605] Lindsey, Nedra. 2005. Vote-recount probe raises some issues. *Arizona Republic* Jun. 12, 2005.

[606] Lipari, Bo. 2006. Department of Justice agrees to New York plan to delay HAVA implementation. *VoteTrustUSA website* May 1, 2006. URL http://www.votetrustusa.org/index.php?option=com_content&task=view&id=1246&Itemid=113.

[607] Lipari, Bo. 2008. Counties choose paper ballots despite court ruling. VoteTrustUSA website. Feb. 18, 2008.

[608] Lipmaa, Helger. 2011. Paper-voted (and why I did so). Helger's Cryptoblog. Mar. 5, 2011. URL http://helger.wordpress.com/2011/03/05/.

[609] Lockyer, Bill. 2005. Attorney General Lockyer files suit to ensure that the disabled in Kern and Santa Cruz Counties have access to polling places and can exercise right to vote. California Attorney Gen. press release. Oct. 17, 2005. URL http://ag.ca.gov/newsalerts/release.php?id=1228.

[610] Loevy, Robert D. 1962. Dirty work on the voting machines. *Life* 53(17): 17–18. Oct. 26, 1962.

[611] Lofgren, Zoe. 2009. H.R. 1719: Voter Registration Modernization Act of 2009. Introduced, 111th Congress. Mar. 25, 2009.

[612] Lohr, Steve. 2010. *Companies Fight Endless War Against Computer Attacks. N.Y. Times* Jan. 17, 2010.

[613] Lombardo Consulting Group. 2004. Voters prefer take-home "ATM style" receipt to prove their vote was counted accurately. press release. Nov. 10, 2004.

[614] Loomer, Jan. 1990. Letter to William Elrite. Anoka Co. public records. Dec. 5, 1990. Unisys account representative.

[615] Los Angeles Voter Empowerment Circle. 2003. Working paper: Voting technology. Politech posting by Thomas Leavitt. Apr. 2003. URL http://www.politechbot.com/p-04698.html.

[616] L.A. Times. 2000. A 'modern' democracy that can't count votes. *Los Angeles Times* Dec. 11, 2000.

[617] L.A. Times. 2000. A place in politics for salesmen and wares. *Los Angeles Times* Dec. 11, 2000.

[618] Lovett, William. 1838. Unto the honourable the Commons of the United Kingdom of Great Britain and Ireland in Parliament assembled, the petition of the undersigned, their suffering countrymen. Jul. 1838.

[619] Lovett, William. 1848. *The People's Charter with Address to the Radical Reformers of Great Britain and Ireland and a brief sketch of its origin*, chapter The People's Charter, 1838. C. H. Elt & Charles Fox.

[620] Ludington, Arthur C. 1911. *American Ballot Laws, 1888-1910*. Univ. of the State of New York, Albany.

[621] LWVUS Board. 2004. Memo to state and local League presidents. Jan. 30, 2004.

[622] M86 Security. 2010. Cybercriminals target online banking customers. press release. Aug. 2010.

[623] M86 Security. 2010. M86 Security Labs discovers customers of global financial institution hit by cybercrime. press release. Aug. 10, 2010.

[624] Macrotrends. 1990. Macrotrends Accu-Vote election successful. PR Newswire. Sep. 14, 1990.

[625] Mahoney, Martha R. 2010. Comment on pilot project testing and certification. EAC website. Apr. 30, 2010. URL http://www.eac.gov/assets/1/AssetManager/Martha%20Mahoney%20-%20Comment%20on%20Pilot%20Project%20Testing%20and%20Certification.pdf.

[626] Mahoney, Martha R. 2010. Looking for trouble in all the wrong places: Security and secrecy problems in the 2008 Internet voting pilot. Unpublished Manuscript.

[627] Mancini, Mary. 2010. Bill to delay Tennessee Voter Confidence Act passes. *Liberadio(!) blog* Jan. 12, 2010. URL http://www.liberadio.com/2010/01/12/bill-to-delay-tennessee-voter-confidence-act-passes/.

[628] Manjoo, Farhad. 2003. Another case of electronic vote-tampering? Representatives of the computer vote-counting industry are unfairly dominating the standard-setting process, say critics. *Salon* September 29, 2003. URL http://www.salon.com/tech/feature/2003/09/29/voting_machine_standards/index.html.

[629] Manza, Jeff and Christopher Uggen. 2004. Punishment and democracy: Disenfranchisement of nonincarcerated felons in the United States. *Perspectives on Politics* 2(3): 491–505. Sep. 2004.

[630] March, Jim. 2003. A deconstruction of a Doug Lewis / Election Center review of the potential for electronic vote fraud. Sep. 9, 2003. URL http://www.ninehundred.net/~equalccw/lewisdeconstructed.pdf.

[631] March, Jim. 2003. Diebold's vote-tally software – security review instructions. Sep. 17, 2003. URL http://web.archive.org/web/20031008104729/http://www.equalccw.com/dieboldtestnotes.html.

[632] Margolick, David, Evangelina Peretz, and Michael Shnayerson. 2004. The path to Florida. *Vanity Fair* Oct. 2004.

[633] Maricopy Co. Superior Court. 2004. Emergency hearing in the matter of the September 7, 2004, Primary Election for State Representative – District 20 Republican Primary, John McComish and Anton Orlich, candidates, before the honorable Edward P. Ballinger, jr. Sep. 23, 2004.

[634] Marimow, Ann E. 2006. Md. official resists call to change voting system. *Washington Post* Feb. 17, 2006.

[635] Marriott, Edward E. 1915. Affidavit. In *Chicago Voting Machine Investigation: Report of the legislative committee appointed under House joint resolution no. 23 of the forty-eighth Illinois General Assembly*, pages 31–35. Illinois General Assembly. Affidavit dated Aug. 13, 1913.

[636] Marsan, Carolyn Duffy. 2009. Feds to shore up net security. *About.com* Jan. 10, 2009. URL http://pcworld.about.com/od/securit1/Feds-to-Shore-\\Up-Net-Security.htm.

[637] Martin, Roy A. and Clarence E. Pittman. 1974. U.S. Pat. 3,787,662: Voting machine. Jan. 22, 1974.

[638] Maryland Board of Elections. 2004. Maryland's better way to vote – electronic voting: Myth vs. fact.

[639] Mascher, Andrea L., Paul T. Cotton, and Douglas W. Jones. 2010. Towards publishable event logs that reveal touchscreen faults. In *Proc. EVT/WOTE'10, the Electronic Voting Tech. Workshop / Workshop on Trustworthy Elections*.

[640] Massachusetts, State of. 1893. *Laws Relating to Elections*, chapter 465: An Act to Authorize Towns to use the McTammany Automatic Ballot Machines at Elections of Town Officers, pages 125–127. Wright & Potter.

[641] Massachusetts, State of. 1897. *Public Documents of Massachusetts*, volume I. Wright & Potter.

[642] Matteson, Andre. 1895. Peculiarities of our election laws. In *Proc. of the Illinois State Bar Assoc. at its Eighteenth Annual Meeting*, pages 168–180. Illinois State Register.

[643] Mauer, Marc. 2004. Felon disenfranchisement: A policy whose time has passed? *Human Rights* 31(1). Winter 2004.

[644] Maurer, Marc. 2004. Presidential report 2004. *Braille Monitor* 47(8). Aug./Sep. 2004.

[645] Maurer, Marc. 2004. The topography of technology, blindness, and the luddite. *Braille Monitor* 47(6). Jun. 2004.

[646] Maurer, Marc. 2005. Presidential report 2005. *Braille Monitor* 48(8). Aug./Sep. 2005.

[647] Maxwell, Kay. 2003. Applying League positions. LWVTopics email posting. Jul. 25, 2003.

[648] Maxwell, Kay. 2003. Letter to the editor. N.Y. Times. Jun. 5, 2003.

[649] Maxwell, Kay. 2003. Letter to the editor. N.Y. Times. Dec. 15, 2003.

[650] Mazzella, Christopher. 2002. Inquiry into the circumstances surrounding the September 10, 2002, election in Miami-Dade County. Miami-Dade Co. Inspector General. Sep. 20, 2002.

[651] Mazzella, Christopher. 2002. OIG final report of the Miami-Dade voting systems contract RFP no. 326. Miami-Dade Co. Inspector General. Sep. 20, 2002.

[652] Mazzolini, Joan. 2006. Prosecutor says Cuyahoga skirted rules. *Cleveland Plain Dealer* Apr. 6, 2006.

[653] McClure, Neil and Kermit Lohry. 2001. U.S. Pat. 6,250,548: Electronic voting system. Jun. 26, 2001.

[654] McClure, Neil, Ralph D. Wieland, Victor L. Babbitt, and Robert A. Nichols. 2006. U.S. Pat. 7,032,821: Precinct voting system. Apr. 25, 2006.

[655] McCormack, Conny B. 2005. Written testimony. Senate Comm. on Rules and Admin. Hearing on Voter Verification in the Federal Election Process. Jun. 21, 2005.

[656] McCormack, Conny B. 2010. Re-counting the vote: What does it cost? *Pew Charitable Trusts* Oct. 2010. URL http://www.pewcenteronthestates.org/uploadedFiles/MN_WA_recounts_report.pdf.

[657] McCormick, Erin. 2002. Scavenged ballot box lids haunt S.F. elections. *SFGate.com* Jan. 7, 2002. URL http://articles.sfgate.com/2002-01-07/news/17528873_1_lids-absentee-ballots-elections-director-haygood.

[658] McDermott, John E. 2005. Form letter on the stationary of Howrey Attorneys at Law. Randy Riddle, office of California Sec. of State. Aug. 11, 2005. URL http://www.calelectionlaw.com/miscellaneous/McDermottAutoMARKLetter.pdf.

[659] McDonald, Laughlin. 2010. Email to Barbara Simons, subject: ACLU policy. May 12, 2010. McDonald directs the ACLU Voting Rights Project.

[660] McDonald, Laughlin, Nancy Abudu, Meredith Bell-Plats, et al. 2009. Voting rights in Indian Country. ACLU Voting Rights Project. Sep. 2009.

[661] McDonald, Laughlin and Daniel Levitas. 2006. The case for extending and amending the Voting Rights Act: Voting rights litigation, 1982-2006. Technical report, ACLU Voting Rights Project. Mar. 2006. URL http://www.aclu.org/pdfs/votingrightsreport20060307.pdf.

[662] McGaley, Margaret and J. Paul Gibson. 2006. A critical analysis of the Council of Europe recommendations on e-voting. In *Proc. EVT'06, the USENIX/ACCURATE Electronic Voting Tech. Workshop.*

[663] McHugh, Pete. 2003. Implementation of the direct recording electronic (DRE) voting system. Memo to the Santa Clara Co. Board. Feb. 25, 2003. Motion based on memo passed unanimously.

[664] McKay, Richard H., William R. Smith, and Herman Deutsch. 1977. U.S. Pat. 4,025,757: Voting system. May 24, 1977.

[665] McKay, Richard H., Paul G. Ziebold, James D. Kirby, Douglas R. Hetzel, and James U. Snydacker. 1974. U.S. Pat. 3,793,505: Electronic voting machine. Feb. 19, 1974.

[666] McKenzie, Angus. 1903. U.S. Pat. 730,788: Voting-machine. Jun. 9, 1903.

[667] McKenzie, Angus. 1907. U.S. Pat. 853,822: Voting-machine. May 14, 1907.

[668] McKenzie, Angus. 1907. U.S. Pat. 855,334: Voting-machine. May 28, 1907.

[669] Mckenzie, Angus. 1910. U.S. Pat. 945,405: Voting-machine. Jan. 4, 1910.

[670] Mckenzie, Angus. 1912. U.S. Pat. 1,031,139: Voting-machine. Jul. 2, 1912.

[671] Mckenzie, Angus. 1916. U.S. Pat. 1,198,563: Voting-machine. Sep. 19, 1916.

[672] McLaughlin, Alysoun. 2007. County lobbying effort stalls 'HAVA II'. *Government Technology* Sept. 19, 2007. URL http://www.govtech.com/gt/146143?topic=117671.

[673] McMillan, Robert. 2010. FBI Director: Hackers have corrupted valuable data. *IDG News Service* Mar. 5, 2010.

[674] McMillin, John V. and Dale W. Schroeder. 1981. U.S. Pat. 4,300,123: Optical reading system. Nov. 10, 1981.

[675] McMillin II, John V. 2006. Email to Douglas Jones. Aug. 21, 2006.

[676] McMillin II, John V. 2006. Email to Douglas Jones. Aug. 21, 2006.

[677] McMillin II, John V. 2006. WLC ballot scanning days. University of Iowa Special Collections, Papers of John V. McMillin II, Box I, Folder 36. Aug. 28, 2006. URL http://www.lib.uiowa.edu/spec-coll/archives/guides/RG99.0023.htm.

[678] McPherson. 2005. McPherson toughens up on voting machine makers. Aug. 3, 2005. URL http://www.americanchronicle.com/articles/viewArticle.asp?articleID=1623.

[679] McPherson, Bruce. 2006. Secretary of State grants certification to Diebold with conditions. California Sec. of State press release. Feb. 17, 2006. URL http://votetrustusa.org/index.php?option=com_content&task=view&id=941&Itemid=113.

[680] McTammany, John. 1881. U.S. Pat. 242,786: Mechanical musical instrument. Jun. 14, 1881.

[681] McTammany, John. 1881. U.S. Pat. 244,069: Mechanical musical instrument. Jul. 12, 1881.

[682] McTammany, John. 1881. U.S. Pat. 248,943: Mechanical musical instrument. Nov. 1, 1881.

[683] McTammany, John. 1892. U.S. Pat. 480,691: Voting machine. Sep. 13, 1892.

[684] McTammany, John. 1893. U.S. Pat. 502,743: Balloting device. Aug. 8, 1893.

[685] McTammany, John. 1893. U.S. Pat. 502,744: Vote-recording machine. Aug. 8, 1893.

[686] McTammany, John. 1895. U.S. Pat. 550,053: Voting machine. Nov. 19, 1895.

[687] McTammany, John. 1895. U.S. Pat. 550,054: Pneumatic vote counting machine. Nov. 19, 1895.

[688] McTammany, John. 1895. U.S. Pat. 550,055: Voting machine. Nov. 19, 1895.

[689] McTammany, John. 1904. U.S. Pat. 749,446: Apparatus for detecting fraudulent or improper votes. Nov. 11, 1904.

[690] McTammany, John. 1904. U.S. Pat. 749,446: Vote counting machine. Jan. 12, 1904.

[691] McWilliams, Brian. 2003. New security woes for e-vote firm. *Wired* Aug. 7, 2003.

[692] Mehta, Seema. 2004. Exerts Sought in Vote Dispute. *L.A. Times* Apr. 12, 2004.

[693] Mehta, Seema. 2004. Official's travel gift questioned. *L.A. Times* Mar. 31, 2004.

[694] Mehta, Seema. 2004. Put registrar on paid leave, county urged. *L.A. Times* Apr. 2, 2004.

[695] Menken, Christopher. 2005. Diebold Election Systems submits voter-verifiable paper audit trail printer for Federal qualification. Oracle Journal. Jan. 27, 2005.

[696] Mercuri, Rebecca. 2000. *Electronic Vote Tabulation Checks & Balances*. Ph.D. thesis, U. of Pennsylvania.

[697] Mercuri, Rebecca T. 1992. Electronic voting machines alert. *Risks Digest* 13(72). Aug. 12, 1992.

[698] Mercuri, Rebecca T. 1992. Inside risks 29: Voting machine risks. *Comm. ACM* 35(11). Nov., 1992.

[699] Mercuri, Rebecca T. 1992. Physical verifiability of computer systems. In *Proc. Fifth Int'l Computer Virus and Security Conference*. URL http://www.notablesoftware.com/Papers/PhysVerify. pdf. Reprint with added notes, 2005.

[700] Mercuri, Rebecca T. 2002. A better ballot box. *IEEE Spectrum* pages 46–50. Oct., 2002.

[701] Mercuri, Rebecca T. 2002. Explanation of voter-verified ballot systems. *Risks Digest* 22(17). Jul. 24, 2002.

[702] Mercuri, Rebecca T. 2011. Email to Barbara Simons re: Woops – I sent an unedited version re P1583. unpublished. Apr. 10, 2011.

[703] Messmer, Ellen. 2009. America's 10 Most Wanted Botnets. *Network World* Jul. 22, 2009.

[704] Metropolitan News-Enterprise. 2002. Judge orders punch-card voting be replaced by 2004 general election. Feb. 14, 2002.

[705] Michigan, State of. 1997. Act 116 of 1954, as amended, 168.803(2). Michigan Election Law. Nov. 17, 1997.

[706] Michigan, State of. 2004. Act 116 of 1954, as amended. Michigan Election Law. Apr. 26, 2004.

[707] Military Postal Service Agency. 2011. 2010 analysis of the Military Postal System compliance with the MOVE Act. Aug. 2, 2011. URL http://www.fvap.gov/resources/media/2010_MPSA_after_action_report.pdf.

[708] Mill, John Stuart. 1860. *Considerations on Representative Government*, chapter X: Of the Mode of Voting. London: Parker, Son, and Bourne.

[709] Miller, Kevin. 2011. Maine voter registration system breached. *Bangor Daily News* Aug./ 25, 2011.

[710] Miller, Worth Robert. 1995. Harrison County methods: Election fraud in late nineteenth century Texas. *Locus: Regional and Local Hist.* 7(2): 11–28.

[711] Mills, Elinor. 2009. Spam offers to let people use their PC to attack Obama site. Aug. 18, 2009. URL http://news.cnet.com/8301-1009_3-10312641-83.html?tag=nl.e757.

[712] Minnite, Lorraine C. 2007. An analysis of voter fraud in the United States. Demōs publications. URL http://archive.demos.org/pubs/Analysis.pdf.

[713] Mississippi. 1987. Section 23-15-403: Authority to purchase or rent voting machines; construction of voting machines. Mississippi Code of 1972, as amended through 1987.

[714] Mitra, Maureen N. 2003. Orange polls residents on new voting technology. *Middletown Times Herald-Record* Jul. 30, 2003.

[715] Moldovan, Michael T., Charles J. Lindross, Lawrence L. Anderson, Robert D. Wescott, and Richard J. Cusimano. 1974. U.S. Pat. 3,847,345: Electronic voting machine. Nov. 12, 1974.

[716] Moloney, Martha A. 1975. Mechanized vote recording: A survey. Technical Report 116, Kentucky Legislative Research Commission. May 1975.

[717] Monaghan, Robert E. 1848. U.S. Pat. 5,469: Mode of taking yeas and nays in legislative bodies. Mar. 14, 1848.

[718] Monteagudo Jr., Luis and Helen Gao. 2004. Some votes miscounted in primary, officials say. San Diego Union-Tribune Apr. 8, 2004.

[719] Montgomery County Elections Board. 2004. 2004 presidential general election review – lessons learned. Dec. 2004.

[720] Morganstein, Sanford J. 2007. U.S. Pat. 7,284,700: Advanced voting system and method. Oct. 23, 2007.

[721] Mummert III, Thomas C. 2009. Avante International v. Premier Election Systems and Sequoia Voting Systems: Order, findings and conclusions on the obviousness of the '944 and '313 patents. U.S. Dist. Court, Eastern Dist. of Missouri, Eastern Div. Mar. 17, 2009.

[722] Munro, Ralph. 1977. Report of the Secretary of State on the examination and evaluation of an optical scan electronic vote tallying system. State of Washington. Dec. 22, 1977.

[723] Munro, Ralph. 1985. Examination and evaluation of voting equipment: Report of the Secretary of State. State of Washington. Apr. 15, 1985.

[724] Murray, Matthew. 2007. Hill will examine voting machines. Roll Call Jan. 16, 2007.

[725] Myers, Jacob H. 1889. U.S. Pat. 415,548: Voting machine. Nov. 19, 1889.

[726] Myers, Jacob H. 1889. U.S. Pat. 415,549: Voting machine. Nov. 19, 1889.

[727] Myers, Jacob H. 1890. U.S. Pat. 424,332: Voting machine. Mar. 25, 1890.

[728] Myers, Jacob H. 1893. U.S. Pat. 494,588: Voting machine. Apr. 4, 1893.

[729] Narey, James O. 1989. U.S. Pat. 4,813,708: Ballot for use in automatic tallying apparatus and method for producing ballot. Mar. 21, 1989.

[730] Narey, James O. and William H. Saylor. 1977. U.S. Pat. 4,021,780: Ballot tallying system including a digital programmable read only control memory, a digital ballot image memory and a digital totals memory. May 3, 1977.

[731] Nast, Thomas. 1871. That's what's the matter. Harper's Weekly page 944. Oct. 7, 1871.

[732] Nathan, Harriet. 1983. Joseph P. Harris: Professor and practitioner: Government, election reform, and the Votomatic. Univ. of California at Berkeley Bancroft Library, Regional Oral Hist. Office, Univ. Hist. Series. Interview conducted by Harriet Nathan in 1980.

[733] National Association of Counties. 2007. Toolkit on 'HAVA II'. website. Mar. 2007. URL http://www.naco.org/Template.cfm?Section=Finance_and_Intergovernmental_affairs&template=/ContentManagement/ContentDisplay.cfm&ContentID=23204.

[734] National Association of Secretaries of State. 2010. NASS position on funding and authorization of the U.S. election assistance commission. Jul. 20, 2010.

[735] National Conference of State Legislatures. 2001. Voting in America: Final report of the NCSL elections reform task force. URL http://www.ncsl.org/programs/press/2001/electref0801.htm.

[736] National Inst. of Standards and Technology. 2003. Building trust & confidence in voting systems. Dec. 10-11, 2003. URL http://www.nist.gov/itl/vote/symposium121004.cfm.

[737] National Security Agency Information Assurance Group. 2010. Defense in depth: A practical strategy for achieving information assurance in today's highly networked environments. URL http://www.nsa.gov/ia/_files/support/defenseindepth.pdf.

[738] National Senior Citizens Law Center. 2008. *Court Decisions from 2006*, chapter No 1983 Right in Voting Rights Case, page 32. NSCLC Federal Rights Project.

[739] Nat. Fed. of the Blind. 2002. National Federation of the Blind, Inc., et al. v. Diebold and Rite Aid. Washington Lawyers' Committee for Civil Rights and Urban Affairs. Oct. 31, 2002. URL http://www.washlaw.org/projects/disability_rights/dr_lawsuits.htm.

[740] Nat. Fed. of the Blind. 2004. NFB Resolution 2004 01 regarding: Maintaining accessible voting for blind people. Braille Monitor. Aug./Sep. 2004. URL http://www.nfb.org/Images/nfb/Publications/bm/bm04/bm0408/bm040813.htm.

[741] Nat. Fed. of the Blind. 2006. National Federation of the Blind hails passage of bill to help fund Braille literacy campaign. Aug. 2, 2006. URL http://www.jfanow.org/jfanow/index.php?mode=A&id=2861;&sort=D.

[742] Nat. Fed. of the Blind. 2010. About the National Federation of the Blind. NFB website. URL http://www.nfb.org/nfb/About_the_NFB.asp?SnID=356728093.

[743] Nat. Fed. of the Blind of Ohio. 2002. Resolution 2002-04. *Buckeye Bulletin* Winter 2002. URL http://www.nfbohio.org/w02.html.

[744] Nedap N.V. 2003. Nedap Powervote frequently asked questions. May 2003. URL http://powervotelive.clientweb.net/about-faq.htm.

[745] Neely, Francis, Lisel Blash, and Corey Cook. 2004. An assessment of ranked-choice voting in San Francisco 2004 election. Public Research Inst., San Francisco State U. Dec. 2004. URL http://pri.sfsu.edu/reports/SFSU-PRI%20Ranked%20Choice%20Voting%20Preliminary%20Report.pdf.

[746] Nelson, Bill. 2007. Congress gets new election bill to ban controversial machines. Senatorial website. Nov. 1, 2007. URL http://billnelson.senate.gov/news/details.cfm?id=286542&.

[747] Nelson, Bill. 2007. S. 559: Vote Integrity and Verification Act of 2007. Introduced, 110th Congress. Feb. 13, 2007.

[748] Neumann, Peter G. 1995. *Computer Related Risks*. ACM Press / Addison Wesley.

[749] New York, State of. 1777. Constitution of the State of New York.

[750] New York, State of. 2005. Election reform and modernization act of 2005. N.Y. Board of Elections. Jul. 12, 2005.

[751] New York Board of Aldermen. 1878. *Report of the Special Committee of the Board of Aldermen Appointed to Investigate the [Tweed] "Ring" Frauds together with the Testimony Elicited During the Investigation – Document No. 8*, chapter Seventh Day: September 18–2: 8 o'clock P.M., pages 133–134. Martin B. Brown.

[752] New York Board of Elections. 2005. Draft subtitle v part 6209 voting system standards. Nov., 2005.

[753] Newman, Terry. 2003. Tasmania and the secret ballot. *Australian J. of Politics and Hist.* 49(1): 93–101.

[754] Newton, Casey. 2006. FBI seizes ballots in close '04 legislative race. *Arizona Republic* Feb 1, 2006.

[755] *N.Y. Times.* 1856. New-York City: A wire ballot box. *New York Times* Aug. 19, 1856.

[756] *N.Y. Times.* 1856. New-York City: The Board of Aldermen. *New York Times* Sep. 17, 1856.

[757] *N.Y. Times.* 1857. Law intelligence: The glass ballot-boxes: The mayor to be examined. *New York Times* Nov. 28, 1857.

[758] *N.Y. Times.* 1860. Law reports: The ballot-box case. *New York Times* May 15, 1860.

[759] *N.Y. Times.* 1871. How Tweed was elected. *New York Times* Nov. 9 1871.

[760] *N.Y. Times.* 1887. Electoral reform. *New York Times* Nov. 10, 1887.

[761] *N.Y. Times.* 1888. No chance to repeat here. *New York Times* May 30, 1888.

[762] *N.Y. Times.* 1889. Voting by machinery: An ingenious reform device invented by a Rochester man. *New York Times* Nov. 24, 1889.

[763] *N.Y. Times.* 1892. Republicans carry Lockport: The new voting machine submitted to a practical test. *New York Times* Apr. 13, 1892.

[764] *N.Y. Times.* 1893. Voting by machine: The Myers device gives great satisfaction in Niagara County. *New York Times* Apr. 12, 1893.

[765] *N.Y. Times.* 1896. Voting machine abandoned. *New York Times* Nov. 29, 1896.

[766] *N.Y. Times.* 1899. Voting by machinery. *New York Times* Dec. 24, 1899.

[767] *N.Y. Times.* 1912. Hearst accused in Chicago: Charge of conspiracy to defraud city in voting machine contract. *New York Times* Apr. 9, 1912.

[768] *N.Y. Times.* 1913. Accuse Hearst man of $105,000 graft: Andrew M. Lawrence charged with demanding that sum for his "influence". *New York Times* Aug. 15, 1913.

[769] *N.Y. Times.* 1922. Sees fraud on city in voting machines: Hirshfeld declares consignment had been rejected by Chicago in 1912. *New York Times* May 9, 1922.

[770] *N.Y. Times.* 2004. Editorial: Denying the troops a secret ballot. *New York Times* Sep. 3, 2004.

[771] *N.Y. Times.* 2004. Editorial: The disability lobby and voting. *New York Times* Jun. 11 2004.

[772] *N.Y. Times.* 2005. Editorial: Making votes count – jne last election lesson. *New York Times* Jan. 18, 2005.

[773] *N.Y. Times.* 2009. Editorial: How to trust electronic voting. *New York Times* Jun. 21, 2009.

[774] Ney, Robert W. 2004. Chairman Ney's response to the New York Time editorial of Jun. 11, 2004. Comm. on House Admin. Oversight Hearing on Electronic Voting System Security, House of Representatives, 108th Congress. Jul. 7, 2004.

[775] Ney, Robert W. 2006. Extended quote in: U.S. House passes Braille commemorative coin bill. Braille Monitor. May 2006.

[776] Ney, Robert W. and Steny Hoyer. 2001. H.R. 3295: The Help America Vote Act of 2001. Introduced, 107th Congress.

[777] Ney, Robert W., Steny Hoyer, Mitch McConnell, and Christopher J. Dodd. 2004. Dear colleague letter. Committee on House Administration. Mar. 3, 2004.

[778] Nichols, Jim. 2007. Election workers plead no contest in deal. *Cleveland Plain Dealer* Nov. 6, 2007.

[779] Nicolls, Willoughby H. 1877. U.S. Pat. 185,950: Registering ballot-box. Jan. 2, 1877.

[780] Nielsen, Chris. 2001. High-tech voting devices an asset for Clay county. *Spencer Iowa Daily Reporter* Nov. 14, 2001.

[781] Supreme Court of Arizona. 1918. Hunt v. Campbell (no. 1588). In *Pacific Reporter*, volume 169, pages 596–616. West. See page 603 for short pencil use.

[782] Attorney General of New Jersey. 2006. 2006 New Jersey chronological elections guide. Div. of Elections. Jan. 20, 2006.

[783] Norden, Lawrence, Aaron Burstein, Joseph Lorenzo Hall, and Margaret Chen. 2007. Post-election audits: Restoring trust in elections. Technical report, Brennan Center for Justice. Aug. 9, 2007. URL http://www.brennancenter.org/page/-/d/download_file_50228.pdf.

[784] Norden, Lawrence D., Aaron Burstein, Joseph Lorenzo Hall, and Margaret Chen. 2007. *Post Election Audits: Restoring Trust in Elections.* Brennan Center for Justice.

[785] Norden, Lawrence D. and Eric Lazarus. 2006. *The Machinery of Democracy: Protecting Elections in an Electronic World.* Acadamy Chicago.

[786] Norwegian Ministry of Local Government and Regional Development. 2010. 11 municipalities to try out e-voting in 2011. press release. Jan. 27, 2010. URL http://www.regjeringen.no/en/dep/krd/press/press-releases/2010/11-municipalities-to-try-out-e-voting-in-2011.html?id=591610.

[787] Nussbaum, Bruce. 1999. A decade of design. *Business Week* Nov. 29, 1999. Silver Winners: AVC Advantage Electronic Voting Machine.

[788] Nutt, Michael. 2004. Electronic voting in the 2004 election. *Voice of the Nation's Blind* Dec. 1, 2004.

[789] Oberheide, Jon, Evan Cooke, and Farnam Jahanian. 2008. CloudAV: N-version antivirus in the network cloud. In *USENIX Security Symposium*, pages 91–106.

[790] Obradovic, Goran, James Hoover, Nick Ilonmakis, and John Poulos. 2006. Election workflow automation: Canadian experiences. In *Proc. 2nd Intl. Workshop on Electronic Voting: Lecture Notes in Informatics P-86*, pages 131–141. Gesellschaft für Informatik.

[791] O'Brien, Shawn Casey. 2004. AAPD – a costly lack of leadership. *Citizen S.O'B (blog)* Jul. 14 2004. URL http://citizensob.blogs.com/citizensob/.

[792] O'Brien, Shawn Casey. 2004. Another costly lack of leadership. *Citizen S.O'B (blog)* Jul. 15 2004. URL http://citizensob.blogs.com/citizensob/.

[793] Office of Management and Budget. 2008. Statement of administration policy: H.R. 5036 – Emergency Assistance for Secure Elections Act of 2008. Office of Management and Budget. Apr., 15 2008.

[794] O'Malley, Martin. 2010. Supplemental Budget Summary. Apr. 5, 2010. URL http://www.dbm.maryland.gov/agencies/operbudget/Documents/2011/FY2011SupplementalBudgetNo1.pdf.

[795] O'Neal, Cothburn M. 1971. U.S. Pat. 3,630,434: Voting machine with punch card attachment. Dec. 28, 1971.

[796] O'Neal, Cothburn M. 1976. U.S. Pat. 3,934,793: Voting machine. Jan. 27, 1976.

[797] O'Neal, Cothburn M. 1977. U.S. Pat. 4,025,040: Voting machine with punch card attachment. May 24, 1977.

[798] Open Rights Group. 2007. May 2007 election report: Findings of the Open Rights Group election observation mission in Scotland and England. Jun. 2007.

[799] Oreskovic, Alexei. 2004. Leaked Jones Day memo triggers suit against newspaper. *New York Lawyer* Apr. 26, 2004.

[800] Organization for Security and Cooperation in Europe. 2006. Expert visit on new voting technologies: 8 October 2006 local elections, Kingdom of Belgium. Technical Report ODIHR 22450, OSCE. Nov. 22, 2006.

[801] Organization for Security and Cooperation in Europe. 2007. Parliamentary elections, 22 November 2006, the Netherlands – OSCE/ODIHR election assessment mission final report. Technical report, OSCE. Mar. 12, 2007.

[802] Organization for Security and Cooperation in Europe. 2011. Estonia: Parliamentary elections, 6 mar. 2011 – OSCE/ODIHR Election Assessment Mission Report. May 16, 2011. URL http://www.osce.org/odihr/77557.

[803] Organization of American States. 2001. Inter-American democratic charter. Sep. 11, 2001.

[804] OSDV. 2010. District of Columbia's Board of Elections and Ethics adopts Open Source Digital Voting Foundation technology to support ballot delivery. Business Wire. Jun. 22, 2010. URL http://www.businesswire.com/portal/site/home/permalink/?ndmViewId=news_view&newsId=20100622006238&newsLang=en.

[805] Ostgaard, Kolleen, Chris Smart, Tom McGuire, Madeline Lanz, and Timothy A. Hodson. 2000. The LegiSchool project. the Japanese-American internment during WWII: A discussion of civil liberties then and now. Technical Report 1028-S, California Senate. May 2, 2000. URL http://bss.sfsu.edu/internment/rightsviolated.html.

[806] Padova, John R. 2001. Draft memo and court order: National Organization on Disability, et al., v. Margaret M. Tartaglione, et al. Oct. 2001. URL http://www.paed.uscourts.gov/documents/opinions/01D0788P.pdf.

[807] Palmer, Chris. 2011. Unqualified names in SSL Observatory. Electronic Frontier Foundation Deeplinks blog. Apr. 5, 2011. URL https://www.eff.org/deeplinks/2011/04/unqualified-names-ssl-observatory.

[808] Paralyzed Veterans of America. 2006. Press release. AAPD Disability Vote Project web site. Aug. 1 2006. URL http://www.aapd-dc.org/dvpmain/votemachines/060802ca.htm.

[809] Park, Stephen K. and Keith W. Miller. 1988. Random number generators: Good ones are hard to find. *Comm. of the ACM* 31(10). Oct. 1988.

[810] Pearson Educational Measurement Group. 2008. History. URL `http://www.pearsonedmeasurement.com/aboutus/history.htm`.

[811] Pennsylvania Dep. of State. 2005. Electronic voting systems certified prior to the Help America Vote Act of 2002. Jul. 27, 2005.

[812] People for the American Way. 2004. Protecting the integrity and accessibility of voting in 2004 and beyond – a statement of principles on voting systems and voter verification. PFAW position paper. March, 2004. URL `http://votingmachines.procon.org/sourcefiles/PFAWvotingsystemprinciplesMarch04.pdf`.

[813] Petri, Tom. 2005. Safeguarding elections. Congressional website. Jun. 24, 2005. URL `http://petri.house.gov/weekly/jun24_05.shtml`.

[814] Pfeifer, Stuart. 2004. Some counties might sue over e-voting orders. *L.A. Times* May 4, 2004.

[815] Pfeifer, Stuart. 2004. State blocks digital voting. *L.A. Times* May 1, 2004. URL `http://www.latimes.com/la-me-machines1may01,1,697635.story`.

[816] Pfeifer, Stuart. 2004. State joins suit over voting machines. *L.A. Times* Sept. 8, 2004.

[817] Phair, Ryan P., Kathryn R. Debord, Daniel M. Nelson, John B. Isbister, Daniel S. Katz, and Richard D. Rosenthal. 2004. Complaint: Linda Schade et al. v. Maryland State Board of Elections and Linda Lamone. Arundel Co. Maryland Circuit Court. Apr. 22, 2004.

[818] Phillipo, Thomas E. De. 1977. U.S. Pat. 4,015,106: Electronic voting machine. Mar. 29, 1977.

[819] Pichaske, Pete. 2004. Discarded paper ballot draws ire of voter. *Howard Co. Times* Apr. 22, 2004.

[820] Pierce, Barbara. 2002. 2002 Convention roundup. *Braille Monitor* 45(7). Aug./Sep. 2002.

[821] Pierce, Barbara and Daniel F. Goldstein. 2004. National Federation of the Blind withdraws complaint. NFB press release. Jun. 14, 2004.

[822] Pierre, Robert E. 2001. Botched name purge denied some the right to vote. *Washington Post* May 31, 2001.

[823] Pinkham, Paul. 2010. Federal appeals court again dismisses Duval blind voter lawsuit. *Florida Times-Union* May 13, 2010.

[824] Powell, Alden L. and Emmett Asseff. 1951. *Registration of Voters in Louisiana*. Bureau of Government Research, Louisiana State University.

[825] Premier Election Solutions. 2007. Diebold Election Systems to become Premier Election Solutions. press release. Aug. 16, 2007. URL `http://www.premierelections.com/newsroom/premier81607.htm`.

[826] Proposition 41. 2002. Proposition 41, Voting Modernization Bond Act of 2002. California Sec. of State. URL http://www.ss.ca.gov/elections/vma/home.html.

[827] Public Opinion. 1896. The trial of ballot machines. *Public Opinion* XXI(22): 679–680. Nov. 26, 1896.

[828] Pynchon, Susan. 2005. Volusia County update on NFB lawsuit. Verified Voting Foundation website. Jul. 15, 2005. URL http://www.verifiedvotingfoundation.org/article.php?id=6134.

[829] Pynchon, Susan. 2005. Volusia county's recurring nightmare (part 2). *VoteTrustUSA website* Dec. 12, 2005. URL http://www.votetrustusa.org/index.php/index.php?option=com_content&task=view&id=484&Itemid=1042.

[830] Pynchon, Susan. 2006. Florida: Ion Sancho fights back. *VoteTrustUSA* Mar. 8, 2006. URL http://votetrustusa.org/index.php?option=com_content&task=view&id=1015&Itemid=113.

[831] RABA Technologies LLC. 2004. Trusted Agent Report Diebold AccuVote-TS Voting System. Technical report, Maryland Dept. Legislative Services. Jan. 20, 2004.

[832] *Ragged Edge online*. 2001. Crips sue DC for voting rights discrimination. *Ragged Edge Online* Sep. 5, 2001. URL http://www.raggededgemagazine.com/drn/drn090501votedcsuit.htm.

[833] Railsback, Horace E. and Harold W. Stewart. 1965. U.S. Pat. 3,226,018: Rapid preference system. Dec. 28, 1965.

[834] Rao, GVL Narashima. 2010. *Democracy at Risk.* Veta.

[835] Rathbun, George D. 1944. U.S. Pat. 2,364,097: Voting machine. Dec. 5, 1944.

[836] Rathbun, George D. 1944. U.S. Pat. 2,364,098: Voting machine ballot parts. Dec. 5, 1944.

[837] Reed, Sam. 2003. Report of the Secretary of State on the examination and evaluation of an direct recording electronic vote tallying system. State of Washington. Jul. 7, 2003.

[838] Rein, Lisa. 2007. Elections chief stars in Diebold promotion. *Washington Post* Jun. 28, 2007.

[839] Reiterman, Tim. 2005. Secretary of State Shelley steps down. *L.A. Times* Feb. 5, 2005.

[840] Reiterman, Tim and Peter Nicholas. 2003. Ex-officials now behind new voting machines; those who led the state's ballot-count reforms now work for the firms making the equipment. *L.A. Times* Nov. 10, 2003.

[841] Remote Voting Project. 2007. II. Evaluatie van het experiment Internetstemmen, Tweede Kamerverkiezingen 2006 (Evaluation of the Internet voting experiment, 2006 Parliamentary elections). Netherlands Ministry of the Interior & Kingdom Relations. Jun. 2007.

[842] Remote Voting Project. 2007. III. Verslag van uitvoering: Experiment Internetstemmen, Tweete Kamerverkiezingen 2006, (Performance report: Internet voting experiment 2006 Parliamentary elections). Netherlands Ministry of the Interior & Kingdom Relations. Jun. 2007.

[843] Remotegrity. 2011. Remotegrity Website. URL https://demo.remotegrity.org/.

[844] Reynolds, Dave. 2002. DC to have accessible voting. *Ragged Edge online* Aug. 15, 2002. URL http://www.raggededgemagazine.com/drn/08_02.shtml#432.

[845] Reynolds, John F. and Richard L. McCormick. 1986. Outlawing "treachery": Split tickets and ballot laws in New York and New Jersey. *J. of American Hist.* 72(4): 835–858. Mar. 1986.

[846] Rhines, John W. 1890. U.S. Pat. 422,891: Vote-recording machine. Mar. 4, 1890.

[847] Rich, Eric. 2004. Court dismisses lawsuit requiring paper receipts for Diebold electronic voting machines. *Washington Post* Sep. 2, 2004.

[848] Ricknas, Mikael. 2008. Finnish voting machines slated by usability experts. *PC World* Oct. 31, 2008.

[849] Riddle, Randy. 2007. Telephone interview with Barbara Simons. Sept. 26, 2007.

[850] Riverside Co. 2004. Riverside County and disabled sue Secretary of State Kevin Shelley; more counties likely to follow. press release. May 6, 2004. URL http://etopiamedia.net/empnn/pdfs/howrey1.pdf.

[851] Rivest, Ronald L. 2008. On the notion of 'software independence' in voting systems. *Phil. Trans. Royal Soc. A* 366: 3579–3767. Aug. 6, 2008.

[852] Rivest, Ronald L. 2009. Email to Barbara Simons. Nov. 11, 2009.

[853] Rogers, Horatio. 1897. (19 R.I. 729) opinion of the Justices in re voting machine: dissent. *Atlantic Reporter* 36: 716–717.

[854] Roney, Alexander. 1878. U.S. Pat. 211,056: Improvement in registering ballot-boxes. Dec. 17, 1878.

[855] Rose, Carol V. and Stanley J. Eichner. 2007. Letter to William Francis Galvin: Purchasing accessible and secure voting machines in Massachusetts. Jan. 30, 2007. URL http://www.aclum.org/news/ACLUM_DLC-Galvin.pdf.

[856] Rosenwald, Julius and Harris S. Keeler. 1913. The voting machine contract: A protest against the recognition in any form by the City Council of the City of Chicago. Technical Report 20, Chicago Bur. of Public Efficiency. Jan. 1, 1913.

[857] RTI International. 2010. Maryland Voting Systems Study. Dec. 2, 2010. URL http://mlis.state.md.us/2010rs/misc/2010VotingSystemsStudyReport.pdf. Prepared for Maryland Department of Legislative Service.

[858] Rubin, Aviel D. 2006. *Brave New Ballot*. New York: Morgan Road Books.

[859] Rubin, Aviel D. 2006. My Day at the Polls – Maryland Primary '06. *blog* Sep. 12, 2006. URL http://avi-rubin.blogspot.com/2006/09/my-day-at-polls-maryland-primary-06.html.

[860] Ruelas, Richard. 2005. Some pens mightier than others in election kerfluffle. *Arizona Republic* Sep. 5, 2005.

[861] Runyan, Noel. 2009. Collection of my electronic voting experiences on the Sequoia Edge II. Verified Voting Foundation website. Sep. 24, 2009. URL http://verifiedvotingfoundation.net/article.php?id=6717.

[862] Runyan, Noel. 2011. Telephone interview with Barbara Simons. Apr. 7, 2011.

[863] Runyan, Noel and Jim Tobias. 2007. Accessibility review report for California top-to-bottom voting systems review. California Sec. of State. Jul. 26, 2007. URL http://www.sos.ca.gov/elections/voting_systems/ttbr/accessibility_review_report_california_ttb_absolute_final_version16.pdf.

[864] Runyan, Noel and Jim Tobias. 2007. Accessibility review report for California Top-to-Bottom Voting Systems Review. California Sec. of State. Jul. 26, 2007.

[865] Runyan, Noel and Jim Tobias. 2008. Election System & Software, Inc., Unity 3.0.1.1, Access review. California Sec. of State. Feb. 14, 2008.

[866] Runyan, Noel et al. 2007. Americans with disabilities call for election systems featuring both accessibility and security. Public statement. Mar. 19, 2007. URL http://web.archive.org/web/20070706164407/http://www.voteraction.org/Accessible_AND_Secure_Voting.htm.

[867] Russell, Ron. 2003. Blowing it: How San Francisco elections officials dropped the ball on instant runoff voting. *San Francisco Weekly* Sep. 17, 2003. URL http://www.sfrcv.com/articles/sfweekly.htm.

[868] Saltman, Roy G. 1975. Effective use of computing technology in vote-tallying. Technical Report Spec. Pub. 500-30, National Bureau of Standards. Mar. 1975.

[869] Saltman, Roy G. 1988. Accuracy, integrity, and security in computerized vote tallying. Technical Report Spec. Pub. 500-158, National Bureau of Standards. Aug., 1988.

[870] Saltman, Roy G. 2007. Improving the voting process: A multidisciplinary and politicized problem. Technical report, National Inst. of Standards and Technology. Sept. 21, 2007.

[871] San Diego Co. 2007. County appoints new registrar of voters. press release. May 11, 2007.

[872] Sancho, Ion. 2008. Email to Barbara Simons. Jun. 11, 2008.

[873] Sanders, Jim. 2007. Bowen faces vote lawsuit. *Sacramento Bee* Dec. 20, 2007.

[874] Sandler, Daniel and Dan S. Wallach. 2007. Casting votes in the auditorium. In *Proc. EVT'07, the USENIX/ACCURATE Electronic Voting Tech. Workshop.*

[875] Sarasota Herald Tribune. 2006. Careful with that voting: Check touchscreen review page to verify selections. *Sarasota Herald Tribune* page A18. Nov. 4, 2006.

[876] Sarrias, Pablo and Scytl Corp. 2008. Okaloosa – cost estimation 200712. Okaloosa Co. Fl. Public Records. Oct. 10, 2008.

[877] Savage, James S. 1873. U.S. Pat. 142,124: Registering ballot-boxes. Aug. 26, 1873.

[878] Save our Votes. 2011. Analysis of the Cost of Procuring and Implementing an Optical Scan Voting System in Maryland. Mar. 4, 2011. URL http://www.saveourvotes.org/reports/2010/2010-3-04sov-costanalysis.pdf.

[879] Schulte, Brigid. 2003. Group mobilizes opposition to new voting machines. *Washington Post* Dec. 14, 2003.

[880] Schultz, Jeffrey D., Kerry L. Haynie, Anne M. McCulloch, and Andrew L. Aoki. 2000. *Encyclopedia of Minorities in American Politics, Volume 1: African Americans and Asian Americans.* Greenwood Publishing Group, Inc.

[881] Schumer, Charles E. 2009. Schumer urges Justice Dept. to probe Diebold's proposed sale of election machine business to its biggest competitor; says deal could have 'adverse consequences' for how America votes. press release. Sep. 14, 2009. URL http://schumer.senate.gov/new_website/record.cfm?id=317761.

[882] Schwartz, John. 2003. Computer voting is open to easy fraud, experts say. *N.Y. Times* Jul. 24, 2003.

[883] Schwartz, John. 2004. High-tech voting system is banned in California. *N.Y. Times* May 1, 2004.

[884] Science Applications International Corp. 2003. Risk Assessment Report: Diebold AccuVote-TS Voting System and Processes. Technical report, Maryland Dept. of Budget and Management. Sep. 2, 2003.

[885] Scott, Jeffrey M. and Robert W. Meek. 2003. Notice of hearing and proposed settlement: National Organization on Disability, et al., v. Margaret M. Tartaglione, et al. Aug. 15 2003. URL http://www.nod.org/resources/PDFs/nod_classaction.pdf.

[886] Scytl. 2008. Comments on the review report of Phyx.core ODBP 1.0, software review and security analysis of Scytl remote voting software. Sep. 19, 2008. URL http://election.dos.state.fl.us/voting-systems/pdf/FinalReportSept19.pdf.

[887] Seelye, Katherine Q. 2004. The 2004 campaign: Online voting; Michigan's online ballot spurs new strategies for Democrats. *N.Y. Times* Jan. 10, 2004.

[888] Seina, Robert. 2008. Julie Lee pleads guilty to all state counts. *San Francisco Chronicle* Jul. 17, 2008.

[889] Selker, Ted. 2008. Study shows ballot design and voter preparation could have eliminated Sarasota Florida voting errors. MIT Caltech Voting Project Working Paper 61. Feb., 2008.

[890] Selker, Ted and Sharon Cohen. 2005. An active approach to voting verification. Working Paper 28, MIT Caltech Voting Project. May 2005.

[891] Sentencing Project. 2007. Felony disenfranchisement laws in the United States. Apr. 2007. URL http://www.sentencingproject. org/pdfs/1046.pdf.

[892] Sequoia Election Systems. 2003. Sequoia Voting Systems to provide uniform statewide electronic voting system for Nevada. Business Wire. Dec. 10, 2003.

[893] Sequoia Voting Systems. 2002. Assistant Secretary of State joins Sequoia Voting Systems, the Oakland-Based provider of touch screen voting systems. press release. Aug. 22, 2002.

[894] Sequoia Voting Systems. 2007. Response from Sequoia Voting Systems to the California Secretary of State's office on the top-to-bottom review of voting systems. Public Hearing, California Sec. of State. Jul. 30, 2007. URL https://www.sos.ca.gov/voting-systems/ oversight/ttbr/archive/comments/sequoia.pdf.

[895] Sequoia Voting Systems. 2008. OGS bid submission executive summary. bid to sell ImageCast accessible voting systems to N.Y. State. Aug. 8, 2008.

[896] Serebrov, Job, Tova Wang, et al. 2006. Election crimes: An initial review and recommendations for future study. Election Assistance Comm. Dec. 2006.

[897] Serebrov, Job and Tova Andrea Wang. 2007. Draft: Voting fraud and voter intimidation. U.S. Election Assistance Comm. obtained by the *N.Y. Times.* Apr. 9 2007. URL http://graphics8.nytimes.com/ packages/pdf/national/20070411voters_draft_report.pdf.

[898] Shaljian, Keith. 2004. Court dismisses lawsuit requiring paper receipts for Diebold electronic voting machines. *Montgomery Co. Sentinel* Jun. 10, 2004.

[899] Shamos, Michael I. 2004. Paper v. electronic voting records – an assessment. In *Proc. CFP 2004, 14th Conf. on Computers Freedom and Privacy.*

[900] Shamos, Michael I. 2006. Testimony. House Admin. Comm., 109th Congress, Hearing on Verification, Security and Paper Records. Sept. 28, 2006.

[901] Shamos, Michael I. 2008. Deposition: Reed Gusciora, et al. v. Jon S. Corzine, et. al. Mercer Co. New Jersey Superior Court No. L-2961-04. Nov. 24, 2008.

[902] Shamos, Michael I. 2008. Rebuttal report: Reed Gusciora, et al. v. Jon S. Corzine, et. al. Mercer Co. New Jersey Superior Court No. L-2961-04. Sep. 30, 2008.

[903] Sharkey, Mike. 2005. 'Pro bono' becomes $2.2 million. *Financial News & Daily Record* May 13, 2005.

[904] Sharpe, Gary L. 2008. Supplemental remedial order: U.S. v. N.Y. State Board of Elections et al. U.S. Dist. Court, N. Dist. of New York, No. 06-CV-0263. Jan. 16, 2008. URL http://www.nyvv.org/newdoc/doj/DOJvNYOrder011608.pdf.

[905] Shelley, Kevin. 2000. Position on touch screen voting machines. URL http://www.ss.ca.gov/elections/touchscreen.htm.

[906] Shelley, Kevin. 2004. Decertification and withdrawal of approval of certain DRE voting systems and conditional approval of the use of certain DRE voting systems. California Sec. of State. Apr. 30, 2004.

[907] Shelley, Kevin. 2007. Email to Barbara Simons. Oct. 2, 2007.

[908] Shelley, Kevin. 2007. Telephone interview with Barbara Simons. Sept. 25, 2007.

[909] Shelley, Kevin. 2008. Telephone interview with Barbara Simons. Feb. 1, 2008.

[910] Shelley, Kevin, Barbara Inatsugu, and Bill Jones. 2002. Argument in favor of Proposition 41. California Sec. of State Voter's Guide,. Oct. 1, 2002.

[911] Sherman, Jerome L. 2006. DOJ threatens to sue Pennsylvania over non-compliance with HAVA. *Pittsburgh Post-Gazette* Feb. 26, 2006.

[912] Shinn, Miles J. 1860. U.S. Pat. 30,503: Apparatus for detecting fraud in ballot-boxes. Oct. 23, 1860.

[913] Silver, Andrew. 2005. Email to Barbara Simons. Sep. 21, 2005.

[914] Silvernail, William H. (ed.). 1897. *Code of Election Laws of the State of New York*. Banks & Brothers.

[915] Silverstone, Barbara. 2004. A verifiable, accessible vote. *N.Y. Times (Letters)* Jun. 14, 2004.

[916] Simmons Attorneys at Law. 2006. Inventor of electronic voting verification system takes industry giants to court for patent infringement. press release. Jun. 28, 2006.

[917] Simons, Barbara. 2004. A response to the League of Women Voters of the United States questions and answers on direct recording electronic (DRE) voting systems. Feb. 2004. URL http://www.leagueissues.org/lwvqa.html.

[918] Sink, Mindy. 2000. Electronic voting machines let disabled choose in private. *N.Y. Times* Nov. 2, 2000.

[919] Slack, Donovan and Yvonne Abraham. 2006. US is said to probe Bay State elections. *Boston Globe* Nov. 30 2006.

[920] Slockett, Tom. 2007. Interview with Douglas Jones. Jun. 14, 2007. Johnson Co. Iowa Auditor.

[921] Smith, Darrell and Jake Henshaw. 2004. Electronic voting blocked. *Palm Springs Desert Sun* May 1, 2004.

[922] Smith, Erica D. 2003. E-vote vendors may form a team. *Akron Beacon Journal* Aug. 23, 2003.

[923] Smolka, Richard G. 1988. Election center research projects to address computerized elections. *Election Administration Reports* 18(11): 6. May 30, 1988.

[924] Smolka, Richard G. and Kimball W. Brace. 1976. A case study: Polling place consolidation and use of electronic voting. *Election Administration Reports* 6(7): 8–12. Mar. 31, 1976.

[925] Smolka, Richard G. and Kimball W. Brace. 1976. Washington focus. *Election Administration Reports* 6(2): 1–2. Jan. 21, 1976.

[926] Smyth, Julie Carr. 2003. Voting machine owner committed to give votes to Bush. *Cleveland Plain Dealer* Aug. 30, 2003.

[927] Soaries, Deforest B. 2004. Prepared statement. House Appropriations Comm. Subcommittee on Transportation, Treasury and Independent Agencies. May 12, 2004.

[928] Soaries Jr., Deforest. 2006. Interview transcript. CNN Lou Dobbs Tonight. Oct. 23, 2006.

[929] Solano Co. 2002. Minutes of the Solano County board. Sept. 30, 2002.

[930] Songini, Marc. 2006. New database rejects eligible Calif. voters. *Computerworld* Apr. 7, 2006.

[931] Songini, Marc L. 2007. Judge denies Diebold request to block ES&S pact with Massachusetts. *ComputerWorld* Mar. 27, 2007.

[932] Soubirous. 2004. Linda Soubirous et al. v. County of Riverside et al. Riverside Co. Superior Court. Jul. 16, 2004.

[933] Spitzer, Eliot. 1999. Suit filed in federal court over inaccessible polling sites. New York Attorney Gen. press release. Dec. 29, 1999.

[934] Spoonamore, Stephen. 2007. Email to Barbara Simons. Jun. 20, 2007.

[935] Spoonamore, Stephen. 2008. Diebold coverup, say SAIC report and stephen spoonamore. Velvet Revolution. Aug. 26 2008. URL http://www.youtube.com/watch?v=j8EeaFyY4y4.

[936] Spratt, Henry. 1875. U.S. Pat. 158,625: Improvement in voting apparatus. Jan. 12, 1875.

[937] Stark, Philip B. 2010. Audits: The after-math of election reform. Conf. on Innovative Electoral Reforms and Strategies. Dec. 10-11, 2010.

[938] Stark, Philip B. 2010. Risk-limiting vote-tabulation audits: The importance of cluster size. *Chance* 23(3): 9–12. URL http://statistics.berkeley.edu/~stark/Preprints/auditingChance10.pdf.

[939] Stark, Philip B. 2010. Super-simple simultaneous single-ballot risk-limiting audits. In *Proc. EVT/WOTE'10, the Electronic Voting Tech. Workshop / Workshop on Trustworthy Elections*.

[940] Stark, Philip B. 2011. Email to Barbara Simons. Mar. 9, 2011.

[941] Stark, Philip B. 2011. Email to Barbara Simons. Oct. 12, 2011.

[942] Steele, Lori, Meredith Gowan, Nick Handy, and Katie Blinn. 2009. Introduction (email thread). Washington Sec. of State Public Records. Jan. 22-28, 2009. URL http://www.votersunite.org/info/WA-PRR-Email-GowanLeGoff.pdf.

[943] Stein, Gary C. 1972. The Indian Citizenship Act of 1924. *New Mexico Historical Rev.* 47(3). Jul. 1972.

[944] Steinbach, Sandy. 2005. Voting system qualification: How it happens and why (presentation slides). In *Voting Systems Testing Summit.*

[945] Stevens, Anthony. 2011. Email to Barbara Simons. Mar. 30, 2011.

[946] Stewart, James D. 1993. U.S. Pat. 5,248,872: Device for optically reading marked ballots using infrared and red emitters. Sep. 28, 1993.

[947] Stewart, Warren. 2007. Nelson and Whitehouse introduce bill that would prohibit DREs in 2012. VoteTrustUSA website. Nov. 1, 2007. URL http://www.votetrustusa.org/index.php?option=com_content&task=view&id=2621&Itemid=26.

[948] Stewart, Warren. 2007. Telephone interview with Barbara Simons. Sept. 25, 2007.

[949] Supreme Court. 1985. Hunter v. Underwood, 471 U.S. 222. Apr. 16, 1985.

[950] Swarthmore Coalition for the Digital Commons. 2003. Excerpts from the Diebold Documents. Why-War.com. Oct. 2003. URL http://www.why-war.com/features/2003/10/diebold.html#excerpts.

[951] Swarthmore Coalition for the Digital Commons. 2003. Targeting Diebold with electronic civil disobedience. Why-War.com. Oct. 2003. URL http://why-war.com/features/2003/10/diebold.html.

[952] Swenson, Steve E. and Shellie Branco. 2006. Malfunctioning cards delayed poll voting Tuesday morning in Kern County. *Bakersfield Californian* Jun. 6, 2006.

[953] Symantec Corporation. 2009. The Conficker worm. URL http://www.symantec.com/norton/theme.jsp?themeid=conficker_worm#do.

[954] Tashima, Wallace. 2010. Opinion: Muhammad Shabazz Farrakhan, aka Ernest S. Walker, et al. v. Christine O. Gregoire, et al. U.S. Court of Appeals, 9th Circuit. Jan. 10, 2010. URL http://blogs.sos.wa.gov/FromOurCorner/wp-content/uploads/2010/01/010509-opinion.pdf.

[955] Taylor, Marion. 2003. No LWV position on "paper trail". LWVCNews email posting. Apr. 30, 2003.

[956] Technical Guidelines Development Committee. 2007. *Voluntary Voting System Guidelines Recommendations to the Election Assistance Commission.* United States Election Assistance Commission.

[957] Tennessee Sec. of State. 2010. Tennessee voting systems. Oct. 12, 2010.

[958] Texas Civil Rights Project. 1997. Two Texas civil rights organizations announce major voting rights legal initiative against Texas counties to assure secret ballot for blind voters. press release. Jan. 26, 1997.

[959] Texas Civil Rights Project. 2006. Voters file for injunction to prevent State Of Texas from using unreliable electronic voting. press release. Jun. 17 2006.

[960] Thompson, Clive. 2008. Can you count on voting machines? *N.Y. Times Magazine* Jan. 6, 2008.

[961] Tjoflat, Gerald B. 2000. Dissenting opinion: Robert C. Tuchston, Deborah Shepperd, et al. v. Michael McDermott, Ann McFall, et al., no. 00-15985. U.S. Court of Appeals for the 11th Circuit. Dec. 6, 2000.

[962] Tokaji, Daniel P. 2002. Testimony to Voting Modernization Board – ACLU Foundation of Southern California. Jun. 17, 2002. URL http://www.ss.ca.gov/elections/vma/pdf/vmb/documents/test_vmb_tokaji.pdf.

[963] Tomlinson, Charles and A.C. Hobbs. 1858. *Locks and Safes*, pages 2–3. Virtue & Co.

[964] Townsend, Mischelle and Scott O. Konopasec. 2004. Electronic voting systems secure. *Riverside Press-Enterprise* Feb. 29, 2004.

[965] Traxler, Arthur E. 1940. Planning and administering a testing program. *School Rev.* 48(4): 253–267. Apr. 1940.

[966] Trone, Kim, Steve Moore, and Rocky Salmon. 2007. Local officials react to decertification. *Riverside Press-Enterprise* Aug. 4, 2007.

[967] Trusteer Inc. 2009. Measuring the in-the-wild effectiveness of antivirus against Zeus. Sep. 14, 2009. URL http://www.trusteer.com/files/Zeus_and_Antivirus.pdf.

[968] Tuteur, John. 2007. Oral testimony. Public Hearing, California Sec. of State. Jul. 30, 2007.

[969] Uggen, Christopher and Jeff Manza. 2002. Democratic contraction? the political consequences of felon disenfranchisement in the United States. *Amer. Sociological Rev.* 67(6): 777–803. Dec. 2002.

[970] Underwriters' Laboratories. 2003. UL milestones in product safety certification and UL's contributions to advancement of new technologies. URL http://www.ul.com/about/history/.

[971] Unisys. 1989. Electronic voting system becomes more secure with new optical scanning system from Unisys. PR Newswire. Apr. 3, 1989.

[972] *U.S. Census Bureau News.* 2008. Facts for features – American with Disabilities Act: Jul. 26. Technical Report CB08-FF.11, U.S. Census Bureau. May 27, 2008. URL http://www.census.gov/Press-Release/www/releases/pdf/cb08ff-11_disabilityact.pdf.

[973] Urbina, Ian. 2007. Panel said to alter finding on voter fraud. *N.Y. Times* Apr. 11, 2007.

[974] U.S. Court of Appeals for the 1st Circuit. 2005. Opinion en banc – Gregorio Igartúa-de la Rosa v. United States of America. Aug. 3, 2005.

[975] USACM. 2003. Preliminary program for Denver workshop. Verified Voting website. Jul. 24 2003. URL http://www.verifiedvoting. org/article.php?id=72.

[976] USACM. 2003. USACM sponsored workshop on voter-verifiable election systems. Verified Voting website. Jul. 2003. URL http: //www.verifiedvoting.org/article_text.asp?articleid=46.

[977] Vanderheiden, Gregg. 2005. Comments made at accessible voting interactive web conference. May 12, 2005. URL http://www. verifiedvotingfoundation.org/article.php?id=6029.

[978] Vascellaro, Jessica E. and Jay Solomon. 2010. *Yahoo Was Also Targeted in Hacker Attack.* The Wall Street Journal Jan. 14, 2010.

[979] Verified Voting. 2007. Statement re: Manager's amendment. website. Aug. 1, 2007. URL http://www.verifiedvoting.org/article.php? id=5884.

[980] Verified Voting Foundation. 2006. 2006 voting process accessibility questionnaire. website. Oct. 27, 2006. URL https://www. verifiedvotingfoundation.org/article.php?id=6401.

[981] Verified Voting Foundation. 2006. Election transparency project. Sept. 2006. URL http://www.verifiedvotingfoundation.org/ article.php?id=6389.

[982] Verified Voting Foundation. 2010. Military & overseas voting 2010. URL http://www.verifiedvotingfoundation.org/article. php?list=type&type=27.

[983] VerifiedVoting.org. 2007. How long does it take to change voting systems? Verified Voting website. May 9, 2007. URL http://www. verifiedvoting.org/downloads/VotingSystemChange.pdf.

[984] Vermont, State of. 1977. Title 17: Elections, chapter 51: Conduct of elections, 17 V.S.A. section 2585. Ballots not to be written upon. Vermont Statutes.

[985] Verton, Dan. 2004. Federal court upholds California e-voting ban. *ComputerWeekly* Jul. 9, 2004.

[986] VotersUnite.Org, Vote Trust USA, Voter Action, and Pollworkers for Democracy. 2007. E-voting failures in the 2006 mid-term elections. Jan. 2007. URL http://www.votetrustusa.org/pdfs/ E-VotingIn2006Mid-Term.pdf.

[987] Wagner, David, David Jefferson, Matt Bishop, Chris Karlof, and Naveen Sastry. 2006. Security analysis of the Diebold AccuBasic interpreter. California Sec. of State. Feb. 14, 2006. URL http://nob. cs.ucdavis.edu/bishop/notes/2006-inter/2006-inter.pdf.

[988] Wagner, David A. 2006. Written testimony. House Admin. Comm., 109th Congress, Hearing on Voting System Standards. Jul. 19, 2006.

[989] Wagner, David A. 2010. Voting systems audit log study. http://www.cs.berkeley.edu/~daw/papers/auditlog-ca10.pdf. Jun. 1, 2010.

[990] Wallace, Henry E. 1901. *The Manual of Statistics: Stock Exchange Handbook.* Charles H. Nicoll. Notice of formation of U.S. Standard Voting Machine Co.

[991] Wallsten, Peter. 2011. Fla. Republicans make it harder for ex-felons to vote. *Washington Post* Mar. 9, 2011.

[992] Wang, Tova Andrea, Guy-Uriel E. Charles, et al. 2005. *Balancing Access and Integrity.* Century Foundation Press. URL http://www.tcf.org/Publications/ElectionReform/baicomplete.pdf.

[993] Warchol, Glen. 2006. Emery County: Ex-clerk at center of machine politics. *Salt Lake Trib.* Jun. 2, 2006.

[994] Ware, Alan. 2000. Anti-partism and party control of political reform in the United States: The case of the Australian ballot. *British J. of Poli. Sci.* 30(1): 1–29. Jan. 2000.

[995] Warren, Richard. 1939. U.S. Pat. 2,150,256: Record controlled statistical machine. Mar. 14, 1939.

[996] Washington Post. 2006. Editorial: Paper-trail politics. *Washington Post* Feb. 20, 2006.

[997] Washington Technology. 1996. Voting becomes more sophisticated. Mar. 7, 1996.

[998] Washington U. in St. Louis Record. 2004. Historic place. *Washington University in St. Louis Record* 29(12). Oct. 28, 2004.

[999] Het Waterschapshuis. 2008. Reaction het Waterschapshuis. published by Gonggrijp, et al, 2008 [397].

[1000] Webb, Kenneth D. 1988. U.S. Pat. 4,774,665: Electronic computerized vote-counting apparatus. Sep. 27, 1988.

[1001] Weik, Martin H. 1961. A third survey of domestic electronic digital computing systems. Technical Report 1115, Ballistic Research Labs, Aberdeen Proving Ground. Mar. 1961.

[1002] Weinstein, Henry. 2002. Court orders California counties to replace voting machines. *L.A. Times* Feb. 14, 2002.

[1003] Weiser, Wendy, Michael Waldman, and Renée Paradis. 2009. Voter registration modernization: Policy summary. Technical report, Brennan Center for Justice. Mar. 27, 2009. URL http://www.brennancenter.org/content/resource/voter_registration_modernization/.

[1004] Weiss, Todd R. 2004. Pentagon drops online votes for armed forces. *Computer Weekly* Feb. 6, 2004.

[1005] Weiss, Todd R. 2007. Ohio brings in experts to review troubled e-voting systems. *Computer World* Oct. 16, 2007.

[1006] Wikipedia. 2010. Conficker. Aug. 10, 2010.

[1007] Wilcox, Dawn. 2004. Silicon Valley Council of the Blind (SVCB) voting machine problems survey. Verified Voting website. Mar. 20, 2004. URL http://www.verifiedvoting.org/article.php?id=2117.

[1008] Wilkey, Thomas R. 2003. History of the voting system standards program. In *Building Trust & Confidence in Voting Systems*. National Inst. of Standards and Technology.

[1009] Wilkey, Thomas R. 2004. Testimony. House Science Comm., Environment, Technology, and Standards Subcomm. Jun, 24, 2004.

[1010] Wilkey, Thomas R. 2006. Biography. http://www.eac.gov/docs/Wilkey\%20bio.pdf.

[1011] Wilkey, Thomas R. 2011. Telephone interview with Douglas Jones. Aug. 30, 2011.

[1012] Williams, Brit. 2006. Biographic sketch. http://vote.nist.gov/bios/williams.htm.

[1013] Williams, Britain J. 2003. Security in the Georgia voting system. Apr. 23, 2003. URL http://www.votescount.com/georgia.pdf.

[1014] Williams, Morris. 1877. U.S. Pat. 200,495: Improvement in ballot-boxes. Feb. 19, 1877.

[1015] Wilson, Chris. 2003. Ohio's history of certification granted by the Secretaries of State on recommendation of Boards of Voting Machine Examiners: 1931 through 2001. Feb. 26, 2003.

[1016] Witt, Louise. 2003. More calls to vet voting machines. *Wired* Aug. 4, 2003.

[1017] Wood, Erika. 2009. Email to Barbara Simons. Apr. 8, 2009.

[1018] Wood, Erika. 2009. Restoring the right to vote, 2nd ed. Technical report, Brennan Center for Justice. May 11, 2009.

[1019] Wood, Frank S. 1898. U.S. Pat. 616,174: Electric voting-machine. Dec. 20, 1898.

[1020] Woods, Harry. 1913. *Illinois Election Laws*, chapter 83 Article XX Voting Machines: Use Authorized, page 443. Illinois Sec. of State. For time limit, see parts 1 and 8 of the 1903 law.

[1021] Wormeli, Natalie. 2004. Written testimony. California Sen. Elections and Reapportionment Com. Hearing. May 5, 2004. URL http://www.wheresthepaper.org/NatalieWormeli.htm.

[1022] Wyle Laboratories. 2006. Wyle corporate overview. URL http://www.wylelabs.com/aboutwyle/co.html.

[1023] Yee, Ka-Ping. 2007. Extending prerendered-interface voting software to support accessibility and other ballot features. In *Proc. EVT'07, the USENIX/ACCURATE Electronic Voting Tech. Workshop*.

[1024] Yee, Ka-Ping, David Wagner, Marti Hearst, and Steven Bellovin. 2006. Prerendered user interfaces for high-assurance electronic voting. In *Proc. EVT'06, the USENIX/ACCURATE Electronic Voting Tech. Workshop*.

[1025] Yoon, Robert. 2004. CNN asks Florida court for ineligible voters list. *CNN Washington Bureau* May 28, 2004. URL http://www.verifiedvotingfoundation.org/article.php?id=2256.

[1026] Zerhusen, James A. 2009. Indictment: United States of America v. Russell Cletus Maricle, Douglas C. Adams, Charles Wayne Jones, et al., no. 09-16-art. Mar. 3, 2009.

[1027] Zetter, Kim. 2003. Calif. halts e-vote certification. *Wired* Nov. 11, 2003.

[1028] Zetter, Kim. 2003. E-voting undermined by sloppiness. *Wired* Dec. 17, 2003.

[1029] Zetter, Kim. 2004. Diebold and the disabled. *Wired* Oct. 12, 2004.

[1030] Zetter, Kim. 2004. Diebold may face criminal charges. *Wired.com* Apr. 23, 2004.

[1031] Zetter, Kim. 2004. Diebold rep now runs elections. *Wired* Sept. 30, 2004.

[1032] Zetter, Kim. 2004. State sets standard for e-voting. *Wired* Jun. 15, 2004.

[1033] Zetter, Kim. 2007. Maryland election official endorses Diebold machines in marketing literature – updated. *Wired* Jun. 26, 2007.

[1034] Zetter, Kim. 2009. Voting machine audit logs raise more questions about lost votes in CA election. *Wired* Jan. 13, 2009.

[1035] Zetter, Kim. 2009. Vulnerabilities Allow Attacker to Impersonate Any Website. *Wired.com* Jul. 29, 2009.

[1036] Zitner, Aaron. 2000. Decision 2000 – America waits. *L.A. Times* page A26. Nov. 17, 2000.

[1037] Zuckerman, T. David. 1925. *The Voting Machine: Report on the History, Use and Advantages of Mechanical Means for Casting and Counting Ballots.* Political Research Bur. of the Republican County Comm. of N.Y.

[1038] Zuckerman, T. David. 1927. The voting machine extends its territory. *American Poli. Sci. Rev.* 21(3): 603–610.

[1039] Zworykin, Vladimir K. 1964. Communications and government. *New Scientist* (381): 603–604. Mar. 5, 1964.

Index

5454